ONTARIO

ST. LAWRENCE RIVER

•OGDENSBURG

BROCKVILLE•

NEW YORK

CATARAQUI
LAKE

KINGSTON

Thousand
Islands

•LE
QUINTE

CARLETON
ISLAND

CAPE
VINCENT

PICTON

ONT.
N.Y.

BLACK RIVER
•WATERTOWN

SACKETS
HARBOR

N

OSWEGO

Oswego R.

SODUS
BAY

•Utica

ERIE CANAL

SENECA
LAKE

CAYUGA
LAKE

OWASCO
LAKE

SKANEATELES L.

KEUKA
L.

D1214580

0    5    10   15   20   25

*Scale of Miles*

# THE AMERICAN LAKES SERIES

*Published:*

*In Preparation:*

# LAKE ONTARIO

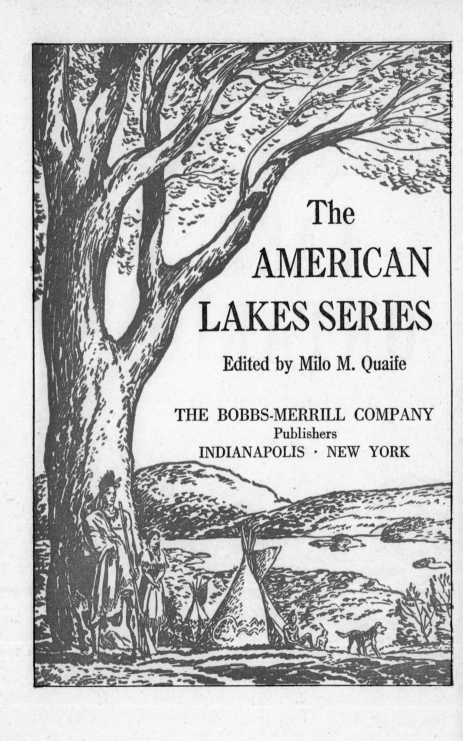

The

# AMERICAN

# LAKES SERIES

Edited by Milo M. Quaife

THE BOBBS-MERRILL COMPANY
Publishers
INDIANAPOLIS · NEW YORK

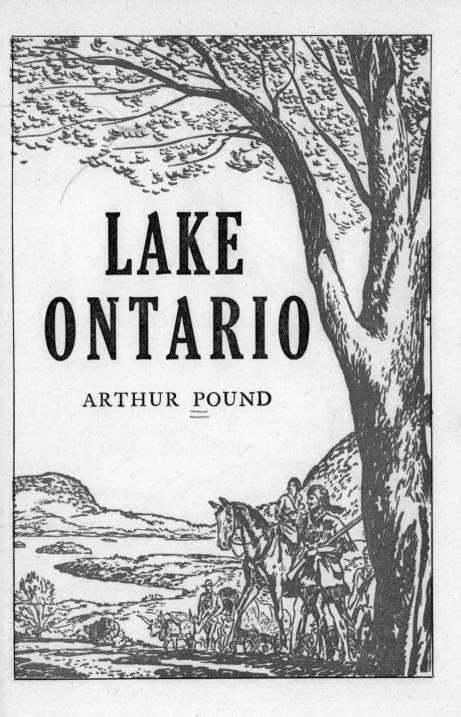

# LAKE ONTARIO

ARTHUR POUND

THIS BOOK IS DEDICATED TO MY FRIENDS IN OSWEGO AND ROCHESTER WHO GUARD LOFTY HISTORIC TRADITIONS FOR THE DELIGHT OF THEIR COMMUNITIES AND THE JOYFUL EDUCATION OF THEIR CHILDREN GENERATION UNTO GENERATION. WHO CAN BREATHE SUCH AIR WITHOUT FEELING HIS VERY SOUL EXPAND?

# EDITORIAL INTRODUCTION

SMALLEST of the Great Lakes, Ontario leads them all in its wealth of historic and human associations. Although but little more than one-fifth the size of Superior and less than one-third that of Huron or Michigan, Ontario is one of the deepest of all the Great Lakes; and since its surface is less than 250 feet above sea level, the great bulk of its cold dark water lies below the level of the ocean. Like Michigan, most of Ontario's shore line is remarkably regular and its surface unspotted by islands. Chief exception to this statement is the lake's northeastern section where numerous headlands and islands combine to create a pleasing diversity of scenes.

Striking indeed is the contrast between Ontario's poverty of present-day commerce and its wealth of history. Reasons governing the former are adequately marshaled, perhaps for the first time, by Arthur Pound in the chapters that follow this introductory note. The founding of Quebec in 1608 as a way station between France and China insured that Lake Ontario should occupy the early pathway of westward French expansion. More accurate, perhaps would be the statement that the Glacial Age which gave to the Great Lakes their present form and outlet insured the westward march across Lake Ontario of whatever nation might obtain a foothold at the mouth of the St. Lawrence. Although the earlier French explorers of the interior were deflected from Ontario temporarily by the hostility of the Iroquois Confederacy which occupied its shores, this opposition was eventually overcome and the existing geographic and economic forces gained full sway.

So it came about that Ontario was discovered in 1615 by Etienne Brulé, who was quickly followed by his leader, Champlain. In 1667 a peace with the Iroquois which endured for a decade and a half was imposed by the French, and for the first time the Great Lake was opened to French exploitation. By the driving energy of Count Frontenac, Fort Frontenac was established at present-day Kingston in 1673 and within a few years his lieutenant, La Salle, placed a few tiny sailing ships on the lake, their advent marking the beginning of navigation—other than in open boats—of the Freshwater Seas.

Repeatedly during the long warfare which raged more or less constantly from 1609 to 1701, French expeditions invaded the Iroquois country south of Ontario. The English, meanwhile, rivals of the French in both Old and New Worlds, came to the support of the hard-pressed Iroquois. They established Oswego as a counterpart to French Fort Frontenac and disputed the French pretension to dominion over Niagara and the Upper Ohio Valley. From 1689 to 1763 four great wars were waged, filling almost half of the seventy-four-year period. New France was conquered at last, and in 1760 British rule replaced French dominion over all the Great Lakes. Barely a decade and a half later, however, the American Revolution began and eight years of warfare were followed by Lake Ontario's permanent division between Great Britain and America. Henceforth, as of old, the northern shore would belong to one great nation and the southern to another; and another painful war would be waged on Ontario's waters before the rival nations could perceive their mutual advantage in adhering to the peace which now has endured for more than a century and a quarter. In 1917 and again in 1941 the two nations became allies in arms, and as these lines are written Canadian and American armies united under one common leader are driving the German legions from the Low Countries and storming their battlements along the Rhine.

As with all others in *The American Lakes Series,* Ontario's story is the story of the lake in its human and historic setting. Selection of Dr. Pound as its narrator was dictated by obvious considerations. A native of Michigan and a graduate of her state university, he spent his formative years close beside the Great Lakes. He has written a group of novels laid in the Great Lakes region and many illuminating economic discussions. In the field of history he has written a biography of Sir William Johnson, a history of General Motors, and another of Detroit, within a few miles of which he grew to manhood. He has served in editorial capacities on both newspapers and magazines, and for several years has held the post of State Historian and Archivist of New York. No less important than the foregoing is his familiarity with Canadian history which is essential to the writing of Lake Ontario's story. If any remotely comparable book about Lake Ontario has been published hitherto, its existence is unknown to the present writer. To sponsor Dr. Pound's fine narrative is a pleasant editorial privilege.

—M. M. Quaife,
Detroit Public Library.

# TABLE OF CONTENTS

## Part I

## VORTEX OF EMPIRE

## Part II

## WARS AND RECONSTRUCTION

# TABLE OF CONTENTS — *Continued*

## Part III

## SHORE JOURNEY

# LIST OF ILLUSTRATIONS

# LIST OF ILLUSTRATIONS—*Continued*

# Part I

## VORTEX OF EMPIRE

# Chapter 1

# Lake Ontario, Its Shores and People

*Ye say they all have passed away,*
*That noble race and brave;*
*That their light canoes have vanished*
*From off the crested wave;*
*That mid the forests where they roamed*
*There rings no hunter's shout;*
*But their name is on your waters,*
*Ye may not wash it out.*

*'Tis where Ontario's billow*
*Like Ocean's surge is curled,*
*Where strong Niagara's thunders wake*
*The echo of the world.*

—LYDIA H. SIGOURNEY

LAKE ONTARIO has seldom had what the British call a good press. Its white discoverer, the unlettered Etienne Brulé, who crossed only the narrow western reach, left no record of his find. Had he been an eloquent clergyman, like Father Hennepin before the wonders of Niagara in 1678, perhaps his first view of the big blue water would have stirred him to memorable rhetoric. But to Brulé the push across thirty miles of dead water was probably no more than a burdensome phase of his extraordinary journey from the Ottawa southeastward to Chesapeake Bay by way of the Susquehanna and its tributaries.

Brulé's crossing occurred in 1615, the same year that Champlain discovered Lake Huron. It was only eight years after the settlement at Jamestown, Virginia, six years after Champlain entered the lake which bears his name, and somewhat less than six years after Henry Hudson had given his employers, the Dutch West India Company, a claim which later matured in their settlement of New Netherland. Thus early did the white invaders discover the easternmost of the Great Lakes.

17

To Brulé's coppery companions and their neighbors, Ontario meant unlimited fish for food, easy access to hunting grounds rich in furs and open pathway for war. In this region the native American Hundred Years' War had been fought between the Huron north of the lake and the Iroquois south of it before the French, British and Americans added nearly another century of intermittent strife for North American empire.

Tribesmen traversed the lake in bark canoes or dugouts to take from its deep, cold waters toothsome whitefish and fat trout, and to this day there are occasional seasons when largemouthed black bass fairly race for the bait off reef and shore. Those weather-wise primitive voyagers knew that Ontario is more dependable than the shallow, larger Erie. Ontario's storms can be severe and prolonged but its depths take a deal of rousing before they answer to a whipping wind. Westerly storms may be seen afar but not so those from the cold northeast, which descend suddenly and ferociously. Shores are for the most part kindly, gently shelved and with few reefs. Except in storms, canoes can be landed safely nearly anywhere, and when the waves are high there are numerous creek and river inlets to serve as small harbors. All these things the first Americans knew in infinite detail.

But there were many things about Ontario that its aborigines could hardly know. Their ideas of time and space were beautifully elastic— they measured according to so many days of good-weather travel by foot or canoe. As to numbers they could be depended upon for a certain count of double hands or "tens," beyond which they had recourse to poetic similes such as "the leaves of the forest" and "the sands of the shore." They lacked not only the wheel, most serviceable and educational of tools, but also statistics; without these man is helpless to cope with nature in the rough and remains its drudge if not its slave.

Ontario, fifth of the Great Lakes but by no means the least (for St. Clair, Nipigon and myriad smaller ones are part of that marvelous water chain) is 193 miles long from east to west as the gulls fly, but only 180 miles on its major axis in a direct line. Its breadth from north to south is 53 miles at the widest, 40 on the average at the waist, and its circumference about 500 miles. In shape it somewhat resembles one of those medieval shoes of soft leather with a pointed toe. Poetic fancy has likened it to an Indian moccasin; but actually Ontario is more shapely than any modern-day Indian's shoe toggery, whatever grace that footwear may have had in the days of old.

Of this shoeful of soft blue water the United States owns 3,560 square miles and the Dominion of Canada 3,980 square miles, total 7,540 square miles. A precisely equal division is impossible. The Niagara River is the natural international boundary but Lake Ontario runs on westward from the Niagara outlet, diminishing as it goes into pointed Burlington Bay, unmistakably Canadian in both geography and sentiment. The lesser half of Ontario's surface, although federal water for purposes of international trade, is wholly in the territory of New York, the truly named "Empire State" whose northern shore is washed for 170 miles by Lake Ontario itself and for another 108 miles by the same waters on their way to the sea.

On the map Ontario lies between 43° 11' and 44° 12' north, and between 76° 12' and 79° 49' west. In about the same latitude lie northern Italy, the Balkans, the Caspian Sea and Lake Baikal, northern Japan, Oregon and South Dakota.

In longitude the lake is directly north of the District of Columbia and a little east of the Panama Canal. A more practical journey on a direct longitude would be 600 miles northward to James Bay, southern arm of Hudson Bay, which can be reached in almost a straight line due north by train, canoe and carry from Toronto.

With binoculars I suppose a man high aloft in an airplane over the middle of the lake might look from one shore to the other of this fresh-water sea. If so, he would behold a peaceful and almost flat vista, for both shores are low, there are no near-by mountains and the level country extends inland for a considerable distance. Except at the eastern end the lake is almost without islands, and only at the western end are bold elevations close to the shore. To the eastward can be seen the distant Laurentians and Adirondacks. But though shorn of picturesqueness in the perpendicular, the horizontal aspect of this bird's-eye view offers variety in colorful crop and orchard land, and winding streams, and off to the northeast lies a maze of forests, lakes and isles almost beyond compare.

The most remarkable view of Lake Ontario is one never yet beheld by man, and only to be portrayed imaginatively in one of those startling relief maps which present the solid earth without a drop of water to clothe its dry body and bones. In every offshore part Ontario is deep, from 500 feet to a maximum of 778 feet, yet its surface is normally only 248 feet above sea level. Therefore about two-thirds of its contents lie below sea level and are entirely untouched by the surface winds and currents. A persistent surface current moves from west to east at the rate of about eight miles a day, strongest along the south shore. Superficially Lake Ontario is a slow, wide river; geologically it is a lobe of a great glacier over which succeeding glaciers moved. Now these glacial waters, released from icy bondage but still prisoned in their ancient bowl, remain immune to transient phenomena. That is why heavy rollers are slow both to rise and to subside.

Think of Lake Ontario as a great basin twice as long as it is wide. Through the giant spillway or gorge of foaming Niagara River the waters of the northwestern river-and-lake system rush into it. Other river systems add their lesser quotas. Not inconsiderable are the flows into Lake Ontario of the Genesee; the Oswego-Onondaga-Seneca system draining the Finger Lakes; the Black, outlet for the rainy western watershed of the Adirondacks; the Cataraqui with the Rideau Lakes for reservoirs; the Trent draining the Peterboro Lakes; plus innumerable lesser rivers and creeks. These accumulating waters from west, south and north spill continuously over the eastern edge of the deep basin through one of the most picturesque island groups in the world. The St. Lawrence outlet is somewhat screened by these islands which for some thirty miles downstream cumber and divide the waters of the great flow—rightly called *fleuve* by the French rather than the lesser *rivière*. The Thousand Islands form a sieve through which the waters of mid-America pour over the edge of Ontario's deep bowl to race seaward through a hundred miles of rapids.

Ontario freezes only near the shore, but all its harbors are closed for about five months, December to April. Its surface being cooler than the air from early spring to mid-July and warmer from September on, the lake noticeably moderates the climate, particularly of the southern and eastern shores. Untimely thawing is prevented at one end of the season and untimely frosts at the other. The isles and indented eastern corner seldom know a really hot day, and the temperature of the south shore is so tempered that on both sides of the border, fruit culture is the preferred husbandry.

Along this balmy littoral the offshore water, because of floating ice from the Upper Lakes, is normally only seven degrees above freezing in May, while in October the water temperature is six degrees above that of the shore air. Sunshine and rainfall, frost, mist and fog combine in ideal proportions for shrub, bush and tree. A little farther south the vegetables take over, and berries, peaches and pears are supplanted by celery, onions and cabbage, with apples on the upland slopes and sentinel drumlins.

Not until the central plateau is reached does one encounter the herds of milch cattle so characteristic of "York State's" rural scene. Throughout the Essex Peninsula of Canada the same rural economy prevails in sequences roughly similar. On the north shore one would witness a like transition, but there the zones narrow to the eastward, widen toward the west. The effects of soil and climate will be discussed at some length later, as they deserve to be. For the present think of Ontario's calm blue waters surrounded by fertility, layer on layer in this order: fruit, vegetables, milk, grain, forest.

Arthur C. Parker, Director of the Rochester Museum of Arts and Sciences and former New York State Archaeologist, relates these influences of scene and climate to human behavior when he says:

"The area lies in the isothermal belt characterized by the most vigorous people in the world. Climate as well as landscape in the light of history has certainly left an indelible imprint upon every group of humanity that has inhabited this region."

The Lake Ontario region today bulks larger in Canadian affairs than it does in those of the United States. In the counties of the Canadian shore live nearly 1,500,000 persons, more than one-eighth of the Dominion's total population. The corresponding figure for the counties on the United States shore is 700,000, only half of one percent of the United States population. Canadian population around Lake Ontario is denser than in any other area excepting Montreal and its environs. Actually the proportion of Canadians living around the lake is three times as great as the proportion of New Yorkers living on the south shore. Every eighth Canadian lives in an Ontario-shore county, while only one in twenty-six York Staters is similarly situated.

Except for industrial Rochester which touches the lake shore only with the hem of its recently added outskirt (the former village of Charlotte), Ontario's south shore boasts no cities between Oswego and the Niagara. To the water's edge cling occasional resorts and infrequent summer homes, but only parts of Ontario have been developed for "summer people." There are old port towns gone dead and once-new ports that never quite arrived. Inland a few miles on the unique and unforgettable Ridge Road are pretty villages, trading towns for thrifty farmers whose holdings are small and prosperous. A few acres under fruit keep a man busy and a well-populated countryside has its social and educational advantages. On the main roads one is seldom out of sight of half a dozen residences, the largest of which is likely to be built of cobblestones. Canada's best fruit lands on the Niagara Peninsula reveal the same ample living on small holdings, with surpassing trimness of homestead and hedgerow. In Canada, farming—whether small or large—retains its dignity, perhaps because it shares in the genteel British tradition of respect for land ownership.

Ontario's north shore, however, is dotted with Canadian ports and cities and lined three-deep with railroads. In the 200 miles from Kingston to Hamilton a dozen communities throb with industry. Here is Toronto, giant manufacturer and clearinghouse for American-Canadian trade; Oshawa, seat of General Motors of Canada; Cobourg, entrepôt for American coal. This is the part of Canada which is nearest the States in methods and interests, yet in political feeling it is of all the provinces most intensely "royal and loyal." For the Canada of Ontario's north shore is an important segment of her water-level route from the seaboard to the interior. Whereas on the American side the water-level route lies eight to thirty miles south of the lake, Canada's crowds close to the waterway throughout the 400-mile stretch from tidewater at Montreal to Hamilton and on to the Detroit-Windsor strait.

This level route north of the lake has conditioned Canadian development in the same way that the New York route, through the Hudson-Mohawk River system and the lake's south-shore plain, influenced America's history and economics. Both the Canadian and American routes required in turn the development of canals, railroads and finally modern highways for motor transport.

It has been the fate of these two great parallel arteries of travel to develop in competition with each other. Only for the brief period of sixteen years—1760-1776—was the whole of this rich, fertile region under one sovereignty, and even then the administration was divided and discordant.

On both sides of the international border, habit disregards the patent fact that the Lake Ontario region is physically a unit. This broad water level from the Atlantic into the heart of the continent is really a single thoroughfare with two divergent entrances—to the north the mighty but frost-bound St. Lawrence, to the south the lesser Hudson with its ice-free mouth at New York City. The mountain mass of the Adirondacks divides these branch routes, but after they join west of those mountains no height of land breaks that geophysic unity until the Mississippi and Hudson Bay watersheds are reached.

What nature has done, man has undone. We hear overmuch of peace on this border for more than a century; but the best part of peace is the doing of great deeds in a spirit of comity while peace prevails. Except for the presence here of an international boundary, the whole route no doubt would have developed with its north and south pathways complementary instead of competitive.

The charming quiet which invests so many shore regions of this most easterly of the lakes is the waiting calm of an unappreciated asset. A drowsy beauty awaits the advent of a lusty young Industry. The other Great Lakes carry a growing traffic because their waters connect lively trading areas in both sovereignties. Duluth, Superior, Two Harbors exchange goods with Gary, Detroit and Cleveland as well as with Windsor, Toronto and Montreal over 2,000 miles of navigable water and supplementary rail. Of course, notwithstanding all barriers, the two customs areas trade with each other hugely, but even if they did not the domestic areas available for the exchange of products and services would still be considerable.

For Lake Ontario, however, the situation is far less favorable. Foodstuffs and manufactures now mostly slide past Ontario ports without stopping. Neither north nor south shore produces the decisive industrial minerals—iron or coal—and the two shores practically duplicate each other in agriculture. Nevertheless, there might be livelier small ports on Ontario's shores if products suffered no impediment in flow. Eventually some mutually advantageous way will be found to ease the flow of trade across an international border which has become a bit of a nuisance to friendly peoples who have learned to trust each other for both peace and war.

Once that border was established by treaty in 1815, the friendliest possible relations between the Dominion and the States—and they were not always so fortunate as they are today—could not keep the Lake Ontario region from developing frustrations somewhat like those we associate with a split personality. Here are some of the lamentable results contrary to the spirit of progress as otherwise manifested in both countries.

The best of United States ports on Lake Ontario in location and potential capacity, Oswego, has seen better days and, marinewise, is but the shadow of its former lusty self. A century ago it was already nearly half as large as it is today and relatively far more important. The liveliest American city near the lake, Rochester, uses the shore more for play than for work, and grows southward toward the hills faster than it does toward the lake—in spite of the milder airs and more even temperature of the shore region.

Cross-lake traffic runs chiefly to bulky specialties like coal. It would never occur to a Rochester manufacturer to ship goods by water to Ontario or to another American port on the lake because there is no regular freight service. The only passenger vessels plying the lake regularly are Canadian. If you want to go from one point to another along the American shore, take a bus and plenty of time.

These are evidences that Lake Ontario's present is not quite so vivid as its past, when for a century and a half it was the center of a decisive theater of exploration and warfare. Then it was a focus of empire; now it is on the remote edge of the great industrial whirlpool of mid-America which stretches from west of Chicago to Oshawa, and from London, Ontario, to St. Louis, Missouri. Yet the busy American midland could never have escaped from the wilderness stage except for certain events which occurred on Lake Ontario and which are now to be related.

# Chapter 2

# Red Man's Country

*The hand of Providence is undoubtedly in this surprising evidence of mortality among the Indians to make room for the English. Comparatively few have perished by wars. They waste and molder away, they in a manner unaccounted disappear.*
—JEDIDIAH MORSE

LAKE ONTARIO received its musical name long before white voyagers saw it. Indian words, like our own, keep changing their meanings. We are told that within the centuries of white acquaintanceship with this region, "Ontario," which originally meant "great lake," has come to mean "beautiful lake."

Other Indian tribes, deferring to Iroquois claims, called Ontario the "Lake of the Iroquois." Then for a time colonial Frenchmen, notably missionaries, in their letters and reports referred to it as "Lake Saint Louis" in honor of Louis IX. Lake Cadaracqui is another whilom name long used.

Was the original journey of Indian discovery made by raft or dugout in tedious course from the farther inland seas as the red folk forged eastward? Or did land trails from the southeast open to restless nomads this lake of romance and utility? Did moccasined feet press first the soil of Canada or of what would be eventually called in folksy pioneer phrase, "York State"? And when did the red man come first to Ontario?

Tantalizing questions these. We cannot identify the first men who walked the wooded shores, but we can see their shadowy forms as part of one of the great folk migrations in human history. For thousands of years warring peoples of the red race would flow from Alaska to the south and east, wave on wave over the continent, crushing the settlements and obliterating the arts of their predecessors. Each wave would set up amid the shards of a vanished culture its own way of life, its own concept of authority over life and death. On and on came the warlike tribes until the Iroquois, uniting, in prowess

25

and statesmanship, authoritative rule with primitive communism, encountered near Lake Ontario the tidal power of the conquering white. Notice of the doom to come was served by crack of a French musket. Decimated by foe, deluded by allies, racked by disease and liquor, they found no way out except slow decline, eventual surrender. Wards now, where once they ruled forest and lake.

Firstcomers to these Ontario shores are thought to have been of the Algonkian linguistic stock arriving by way of the Niagara Peninsula. Relics of their archaic culture excavated near these shores reveal that they were hunters and fishermen of no mean skill, no small equipment. So likewise were their dispossessors, the Laurentians whose artifacts of ground slate knives, broad blades and the like have been found widely through New York and in Canada. These wanderers apparently crossed Canada high up, and came down into the Ontario region, remaining there until they were in turn driven out, apparently down the St. Lawrence and Hudson valleys.

The Vine Valley people arriving from the West took pride in handicraft and nursed well their small flame of culture. Some of their pottery, tools fashioned of bones and antlers and polished stone implements, preserved in museums, have been witness to their development. In succession came the mysterious Mound Builders with their unexplained passion for earthy engineering. Their territory, or perhaps one might better say their influence, extended from the Mississippi eastward into the Empire State. Mounds have been found in Niagara, Wyoming and Genesee Counties, New York, but they lack the Buckeye and Hoosier bulk.

These long and difficult migrations we moderns dismiss in a phrase based on a single and minor fact. Because some bits of good pottery were found near Lake Owasco, we group Indian centuries together under the term "Owasco Aspect." The Owasco people followed a rising arc of facility in the decorating of pottery and clay smoking-pipes, in the fashioning of triangular arrowheads and in the culture of beans and corn. This phase may have endured for several centuries before A.D. 1300.

When the whites arrived they found Algonkins in possession of the Atlantic coast line from the St. Lawrence southward to Georgia, and altogether the Algonkian occupation of the Ontario section may have lasted several thousand years. The final Algonkian wave surging east-

ward was likely that of the Lenni-Lenape, renamed the Delaware by
the white pioneers in Pennsylvania and New Jersey. These intelligent Indians, who dwelt in villages and pursued farming, ventured
northward into the Hudson Valley, but they were stopped short of
Lake Ontario by the Iroquois who had already established themselves there and who were not merely holding their own but pushing
their dominion in all directions.

In this region are far more remnants of Iroquois earthworks and
stockaded enclosures than of early Algonkian equivalents. More
than a hundred earthworks exist in northern and western New York.
They include embankments, ditches and circular enclosures. As a
base for a stockaded wall, tree trunks fifteen to twenty feet high were
planted six to twelve inches deep and the earth packed up about
them. The enclosures range in size from one-eighth of an acre to
seven or eight acres. The works are similar to those erected by the
Huron in Canada and in Ohio but are less extensive than the latter.
Of the weapons found, knives predominate in number over spear-
heads. The Iroquois eschewed the flint fancied by the Algonkins,
preferring to work with other materials.

These haughty red aristocrats were conditioned for conquests by the
rigors of long migration. Oddly, there are few Iroquois migration
myths, but one of them says that the first tribe of Iroquois came to the
Ohio country from "the land of the tree with leaves like swords."
This suggests the palm trees of the South and similarities have been
noticed between the Iroquois and the Aztecs of old Mexico. Most
legends of the earlier life of the Iroquois relate to the Southwest. In
addition are many folk tales of war forays up and down the Ohio
River, sagas of long wars waged in the Mississippi region and a few
stories of the gloomy North.

One or perhaps two Huron-Iroquois tribes settled near the mouth
of the Ohio River. Pressed by Caddoe, Muskoghee, Sioux and Algonkin, they took to canoes in mass migration and paddled up the Ohio.
Some pushed eastward to the Carolinas but the main body continued
northeastward. In their wake came other Iroquoian tribes trying to
pass northward through Mound Builder lands in Ohio. After a long
war they overcame the Mound Builders and took on some of their
culture. Eventually they followed the vanguard toward the Ontario
country, fighting off Cherokee raids which drove some of them south-

ward across the Appalachian range to found the Tuscarora branch later reunited with their elder brothers.

Huron-Iroquois bands crossed the Detroit River to people the peninsulas between Lakes Huron, Erie and Ontario. Both Huron and Iroquois are names applied not by the tribesmen concerned but by others. Huron was bestowed by the French in tribute to the characteristic roached "hair-do"—*huria* being Old French for "hair." Iroquois means "destroyers" or "eaters" and was bestowed by the enemies of those who spoke of themselves as Ongwehoweh, "The True People" or "Men of Men."

Huron and Iroquois were of the same linguistic and racial stock, could be understood by each other in conversation and apparently remained allies throughout the period of migration and down to the split over confederation. The Huron settled south of Lake Simcoe, north of Lake Ontario. An allied tribe, Attawandaronk or Neutral, accredited parent of all Huron-Iroquois stock, took possession of the region south and east of the Huron holdings and were long left there undisturbed, while the more aggressive Huron fought their way along the north shores of Erie and Ontario to the mouth of the St. Lawrence. Schoolcraft shows that Cartier, visiting Hochelaga, the site of Montreal in 1535, found Indians, probably Huron, who spoke basic Iroquois.

Long before the white invasion began in 1619 other Iroquois bands had moved southward. In history they have become known as Onondaga and Mohawk. It may have been about A.D. 1300 when they crossed the St. Lawrence to seek new homes among the hills east of Lake Ontario in the present counties of Jefferson and St. Lawrence.

Along the Indian River above the village of Theresa in Jefferson County is a rugged spot where limestone rocks shelve gradually down to the riverside. Many aboriginal relics have been found in the vicinity. A series of potholes and open ovens, the latter rock-walled at their backs to shield the flames from the winds, attest the vanished Indian occupation. These camping comforts are situated well down the slope and not far from the river where canoes of the red hunters used to return in the evenings. This spot lies not far from the western boundary of St. Lawrence County wherein the migrant Mohawk made their home for an indeterminate time before continuing to the more southerly valley named for them. Along some twenty miles of the lower Black River, from a point above Watertown to its Lake

Ontario mouth in the village of Dexter, stretch caves and twisting galleries, worn by swift waters eroding the limestone. Traditions mark these caverns as favorite hiding places during Indian wars.

Meanwhile, other Iroquois bands from the Midwest had advanced against resistance along the south shores of the Lower Lakes. The Erie claimed the south shore of the lake which bears their name. The Seneca took the terrain from the Genesee River to Lake Canandaigua. The Conestoga or Andaste tribe swung into northern Pennsylvania and ranged southward to Harrisburg; while the Susquahannocks, to whom white folklore assigned the stature of giants, appropriated for a time the beautiful valley which cleaves middle Pennsylvania. Even during these wholesale migrations there was a tendency to amicable intercourse between the various Iroquois nations which expressed itself in loose alliances interrupted by frequent warfare.

Gradually the transplanted Laurentian Iroquois—Mohawk, Onondaga and Oneida—found it profitable to cease fighting among themselves. They were surrounded by hostile tribes which finally compelled withdrawal of the Onondaga to the valley which perpetuates their name immediately below present Syracuse. The Laurentian Huron swarmed down upon the Mohawk in St. Lawrence County and drove them into the Mohawk Valley. The Oneida moved westward into Madison County between the Mohawk and Onondaga.

On this strategic line between the Atlantic tidewater and the Great Lakes, a land convenient for waterways and rich in fertility, the three Eastern Nations of the Iroquois took their historic stance. In time the Cayuga and Seneca extended the Iroquois front westward to the Genesee. It was a prize selection as a homeland, whether for peace, war, agriculture or the chase of fur and meat. By easy portages canoers could travel from the Mohawk and Genesee to the Great Lakes, the Illinois, the Ohio, the St. Lawrence, the Hudson, the Susquehanna and Chesapeake Bay. With correct military vision these nations had chosen for home sites the easy water-level pass from the seaboard to the Great Lakes, a pathway of empire which gives to its possessors the control of mid-America. There they built their long bark-sided houses, held their councils, tilled their corn and squashes and occasionally ate human flesh when other supplies failed. There they established that remarkable institution—the League or Confederation of the Long House.

## Chapter 3

# Iroquois Rule the Waves

---

*It would be a very strange thing, if Six Nations of ignorant savages should be capable of forming a scheme for such a union, and be able to execute it in such a manner, as that it has subsisted ages, and appears indissoluable, and yet that a like union should be impracticable for ten or a dozen English colonies, to whom it is more necessary and must be more advantageous, and who cannot be supposed to want an equal understanding of their interests.*

—BENJAMIN FRANKLIN

---

THE historic Iroquois League of the Hodenosaunee or Long House was no sudden inspiration. Its precise adjustments in precedence, its delicate balance of forces indicate that this enduring political institution must have grown out of a long process of trial and error. A more rudimentary confederation of some kindred nature, perhaps itself in being for centuries, must have provided the experience for the later compact of Five Nations which the whites encountered, studied and envied.

This conclusion seems inescapable even though it removes some of the glamour from the legend of the League's founding by Hiawatha or Hayonwatha, the Onondaga orator, and his convert, the philosophic Dekanawida who hailed from the Bay of Quinte on Lake Ontario. The two are said to have spent five years in promoting the League as an instrument of mutual peace and defense for war-weary Iroquois nations of similar tongues and customs. At any rate, whether years or centuries went into the formation of the League the five contiguous New York tribes joined up somewhere between 1520 and 1570. The other Iroquois groups refused to limit their independence of action and thenceforth were considered enemies by the confederated tribes.

Hiawatha's mission to unite all Indian peoples in a brotherhood of peace, if he really possessed that vision, at least had this practical

30

result—five small nations, growing strong through an enduring union, terrorized and destroyed their neighbors so successfully that except for the white invasion the Iroquois might well have come to dominate America east of the Mississippi. At the peak of their numbers, there were probably never more than 15,000 Iroquois, of whom about 5,000 were in the Five Nations composing the League. One marvels at the military prowess and political sagacity of so small a group.

Culturally the Iroquois were in the Old Stone Age and artfully waged war with stone hammers until the competing white traders equipped them with iron tomahawks. They had no written language, but were evidently approaching that art in their drawings of totem animal signs and other symbols. These symbols they drew cleverly, for they had instinctive skill in design and coloration. They made pottery by shaping clay on foundations of grass rope. Their lack of the wheel, even the potter's wheel, kept them from developing easy ways of doing things; with labor so difficult they preferred war and the chase, those forms of toil which involved most excitement and least drudgery, leaving agriculture to the women and old men.

Iroquois women were excellent farmers, adept with the hoe. Theirs was the "green thumb" for corn, squash, pumpkins, beans, tobacco and Jerusalem artichokes. John Ball, who went early from eastern New York to western Michigan, says that for townsites nothing equaled an Indian garden clearing. "The Indian," he wrote, "is too good a farmer to ever till a poor soil."* Patient Indian women could beat the careless white man's growing of corn while competition stood even as to tools and seed, "for the squaws were very good with the hoe."† No doubt it was this traditional care of the land which gave women headship in the subordinate clans, component parts of the tribe which traditionally held the land in trust for the children. Descent was reckoned through the mother, a most sensible and realistic provision in a society where husbands were forever wandering on distant wars and hunts.

While it can hardly be said that the Iroquois pampered their women as mates, it was thought that age gave women a special lien on wisdom. Old women could speak up in the Grand Council of the

---

* Franklin Everett, A. M., *Memorials of the Grand River Valley* (Chicago, 1878), p. 25.
† *Ibid.*, p. 36.

Confederacy, and often did so to counsel peace. Since there were no written minutes, theirs was the duty, too, of remembering all things done and said in council and of treasuring and teaching the lore of myth, history, tradition, treaty. Only a man of one of the Royaneh or aristocratic families could be a Confederate lord or sachem, but the women of his clan passed on his fitness, placed the antlers of authority on his brow and removed them when through old age, sickness or evil he was no longer considered a proper representative.

Villages were spaced from ten to twenty miles back of Ontario's shore line on high ground with access to good canoeing water. Usually soil fertility was spent and firewood cut away in about ten years. Then a new village would be built elsewhere but kitchen middens on abandoned sites still reward archeological research.

With life's battle ended, the body of a dead warrior was sometimes promptly interred, or it might be swathed in blankets or skins and placed in the branches of a tree. Some burial houses were maintained where bodies lay until only bones remained; these were bound together and buried. When a body was interred it was placed flexed on its side, but in some stone graves on the lake's south shore the skeletons—probably pre-Iroquoian—lie on their backs.

In Iroquois folklore life and its beginnings were more than death. The Attawandaronk, revered as parents of all Huron-Iroquois, displayed in one of their villages near the Niagara River a crude statue of a woman, Ji-gon-sa-seh, "the Mother of Nations." She was considered the lineal descendant of earth's first woman. That original creature, according to an Onondaga tradition, was created together with the first man in a "garden of Eden" located on one of the two branches of Sandy Creek which merge to flow northward to Lake Ontario. This mythical cradle occupies the borders of Jefferson and Oswego Counties.

Another myth of the creation, more celebrated than the Sandy Creek fable, concerns a pregnant woman who fell from heaven to the back of a giant turtle which expanded swiftly into the continent of North America. The woman bore twin sons, the Dark One and the Good One. Quickly maturing, they wrestled for mastery. Their struggle shook the earth and caused a mighty storm to be loosed with winds that scooped the earth into valleys and raised rocks and soil to form hills. The Good One finally threw the Dark One down

PORT DALHOUSIE HARBOUR, MAY 1878

Note the schooner *Ayr*, the first ship the Muirs began building in 1854, launched March 3, 1855.

A CARGO OF LUMBER FROM BRITISH COLUMBIA IN
TORONTO HARBOR

LIMESTONE BEING UNLOADED IN TORONTO HARBOR FOR STEEL
AND CHEMICAL FACTORIES

with such force that he crashed through the floor of the world and fell into the fiery lake that is the molten core of the earth. From his endless torment the Dark One eternally sends up troubles for the Good One and tribulations to his children.

White students have traced in many of these Iroquois myths influence of Christian teachings of early missionaries. Red listeners would absorb Bible stories and twist them into the more fantastic forms suggested by their vivid imaginations. It has been found, too, that the Iroquois watched intently the white pioneers, assayed their doings according to tribal fancy and concocted myths even wilder than those told by their forefathers.

As an instance, there is the comparatively modern legend of Hiawatha crossing Ontario in his white canoe. Upon the south shore he took in two Onondaga who had been standing there watching his approach. The trio paddled up the Oswego River to found the Confederacy among the Pompey Hills. In the Onondaga Nation's fancy a cable stretched across the Oswego River by white engineers became a giant obstructing serpent waiting to be slain by Hiawatha. Some of these wonder tales may have originated in moods of Iroquois humor for the ears of credulous white folk taking notes in the wilds.

Iroquois legends of the North are filled with blood, gloom and gooseflesh, fit to send the listener whistling past a graveyard. Stone giants, awesome wraiths of Iroquoian mythology, leer and roar from storms of thunders and lightnings. Hell's feminine furies, hags with yellow fangs and streaming hair, lurk in dark and silent places to pounce upon the hapless pilgrim. The brave or the fair who ventures out at night risks annihilation by rending claws of unseen but virile ghosts.

Despite missionary efforts zealously prosecuted in spite of torture and frequent killings, the average Iroquoian was stubborn material for conversion to Christianity. He was deeply religious but his true worship went to the Divine Spirit which was daily revealed blossoming, withering or freezing in the changing seasons. A nature worshiper, he endowed animals and trees with personality, soul and variant degrees of divinity. There were lesser godlets, too, and a well-developed cult of animal guardians who especially aided the clans for which they were named. The good spirits brought the harvests. Evil spirits sought to blight them and bring famines.

Heroes wrestled with demons. Light fought with darkness. Not only did the Iroquoian believe in a life beyond the grave; his daily life was itself a series of religious acts and incidents. As a pagan he sought with charms and incantations and strange dances to propitiate unseen gods ruling the mortal scheme. Many Iroquois adhered to Christianity but most of them did so fitfully and with reservations. There were some truly devout Christians among the converts, but these were never numerous enough to please the missionaries who risked all to bring salvation. The Jesuit *Relations* might well be termed "Lamentations" because of the sorrowful note of failure so consistently sounded by the disappointed white fathers of Indian flocks.

Slow and backward in other lines, the Iroquois shone in arts of war and politics. In the latter field particularly they could instruct the whites of their day as Benjamin Franklin pointed out in the letter quoted at the beginning of this chapter; and even yet we have not altogether caught up to their ingenious devices for securing harmony of action among discordant peoples.

Secretary of State Robert Lansing in *The Independent,* issues of October 4 and October 11, 1924, analyzed the Iroquois League as a political institution and gave details of its procedure. Though crudely organized, he wrote, it rested squarely on principles with which modern students of international organization are familiar. Control of affairs affecting all five nations rested with a joint council of fifty sachems, while administration of local matters was left to each separate nation. Mr. Lansing saw the League as "an amazing development in political theory among a race still in the savage state." The scope of control was liberal enough for the times. A member nation of the body might launch a war against any one of the hostile tribes encircling the League, notwithstanding that its brother nations might remain passive. Contrariwise, it might make peace while its fellows continued at war. It was enjoined, however, against making offensive or defensive alliances against any other nation of the Iroquois, and this rule was never violated. "The League was a league of peace between its members. Bloody as its history is, peace was its central idea and purpose."

Secretary Lansing listed the following fundamentals of the Iroquois

Confederation as combining "all the elements necessary to an international association."

1. Permanent peace between members, and no offensive alliance by one nation with an outsider.

2. Freedom of national action otherwise, both as respects the internal affairs of each nation and toward all nations not members.

3. Mutual discussion and decision regarding subjects of common interest by a council of representatives of the nations composing the League.

4. Unanimity in decisions of the council.

5. Publicity of the discussions in the council.

Lansing, much of whose leisure was given to study of the Iroquois history and philosophy, emphasized in his articles that the white man owes a debt of gratitude to present-day Indians "whose forefathers laid the cornerstone of a mighty nation behind the battered and war-torn walls of the Long House. Even now it is not too late to acknowledge the debt. And not only should their services be recognized and their achievements be given a proper historical value, but the constitution and functions of their great league should be studied and analyzed with that care to which every international organization is entitled that is proven to be practicable and efficient."

The League's underlying principles deserve special consideration, declared Mr. Lansing, "because, when applied, they worked. They stood the test of actual experience. . . . We can learn much from these savage hunters of the neolithic age in America, who in the twilight preceding the dawn of recorded history had developed a League of Nations with the purpose of preserving peace between its members, a purpose which was attained, thus proving the soundness of its principles and the practicability of its organization and functions."

After being transmitted orally for three centuries the laws and constitution of the Five Nations were recorded by Dr. A. C. Parker and Seth Newhouse. Here are two significant passages:

"Our Creator, the Great Ruler, never intended that man should engage in any such work as the destruction of human life. There are many who have perished in the direction you are facing, and these lords have come to induce you to join them so that the shedding of human blood might cease and the Good Tidings of Peace and Power prevail."

\*      \*      \*      \*      \*      \*

"We shall now combine our power into one great power which is this confederacy and we shall therefore symbolize the union of these powers by each nation contributing one arrow, which we shall tie up together in a bundle, which when it is made and completely bound together, no one can bend or break."

After the early onset of enemy peoples had been met, union soon brought military security to League members. Thereafter its lands were seldom invaded by red foes. The last Mohican attack on the Mohawk occurred in 1669 when a sanguinary battle in Wolf Hollow near present Amsterdam, New York, so decimated the invaders that they never recovered their strength. From 1615 on, the French made several descents from Canada upon the Five Nations, but the Iroquois remained unconquered and recurrently invaded Canada to attack Montreal, Three Rivers and Quebec.

Evidence of the military prowess of the League may be read in distant triumphs. Both Lake Superior and the Illinois country were invaded and the Twightwees of the Miami almost destroyed. From the Cherokee the Iroquois wrested everything south from the Ohio to the Great Bend of the Tennessee River. Iroquois rights to this land were acquired by the British Crown for £10,000 in 1768. This explains why the first British-American settlements beyond the Appalachians were made in that region. Southeastward the Iroquois raided to the Santee and Catawba in the Carolinas and broke the power of the Powhatan in Virginia. Nearer home they collected regular tribute from the wampum makers of the lower Hudson, Long Island and Connecticut shores. The once proud Delaware of Pennsylvania were deprived of the power to make treaties; to them was sent an Iroquois with the odd title of Half-King to serve with the Delaware's own leader. The Huron north of Ontario were almost destroyed as a united, independent people.

Thus toward every point of the compass the Iroquois extended their power and so improved the safety of their homelands. Many of their later military adventures were for the purpose of extending and maintaining a monopoly of the Lake Ontario fur trade in which the Iroquois acted as middlemen between the interior tribes and white buyers. The League's life tenure of more than two centuries was marked especially by a steady growth in power and prestige during the 130 years from 1570 to 1700. After 1701, says Mr. Lansing, the League declined in independence and became a variable and subsidized factor in the great game of power politics played by France and Great Britain for the possession of North America.

Iroquois tradition or history records no instance of any member nation seeking to secede from the League, and until white conflicts invaded the Iroquois sphere no Iroquois nation ever fought with another. Such conflicts as occurred thereafter were slight and soon mended, at least until the American Revolution, when the Oneida, under the influence of Samuel Kirkland, a Congregationalist missionary, helped the patriots while the other nations clung to the old covenant with the British. For the Iroquois our Revolution was truly a civil war.

Of the Five Nations three were senior and two were junior. The Mohawk, fierce in war and ancient in dominion over a fertile valley, held the eastern door of the Long House against the more numerous Algonkins. Westward and adjoining lived their younger brothers, the Oneida. The Cayuga similarly were junior to the mighty Seneca at the western gate. The Seneca were the strongest in numbers of the Five Nations because of their conquests and subsequent mass adoptions. Between the two junior nations resided the third senior nation, the Onondaga, occupying a unique position in the hierarchy. This central nation was the proud keeper of the Sacred Fire, around which gathered the sachems in the Great Councils on Pompey Hill in days before the whites came to trade and conquer. The Tuscarora, a kindred though somewhat mongrelized people hard pressed in the South, sought protection from the Iroquois League and were admitted to limited partnership, sitting humbly apart at councils of the lordly League.

Here then was a practical hierarchy of nations, a League with graded powers, privileges and responsibilities with dominion over the great lake which for a century bore their dreaded name.* When the whites arrived the Iroquois were strong enough to resist them for a time and even to expand their own empire by means of improved weapons bought from the whites with proceeds of the chase and fur trade. The history of Lake Ontario for nearly 150 years thereafter is Iroquois history no less than British, French or American.

---

* Seymour Dunbar, in his monumental *History of Travel in America* (New York, 1937) relates (pp. 69-71) how Iroquois control of trails and trade routes earned them the title of "Keepers of the Highway," and says that royal governors of Virginia, Maryland, Pennsylvania and New York visited their councils to treat for rights of passage.

# Chapter 4

## The Conquerors Arrive

*Now under the name "Mission of the Hurons," we compre-
hend all these vast countries (the Great Lakes and Hudson Bay
regions); and our design was, never to stop in seeking out of
new peoples,—to whom we hoped that a colony in the country
of the Hurons might be a key—had not the inscrutable judg-
ments of God decreed otherwise.*
    —FATHER FRANCESCO GIUSEPPE BRESSANI

T HE first white commander to see Lake Ontario was the first
governor of Canada, Samuel de Champlain, gentleman of
Saintonge in France. Several others preceded him in authority
in Acadia and along the Atlantic shore where he himself spent five
years. But in the officially accredited list of Canada's governors
Champlain deservedly stands first, for he was the founder of Quebec
and the pathfinder who led the way toward the interior of the continent.

As for Canada, the name still puzzles. The most logical deriva-
tion is the Iroquois designation for a village or group of huts. Other
origins more fancifully attribute it to Spanish voyagers and French
punsters. At any rate, the name as used officially in Champlain's
time and for generations afterward meant all of the Great Valley of
the St. Lawrence, including the Great Lakes and most of the Ohio,
Wabash and Illinois Valleys, but not that of the Mississippi, where
Louisiana began at the confluence of the Illinois. For a time (1698-
1710) Canada and Louisiana had joint administration.

Champlain, first high French official to see Lake Ontario, founded
Quebec in 1608. He had arrived in Acadia in 1603. Five years of
experience on the rock-bound coasts from Labrador to Maine had
convinced him that the future of France in America lay inland on
the great river and its connecting lakes. The exposed situation of
Acadia invited attack from the sea while the interior remained immune to British aggression for a century and a half.

39

In 1632 Champlain reviewed exploration in Canada, his own and others', in a memoir written for Louis XIII. He held that France had true claim to the American shore by reason of the voyages of Verrazano and Gomez in 1524 and 1525. Except for the hesitant Verrazano's failure to find and ascend the Hudson after getting into its very mouth in New York Bay, no doubt the French would have made their bid for American empire there instead of in the St. Lawrence. Gomez found the St. Lawrence, entered it and traded with the Indians on its lower shores, apparently unaware that the gulf extended far inland. Jacques Cartier sailed deep into the interior in 1535 while looking for the Northwest Passage to Asia. What he found was the nearest thing to it, a waterway leading for 2,000 miles into the heart of the continent by way of a series of inland seas and their connecting waterways. Cartier followed the river inland until his ship was barred by the rapids at present-day Montreal, parleyed there with friendly Indians and then retreated downstream to avoid ice. A tremendous voyage that of Cartier's, deep into the heart of America seventy-five years ahead of Hudson's northward penetration by means of the more accessible Hudson.

After six years Cartier and Roberval planted an unsuccessful colony on the Isle of Orleans. On the coast of Acadia, however, the French fared better. It is related that the Indians above Montreal, who had witnessed the first coming of the whites, learned in an odd manner that the French had returned to abide in the land. Sharp eyes saw a new insect at work—the honey bee brought from Europe had moved inland faster than the French.

Champlain's memoir on the subject of these discoveries reveals him as just and discriminating, capable of taking a judicial point of view the more remarkable because the British had then been holding his beloved Quebec for three years and returned it only because Charles I, quarreling with Parliament, needed the equivalent of $240,000. But Champlain evidently thought that North America was big enough for both powers. Modestly he related having himself "discovered and caused to be discovered ... divers countries, over 4 to 500 leagues inland." He concluded that the British, by priority of discovery, held the best claims to the north side of Labrador and beyond, the Hudson Bay country; but that France had an equally good claim to the coast from Labrador to the Virginias. Too many English, he admitted, had settled in Massachusetts and Virginia to let the French get a footing, whatever Gallic rights by discovery might be. Therefore he advised that France should develop the interior, which was rich in furs and of vast extent.

Relations of New France and New England remained peaceful thereafter as long as the Stuart kings occupied England's throne. Indeed, there were once French overtures for a union with New England whites against the Iroquois. Champlain had set a good example in moderation, and because of distance neither side felt as yet commercial or political pressure from the other.

Champlain's first exploration toward the west took him into the lake which now bears his name. Before concentrating on western exploration beyond Montreal he tried a push southward, only to encounter there a foe whose opposition would color the whole future of Canada. There, on July 30, 1609, his southward move was brought to an end by Iroquois opposition. By long custom a certain mountain range marked the hunting grounds of his Algonkin companions off from those of the Mohawk, leaders of the Iroquois Confederacy. By a night march Champlain pushed beyond this line and drove off challenging Mohawk. With his arquebus he killed two chiefs and wounded a third. He is generally blamed for this skirmish, as an error of judgment forever alienating the Mohawk, but it may be that he had no choice. An official memoir written many years later, in 1671, says: "It is necessary to know that the French are established in New France, in a Canton belonging to Indian people named Algonquins, who received us among them in order that we should aid them against another people, called the Iroquois, of whom they were for a long time the enemies." But no doubt the chief cause for the long enmity between the Iroquois and the French lay in desire to control the fur trade arising among the interior tribes.

As if clairvoyantly aware that his way southward was barred, Champlain never took that route again. That little skirmish in the wilderness is one of the turning points in American history. Its effect in fixing Iroquois hatred of the French may be exaggerated. What is more important, when Champlain gave up his advance to the south he was approaching the headwaters of the Hudson, more than two months before Henry Hudson sailed up the river from the opposite direction in the Dutch vessel *Half Moon*. In those two months there was plenty of time for Champlain to navigate that river to the Lower Bay, thereby giving substance to the shadowy French claims established by Verrazano and Gomez in 1524 and 1525. In that case there could hardly have been a weak Dutch colony along the Hudson to be easily overcome by the British, and American colonial history would have developed quite differently.

At Quebec Champlain heard news of western waters which he eagerly noted and reproduced on maps better known for beauty of delineation than for accuracy. He was told of Lake Ontario and of La Mer Douce, or Huron, the sweet-water lake which he judged to be the true Western Sea near whose farther shores lay Cipango, Cathay and the Spice Indies.

Forced to make several journeys to France to secure backing for his journeys, Champlain moved westward by various delayed stages. In 1611 he founded a post at the confluence of the St. Lawrence and Ottawa Rivers. Two years later he made a reconnaissance along the Ottawa, reaching present Portage du Fort, about a hundred miles upstream, on June 6. On June 7 he lost his astrolabe, an instrument by which latitude and longitude readings can be calculated. Thereafter the narrative is less definite on locations; and apparently this journey developed no major importance beyond solidifying Indian relations. But it is a curious fact that an astrolabe of 1603 was found near Portage du Fort on the Champlain route in 1867 close to present North Renfrew. Identified as Champlain's missing astrolabe, it has been admitted to the collections of the New York Historical Society.

The next year Champlain visited France to lay before his patrons and the Ministry of Marine his plan to explore the West and convert the heathen. He brought back with him three Récollet friars—Denis Jamay, Jean d'Olbeau, Joseph le Caron, priests—and a lay brother, Pacifique du Plessis, first missionaries on the St. Lawrence. Le Caron went to the Huron with the Western expedition, D'Olbeau sojourned among the Montagnais, while the others remained in Quebec.

In the summer of 1615 Champlain and two white followers set out toward the Western Sea of the Huron, guided by members of that tribe, who were hopeful that he would help them against the Iroquois. Champlain from 1610 on had encouraged some French youths to live among the natives in order to accustom themselves to the language, customs and folklore. Among them was Etienne Brulé, who accom-

panied his master again. The Huron led the party northward from
the Montreal region by way of the Ottawa River, a route which Champlain had already followed part way and which has since become
noted in colonial history as that followed in the founding of early
French settlements on the Upper Lakes and the later settlement of
Detroit in 1701.

This time the intrepid Frenchman was not to be stopped. He
visited the tribes at the headwaters of the Ottawa, and then went on
to Georgian Bay, where he became the first French commander to
see Lake Huron. From its shore, at the mouth of the French River, he
looked westward toward what he truly believed was the fabled
Northwest Passage and, believing this vista led to limitless expanses
beyond, named the waters "La Mer Douce."

The homeward journey took him southeastward through a country which he considered very beautiful and pleasant, with abundant
shallow lakes and safe water, good hunting and fishing. Champlain
was in no hurry; in fact a little delay might be helpful. Having decided to attack an Iroquois stronghold, as he had promised his
Huron allies, the commander had dispatched his protégé Brulé to the
Susquehanna in hope of getting certain of the tribes there to join the
Huron in the projected attack.

No one knows precisely Brulé's route or how far he went. Champlain said his objective was to bring in the Carantouans who lived on
the headwaters of the Susquehanna; but as none of these Frenchmen
knew where the headwaters of the Susquehanna might be, almost
any part of southwestern New York from Binghamton to Buffalo
can claim an introduction to history by Brulé. In view of all the circumstances of his journey—the hostility of the Seneca and his need
for haste—it seems likely that the voyageur kept west of the Genesee
until quite well south and then crossed its headwaters into either the
Tioga or Cohocton Valley, both of which feed into the Susquehanna
through the Chemung.

A reasonable conjecture is that he was seeking the Andastes, then a
strong people holding the middle, or east-west, reach of the Susquehanna before the river definitely turns south to bisect Pennsylvania
and eventually reach Chesapeake Bay. That Brulé ever reached the
bay itself is doubtful but continues to be strongly stated. At any rate,
his mission failed; when time came to attack, Champlain's southern

allies were missing. Apparently they were willing, but Brulé could not get the message through in time. What gives this hardy young woodsman's journey significance for this book is that he and his Huron guides could hardly have reached the Susquehanna without crossing Lake Ontario, so it is quite certain that he saw the lake itself before his famous commander did.

While Brulé was making hard going of it through a wilderness strange even to his guides, his recent companions took the far easier way through one of the lovelier waterways of the earth, a lake country drained mostly by the River Trent. No doubt a meandering journey on the Trent from present Simcoe Lake through the heart of Ontario to Lake Ontario at the sand dunes of Quinte could have been easily accomplished with few portages when that moist land still lay under the shelter of primeval forest. Since there was for once no need for haste and no danger of enemies, this phase of the journey must have been one of the most serene explorations ever undertaken. Here was the heart of Huronia, as yet unravaged by the fearsome Iroquois, and in the whole Northeast no land was better suited to Indian living.

In the Bay of Quinte the expedition had the shelter of sandy Quinte Peninsula for their stealthy movement of surprise. Soon they were shielded by the islands near the outlet where they made their crossing. Coasting along the eastern shore for fourteen leagues, they made camp at the mouth of the Salmon River in present Oswego County, a favorite stopping place for Indian travelers and later for French expeditions. No doubt the fact that the Salmon flows from the east caused Champlain to select this site as his base. Unlike the Oswego outlet it would not be closely watched, but from the Salmon to the Iroquois country was still a good twenty-five or thirty leagues of stiff marching through tangled woods and mazy waterways with which the Huron guides were unacquainted. The marauders took five days on the way to their objective—one of the fortified castles of the Oneida at Nichols Pond in present Fenner Township, Madison County, New York. The Oneida had never been directly in conflict with the French as yet, but no doubt frequently warred against the Huron. At any rate, as "younger brothers" of the Mohawk they would be considered fair game by the French even though from present standards the attack seems to have been without sufficient military justification. If the place fell, the victors could not hold it; the best they could hope to do was to destroy a simple little community of primitive men who lacked firearms.

What the defense lacked in armament, however, it made up in courage. The village was well fortified in the Indian manner, with four rows of palisades made of large timbers closely interlaced. The chief stockade is said to have been "thirty feet high with galleries running around like a parapet." The "shooting-pole" of civilization was no longer a complete surprise to aborigines. Oneida scouts had given warning, the women and children were sent away into the woods and the red men stood firm behind their timbers, showering arrows down on the attackers.

The defenders held on even though Champlain surprised them by having a tower built as high as the fortifications, from which his musketeers and armored archers could shoot directly into the stockade. On the other hand the attacking Huron, though keen for loot, proved unmanageable, would not obey orders, rushed foolhardily into the open and then retreated. Characteristic of Indian warfare is inability to stand heavy losses. Where men are scarce and irreplaceable, as throughout aboriginal America, battles are mercifully short. This one lasted three hours. For three days the invaders remained near by, but, with provisions and powder running short, they had to depart. Then Sieur de Champlain entered upon one of his periods of greatest danger. So angry were his Huron allies over their losses that the commander was forcibly detained in the Huron country over the winter. By spring he had argued his way out of custody and returned to Montreal where he had been given up for dead. Actually he may have enjoyed his first winter free from responsibility, for Champlain was above all a patient man accustomed to hard living and of serene religious faith.

This journey was Champlain's last voyage of discovery; the remaining twenty years of his life were spent in wrestling with a niggard court and a stubborn forest. His colony was pitifully small and poor, for all fur-trade profits were absorbed by the Company of Rouen and St. Malo, an association of merchants headed by the De Caens. Early profits ran close to forty percent and the fur trade so engrossed all activities that at one period only one family at Quebec tilled the soil. A shake-up came with the rise to power of Cardinal Richelieu, but what with war and the capture of Quebec by the freebooting Kirkes, Champlain perforce left Lake Ontario in its primeval silence.

Catholic missionaries took hold of the Western cause at last. As we have seen, the Récollets were first on the ground but the most determined representatives of Christianity were later arrivals, members of the crusading Society of Jesus, commonly called Jesuits. That powerful order was less than a century old when the first "black robes" reached Quebec in 1625. One of them, Father Jean Brébeuf, labored among the Huron from 1626 to 1629, when war with England compelled him to retire to France. Five years later, accompanied by Father Chaumonot, an assistant, he returned to his former station. On leaving France, Brébeuf had testified to "inexpressible joy at the prospect of a living and dying martyrdom." Fate spared neither; both underwent intense privations and sacrifices. But they and their followers effected wholesale conversions among the Huron. This promising beginning was frustrated by Iroquois invasions which shattered the Huron almost to complete extirpation. Henceforth they were a broken and divided people. Many Jesuits perished; others returned to France; still others went on to explore America to the northwest.

History has to thank these missionaries for their extensive reports published as the Jesuit *Relations*. At last the wilderness had found its chroniclers in educated men who dutifully gave account of their travels and labor.

The account of Brébeuf's and Chaumonot's journey to the Neutrals in 1640-1641 contains the first authentic knowledge the whites had that the waters of Lake Huron were connected with the St. Lawrence watershed, and also that beyond the lakes there stretched an area of vast extent. These priests estimated that there were at least 12,000 souls for them to save in the country between Lake Huron, the St. Lawrence chain of Erie, Ontario and the river, and Hudson Bay. Notwithstanding wars, famine and sickness they thought these loyal Canadian Indians could muster 4,000 warriors. This fighting strength was divided among many tribes, some as yet unvisited, but "we have every reason to believe that not long ago, they all made one people,— both Hurons and Iroquois, and those of the Neutral Nation; and that they came from one and the same family."* This conclusion is now fully adopted by scientific ethnology.

Father Francesco Giuseppe Bressani's account of 1653 contains quite accurate geographic detail and ends on a note of high endeavor—on and on to the west—as indicated by the quotation at the head of this chapter.

Although the Mohawk and Oneida had reason for hostility, the other three Iroquois nations were not hostile to French missionaries in this early period. A mission of Father Simon Le Moyne to the Onondaga in 1653-1654 received a warm welcome and continued for nearly thirty years, although an interruption occurred after five years when the missionaries and some of their converts fled at night, fearing a plot. Later the mission was re-established.

To the west the missionaries were well received, but at the eastern gateway the Mohawk, Champlain's original adversaries, twice tortured and finally murdered Father Isaac Jogues at Auriesville, now a great Catholic shrine on the beautiful south shore of the Mohawk. Since his martyrdom occurred on the soil of the United States, sanctification made this French missionary the first American saint, but other saints precede him in Canada, both in year of martyrdom and year of sanctification. Even the Mohawk, however, were split by Jesuit zeal and persistence, and many converts went north to the St. Lawrence to abide in the folds of the church. Among them was Tekakwitha, Indian maiden now beatified, with a Shrine church near Fonda, New York.

Father Jogues' martyrdom seems to have had no effect on the more western missions, for Fathers Garnier and Gavreau received Indian hospitality on their way to the western tribes, as did Fathers Chaumont and Dablon while en route to the Onondaga, who made them welcome.

Fisherman will relish this clerical description from the Jesuit *Relations* of the yield of the Salmon River as it neared Lake Ontario: "In the spring as soon as the snows melt it is full of gold-colored fish; next come carp, and finally *achigen* (black perch or black bass). The latter is a flat fish half a foot long and of very fine flavor. Then comes the brill and at the end of May, when strawberries are ripe, sturgeon are killed with hatchets. All the rest of the year until winter the

---

* Jesuit *Relations*, XXI, 195.

salmon furnishes food to the village Onontae. We made our bed last night on the shore of a lake where the natives toward the end of winter, break the ice and catch fish,—or rather draw them up by the bucketful."

This fisherman's heaven has been identified as the same harbor where Champlain landed on his voyage across the lake on his way to attack the Oneida. It was a common meeting and trading place, a "resort of all nations," as Le Moyne described it in 1654. Popularity for trade may have begun with plentiful fish for food and continued because at this early period the Salmon lay on the edge of land not in the Iroquois domain. Here Iroquois met hunters of other tribes and exchanged Dutch merchandise for furs which they carried to the white traders at Fort Orange (later Albany).

In this manner the Dutch blunderbuss and tomahawk, the latter a neat little number lighter and better balanced than the English hatchet, were distributed, and likewise Holland gin, rum and such other hard liquors as the Dutch could spare for the comfort of the natives. The liquor, however, rarely passed far through Indian hands, being liable to instant consumption by the Mohawk who usually were in on the final transactions with the whites. Needless to say, the Mohawk soon began to decline in health and numbers, though not so swiftly as the Narragansett and Mohican under the more generous and headier libations provided by the Saints of Massachusetts. Salmon Bay did not long retain its good fishing. Probably the place was fished out as trade increased, for later it well earned the reputation of a starving-place and became known as La Famine, Famine Bay and Hungry Bay. By 1688 the "large clearing" had become a favorite meeting place for French traders and Iroquois hunters; Coronelli's map of that year says that there "most of the Iroquois disembark to trade their beaver." They preferred not to have French traders enter their country as the Yorkers and British were easily roused thereby.

Why the long enmity between French and Iroquois? Champlain's first shot could hardly have been a controlling factor for a century and a half. Was it religion? Indians knew little and cared less about the differences between Catholicism and Protestantism. The red men, like most primitives, were incurably religious and enjoyed symbolism but they had no talent for complex, disputatious theology. Both of the Christian creeds were offered to them on the platter of high politics. The priests were not merely Catholic but also infallibly French by blood or adoption; the parsons were not merely Protestant but also champions of Holland or Britain as the case might be, and all were to some extent advance agents for trade.

The ninth governor, Pierre Dubois, Baron d'Avaugour, rather lets the cat out of the bag in a memoir to the Minister of Marine of August 1663: "In his [Dumont's] Instruction I noted that it was politic to exaggerate more than ever the cruelties of the Iroquois, in order better to conceal the designs that might be adopted by this country; fearing lest English ignorance and Dutch weakness might be alarmed and have their jealousy excited. . . . It is important to preserve henceforward the secrets of the designs of this country. . . . Therefore it will be expedient to make public in every way the extreme cruelty of the Iroquois in order that we may, by that truth, succeed more easily in establishing the Gospel in the most healthy and favorable climate in the world."

French officials very early appreciated the size of the interior and schemed to win and develop it. A hundred years later the British had not yet arrived at so correct a judgment on mid-American values as that expressed by Governor d'Avaugour in his letter of 1663 to the Minister of Marine: "The settlement there [New Netherland] . . . properly speaking is but a fishing Coast of small consideration compared with the Great State of America, of which the River St. Lawrence is, as it were, the centre, traversing it from one end to the other."

D'Avaugour promised the minister that 3,000 soldiers, 100,000 écus for fortifications and 100,000 francs for munitions would make New France so strong in three years' time that no opposing power on earth could capture it. This doughty governor, considering it useless to traverse 200 leagues of hard going in order to fight the Iroquois, suggested getting permission from the Dutch to send troops up the Hudson to Fort Orange. He recalled also that the mayor of Boston had once proposed to destroy the Iroquois for 20,000 francs.

This transaction was no doubt connected with negotiations, opened in 1648 and reopened in 1651, between Quebec's supreme council and New England's commissioners for an offensive and defensive alliance against the Iroquois and a "union" for mutual trade.

In 1712, after New France and New England had been foes in

two considerable wars, these forgotten documents of the "Ancient Council" apparently were discovered and looked upon somewhat as we would view a historical find. But D'Avaugour, a veteran government servant, recalled in 1663 the negotiations of twenty years earlier and, the situation not having been fundamentally changed in the meantime, desired to have the Iroquois attacked simultaneously by both New England and New France. Very soon the situation changed drastically through Britain's seizure of New Netherland, but while the Dutch held the Hudson River, New England had almost the same grievances against the Iroquois that the French had, namely interference with the fur trade in favor of Albany, and occasional raids on frontier settlements.

Louis XIV in 1665 resolved to carry war even to Iroquois firesides. To that end His Majesty sent Sieur de Prouville, Marquis de Tracy, veteran general, from the Antilles with four companies of regulars, and in addition "one thousand good men [the Carignan regiment] are coming from France under command of their Marshal du Camp Salière with all munitions of war and equipment."

De Tracy's expedition of 1666 is credited with the capture of a principal Indian village or "castle" at the juncture of Schoharie Creek and the Mohawk, always a strategic site and later protected by Fort Hunter, name of the present village forty miles west of Albany. As the inhabitants fled, the French put the torch to the Indian bark houses and stores of grain. Although the expedition then retired without finding anyone to oppose, it can be counted a complete success. France had proved possession of a long arm able to punish the marauders who had terrified Huron and habitants alike. The Iroquois begged for a treaty, were accorded one and continued tractable for almost twenty years, though other expeditions were sometimes necessary, as we shall see.

To understand this quick reversal of the military situation, it is important to remember that the British had acquired New York by conquest only two years before, thereby supplanting the Dutch who had kept strong the Great Covenant Chain with the Iroquois. The British entered into the same relationship but not vigorously enough at first to forestall the French, who took rather prompt advantage of the confusion in New York. It has since come to light that both King Charles II and his brother the Duke of York, Lord Proprietor of New York, were in the pay of France, and temporarily a free hand for France on the New York frontier followed these undercover transactions between the Bourbon and Stuart courts.

De Tracy, senile and rapacious, held office only two years, and then returned to France. A lasting influence from his period proved to be settlement on the land of the famous Carignan regiment, or as it is often called Carignan-Salières. The king intended them to remain and populate the country. As a census of 1668 shows there were 5,870 persons in all Canada and only 2,000 men capable of bearing arms, the Carignan regiment obviously was a tremendous reinforcement both to immediate defense and later increase.

Western exploration revived with the coming of Intendant Talon. Hitherto discovery had been motivated by religious and military considerations, but Talon urged action for profit and trade. He was eager to develop the interior, which he described as of such vast extent that he knew not its limits. The climate, though indeed cold, he declared to be so salubrious that sickness was infrequent, harvests abundant and fruit plentiful. Mineral wealth, too, was so abundant that Talon promised large returns on state funds invested in their search. But Louis bade him concentrate on copper and nurse his broader plans in patience for a while.

Ambitious Talon sought aid next from Colbert, greatest of the Sun King's ministers. Colbert's sole weakness seems to have been that he wanted to manage everything and everybody, bringing France eventually to the point where, as Buckle says in his *History of Civilization,* the king hired 800,000 functionaries to trouble the rest of the inhabitants. Managing New France on this precise pattern called for so many regulations that the English, aided by better manufactured goods at lower prices, usually secured more furs from Indian hunters at less expense. Punitive expeditions, treaties and subsidies had only temporary effect. The steady economic pull of prices usually overcame these effects and dominated the fur market because the trade covered such vast extent that it escaped control.

Returning to France, Talon drove hard for development of the Lake Ontario region and beyond. He reported that he had sent out "Adventurers for the Discovery of New Countries who are to keep journals, take possession and display the King's Arms." In his opinion an establishment should be set up on Lake Ontario, two posts on either side of the lake and a small vessel or galley to move either by sails or oars in order to deter the Iroquois from taking furs to the English and Dutch. The Iroquois, he noted, have already exhausted their country of elk and beaver skins, "the latter by far the most popular fur, and so must trespass on their neighbors north of the Lake, yet they furnish the bulk of beaver to Boston, Orange and Manathe [Manhattan] to a value of 1,200,000 livres, almost all dry and in condition the best."

Talon also related that the Sulpician missionaries from Montreal—Dollier and Galinée—had returned from visiting all the tribes around Lake Ontario. The missionaries posted the usual notices of possession, but the Iroquois—impious wretches—pulled down the placards and coats of arms. Talon was convinced nothing could be done with these *canaille* except to hit them again.

In February 1671, Colbert approved Talon's sending two of the greatest Canadian discoverers westward to find the South Sea—"Sieur La Salle to the South and Sieur de St. Lusson to the North." The minister evidently thought they had small chance of accomplishing that objective, but counseled that they ought to look particularly for copper because such discoveries would encourage Frenchmen to emigrate.

Nine months later St. Lusson was reported back, after reaching a point which he believed to be "only 300 leagues from the Vermilion or South Sea and a like distance from the West Sea, and from the West Sea it is a mere 1500 leagues" of navigation to Tartary, China and Japan. Although the thrifty explorer had not found the copper mine as ordered, the voyage had cost nothing since seventeen newly discovered Indian tribes had presented him with enough beaver to pay expenses.

This voyage confirmed the optimistic official view of the interior. "I am no Courtier," wrote Talon, "and assert, not through mere desire to please the King nor without just reason, that this portion of the French Monarchy will become something grand."

"Something grand"—majestic prophecy destined to mature in other hands than those of France, whose colonial efforts failed in large part because her functionaries at home refused to back her far-sighted empire builders in America.

In the annals of a tight autocracy like that of colonial France one reads chiefly of educated and eminent persons—officials, envoys, commanders, missionaries. Only occasionally do we catch—and then mostly between the lines—glimpses of humbler actors in the manifold and sporadic enterprises which are grouped under that stirring phrase, the opening of the West. But of a certainty the rugged common man was there with an oar in his hand and a pack on his back. His was the hand that drove the canoe forward, placed the traps and skinned the "varmints" whose pelts paid all of Canada's early bills, plus the shocking graft of so many of her leaders. His was the body tormented by insects and wounded by arrows. His superiors, the men of letters, called him and his mates *"coureurs de bois"*—woods runners or travelers—rated them rough fellows and tried to fetch from France wives for their better governance. Between these termagant civilians and the soldiers existed a gulf, as between the free and the bound in all societies. But to many a common soldier the Canadian service was a way toward freedom. If they escaped being scalped, dying under floggings or being shot as mutineers, they might well become trappers, traders, habitants, men of family and landed possessions.

These men of the people, burden bearers and obeyers, are the ones who in the end made something enduring out of the sacrifices and follies of their masters. With such women as were obtainable, white or red, they begat descendants who took root in the new land and refused to be weeded out by adversity. Those indestructible bloodlines remain, perhaps under names most remarkably altered and now often not identifiable as French. Much of Canada is still peopled by the sons of those farmers, trappers and soldiers who came up the St. Lawrence to Ontario when the forest stood solid just beyond the water long called "Lake of the Iroquois" in token of savage dominion. By fire and sword was that dominion broken, say the history books in all truth; but no less was it broken by clumsy plow, by galled shoulders and the stubborn will of humble men who sought neither wealth nor honors but merely peace, food, homes and, in the end, some decent word above their graves.

# Chapter 5

## Of Captains, Voyages and Wars

*Second only to Champlain among the heroes of Canadian history stands Robert Cavelier de la Salle—a man of iron if ever there was one—a man austere and cold in manner, and endowed with such indomitable pluck and perseverance as have never been surpassed in this world. He did more than any other man to extend the dominion of France in the New World. As Champlain had founded the colony of Canada and opened the way to the Great Lakes, so La Salle completed the discovery of the Mississippi, and added to the French possessions the vast province of Louisiana.*

—JOHN FISKE

NEXT JOURNEY in force to Lake Ontario was that of a new governor, the Chevalier Rémy de Courcelle in the year 1671, pleasantly reported in the *Paris Documents*\* by an unknown scribe. He writes that cascades or rapids on the great St. Lawrence waterways are eight in number, of which six lie between Montreal and Lake Ontario, the seventh is Niagara, and the eighth between Lakes Huron and Superior. He adds:

"What is called a rapid in this country is not a current of water, but a current caused by a pitch so great that the water combs violently up, breaking sometimes three or four feet. I have seen some such leap over eight or ten feet, so that the hair of the head stands on end when one is obliged to pass those places."

To cope with these rapids the French successfully tried out a large plank bateau, apparently the first time so large a vessel had been used for the rough voyage to Lake Ontario. For these tumultuous waters

---

\* *Paris Documents,* I-VIII, 1631-1774. Transcripts of Documents in the archives of the Ministère de la Marine et des Colonies; of the Ministère de la Guerre; and in the Bibliothèque de Roi, at Paris. Translated and edited by E. B. O'Callaghan, M. D., and published as Volume IX of *Documents Relative to Colonial History of the State of New York.* (Procured in Holland, England and France under the direction of John Romeyn Brodhead, agent, under Act of May 2, 1839. Webb, Parsons & Company, Albany, Printers, under Act of March 30, 1849.)

the chronicler considered the fragile Indian canoe altogether too perilous. Passengers had to keep kneeling or sitting because ten pounds on one side more than the other would cause a lurch. Yet canoes were so light that a man or—at most—two could carry them, and with skilled paddlers some of the larger craft could easily support six or eight men with their provisions and baggage. A particular skill was required, and for want of it many greenhorns lost their lives.

Such were the canoes, made of birch bark over a cedar frame. In those frail barks—literally of bark—long and perilous journeys had been undertaken by Frenchmen through two generations to advance trade and war. Welcomed into the land by Indians who desired their aid against the Iroquois, the French at first "found no inconvenience from those wars. They were here only for the Beaver trade without caring about making any settlement or clearing any land." But Courcelle's scribe in 1671 wisely concluded that those simple days were done. Frenchmen had moved out of the fortified areas to live dispersed along the rivers, each on his own farm. Consequently they were open to attack and it was no longer possible to overlook Iroquois hostility.

Notwithstanding distance, fatigue, expense and short supplies, expeditions were required even after a treaty of peace had been forced from the Five Nations in 1667. Thereafter show of force usually sufficed, as with this expedition of Courcelle. Even without heavy fighting, however, troops faced an arduous task. Courcelle's party took ten days for the upstream voyage from Montreal against only three days on the return trip. The St. Lawrence rapids made the beginning the worst part of a trip to the interior. But time after time French expeditions ascended them.

Peace with the Iroquois, though seldom profound, did more than protect habitants on settled beaches; it also gave France a firm take-off for future discovery. Stimulating news came in from the West. Missionaries en route to the great river called Ohio by the Iroquois and Mississippi by the Ottawa, had failed to reach that stream, but learned enough of it to conclude that "the river disembogues into another sea . . . it is probable it waters those countries toward New Spain, which abound in gold and silver." As yet no Frenchman had seen the Father of Waters. This shrewd clerical hint of the existence of a Gulf of Mexico receiving a stream larger than the St. Lawrence may have been influenced by reports heard in the Far Lakes region by Jean Nicolet and St. Lusson, then on the move in the West—"beyond the beyond."

Next strode into power a majestic figure, Louis de Buade, Count de Palluau et de Frontenac, French Canada's greatest ruler after Champlain. Frontenac served two terms—1672-1682 and 1689-1698—being recalled to service because of errors of his successors during the interval.

As usual in the royal instructions to new governors, Frontenac was directed to smite the Iroquois, develop trade and agriculture, encourage exploration and promote marriage of "youths at twenty years and girls at fifteen." In reply the Governor asked for the wherewithal to accomplish these greatly mixed objectives—specifically, 150 girls to wed wifeless men who were fast turning into banditti and buccaneers, and more armament on Lake Ontario, which the new governor recognized as the vital area. French interests required strengthening of the small trading post on the Bay of Quinte, established by his predecessor in office, and also a "row galley" to sweep the waters. If Louis would but provide for these, Frontenac declared no one need fear the Iroquois again.

Frontenac started upcountry in a sloop on June 3, 1673. Accompanying him was Father Claude Dablon, Superior of the Jesuits, a missionary whose fame had spread from Quebec to the Wisconsin tributaries of the Mississippi. He had served among the Onondaga in New York, then in Wisconsin, next with Father Marquette along Superior, and at Sault Ste. Marie, where he represented the Church at the great council convened there by St. Lusson on June 14, 1671. A headland on Lake Ontario's south shore, where he made camp on his first journey westward to the Onondaga, has recently been named Dablon Point in his honor. The Governor was also accompanied by many notables, 400 soldiers and a number of Huron. The expedition, occupying 125 canoes and two bateaux, proceeded in nine sections.

Whoever took that route for the first time was always impressed by the perils of getting a flotilla upstream through the rapids, but in nine days smooth water was reached. Iroquois canoes now arrived to say that 200 of the "most ancient and influential" of the Five Nations awaited the Governor at Quinte. Frontenac sent word to meet him at Cataracqui, near present Kingston, for the map had told his unerring eye that a fort there would command the route by which northwest furs came to Montreal. For twenty years weak governors had flirted with this idea, but Frontenac acted where his predecessors had merely advised.

There at Cataracqui, day after day, the two parties made powwow, delivered magnificent speeches, exchanged wampum, presents and promises. Humbly the Iroquois agreed to everything demanded, including even the sending of some of their children to be educated in Quebec, where they would be so many hostages for the good behavior of their fathers. This was a real sacrifice, for Indian children were deeply beloved, perhaps because there were few of them.

France was winning every trick. Years afterward it developed that all through this period King Charles II had been receiving secret subsidies from France. For the moment the province of New York, an appanage of the king's brother, the Duke of York, would not contest rising French influence on its distant frontier. The Iroquois could not expect even moral support from the British and had to accept the great Count Frontenac as their whilom champion. With the erection of Fort Frontenac at Cataraqui, rapidly built by La Salle, Iroquois monopoly of Lake Ontario ceased. The fort itself remained an important factor in imperial strategy until burned by the English seventy-five years later.

When Jolliet returned from the Mississippi, on which he had embarked with Father Marquette on May 17, 1673, Frontenac grew eager to learn where that mighty stream met salt water. One of America's greatest explorers stood ready to find out. He was Robert Cavelier, Sieur de la Salle, appointed commandant at Fort Frontenac, who promptly petitioned for the seigneury there. The Governor granted it along with a patent of nobility, on condition that La Salle hold himself in readiness to leave for the West as soon as authority could be received from Paris. Previously La Salle's home had been the feudal domain of St. Sulpice, eight miles west of Montreal. Today it bears the name of Lachine (China), said by Abbé Faillon to have been applied in derision because of its master's dream of a westward passage to China.

That expedition has already been mentioned. Little is known of its actual achievement, although many have believed that La Salle reached and explored the upper Ohio. Conceiving his lifework to be the descent of the Mississippi to its mouth, La Salle eagerly awaited royal authority and backing.

Meantime, against many obstacles, he started a promising settlement at his new seigneury on Lake Ontario. His accomplishments there were remarkable. He was granted the site on consideration that he would spend 11,000 livres on the king's account for construction of the fort. Completing his contract took 9,000 more livres. Fifty to sixty settlers and several Récollet missionaries were brought in from France at La Salle's expense, together with livestock, seeds and implements. These feats of colonization between 1673 and 1679 are modestly related in a "Remonstrance to the Minister" penned in 1684 and published in the *Paris Documents.** In this he speaks of "increase in buildings and clearances; encircling the place with a strong wall on the land side and strengthening the palisade toward the water." Of even more importance from the aspect of dominion, La Salle carried out Talon's idea of naval control by having "barks constructed which navigate every part of the Lake, keep the Iroquois in check, deprive the English, without violence, of a part of the trade, and close the passage to the deserters agreeably to the express orders M. de Frontenac had received." In short, it was La Salle who made Lake Ontario for a time as peaceful as a French millpond, by building an impregnable strong point and basing upon it naval strength sufficient to apply French power to every shore.

On May 12, 1678, Louis XIV granted the desired authority but no funds. La Salle was authorized to explore the West for five years and build any forts desired, providing he did so at his own expense and refrained from trading with Indians who habitually brought their furs to Montreal. For compensation he could trade as he pleased in the skins of the "cibolo" or buffalo. Frontenac gave La Salle his steady moral support but little more.

Although already "land poor" and beset by petty jealousies, La Salle proceeded with thorough advance preparations. In late autumn his advance party, commanded by La Motte de Lussière, proceeded along the north shore of Ontario to the Niagara portage with shipbuilding supplies. Garrulous Father Louis Hennepin of the Récollet order accompanied this group as chaplain, and so, as graph-

---

* *Doc. Rel. to Col. Hist. of N. Y.,* IX, 213.

ically related in his lively account, had the good fortune to view the Great Cataract of Niagara in its native splendor. A palisaded warehouse was built in December at present-day Lewiston where the portage path left the Niagara River for the long, stiff carry to Lake Erie's level beyond the Falls. For winter food it is said that La Motte went to Seneca well inland in search of corn which on delivery became the first grain to pass in commerce along those waters later so important in the grain and flour trade.

La Salle came on for a flying visit in the early winter of 1679, and then hurried back to Frontenac to wrestle with finances for the advance in force the following June. At that time he used one of his brigantines for the voyage up the lake and stopped at Irondequoit Bay, where a "chapel of bark" was erected for the Mass of departure. A few years earlier or later, his passage of Lake Ontario and the Niagara portage might have been contested, or at least protested; but the Iroquois had been humbled sufficiently to let French expansion proceed apace in this middle period.

In a rude shipyard on the south shore of Cayuga Creek, at present La Salle, New York, his men built the *Griffin,* a small sailing vessel to be used in navigating the Upper Lakes. This establishment contained several bark houses for soldiers and workmen, one of which was used by Father Hennepin as a chapel and here Mass was said regularly for the first time on the Niagara frontier. But what avails piety and faith against debt? Word came of the seizure of both La Salle's estates by creditors. Resolving to leave his future to a higher court, he began the first navigation by sail of the chain of Upper Lakes. Passing through Erie, Huron and the straits of Michilimackinac, he reached the northern end of Lake Michigan after heavy storms and difficulties of supply.

Here the *Griffin* was sent back to Niagara to pacify La Salle's creditors with a cargo of furs and to bring back a load of urgently needed stores. Neither ship nor crew was ever seen again. Presumably the little ship foundered in one of the late-season gales which still terrorize Great Lakes mariners, but where and how remains a mystery.

After the *Griffin's* departure La Salle led his party on to the Illinois River, where he built a small post called Fort Crèvecoeur. Indian hostility and hunger reduced morale to the point of mutiny. Convinced that no help could be expected from the *Griffin,* the commander, leaving his post to the harsh, iron-handed Lieutenant Tonty, departed with four white companions and one Indian guide—a Mohegan far displaced from his own region—for the East. A meandering route led them for more than a thousand miles back to Lake Ontario and Montreal.

There misfortune of another kind met La Salle head on. A ship from France carrying to him a cargo worth 20,000 livres was wrecked in the dangerous channels of the Gulf. Undeterred, he went back to Fort Frontenac and set about gathering supplies and reinforcements, on credit, for Fort Crèvecoeur. He was outfitting for the West again when word came that the mutinous garrison of Crèvecoeur had deserted. Only Tonty and a few others had remained faithful. It is characteristic of La Salle that his next push was partly a punitive expedition in which he inexorably hunted down the deserters before going to the relief of Tonty's party, which had taken refuge with the friendly Illinois Indians.

The year 1680, however, witnessed a smashing raid against the Illinois by the irrepressible Iroquois, who, restrained in one direction, promptly broke out in another. In the face of this menace Tonty had withdrawn to Green Bay, and when La Salle arrived at Fort Crèvecoeur he found it reduced to ashes. Halted by this catastrophe, La Salle made treaties with the Illinois against the Iroquois in order to render the entire region safe for Frenchmen. In May 1681 he proceeded east again by the water route, picked up Tonty and at last came home to his Ontario seigneury.

At this point La Salle's enemies concluded he was whipped. Apparently he was right back where he started from geographically and far worse off financially than he had been three years before. Actually he had laid deep foundations in knowledge of navigation of the lakes and in better Indian relations in the Illinois country. Far from being disheartened, he started again and this time fortune was with him. Once more he advanced by way of Lake Michigan to the mouth of the Chicago. Descending the Illinois and the Mississippi, on April 9, 1682, La Salle planted the Bourbon fleur-de-lis flag at the mouth of the Father of Waters and in the name of his sullen master annexed the vast empire drained by its waters. The king so richly dowered by his dauntless subject had expressed himself a little prematurely in declaring that La Salle's western explorations were "very useless and such enterprises must be prevented hereafter, as they tend only to debauch the inhabitants by hope of gain, and to diminish the revenue from the Beaver."

The royal tone changed when La Salle, after returning upstream and visiting Canada, continued on to France. His request for a colony to be settled by a naval expedition was granted. Amid a paean of hero worship the hero endeavored to settle his tangled private affairs which had been worsened by the temporary retirement of Count Frontenac from the governorship. Frontenac's successor, La Barre, described as both weak and grasping, aided the vendetta against La Salle by authorizing seizure of the latter's properties in 1684. This inspired his "Remonstrance," already quoted in part.

It would be pleasant to record that full justice was done to La Salle before the end of his tumultuous life, but such is not the way of princes. This great man's life came to an untimely end. The naval expedition to the mouth of the Mississippi lost its way and came to grief upon the coast of Texas, thanks to the wretched navigation of a blockhead captain. La Salle started overland in search of the great river, hoping to ascend it and secure supplies, only to be ambushed and killed by his own mutinous followers. Thus perished miserably in an utter wilderness, in March 1687, at the age of forty-three years, the former master of Lake Ontario and leader in the plan to unite in empire the St. Lawrence and Mississippi watersheds. In the entire history of great captains of explorations there are few to equal Champlain and La Salle in nobility of soul, righteous conduct and inflexible will.

While La Salle had been struggling in the wilderness of the Illinois country, altogether unaware of his patron's departure from Canada, Frontenac returned to France in 1682, La Barre succeeding him. During his three-year term Canada descended again to a "distressful condition." This decline coincided with the increasingly firm policy of Thomas Dongan, Governor of New York. Dongan—although a Catholic like his royal master, the Duke of York—strongly reasserted the British position, and never thereafter did the British Crown and Iroquois Confederacy entirely part company in statecraft.

Presuming upon Frontenac's departure and the absence of the vigilant La Salle, the Iroquois attempted a renewal of their control of the fur trade on Lake Ontario. La Barre moved against them in 1684 with 1,100 French soldiers and Canadian trappers, plus 700 Indian allies. This expedition formed the largest gathering of whites thus far in Lake Ontario history. Their goal was the Onondaga country, heart of the Confederacy and home of a people heartily disliked in Canada for a special reason. After inviting Father Le Moyne to establish a mission, which was done in 1656, the Onondaga by their conduct aroused such suspicion that the missionaries fled secretly by night two years later. Other hostile incidents had so increased the Onondaga reputation for treachery that La Barre intended to settle matters once and for all, after the determined manner of military men who think a show of force solves everything.

His plans soon went awry. At Fort Frontenac his troops suffered losses from sickness. On the simple crossing to the Oswego outlet (Choueguen) the navigators missed the mark and landed instead at the mouth of the Salmon River. Whereas the Oswego led directly to the fields of the Five Nations, the Salmon drained a forest which even today is little more than a cutover wilderness. As a thoroughfare the Salmon led nowhere. More soldiers fell sick there and the site—previously described as rich in fisheries—fully earned its French title of *La Famine* or Hungry Bay. Unable to proceed farther, La Barre put on a brave face and called a council. At first he met defiance from his Indian listeners, who replied that they were freeborn men and would trade with whom they pleased. Next day both sides grew calmer, smoked the peace pipe, uttered the usual flatteries and empty promises. What was left of the army, large for its day and objective, turned homeward without significant accomplishment. La Barre soon gave way to the more vigorous but undiplomatic Denonville.

His administration is notable in the annals of Ontario for the first military expedition by whites against the Seneca, most westerly nation of the Iroquois, and likewise for the founding of famous Fort Niagara at the junction of the lake and the Niagara River. The troops left Montreal on June 11, 1687. They stopped off at Fort Frontenac, treacherously seized Indians who had come to parley, and reached Irondequoit Bay on July 10. It was swift travel for 2,000 Frenchmen and 600 Indians in a fleet of 200 bateaux and as many canoes. Reinforcement of 180 Frenchmen and more than 300 Indians from the

Upper Lakes, under Tonty and La Durantaye, met the larger force at Irondequoit.

Standing in overwhelming strength on the Irondequoit shore, the French were only thirty miles from the Seneca villages, with an easy route thither up the wide valley which once had accommodated the mightier flow of the Genesee. Father Thierry Beschefer in a Jesuit *Relation* described how, landing unopposed, all set to work "to build a fort for the protection of the boats and canoes of the army, which was to march overland to seek the enemy in their own country. As this post was of great importance, 400 men were left in it under the command of Sieur Dorvilliers."

The main body of the army advanced toward a Seneca village. The defenders fought from ambush, inflicting losses in killed and wounded. Seneca villages, then fairly near the lake in present Monroe and Ontario Counties, were found abandoned, with one of them in ashes. The invaders destroyed corn in the fields and burned what was left from the previous year. For nine days the army burned relentlessly, its leader certain that loss of grain stores would cause a deadly famine. In well-rounded, clerical prose the commander's calculations were given to prove that since the Seneca had as many mouths as the other four Iroquois nations combined, their allies could not possibly feed the Seneca for fourteen months. "Those who will disperse through the woods, to live by fishing and hunting, will be liable to be captured and killed by the savages, their foes, who are resolved to seek them everywhere."* And yet in general the French treated Indians rather better than either the British or the American colonials did.

Having demonstrated afresh the superiority of white civilization, Denonville led his army back to Irondequoit, meditating on matters of imperial gravity for both France and America. He decided "it was of highest importance to build a fort at the entrance of the Niagara river, whereby Lake Erie discharges into Lake Ontario, 80 leagues from Cataronky, and over 140 from Montreal." This post, which was to be called Niagara, would dominate the Seneca, serve as a refuge for Indians friendly to the French and anchor French maritime power firmly in the west as Fort Frontenac had done at the

---

* R. G. Thwaites (ed.), *The Jesuit Relations and Allied Documents* (Cleveland, 1896-1901), LXIII, 277.

lake's eastern end. After placing Niagara in a state of defense with a rude structure, Denonville left 100 men there, the largest garrison he felt able to keep supplied, owing to transport difficulties.

The fort at Niagara was built upon the site of a blockhouse erected by La Salle in 1679, on a sightly point between the eastern angle of Lake Ontario and the Niagara River, a spot ever since defended by a succession of forts and now occupied by both old Fort Niagara and a large modern military establishment.

Throughout New France and Old France alike, Denonville's expedition aroused applause, but Father Beschefer, its scribe, believed that Canada remained in great danger, especially as the Iroquois were again being incited by the English. These savages soon attacked several outlying French settlements in revenge for the ruin wrought on their villages and the indignities heaped upon captives.

Thirty-six Iroquois captured while prowling near Fort Frontenac were sent to France to labor in galleys. Iroquois protests were seconded by Governor Dongan, who now claimed the right of protection for all Five Nations, and insisted that the captives should be sent back to America. In this demand he was fully sustained by England's new king, James II. Later when Count Frontenac returned in 1689 to resume governing Canada, he brought back with him the survivors of this hideous cruelty, for to an Indian death under torture would have been much preferred to slave labor far from his beloved homeland.

In the meantime the Iroquois inflicted full retribution, of a kind which brought Denonville's administration to a dismal close. The Confederacy rallied, no doubt with underground British assistance, to avenge Seneca wrongs. Within a year three of the main French settlements were ravaged. Environs of Fort Frontenac were laid waste by 800 warriors; the fort held, but later had to be abandoned for a time. Niagara was so closely besieged that its garrison could not stir outside the walls even to recover their dead. Starvation took heavy toll, and that new outwork of empire also was abandoned as soon as the arrival of spring let the miserable survivors escape by water. Twelve hundred Iroquois descended upon Montreal, and nearly all settlers outside the fortifications perished. Estimates of the Iroquois invasion say that it cost a thousand lives and set the colony back fifty years in population and extent. West of Montreal, French power

GENERAL JOHN SULLIVAN

PETER GANSEVOORT

MARINUS WILLETT

GENERAL

NICHOLAS HERKIMER

SIR WILLIAM JOHNSON

COLONEL GUY JOHNSON

COLONEL JOHN BUTLER

JOSEPH BRANT

crumbled wherever the Five Nations could bring their revived strength to bear.

In this extremity Frontenac was recalled from his retirement in France, and throughout his few remaining years strove valiantly to undo the errors of his two predecessors, restore the old prosperity and defend Canada, which was now in extreme danger. Immediately upon his return, war with the British began on a scale greater than ever before. Previous conflicts between the two great powers in America had been short and often undeclared, but the issue of American empire, now seriously raised for the first time, would not be settled until the end of four world wars in steady sequence.

# Chapter 6

## Empires Won and Lost

---

*It is in those vessels they [the French] carry the soldiers, artillery, ammunition and provisions to the forts and transport to and fro the goods they sell and buy from the Indians. By means only of the mastery of that lake [Ontario] is it that they have acquired and still hold their favor over all the Indians from Canada to Messasippi and thence back to Canada.*

—LIEUTENANT-GOVERNOR GEORGE CLARKE

---

O<small>N SEVERAL</small> occasions, as we have seen, French and British forces clashed in the New World before 1690. Armed conflict had resulted in the British capture of Quebec, and the English Hudson's Bay Company's claim to the fur monopoly of that region had been hotly contested by force of arms. But these struggles are rated as piratical or commercial rivalries rather than official and recognized war. Therefore it is common to call King William's War, 1690-1697, the first intercolonial war.

There is rough justice in naming the American end of the conflict for King William III, Prince of Orange and husband of Mary Stuart, daughter of King James II of England. William, a Protestant Dutchman, succeeded his unpopular Catholic father-in-law on the British throne after a successful bloodless invasion of England and a campaign in Ireland. This English revolution immediately brought war with France, whose great king, Louis XIV, had steadfastly backed the house of Stuart in both exile and restoration. Almost immediately the fires of European war spread to the New World.

Here Britain possessed the advantage in population; France, that of better communications and Indian relations. Her extensive areas were lightly peopled. Only 11,249 French persons, scarcely one-twentieth of the population of the rival English colonies, were listed as dwelling in North America in a census of 1688. Acadia, as distinct from Canada, had only 900 inhabitants from the Kennebec to Hudson Bay. Count Frontenac, once more in harness with the task of

66

defending Acadia as well as Canada, was also charged to recover Hudson Bay and capture Manhattan, which remained a French objective for the next twenty-five years. Also he was advised to strike soon against the Iroquois country, in order to revive French prestige among western Indians disaffected by revived Iroquois strength.

Action soon began along the eastern seaboard and as far inland as Montreal and Schenectady. The little Dutch town on the Mohawk was raided and burned on February 8, 1690. Sixty persons, including seventeen children and ten Negro slaves, were massacred, and the survivors suffered intensely as they fled in deep snow and bitter cold.

It is sometimes argued that this expedition was aimed at Albany, sixteen miles from Schenectady, and of course for military purposes a far more strategic location. The explanation is sometimes given that the drive went astray because the invaders missed the right fork of a trail in the Adirondacks, and found themselves before the wrong settlement when time came to attack. Manifestly Schenectady had no importance as a station on the way to Manhattan, but at least British supplies to the Iroquois were channeled through it and the place had paramount significance to the Mohawks near by. If the expedition were intended merely to daunt the Iroquois, Schenectady would serve the purpose at small risk. The night attack found the village wide open. In addition to the sixty killed on the spot, roughly forty persons froze in the bitter weather, since their houses were burned in a systematic holocaust. Relief militia forces from Albany with Mohawk help chased the expedition back to Canada, inflicting some losses on the way, but once more Frontenac had proved that France used a long arm against distant foes.

Another descent was made into eastern New York, but we are chiefly concerned with the third expedition, the so-called "grand castigation" of 1696, when Frontenac himself descended on the Oneida and Onondaga with 2,000 men, in the last year of the war. This drive was planned as retaliation for an Iroquois shift toward Britain after they had entered into a truce with Frontenac at Quebec two years before. Caught between the French and British imperial millstones, the Iroquois were now being ground down to the point of mere opportunism, yielding allegiance to the latest comer with the largest gifts of cloth, powder and weapons. Frontenac, warned of danger by his agents, decided that a weak policy on the eastern half of Ontario would encourage attacks on more distant places, since the Iroquois were suspected of arousing western tribes. Although the post at Niagara had been rebuilt after a fashion in 1695, it was not strong enough to withstand a siege.

With an energy which belied his years and infirmities, Frontenac prepared his last wilderness campaign. As usual, his flotilla stopped at the fort bearing his name, which his former lieutenant, La Salle, had built. Then it crossed to the Oswego inlet, landed there and pushed on upstream until, by the network of waterways which gave the aborigines their old advantages for war and trade, the French canoes rode the still waters of Lake Onondaga.

Eight or nine miles south of the lake, a day's march brought the invaders to a burned Onondaga village, whose inhabitants had applied the "scorched earth" policy and then departed for the woods. Frontenac, infirm in body but firm in will, journeyed in an armchair, but his progress could hardly have been pleasant over the rough and narrow trails. Perceiving the risk of maintaining so large an army in a burned-out country, he turned back home after dispatching his second-in-command, Philippe de Rigaud de Vaudreuil, to turn eastward and burn Oneida villages, if possible seizing grain before applying the torch.

Although the Onondaga had found and applied the correct defense against invasion by a numerous force unable to maintain itself in hostile country without captured food, the Five Nations soon capitulated anew. Especially were they chagrined by the failure of the British in Albany to get wind of Frontenac's designs in advance and to send help to the threatened Indian "castles." Not yet could Britain fulfill promises in central New York, more easily reached from Fort Frontenac than from Schenectady. Promptly the Iroquois ceased trying to stir up the western tribes and sued for peace. Once more Frontenac had won.

Stalemate ensued after the phantom Peace of Ryswick in 1697. Four years later, when a childless king died in Spain and Louis XIV claimed the succession for a Bourbon prince, the war drums sounded again. Called the War of the Spanish Succession abroad, Queen Anne's War here, the fighting dragged along till 1713. Rather oddly, operations leapfrogged Lake Ontario. British naval operations against Quebec and land operations from Albany toward Montreal both failed; and at Detroit the French so successfully resisted the Foxes from Wisconsin that the latter never recovered from their losses. Nevertheless, the war elsewhere had gone so hard with the French that in the Peace of Utrecht they yielded possession of Acadia according to its ancient boundaries, Newfoundland excepting certain fishing rights, and all claims to Hudson Bay. Another clause of that treaty has a special meaning for us: France agreed not to molest the Five Nations subject to the dominion of Great Britain.

But what were the legitimate domains of the Five Nations? They had always claimed as hunting grounds more land than they occupied effectively, and they held certain other peoples in a fluctuating, uncertain vassalage. Room to quarrel again over that, France and Britain, when the mood for quarreling arrives! And did Cape Breton Island go with Acadia and Newfoundland?

Whether Fort Frontenac should be rebuilt became an issue. Creditors of La Salle urged its restoration as a means of recovering on the dead hero's adjacent landed estate. The opposition asserted that it was badly located for both trade and war. Near-by swamps were declared unhealthful and "forty miles of water in constant agitation" lay between the post and the natural center for future trade at Oswego. Nevertheless, the fort was rebuilt as a small stone structure in the same place—perhaps because Oswego seemed too near the Iroquois for safety.

Proposals to renew effective possession of Niagara by construction of a new fort were made in 1706, a wise decision from every consideration of trade and defense. Together with Fort Frontenac near the eastern gateway, Fort Niagara toward the western end would complete the effective bracketing of the entire lake. Ships could sail back and forth in two days, at a sharp saving of time for transport of goods and furs. Documents of the period note many further advantages: establishing a fortress to keep the Iroquois in check, shelter other Indian allies and keep them from trading with the English; supplying the post of Detroit; and clearing its eastbound furs. A few years earlier, Madame Cadillac and her children had passed that way on their journey to Detroit and had been well received by the Seneca. It is recorded that the warmth of this welcome, which involved savage kisses, rather daunted the French ladies, but no harm came to them. Cadillac himself used the Niagara route on his frequent journeys between Detroit and the East, because the hazards of nature were fewer than by the Ottawa River route. All these considerations led to Niagara's reinstatement on the French military map.

In rebuilding the post the French felt obliged to move softly in order not to affront the Iroquois or arouse the British; shrewdly they sought to confront the latter with a *fait accompli* by backing one of their most successful agents and traders, Louis Thomas de Joncaire or Jonquière, Lieutenant of Marines, who was already partially established at Niagara. Son of a common soldier, Joncaire had risen by his merits in a service which usually paid more heed to birth than to deeds. A bluff, hearty man, he had so bulldozed the Seneca while their prisoner in 1694 that they esteemed him ever after. In Quebec, before Governor de Callières in 1700, their sachems had honored Joncaire by asking that he go to reside among them, in which case he could select any site he desired for his trading post. The wily French saw in this offer an opportunity of managing a delicate affair without noise, as Joncaire could go there "as a private individual intending simply to form an establishment for his family, at first bringing only the men he will need to erect and fortify his dwelling, and afterward in pretext of conveying supplies and merchandise increasing their number insensibly. . . ."*

Thus subtly were Joncaire and his two famous sons, Daniel (Chabert) and Philippe, introduced to the scenes where they became a dynasty of some significance to American history through the next fifty years.

At the outset, however, there were the usual hesitations and difficulties. To make a success of the new post both commercially and politically, the king was advised to furnish at lowest prices 25,000 to 30,000 tons of powder, lead and trade goods for which shipping space should be provided. Necessary also would be regulations "to prevent all the improper carriage hitherto carried on, by the transportation of Brandy into the forest, which has been the cause of all existing disorders and evils."

For ten years adequate fortification was delayed although Joncaire did his part. He and his descendants, intermarrying with the Seneca, almost pulled that powerful people from the British alliance and

---

* *Doc. Rel. to Col. Hist. of N. Y.*, IX, 773.

sometimes nullified the influence of the Great Covenant Chain for years at a time. Rightly did Governor Vaudreuil describe the founder of that famous frontier family as possessing "every quality requisite to insure success. He is daring, liberal, speaks the language with great perfection, hesitates not."

Reports of a special investigator, D'Aigremont, who met Joncaire at Niagara, cast cold water at the whole enterprise and intimated not only that Joncaire profited in the distribution of supplies and presents to the Iroquois, but also that he shared the take with the Governor. But this cool sleuth of the Crown could find no good in the operations of Cadillac, Tonty or anyone else in authority on the French frontier near or far. All were off side in shady practices; all were at odds with one another. Graft ruled where confusion did not, and one suspects the investigator of jealousy against well-known men of action.

During this interval of waiting for funds with which to develop Niagara solidly, Joncaire placed the Governor everlastingly in his debt by disposing of an Indian or half-breed named Montour, who early in May 1709 was bringing ten western sachems to Albany for a powwow. The lurid account of this execution (French version) or murder (English version) gives us at once a measure of Joncaire's mettle and the flavor of desperate times. Tricking Montour out of possession of his knife and tossing it away as a signal, the French agent had one of his minions smite Montour down with his hatchet. This cold-blooded killing went unavenged although the Montour connection—of which further history will be given in later pages of this book—was both vindictive and powerful enough to bestow its name on Montour Falls, Montourstown and Montour Mountain in New York. Usually enlisted in the French interest, they perhaps saw in this British agent a family traitor deserving his fate. It was well for Joncaire's reputation that Governor Vaudreuil took full responsibility, advising New York's Governor Burnet it was impossible to bring the victim in for trial.

M. de Longueuil, Lieutenant Governor at Montreal, became the next champion of Niagara construction. In 1716 he recommended that a small post north of Niagara Falls on Lake Ontario, which could be reached in seven or eight days by canoe from Fort Frontenac, would prevent the western Indians from coming to the

Iroquois to trade after they had hunted in the neighborhood of Lake Erie. All trade, he advised, should be carried on in the king's name and for his profit. Also, M. de Longueuil proposed, a bark should be built to ply between the two posts. By these measures French traders could secure the greater portion of peltries which were then going to the English. Independent traders whose operations were prejudicial to Fort Frontenac would be driven from the lake.

Governor Burnet of New York had news of these proposals through the Mohawk grapevine and entered serious protest, to which Governor Vaudreuil replied that the French claim to Niagara was half a century old and never before had it been questioned. La Salle, he said, had built one fort there, and Denonville another. France had garrisoned the place with a hundred men in 1684, and although that garrison had been removed the site remained a common trading place for the French. As for Joncaire's trying to divorce the Seneca from their British connection, which Burnet also charged, Governor Vaudreuil replied—tongue in cheek, no doubt—that one of Joncaire's character and qualities would never undertake such a rupture of the existing peaceful relations.

Captain Joncaire was popular with the Seneca and a favorite guest in their villages. He even wintered in one, in 1720-1721, when intrigues were raging in connection with the establishments at Niagara and Irondequoit Bay. The latter post, Fort des Sables, at present Sea Breeze ten miles from modern Rochester, was planted about that time, 1716 to 1721, to take advantage of the natural trade route from Lake Ontario to the Seneca country. As part of his aggressive British policy, Governor Burnet sent Captain Johannes Bleecker and David Schuyler, a young scion of the famous Dutch family of Albany, to open trade at that point. Another British agent, Laurence Clawson or Clason, figured in an undercover duel for Seneca influence, along with a Dutch smith, Barent Wemp. The Joncaires, with their own French smith to sharpen Seneca tomahawks and active missionaries to offset the British penetration by pious words, eventually carried the day, and Fort des Sables remained without further competition for many years.

This location on Irondequoit Bay is almost at the southernmost point of the great south-reaching curve of Lake Ontario. It still provides a natural haven for mariners wearied by headwinds, just as it did for untold centuries. Remains of sturgeon bones in long-buried rubbish heaps indicate the presence of man on that beach 1,500 to 3,000 years ago, perhaps when near-by Irondequoit Creek was a mighty river carrying the full flood of the Genesee. In historic times the Genesee, following another channel, has been blocked for navigation by a series of falls and by sand bars at the mouth. But ten miles eastward the old channel provided an easy entrance to the Seneca country. Canoes could travel the smaller waterway to the landing place in what is now Ellison Park, from which the Seneca villages could be reached by a not-too-difficult trail also leading to the Genesee above the falls.

The contest between France and Britain for Irondequoit, Niagara and other strategic locations on the Ontario littoral, remote though it seems today, was once a life-and-death struggle deciding who should rule the interior of America. One of the main causes of contention was the unsettled boundaries between the two powers. It had been agreed that a Treaty of the Limits would soon be negotiated in order to settle all disputes between the two nations forever; but in 1720-1725 this very prospect of settlement drove the rivals to nail down their claims with fortifications before boundaries were run.

French claims and titles to Niagara and Irondequoit the British countered by getting from the Iroquois in 1722 the right to build at Oswego a post which remained for nearly forty years the only British port on the Great Lakes, a vantage point from which they could keep an eye on French commerce, travel and intrigue.

In 1725 the French commissioned their able engineer officer, De Léry, to build the strong citadel of old Fort Niagara which still stands sentry on New York's bold northwest corner where the Niagara River, all tension passed, pours serenely into Lake Ontario. Scarcely was this fortress finished than Britain began in 1727 to fortify Oswego, near the eastern end of the lake.

Thus a quarter-century of friction preceded the War of the Austrian Succession in 1744-1748, generally called King George's War in American history in doubtful memory of George II, one of the duller British kings. The chief American incident was the capture of Louisburg by New England troops, and chief result of the war was the rise of anti-British feeling when the Crown returned that fortress to France to offset cessions in India which seemed trifling to Americans as compared to the citadel captured in the first successful campaign waged by British Americans on foreign soil. On Lake Ontario the French shipping held complete control and consequently France could pick the point of attack. Struggle centered on the Oswego communications, with the French trying to cut off supplies by means of Indian raiding parties. Oswego held out, partly through the ability of a frontier commissary officer, William Johnson, to get supplies through—the humble beginning of his remarkable public career.

All three of these wars were mainly European, with America merely a side show. Each was part of a British balance-of-power pattern, and as such was a mere incident in what the British historian Seeley well calls "the Second Hundred Years' War against France"— a century in which a chief concern of British policy was to keep Bourbon France from controlling Europe.

The fourth intercolonial war was part of the same historic cycle, but with this variation: it began in America and swept outward to Europe, India and the Seven Seas. America was no longer a side show on the international circuit; its destiny had become a chief concern of the great powers. Some lofty rhetoric on this facet of the encounter has clouded the fact that the French and English in 1754 were ready to fight somewhere or anywhere and began their sparring in America.

The first move came from France when a band from the Upper Lakes raided a British-Indian trading post in Ohio. The moot question of Louisiana's extent with relation to the Mississippi watershed was revived when Blainville de Céleron, descending the Allegheny and Ohio, buried at strategic points along the river lead plates which bore the challenging declaration that the French king possessed those valleys by virtue of the peace treaties of Ryswick, Utrecht and Aix-la-Chapelle.

To defend their claim the French built a series of posts on soil claimed by Virginia. This French occupation aroused Governor Dinwiddie of the Old Dominion in 1753 to send a young militia officer named George Washington, then only twenty-one years of age, with an ultimatum calling upon the French to depart. One of the Joncaires entertained the messenger royally at Venango. George delivered the message and returned after a severe journey with the expected answer, "No!" So the next year Dinwiddie, himself a considerable investor in Ohio lands, sent Washington back to the Forks of the Ohio with a small body of militia. The French were beforehand with more troops and more experienced leaders who forced surrender of the Virginians on July 3, 1754, at Fort Necessity in Fayette County, southwestern Pennsylvania. The signal had been sounded for Mars to reassume command of destiny.

At last both contestants were aware of midland America. The French knew it firsthand in infinite detail; the British not so well. By this time both recognized the strategic importance of its strong points as revealed by the study of even a hazy map. These strong points were obviously five in number:

1. Quebec, commanding the lower St. Lawrence.

2. Montreal, at the junction of water-level routes to the southward and westward.

3. Oswego, commanding the entrance to central New York and the outlet to the St. Lawrence, a post balanced by Fort Frontenac in a somewhat similar location on the French side of the lake. The British realized the need for additional fortifications at Oswego and were at work on Fort Ontario, which still stands, and a third smaller fort.

4. Niagara, commanding the portage from Lake Ontario to Lake Erie and the Allegheny-Ohio river system, and threatening the strongest of Britain's Iroquois allies, the Seneca. The French posts on the Great Lakes and in the Ohio country could hardly be captured while Niagara held safe. Iroquois opposition meant that all supplies for Fort Duquesne, the new French post at the Forks of the Ohio, had to pass Niagara before taking the southward turn; but this roundabout course was mostly navigable waterway for seven months of the year and during the open season offered swifter travel for supplies and munitions than the alternative streams and trails blocked off by Iroquois opposition.

5. Fort Duquesne at the Forks of the Ohio (now Pittsburgh), commanding a second easy opening to the West and South. Extremely vulnerable because of its advanced position and the difficulty of supplying it with war materials, it was nevertheless of immense importance since, if it could be held, it would tie Canada and Louisiana into a single system of defense.

Weighing these considerations, the British rightly decided that Niagara was the anchor of the French line of fortifications, but they unwisely decided to proceed to Niagara by way of Fort Duquesne. The plan of campaign had been worked out by a soldier who had never visited America—the Duke of Cumberland, brother of King George. It is possible, also, that the British commander, General Edward Braddock, having landed at Alexandria, was influenced by Virginia speculators in Ohio lands. At any rate, he took the pick of his regulars and set off through the woods and mountains of Maryland and southern Pennsylvania, a hazardous, fatiguing journey against a vigilant enemy.

Meantime, recognizing that an easier way to Niagara existed, Braddock had ordered Governor Shirley of Massachusetts to Oswego with a force composed of hastily recruited troops. From that port an army could be moved to the very ravelin of Fort Niagara in a week of calm water. Shirley was supposed to meet Braddock there in a sweeping pincers movement.

A third army, aimed at Montreal by the Lake Champlain route, was allotted to Major General William Johnson of the New York militia, whose military experience began as commissary officer at Oswego in the previous war. Although no leader knew the intricate waterways of central New York better than Johnson, he was less well acquainted with those of the Lake Champlain sector to which he was assigned by Braddock, while Shirley for his part proved to be dismally ignorant of Ontario's geography. And, curiously, Johnson received numbers of New England militia to command, while some of his own militia, over whom he had been an officer for twelve years, were assigned to Shirley. In both cases lack of confidence and intense jealousy developed on a scale which colored Yorker-Yankee enmity for generations.

Of the three expeditions Johnson's alone scored any sort of victory. Defending their fortified camp at Lake George, his forces beat off a determined attack and captured the enemy commander, Baron Dieskau, French commander in chief in America, after the latter had scored a triumph in "the bloody morning scout." Braddock's larger force of regulars was routed on the Monongahela in the greatest disaster British arms had sustained in America up to that time. Shirley at Oswego experienced neither victory nor defeat, because he dawdled until Braddock's defeat relieved him of the necessity for action. His expedition strengthened Oswego's defenses but was otherwise a sad failure. However, on June 27, 1755, the British built and launched at Oswego their first naval vessel on Lake Ontario, a move suggested by Benjamin Franklin.

Dieskau's successor, Montcalm—Louis Joseph, Marquis de Montcalm, Gozon de St. Véran—arrived at Quebec in May 1756. That great soldier immediately perceived that the easy way to Niagara for the British lay through Oswego, and to forestall that eventuality he proceeded to isolate the British post. In this campaign of 1756 either the advancing French or the retreating British destroyed practically all units of the system of small British posts painfully erected to guard approaches and portage of the Great Carrying Place between the Hudson-Mohawk River system and Lake Ontario through Wood Creek, Oneida Lake, the Oneida and Oswego Rivers. Most spectacular of these losses was Fort Bull, captured with its garrison and 40,000 pounds of powder by 300 skate-and-snowshoe raiders from La Présentation (Oswegatchie, later Ogdensburg). The scene of this daring exploit is now farmland but the fortifications may be easily traced; and the spot deserves equal consideration with the companion post at the foot of Oneida Lake, Fort Brewerton, which has long been taken care of by New York State and the American Scenic and Historic Preservation Society.

While the puerile British commander, General Webb, conducted feeble defensive war in the Mohawk valley, Oswego was being throttled by Captain Coulon de Villiers' systematic encirclement. The gallant little British fleet, outmanned and outgunned, attempted a diversion by attacking three French vessels off Fort Frontenac on June 27, 1756. The smallest British vessel was captured with fifteen men; the others scurried home. Three days later the dauntless Colonel John Bradstreet, one of the heroes of Louisburg, later Quartermaster General of British forces in America, brought through supplies and reinforcements. Literally his bateaux had to fight through the mazy waterways, the scene of the sharpest engagement still bearing the name of Battle Island. Bradstreet brought back to Albany definite intelligence that large French forces were on their way up the St. Lawrence. The grim Scottish commander in chief, Abercromby, then gave orders for Webb to be ready to move north with a single regiment, the Forty-eighth Foot. Webb marched about August 1, but had gone only halfway to the Oneida carrying place, at modern Rome, New York, when he heard that the blow which had been maturing for so long had at last fallen.

On August 6 the French army, reported 5,000 strong, camped at Henderson Harbor on the eastern shore. Acting with his usual speed in his favorite open warfare, the Marquis de Montcalm sent De Villiers, well attended by Chabert Joncaire's Indian guides, to scout the approaches to the British fortress. No doubt it was hard for 600 men under De Villiers to believe that so vital a position would be so callously neglected. But the only Britishers encountered outside the fort were a little band of ships' carpenters trudging toward the post without adequate guard or welcome. It is said these workmen were captured within 300 yards of the fortifications.

In garrison were two new British line regiments, the Fiftieth and Fifty-first, recruited only the year before in the stews of American seaboard cities. The colonel of the Fiftieth, James F. Mercer, was senior in command, a thorough, steady soldier who would have fought it out to the bitter end. The commander of the Fifty-first, Lieutenant Colonel Littlehales, became the villain of the piece. A third officer worthy of note was Colonel Peter Schuyler of the Jersey Blues. Both officers and men considered themselves forgotten and deserted by their generals.

Montcalm's army, well supplied with artillery, appeared on August 10. Within three days he had the place at his mercy in spite of the three forts. Capturing two warships lying helpless because no other Ontario port was in British hands, the French engineers sank them across the river entrance to hinder escape. Trenches surrounded the doomed garrison. By the evening of August 13 the strongest defense point, Fort Ontario, had been so reduced by cannonades that the garrison abandoned it and crossed the river to old Fort Oswego, the name of which had been changed to Fort Pepperell in honor of the captor of Louisburg in the preceding war. The shift of base was undertaken in good spirit, as it had the advantage of conserving stores and ammunition. The third fort, unfinished, could not be considered tenable; officially known as Fort George, its nickname of Fort Rascal sufficiently indicates its condition and repute.

Soon after the troops crossed the river, just as the French had blown a breach in the walls and were mounting an assault, Colonel Mercer was killed. Littlehales, his successor, hoisted a white flag and the 700 survivors surrendered on August 14. The opinion that Little-hales had been bought appears in James Fenimore Cooper's *Path-finder,* written after the author's residence there as a junior officer in 1808-1809, but it is no longer seriously believed. While the defense lacked the dogged resistance worthy of British regulars and seasoned colonials, it must be remembered that the Fiftieth and Fifty-first were young, badly disciplined regiments shoved too fast into an iso-lated position. There they were insufficiently supplied and in the end abandoned to the attack of larger forces led by a master of mobile warfare. Montcalm, on the ground "first with the most," was too certain of victory to spend Bourbon gold, of which he never had more than was needed for his campaigns, on the enrichment of Oswego's second in command.

As shrewd in Indian relations as in warfare, Moncalm made no effort to hold Oswego, which would have been a heavy risk; but instead, after destroying all structures, turned it back to the Iroquois with fair words. The Indians, remembering the benefits promised to them when the British sought to erect the first fort at Oswego and how little those promises had matured, were impressed. For the next two years Sir William Johnson, Superintendent of all Northern Indians, experienced difficulty in recruiting Iroquois scouts, and for nearly two years Lake Ontario was once more a big French pond completely dominated from one end to the other, while the larger struggle continued to the eastward.

But the quiet of defeat could not endure. Once more John Brad-street entered the Ontario region, this time to effect a telling blow. Having covered well the retreat of Abercromby's army from a dis-astrous defeat at Ticonderoga on July 8, 1758, he was selected to lead an expedition against Fort Frontenac. This move was necessary to regain British prestige with the Indians and also to assist General Forbes's expedition through Pennsylvania to the Forks of the Ohio, where Fort Duquesne lay dependent upon supplies and ammunition shipped through Lake Ontario and stored in large quantities at Frontenac and Niagara.

For this raid Bradstreet used 2,600 provincial troops, 40 Indian scouts and a force of armed bateau men. It was an assignment meet for colonial daring, which preferred the "dash and disappear" frontier fighting to continuous campaigning, and thought standing still under fire was a British absurdity.

A journal of the expedition kept by Lieutenant Colonel Charles Clinton, elderly militia leader, founder of the famous Clinton family of New York and father of the state's first governor, reveals the complete surprise achieved by secrecy and speed: "The Destruction of this place [Fort Frontenac] and of the Shipping, artilery and stores is one of the Greatest Blows the French have met with in America Considering the Consequence of it, as it was the store out of which all the forts to the Southward were supplied. . . . It was Concerted and agreed upon in an Instant (tho looked upon by some as a Chimerical Wild Undertaking) Carried on so Secretly that the French never heard of our Coming until they saw us."*

Actually, this important position surrendered after a day's bombardment, with only two wounded and not a single man killed on the British side. Two ships were captured, loaded with supplies, and sailed away to reviving Oswego, together with 150 prisoners. The rest of the stores, the magazines and all structures were burned.

At once Montcalm the all-victorious recognized the peril to his cause: "I am not discouraged; neither are my troops. We are resolved to find our graves under the ruin of the colony." In a single stroke France had lost control of the lake route, an incredible quantity of scarce materials and prestige throughout the Indian world. The fall of Oswego had been revenged!

As far as inland operations are concerned, the raid on Frontenac proved to be the turning point of the war. After nearly five years of surrenders, defeats or drawn engagements in which weight of numbers had been offset by swift movements and keen generalship, at last a well-planned movement had been carried through with dash and precision to unquestioned victory. Soon after the destruction of Fort Frontenac came abandonment of Fort Duquesne to General Forbes, a French defeat somewhat traceable to destruction at Fort Frontenac of stores intended for the Pennsylvania fortress.

In succession to the disappointing Shirley, Loudon, a governor of Virginia who served as commander in chief, and Abercromby,

---

* The original journal was burned in the New York State Capitol fire at Albany in 1911, but copies were saved and are in the New York State Library. It is unpublished.

Britain now had in America a commander who early gained colonial confidence. At home, Sir Jeffrey Amherst, conqueror of Louisburg, was lampooned as overcautious because he took time to mobilize overwhelming forces before starting a campaign. His concentrations need not have been so large, for the enemy was worn thin with campaigning and had few reserves. Montcalm could rarely dispose of more than 3,000 regulars, plus about 2,000 colonials and militia. By contrast, Abercromby commanded 10,000 when beaten at Ticonderoga. Amherst's 1759 campaign involved the simultaneous descent of three columns upon a given objective.

For the expedition against Niagara, Amherst promised three of his best regiments, with a competent artillery train. The regiments were the Forty-fourth and Forty-sixth Foot and a strong detachment of the Royal Americans, recruited largely from Pennsylvania and drilled by painstaking Swiss officers. Top command he gave to a capable officer, Brigadier General John Prideaux (pronounced Priddy). Two battalions of New York provincial troops were led by Sir William Johnson, major general of militia and Indian superintendent who had been made a baronet for his services at Lake George four years earlier. His remarkable influence over the Iroquois brought in 700 Indians.

The column began to assemble at Schenectady on May 15, 1759. Here are its travel stages: left Schenectady May 20; a slow progress up the Mohawk and through Oneida Lake to reach Oswego on May 26; left Oswego July 1; reached Sodus Bay July 2; spent July 3 and 4 at Irondequoit Bay; reached Braddock's Bay on July 5; Johnson's Creek on July 6; Petite Marais, four miles east of Fort Niagara, on July 7.

That this slow journey was not interrupted indicates how far Canada had fallen in resources and morale, but one last despairing effort was made to force a recall of the expedition. Lieutenant Colonel Haldimand, whom we shall meet later in larger authority, had been left at Oswego with a detachment to refortify that post. A surprise assault on his works was driven off and the base for Prideaux's expedition saved.

Actually the westward-bound flotilla encountered no enemy along the lake shore until it approached the landing place, and then opposition was half-hearted. Trench work began on July 10. A premature sally the next day was beaten back and siege operations resumed. Nine days later General Prideaux, while visiting the trenches, was killed by the bursting of a shell from a coehorn mortar—"head blown off," says one account, in narrating the melancholy end of a good officer on the eve of his greatest chance at fame.

After General Prideaux's death a squabble for command, regulars versus colonials, was resolved by the firmness of Sir William Johnson who insisted on taking responsibility until Brigadier General Gage, the new commander, should appear. Johnson's militia major-general-ship so far outmatched the lieutenant-colonelcies held by the ranking British survivors that the latter gave way, perhaps a little daunted by the Indian superintendent's title, which derived directly from the king, as well as by his wealth and reputation, then near their peak. Presently Haldimand appeared from Oswego to request command but was refused. Sir William continued his predecessor's siege operations by means of which trenches crept nearer and nearer to the lightly manned redoubts. On July 22 the parapet of the flag bastion was pulverized under heavy fire.

Commander of the fortress was Captain François Pouchot, hitherto in authority at Irondequoit and Des Sables. His *Late War in North America* is a dependable source book. One of his principal subordinates was Captain Philippe Joncaire, son of the famous French agent who had secured the site of the fortress. Pouchot had put the works in good repair but his defense lacked plan. A hastily gathered reinforcement was on its way from the French posts westward, but instead of waiting for it he had wasted strength in the premature sally. Then when the 1,600 men from the west under D'Aubry drew near and made a desperate effort to break through at the near-by farm of La Belle Famille, the defenders remained in their fortifications and failed to make a diversion when it would have counted most.

To intercept the threat from the West, Johnson sent tested regulars who stood firm against the charge of the ragged, hungry men and held their volleys until they could pour fire at close range into crowded ranks. The French loss was heavy, especially in officers killed and captured; among the latter were D'Aubry, De Ligneris, Marin and De Repentigny. Survivors in the rank and file melted away and are heard of no more in history. Pouchot surrendered his fortress the next day, July 25, and the fleur-de-lis flag of France descended on a site which had become a fortified part of the French empire seventy-three years before. The victors found in service there cannon which had been captured from Braddock on the Monongahela four years before. They were destined, indeed, for Niagara by Braddock, but fell into other hands. Thenceforward for thirty-seven years the British held the captured post. Today, in compliment to the brave who sleep beneath its soil, Old Fort Niagara flies three flags—French, British, American.

Niagara's surrender preceded by seven weeks the fall of Quebec after the battle on the Plains of Abraham on September 13, 1759, where Montcalm and General Wolfe were both mortally wounded. Fort Niagara military reservation now occupies about 300 acres of the extreme northwest corner of New York State. The Niagara River, flowing in from the southward, makes a west turn just before entering the lake so that a small, easily defended peninsula is formed with a steep escarpment on the northern or lake slope. All but some twenty-five acres is occupied by grounds and buildings of the United States Army, which here maintains one of the great peacetime military establishments. Of late years the famous Twenty-eighth Infantry held the post and represented modern America in the historic pageantry so well and frequently presented by the Old Fort Niagara Association. This society holds under Federal lease, subject to military needs, the tip of the peninsula which contains the citadel of 1727, and other buildings now well restored by the Association. Since all roads to the old fort lead through the military reservation, and the reservation has been used as a mammoth induction center for purposes of the Second World War, customary operations in pursuit of history have been curtailed.

Under ordinary conditions, however, the visitor is privileged to see at Niagara an ancient military establishment in all its picturesque detail. He can enter by a drawbridge at the Gate of the Iroquois, visit the pagodalike watchtower, stroll through subterranean defense galleries, and then examine at his leisure the central citadel as built by the French in 1727 and captured by Johnson in 1759. In restoring this and other structures a successful effort has been made not only to recapture authentic historical flavor, but also to accommodate both regimes, the older French occupancy and the later British one. Thus are presented a seventeenth-century Catholic chapel and an eighteenth-century council room which Johnson used for the stately gatherings of frontier notables for many years after he maneuvered its capture.

Despite its isolated position, more than 50,000 persons visit this beautiful and serene historic shrine each year, to enjoy a rare combination of scenery and history.

Wherever Sir William Johnson went among the tribes it was his duty as Superintendent of Indians for the Northern Department (everything north of the Great Bend of the Tennessee River) to hold an Indian council. These were gaudy, expensive affairs, heavy with oratory, compliments, presents, drink. After the capture of Niagara, Johnson called together a council and told the Iroquois to assist Colonel Bouquet—like Haldimand, of Swiss birth—in his move against the enemy's western posts, and to prepare themselves for another campaign next year when France would be driven out of Canada forever. Next, Johnson convened the recent savage allies of France, warned them to behave, assured them of the Crown's good intentions and explained his policy—a friendly concern for the interests of well-behaved Indians, prompt punishment for those ill-behaved toward their new masters. The last flourish of French power on western Lake Ontario occurred when two small French schooners endeavored to halt embarkation of Johnson's army which returned to Oswego in a swift three-day voyage.

In 1760, a year behind schedule, three columns moved upon Montreal. Amherst and Johnson, proceeding through the Mohawk-Oneida waterway to Oswego, led a great flotilla carrying 10,000 men down the St. Lawrence, meeting Murray on September 7. The next day Colonel Haviland's column came in from the south.

Governor Vaudreuil hastily signed a capitulation for all Canada, against the protest of De Levis, doughty soldier who had succeeded Montcalm. Promise of security for property and religion no doubt weighed heavily with the governor, a weak man with a large family. All else he signed away, regardless of the fact that the war elsewhere remained indecisive and that the definitive Treaty of Paris was not to be signed for another three years.

Canada was conquered; continental New France was off the map for good. A small population had bled itself white trying to hold a vast area. Bourbon France had sent insufficient aid, the string was played out, the will to resist had departed. Of fortitude Canada had plenty up to the moment Montreal beheld three armies, each larger than her largest; but of resources and numbers it never possessed enough.

Thus ended a century and a half of French rule in continental North America and over Lake Ontario. For three years more, until the Peace of Paris validated the capitulation of Vaudreuil at Montreal, the Canadians clung to hope of redemption. They had been out-manned and outgunned but not outgeneraled or outnerved. In fact, for so many years numbers and strength had been offset by wile and wit that the citizenry felt no permanence in accepting British rule, even though they conformed to it readily enough in practice. Down to the sale of Louisiana to the United States in 1803, a few die-hards clung to the idea of reclaiming part of the American Northwest for France. Mysterious Frenchmen and occasionally Frenchwomen, some of them of title and quality, moved deviously along the frontier. In the dim background of Indian conferences they stirred the mem-ory of French favors among the tribesmen for a full generation after the capitulation. One reads of encounters with an unexplained Madame Biron, for instance, in the Oneida country five years after Yorktown.

For fifteen years following the capitulation of Canada in 1760, Great Britain ruled eastern America from Florida to the Pole, as far as trade marched and law could tag after. A loose control over the newly won hinterland was maintained by British garrisons in the old French posts, and the Indian trade was sketchily supervised by agents of Sir William Johnson, Indian superintendent. He, of course, was also Crown manager of political relations with the tribes.

Indian peoples soon resented the calm British assumption that whipping the French gave the victors authority over territory which the Indians had never ceded to France and regarded as their own. Major Robert Rogers' journey to Detroit to take possession of that post was not opposed, but British regular officers were less tactful, and their commander in chief, Sir Jeffrey Amherst, gave them a wrong lead by reducing garrisons, lessening subsidies and taking a high tone whenever dissension arose at the posts. British commanders of isolated forts behaved like generals of divisions representing a lofty conqueror race in control of abject subjects. Indian resentment, dampened somewhat by Johnson's conferences at Niagara and Detroit in 1761, burst into flame at Detroit on May 9, 1763, in the sanguinary uprising called, for small reason, Pontiac's War.

The chief war theaters were the western lakes and the Forks of the Ohio. Fort Niagara was invested on June 5. Johnson had long been aware of rebellion brewing among the Cayuga and Seneca, and now exerted all pressure to hold Iroquois participation in the uprising to a minority in those tribes. In this he was successful. When the Niagara garrison held out, that fort became for the British the anchor of defense it had been for the French in their day, of which Parkman wrote: "The immense extent of inland navigation was safe in hands of France as long as she held Niagara."

For Britain in 1763 a Niagara firmly held meant the ultimate defeat of hostile western Indians. Troops and supplies moved from Oswego to Niagara and across the Niagara portage to beset Erie and Detroit. That way passed Captain Dalyell to meet his death in the Bloody Creek sortie at Detroit, and likewise Lieutenant Cuyler and his doomed men to their rendezvous with death at Point Pelee. On September 14 a British force on its way from the recently constructed Fort Schlosser, two miles above Niagara Falls, was ambushed and defeated with heavy losses near the Devil's Hole, a bowl-like depression into which captives and wounded were thrown. But the old fort built by De Léry for the French continued to resist until Sir William pulled the Seneca back to the ancient covenant, and word seeped through from the Mississippi that France had finally yielded all territory east of that stream. Regiments back from the siege of Havana were being rested and reinforced. "The red man knew that he was hungry and thirsty—and whipped. Pontiac drifted off to the Maumee, to the Illinois, to the back of the beyond."[*]

The Indian rebellion, a mere troublesome incident in the current rush of British imperialism, could not be considered closed until its leader made obeisance. For purposes of diplomacy and prestige a lost Chief Pontiac was a continuing danger; no telling what the fellow might be up to, drunk or sober. Accordingly he was sought out in

---

[*] Arthur Pound and Richard E. Day, *Johnson of the Mohawks* (The Macmillan Company: New York, 1930), p. 406.

his Illinois retreat by Johnson's deputy, George Croghan, and persuaded to come east for a peace council at Oswego to which were summoned sachems of all the tribes.

Pontiac's progress along Ontario's south shore, with stops at Niagara and Irondequoit, was alcoholic enough "to ease the broken spirit of a grieving primitive."* His daily bar bill is of record in the *Sir William Johnson Papers* since the ever orderly British Crown paid the reckoning. From Niagara, Benjamin Roberts, commissary, wrote to his superior:

"Pontiac said I had received them very well and given them *Tobacco,* which Indians love . . . & rum which they loved above all things. . . . After having smoked and drank a couple of drams they left me to prepare to set out in the morning. I just now offered . . . the boat should go tonight but he was a little drunk and did not chuse it he kissed me. . . . The whole of them seemed in very good humor."

After all, Pontiac was a French-taught Indian, to whom the male kiss was a symbol of friendship. Presently, at the grand council held near the site of the present Pontiac Hotel in Oswego, the great chief kissed Johnson at the height of emotional oratory. Probably no more impressive or generously supplied Indian council was ever held thereafter, for this one marked fulfillment of a vast imperial conquest. Whatever the rights and peccadilloes, the British Crown would not be challenged by Great Lakes Indians again. No doubt its soldiery would tread the wilderness more circumspectly henceforth, but the red man had been mastered by the redcoat. Henceforth the two would fight as allies, not as foes.

Peace talks ended on the last day of August 1766 at Oswego with a touch of symbolism which contained an abiding truth, when Johnson gave each Indian leader a silver medal inscribed, "A pledge of peace and friendship with Great Britain." Then, as Ralph Faust says in his *Story of Oswego,* the Indians "launched their canoes, loaded with presents, upon Lake Ontario, and with weird chants paddled their way back to the setting sun."

Pontiac himself returned to the obscurity from which he had been dragged. The British could settle down for a time to peaceful exploitation and piecemeal settlement.

---

* *Ibid.,* p. 414.

# Part II

## WARS AND RECONSTRUCTION

## Chapter 7

## Border War—The Oswego Sector

*The finger of God points out a mighty Empire to your sons;
the Savages of the wilderness were never expelled to make room
in this, the best part of the Continent, for idolaters and slaves.*
—New York Journal or General Advertiser,
July 20, 1775.

WITHOUT attempting to explain the rising revolutionary feeling along the American seaboard, it is proper to show that the back country of which Lake Ontario was then a part had a share in causing it. At least two of the important official steps taken by the British government between the conquest of Canada and the American Revolution were aimed at regulation of the as yet misunderstood West by measures distasteful to the Thirteen Colonies.

Having won the interior of America by six years of war, the British were slow to appreciate that they had acquired the richest lightly occupied country on the planet. In 1761 the Lords of Trade and Plantations declared Newfoundland to be worth more for wealth and trade than Louisiana and Canada combined. Seven years later that obtuse body was still committed to the shortsighted mercantilist view that colonial settlements should be confined to the seacoast because the object of colonization was to extend the commerce, navigation and manufactures of Great Britain. To some extent this opinion had been fostered by the Hudson's Bay Company, which preferred Indian hunters to white settlers. But the population of the seacoast colonies had multiplied to a point where land-hunger drove the whites westward.

The Fort Stanwix treaty of 1768, negotiated at the army post at the Oneida carrying place (modern Rome, New York) between the Mohawk Valley and Lake Ontario, embodied a temporary cure. For £10,000 the Iroquois sold to the Crown their rather shadowy hunting-ground rights to the area between the Ohio and the Great

91

Bend of the Tennessee. Except in that transferred area, it was solemnly agreed that white settlers should not cross a line drawn from Fort Stanwix to the Susquehanna, thence to the Allegheny and the Ohio. Thus the westward movement first reached the interior in southern latitudes, while the already rebellious New Englanders had one more grievance in being shut out from a West whose fertility was becoming known, and to which two of their colonies possessed definite claims by charter or royal grant.

Secondly, by the Quebec Act of 1774, the British Parliament extended the Province of Quebec to include practically all of Canada as then known, plus the area one day to comprise the Northwest Territory, and now containing the states of Ohio, Indiana, Illinois, Michigan and Wisconsin. This greater Quebec extended from Labrador to the confluence of the Ohio and Mississippi Rivers. In this vast region, thrice the size of the former province, the Quebec Act formally legalized the Catholic religion and the French language, and set up forms of government which gave no encouragement to the rising democratic spirit. Passed at the height of revolutionary ardor, in the same year that the Port of Boston was closed to trade and garrisoned strongly with British troops, this measure aroused furious resentment throughout British America.

While Catholic emancipation attracted the noisier attention, the fact that the Quebec Act nullified prior grants and cut the northern colonies off from westward expansion also drew sharp criticism. Virginia considered herself wronged in two ways. First, the act gave to Quebec the better part of the rich hinterland in the northwest previously granted to Virginia by royal charter; and secondly, the prospects dwindled for many western speculations entered into by rich Virginians. Syndicates such as the Ohio Land Company and the Vandalia Company were threatened and their shares fell off in value. George Washington and Patrick Henry both stood to lose heavily. No doubt one powerful reason why the leaders of the aristocratic Old Dominion made common cause with democratic Massachusetts in the revolutionary crisis can be discerned in the personal losses and financial fears of Virginia's ruling group.

On the New York frontier these land manipulations, begun before the passage of the Quebec Act, had tragic consequences not fully explained even yet. A short-term royal Governor of New York—1770-1771—John Murray, Earl of Dunmore, had been promoted to the governorship of Virginia. While in New York he had visited Sir William Johnson at the baronet's frontier home in Johnstown. Those historians who paint Sir William as a selfish intriguer hold that a sinister understanding was then reached by the two men on the subject of western lands. Dunmore's part, it is alleged, was to bring on an Indian war in the Ohio Valley and enforce Virginia's claim to Ohio for land settlement, in defiance of the Fort Stanwix Treaty. In order to accomplish this, the Iroquois had to be placated because they claimed overlordship of the Ohio country, and their pretensions were so far recognized that the tribes directly affected would be influenced by the attitude of the Six Nations. Johnson's presumed part in this evil program was to cajole the Iroquois into counseling the Ohio tribes to offer no resistance; or if that failed, to get their promise not to send war parties to aid the Ohio Indians.

The Five Nations had become six in 1713 when the Confederacy admitted the Tuscarora, an Iroquois people that migrated from their homelands along the Neuse River in North Carolina after a disastrous war with the whites. The Tuscarora received lands and protection, particularly from the Oneida, but their status in the League remained humble, as their sachems "sat below the fire" in council and had no voice except by courtesy. Nevertheless, they developed some notable leaders, among them Red Jacket.

Dunmore did in fact bring off his border war on schedule in 1774, and this in spite of having been reprimanded for running surveys across the Ohio. Whether a secret understanding did exist between the Virginia governor and the Superintendent of Northern Indians cannot be proved, but there are enough traces of it to keep suspicion alive. At any rate, Sir William could not bring the Iroquois around. In the torrid heat of July 1774 he held council with their chiefs at Johnstown, overexerting himself so greatly in continued exhortation that he died suddenly on the third day of that protracted argument. A tale that he committed suicide will not down, yet that end seems contrary to his sanguine nature. Whether the issue of that fateful council was merely the usual and legitimate one of limiting the war or whether it included some hidden imperial or selfish design on

Ohio lands, the proceedings show that Johnson was both amazed and distressed by the stubbornness of his usually tractable Iroquois "children."

When Sir William died on July 11, 1774, he held firm control of the great water-level pass to the interior of the continent. With enormous popularity and prestige in war, the warden of the Mohawk no doubt could have maintained his position against the "rebels" and might even have held New York—one of the more conservative provinces—in line for the Crown. In time he might even have placated the Virginians on the land question by eventually bringing the Iroquois around, thereby isolating the revolutionary force in New England.

As revolution flared, the British commanded the inland seas no less than the oceans. They held the sympathy of the major tribes of Indians and could maintain and implement that sympathy by means of grants from a treasury that never failed.

For Lake Ontario the Revolutionary War began and ended at Oswego, near the southeastern corner of the lake, where the outpouring waters of central New York created a broad avenue for war and trade. For both of these purposes the route was already old in use before the white man came, but, as we have seen in the chapters on colonial Canada, the French soon discovered its advantages for chastening the Iroquois in their home lands. How the British secured control of this important location, for long their only post on the Great Lakes and hence a pivot of their diplomatic policy, will be related in a later chapter dealing with Oswego's history.

Preparations for combat were practically complete at Oswego by the spring of 1775. Late in May, Colonel Guy Johnson, successor to his uncle, Sir William, as Superintendent of Indian affairs, removed from the Mohawk Valley to Fort Stanwix. He reached Oswego on June 17. Captain John Butler was also present, likewise Joseph Brant, several Loyalists and a number of Mohawk. Oswego was in one of its frequent slumps. There was no garrison and decay ruled. Johnson sent runners to the three western nations of the League, calling them to a July conference "to feast on the flesh and drink the blood of a Bostonian," as Whigs were characterized by Loyalists.* Johnson explained the cannibalistic bid as meaning merely that his guests were

---

* David Ramsay, *History of the American Revolution* (London, 1793), p. 114.

to devour a roast ox and swallow a hogshead of wine, but it sounded ominous to patriots.

One small sloop brought in ninety barrels of provisions from Niagara, small allowance for the hungry hordes of Indians assembled for the powwow, including squaws and children. Colonel Johnson placed the number of warriors at 1,340, probably an exaggeration to frighten the Americans. The total number of warriors in the four nations which adhered to the British was only about 1,600, and it is hardly probable that so large a proportion of the whole array gathered at Oswego.

Sachems and warriors in council were told that the colonists were scarce and poor, that the rich English king had men at his disposal in numbers rivaling the leaves of the forest, that his gold was as abundant as the dirt the red men's moccasins trod, and that the rum supply was as the lake itself in extent. Plied with arguments and liquor, the red men consented to a piecemeal program. At first they would agree only to defend Lake Ontario and the St. Lawrence from the Americans. As further inducement Johnson gave them new arms and other gifts. For more than fifty years thereafter the Seneca used brass kettles given them by Colonel Johnson during that July war council in Oswego.

Some extremely able Indians listened to these blandishments and pondered the future of their sore-beset peoples. Caught between two warring camps, they had to make a choice; neutrality would destroy them no less than a losing war.

Time and again in the course of this story we shall meet one of the greatest of red men in the Mohawk chieftain, Joseph Brant. Thayendanegea (1742-1807) was then in the prime of his extraordinary powers. His Indian name has many renderings; in Sir William Johnson's last will and testament, for instance, he is bequeathed 1,000 acres and £100 under the name "young Brant, alias Kaghneghata of Canajoharie." He had been educated by Sir William Johnson, whose third consort was Joseph's sister Molly—often known as Brown Lady Johnson. Realizing that the Indians had nothing to hope for from the Colonial side, Brant tried to discredit Samuel Kirkland when that missionary won over the Oneida and Tuscarora. Then he appeared as Mohawk spokesman in a conference with Sir Guy Carleton at Montreal and received a captain's commission.

Later he balked an effort of Red Jacket to persuade the Iroquois to make a separate peace with the Americans. However, Brant at the Oswego council dodged a final decision, and did not fully commit the Mohawk, whose influence on other tribes was decisive, to the British cause until after a journey to England which convinced this astute son of the forest that his people could not possibly recover their country, and hence must side with the white nation whose policy would be less injurious. This meant Great Britain, because American victory would bring prompt occupation of Indian lands.

Make no mistake, Joseph Brant was a great man, of full stature in any company or scene, in battle or council, amid red men or white. His massive head, carved in stone, appears on the façade of the State Capitol at Albany, remarkable tribute from a state against whose founding he stubbornly fought and from which he led his people to Canada after he lost his war.

Another Iroquois prominent during the Revolution was the Seneca chief Cornplanter (1732-1836). A son of an Albany trader, John Abeal, by a Seneca woman, Cornplanter served as a war chief with Brant's marauders. In his later years his hostility to Americans diminished, and he counseled his people to sign the treaty with the Colonies, the "Thirteen Fires," which opened the central and western portions of the state to white settlement. Honored by Washington, Adams and Jefferson, appointed liaison officer between the national government and the Indians, Cornplanter thenceforth stalked in stately uniform, flaunting upon his broad chest medals given him by both British and Americans.

A half brother to Cornplanter played a far different role in the Ontario country. Handsome Lake (1735-1815) reformed after years of drunkenness to follow an opposite mission of peace and good will. He obeyed an apostolic call to reform and purify the ancient worship of the Indian peoples before they had been corrupted by white contacts. Wandering through the villages, Handsome Lake exhorted the Iroquois to temperance, hospitality and humanity. He died from exhaustion while on a pilgrimage and was buried on the Onondaga reservation. His beliefs are held today by most of the western Iroquois, although not openly professed by all.

The Iroquois hesitated to promise all-out aid to the Loyalists.

FORT NIAGARA TAKEN FROM THE BRITISH SIDE OF THE RIVER AT NEWARK, 1814

SIR ISAAC BROCK

SIR GUY CARLETON

Brant's persuasion influenced the Mohawk, Seneca and Cayuga, but they avoided committing themselves completely as yet to the British cause. Later many, but not all, of the Onondaga—a priestly people noted for clairvoyance—joined the British in the struggle which they foretold would bring doom to the Confederation. The Oneida and the Tuscarora, the foundling Sixth Nation, remained passive or pro-"rebel" owing to the Kirkland influence and Red Jacket's impressive oratory in stating his conviction that the Americans would win. Thus the Iroquois League, after 200 years of political unity and military prowess, was broken asunder.

The protracted council dispersed about July 8. The Iroquois mostly returned to their homes, but many Mohawk followed Guy Johnson and other Loyalists to Canada. In all, 220 men embarked for Montreal in a small sloop and several bateaux. John Butler sailed to Niagara. Oswego was again deserted except for a few dependables assigned to take care of the buildings.

The first Indian council was larger than any of its successors, but similar gatherings on a smaller scale were held at many other points on the frontier during the next eight years. In contrast to the almost unending planning and intriguing which went on in this region, military action was infrequent and mostly abortive. Upon Ontario's waters there were no naval sorties or engagements such as had occurred twenty years earlier, because the Americans could not challenge British naval power on the lake. But its lonely wooded shores were trod by many a spy seeking to learn in advance of swoops from these northern bases into the Mohawk or Susquehanna valleys and even into Pennsylvania.

In preparation for these raids and campaigns, white men in red coats foregathered with semi-naked, grotesquely painted native warriors to plan bloody descents on unsuspecting settlements. For thirty years British New York had been buying the scalps of enemies from the Indians. The custom was well established, but long bargaining went forward over the prices to be paid for hairy merchandise. Weapons, food, cloth, blankets, powder—all the materials of war had to be promised and provided. No pretty war, this one where white hired red for butchery and red strove vainly to recover his lost country by aiding the least land-hungry of the foes. Today the forest belt, dominant feature of the revolutionary landscape, is gone; and it requires a lively imagination to clothe with terror Fort Niagara at the lake's head or Fort Ontario near its foot.

By far the most critical campaign to move through Oswego was that of 1777. In preparation for the Ontario phase of this critical military operation, the British, although their ships were unchallenged on Lake Ontario, decided that they needed still more shipping for the large troop movements planned. So to Ontario came one of the master shipbuilders of the Royal Navy, Lieutenant John Schanck, who had won a reputation by swiftly building up the Lake Champlain fleet where he had the 18-gun *Inflexible* of 300 tons ready for battle in the record time of seven weeks. He came to the Great Lakes as "Senior Naval Officer and Commissioner" on Ontario and Erie, but was advanced to the rank of Master and Commander in 1780. Altogether, he built four dockyards in America—at Saint John, New Brunswick, at Quebec, at Detroit and at Carleton Island in the St. Lawrence outlet of Lake Ontario. A most distinguished career awaited this officer, in the course of which he earned credit for various significant inventions, including gunboats with removable sides and the inclined plane for gun carriages, which is rated as one of the most important inventions in gunnery. Schanck rose to the high rank of Admiral of the Blue in 1821. His Revolutionary War activities proved excellent practice for his later ingenious triumphs.

Meantime another famous naval engineer was building flatboats at Three Rivers for St. Leger's upstream push. Lieutenant William Twiss was ordered there on June 3, 1776, with instructions to build numbers of flat-bottomed boats, of the type known as the King's boat or Royal boat, each of which should be capable of carrying thirty to forty men with stores and provisions. One change in design that he introduced has quite a modern ring. The bow of each boat was built square for convenience in disembarking troops on a broad gangboard. This gangboard was pierced by loopholes for musket fire so that it could be carried as a shield by troops advancing across an open beach. This ingenious contrivance was probably not used in the campaign, since the Lake Ontario landings were unopposed. Altogether, the British had enough shipping afloat on the lake to smother any Continental interference with their movement on its waters.

The campaign that crossed Lake Ontario was a part of General

Burgoyne's plan to split New England from New York down the Champlain-Hudson line. Burgoyne himself with the main force was to pierce south directly toward Albany. Meanwhile a large though secondary force under St. Leger was to ascend the St. Lawrence to Lake Ontario, cross to Oswego, come down by way of Lake Oneida to the Mohawk Valley and drive at Albany from the west in a variation of the now-familiar pincers movement. It is with this campaign of St. Leger's that we are chiefly concerned. The stalemate of St. Leger's forces not far southeast of Oneida Lake, at Fort Stanwix and Oriskany, prevented his joining Burgoyne and was a prime cause for the defeat of the main column under Burgoyne at Saratoga.

Colonel Barry St. Leger, of Huguenot descent, came to Canada in the spring of 1776 with troops to reinforce Carleton. As acting brigadier, he led from Oswego a somewhat motley force which was intended as a "fifth column" rather than a fighting column. Oswego's forests again glowed with campfires. Sir John Johnson with his Royal Greens and Colonel Claus, Superintendent Guy Johnson's deputy, arrived at Oswego in June 1777 to prepare for their roles. Brant had been making grim feints on the upper Susquehanna, but led his band northward in July. Seneca also swarmed in. Other Six Nations warriors came in by trail or canoe. In mid-July, Captain John Butler, who apart from his duties as a military commander was also Deputy Superintendent of Indian affairs, arrived from Niagara and pleaded with the Indians to join the coming expedition. Some of the warriors objected, declaring their wish to remain merely spectators in the approaching campaign. Butler, emphasizing loot and playing down the opposition, won them over.

Some historians have held that after this mobilization at Oswego Brant acted as head chief of the Iroquois in the Revolution, but the claim is unsupported by official evidence. British dispatches of record refer to him merely as "Brant" or "the Indian chief." Joseph referred to himself not as "head chief" but proudly as "captain," his Crown-conferred commission. In all its history, the Confederacy never had an over-all chieftain. The Iroquois custom was to choose leaders for separate expeditions, and to this custom the British adhered, since to set Brant formally above the rest would have aroused intertribal jealousy.

Discordant advices from the Butlers on one hand and the Johnsons on the other appear to have confused St. Leger, who lacked firsthand knowledge of Indian character and relations. A commander by no means inspired or inspiring, he expected in this campaign to win high reputation on cheap terms by means of a surprise attack. The cause of his failure to accomplish this was one of those incalculable incidents which confound a military plan based upon synchronizing the movements of small bodies of troops over wide areas.

On St. Leger's route is a State memorial to the keen-eyed scout who wrecked all hope of a surprise attack. From an island in the Little Salmon River a Continental spy, Silas Towne, saw the enemy force disembark on the mainland. That night he paddled down the river and rushed overland by trail to warn Colonel Peter Gansevoort, of the Third New York Continental line regiment, of St. Leger's approach. The island, near Mexico and not far from Oswego, is known as Spy Island. Towne's grave is there, marked by a marble shaft.

Under St. Leger marched 200 regulars, 200 of Johnson's Royal Greens and from 300 to 400 Hessians, more accurately the Wurttemberg Chasseurs. Most of these troops had been boated up the St. Lawrence and across the lake to Oswego. There they were joined by some 500 Indians, giving St. Leger a striking force of from 1,300 to 1,400 men. For armament he had two 6-pounders, two 3-pounders and four 5-inch howitzers, manned by forty artillerymen.

Warned in time by Towne, the Continentals stopped St. Leger in his tracks, both at Fort Stanwix itself and at near-by Oriskany, where General Nicholas Herkimer and his homespun militia met the enemy on August 6 in one of the bloodiest battles of the war. Herkimer was fatally wounded but continued to direct the battle while seated on a saddle under a tree. His men sustained such losses that they could not pursue the British. Many militiamen died because their officers overrode Herkimer's orders and went forward into action too soon, only to meet deadly ambush. Those who obeyed orders then saved the day. Their homespun general was carried home, where his leg was amputated by a young surgeon who was performing his first major operation. On being told there was no hope, the General, who came of rugged Palatine stock, directed some boys to go out and retrieve his buried leg, so that he might appear with both at the last trump. The Herkimer house, a substantial brick mansion on the southern slope of the Mohawk Valley, about ten miles from the city which bears his name, has been restored and is maintained by the state of New York.

The broken British and their Canadian and red allies, their artillery abandoned in the woods, reeled back to brief sanctuary at Oswego while the Iroquois mourned their slaughtered brethren. They had been invited to a picnic and instead found a death grapple. Seldom thereafter could they be brought to the point of hand-to-hand fighting against alert American troops. After a brief halt at Oswego the British army scattered. St. Leger took his regulars back to Montreal, the Butlers and Brant returned to Niagara and Johnson led his Royal Greens to Oswegatchie (Ogdensburg).

St. Leger's defeat in the Mohawk, together with Sir Henry Clinton's failure to drive north from New York City in time to relieve Burgoyne, broke the British pincers and left that unfortunate commander without his expected reinforcements. Carleton later sharply reproved St. Leger for not having properly disciplined his troops on the march, but there is evidence that he had taken some precautions to restrain his Indian allies.

Buying scalps, a commercial practice already touched upon in these pages, was gruesomely high-lighted after St. Leger's frustrated drive. After the battle of Oriskany, American depositions were made that St. Leger offered twenty dollars apiece for Continental scalps. Squire Ferris, an American prisoner at St. John's in 1779, after being released denounced St. Leger as a brutal drunkard who had ordered his prisoners shackled together and had kept them in a dungeon for fourteen days.

In justice a counterincident, to St. Leger's credit, should be told. Believing that the Fort Stanwix garrison might offer to surrender, he sent Lieutenant Bird with an Indian escort ahead of the advancing force with orders not to accept a capitulation but to await approach of the main body. "This is not to take any honor out of a young soldier's hands," he explained, "but by the presence of the troops to prevent the barbarity and carnage which will ever obtain where Indians make so superior a part of the detachment."

The major result of Burgoyne's surrender was France's decision to join the war as America's open ally. On February 6, 1778, a treaty of amity and commerce, with an eventual defensive treaty of alliance, was concluded between Louis XVI and the United States.

Within forty-two hours a spy brought this news to London, but the British government held it secret pending official transmission from the French capital on March 13. Declaration of war between Britain and France soon followed.

After Burgoyne's surrender in October, Oswego stood practically abandoned. It was reported as still unoccupied in March 1778, and remained deserted through the spring except for purposes of a night's sleep or a brief rest by parties passing from the St. Lawrence to Niagara, or the reverse. Early in July of that year Colonel Gansevoort sent Lieutenant McClellan from Fort Stanwix (rechristened Fort Schuyler* at the beginning of the Revolution) to destroy the buildings at Oswego, including Fort Ontario. McClellan found there only a woman and her children and a lad of fourteen. He placed the family with their furniture in an outbuilding, gave them some provisions and then partly burned the other buildings, although with his small force he seems not to have made a thorough job of it. This occurred at about the time of the Wyoming Massacre.

Sir Guy Carleton became disgusted with the shabby treatment he received from London and desired to be relieved. His successor as Governor General and Commander in Chief in Canada from 1778 to 1785 was one whom we have met already at Oswego and Niagara in the "old war" and whose name bulks large in Ontario annals. Sir Frederick Haldimand was one of several thorough Swiss soldiers who joined the British service and came to America in 1756. In 1776 he was a full general and likewise colonel-commandant of the Sixtieth Foot, the "Royal Americans" whom he had helped to organize and train. When advancement came, he was reluctant to accept because of disgust at the treatment accorded his predecessor. As a result, Haldimand did not take office for a year after his appointment and then, on June 21, 1778, did so at Carleton's earnest solicitation, so that the latter would be free to carry the fight against inept leadership to London.

Once in office, General Haldimand concluded that the American colonies could not be recaptured, and concentrated on keeping

---

* The original Fort Schuyler was built in 1758 by the British, close to the river on the tract which is now Main Street of modern Utica. It soon fell into ruin and was abandoned in the 1760's. Then the Americans confused the record by giving the name of Fort Schuyler to Fort Stanwix at Rome, presumably because General Stanwix was a British officer. Hereinafter the post at Rome will be called Fort Stanwix.

Canada British. His military census, Canada's first count of heads, showed only 113,000 population, of whom only 28,000 men were capable of bearing arms. Britain never had a more loyal servant. Foreign birth and long American service let him take an objective view of affairs which English officers were likely to judge in wrath and haste. His administration was never popular, perhaps because he had difficulty getting himself understood. Misunderstandings led to harshness, and he lost some lawsuits based on false imprisonment. Yet, as we shall see, General Haldimand held and applied farsighted ideas on the military and commercial importance of Lake Ontario and the West. This strong, progressive leader is memorialized in Haldimand County on the north shore of Lake Erie.

Oswego remained quiet almost to the end of the war. In later generations residents on both sides of the border believed that the British had maintained a strong garrison at Fort Ontario, and that the Mohawk Valley raids originated there. This was untrue, though it would have been feasible. Instead, Niagara and Carleton Island were developed as principal bases. As for Oswego, the anxious Iroquois sent a group of chiefs to Haldimand at Montreal in the spring of 1779, asking that the fort be re-established. Haldimand informed them that his troops were required at other points.

His decision proved to be a strategic error. Military operations along the Ontario border in the Revolution often had far-reaching consequences. Niagara was a distant hornet's nest but the old trading post of Oswego, a ready entrance and exit for raiders, lay within range of easy reprisal. No doubt Haldimand delayed consent to the Iroquois request for the fort's rehabilitation because he considered that the new post which he established on Carleton Island effectively covered the Oswego inlet, but that fortress, although important later, meant little to the Indians then because it offered them no protection in crisis. Maintenance of a garrison at Oswego might conceivably have averted a hard blow soon struck against the Onondaga.

On April 19, 1779, Continental troops led by Colonels Van Schaick and Willett, noted border leaders, left Fort Stanwix, at present Rome, surprised the Onondaga south of Syracuse, destroyed their villages, burned their provisions and slaughtered their livestock at a time when some of the Onondaga warriors were campaigning with Loyalist forces. The effect of the raid was twofold. Numbers of enraged

Onondaga who had not previously fought hurried to join Brant and the Butlers, and the Indians renewed their pleas to the British that Fort Ontario be re-established at Oswego. The British finally gave serious attention to this plea, but too late to forestall larger troop movements in the making, for this raid on the Onondaga proved to be the preliminary flourish to a major campaign against the Iroquois of western New York. The story of the Sullivan-Clinton expedition will be told in the following chapter.

During the autumn of 1779 the British made a feeble gesture toward reviving hostilities from Oswego. Colonel Guy Johnson and Sir John Johnson arrived there by boat from Niagara to meet a number of Iroquois. An additional body under Brant and some British officers was to march along the shore to join them, but did not arrive. The Canadian Indians then refused to carry out a foray in the Fort Stanwix area. So Butler's Rangers returned to Niagara, the Indians went to winter quarters on the St. Lawrence and at Niagara, and Oswego went into another season's hibernation. Colonel Guy Johnson, reporting this fiasco to the home government, urged that Fort Ontario be re-established in the next spring, as the Indians had it much at heart.

In the autumn of 1780, Sir John Johnson, heading a war party of Indians and whites, again passed through Oswego and ascended the river to Oneida Lake. Hiding their boats on the shore, they reached circuitously the borders of Schoharie County and executed a bloody raid lighted by the torch. Despite hot chase by the New York militia they escaped to Canada.

At long last General Haldimand realized the risks he had run by neglecting Oswego. On February 18, 1782, he directed Major Ross, commanding at Carleton Island, chief British base eight miles down the Saint Lawrence from the lake, to proceed to Oswego as soon as the ice broke in the spring, because a post was to be established there with all speed. Haldimand reasoned that if the Continentals were planning a drive upon Quebec Province, as threatened, possession of Oswego would be of prime importance to them. That risk must be prevented by "a more Early Exertion, and as the first object to be considered is to secure yourself from insults, you will pay your whole attention to it, taking advantage of what remains of the old Bastions and afterwards proceed to Buildings."

Construction plans were outlined in detail. Captain Turis of the Engineers would communicate to Ross his plans for the works and the Adjutant General would advise regarding ordnance, size of garrison and other details. Ross pushed the rebuilding at Oswego though the works there were in bad shape and tools available at Carleton were few. He had visited the Oswego fort twice, he said, and found it rickety. Transport vessels, including the scow *Haldemand,* would be ready to sail from Carleton in April and the troops should know nothing of their destination until they were embarked. For this service nearer the enemy, Ross had requested General Powell* to send from Niagara as many as possible of the Eighth Regiment of British Foot because he found that Cornwallis' defeat had tended to dampen the spirits of his men. This newly constituted garrison narrowly escaped a surprise attack by Colonel Willett's raiders in the last action of the war on the Ontario border. Under special orders from General Washington, Colonel Willett assembled 470 men at Fort Herkimer. In bitter cold, on February 8, 1783, they moved by sleigh to Oneida Lake, then crossed the ice to Fort Brewerton, and reached Oswego River three miles above the falls about February 12. Pausing to make scaling-ladders, they resumed the march that night, treading river ice to the rapids called Bradstreet's Rift, where they took to the woods. After struggling through deep snow for several hours their Oneida guide admitted he had lost his way. In subzero weather they kept moving throughout the night to escape freezing. At dawn, by sheer luck, they found themselves emerging from the woods with Fort Ontario only three-quarters of a mile distant. They were on Oak Hill, near the present intersection of Utica and East Seventh streets in modern Oswego.

Washington had ordered Willett not to attack unless he could surprise the enemy. Retiring for cover to the forest's fringe, the officers debated a plan to build a fire deep in the woods, lurk there through the day and make a rush on the fort that night. Just then five British soldiers, sent from the fort for firewood, approached the hideaway. Willett's men tried to capture them quietly, and caught two, but the other three raced back toward the fort bawling the alarm. Drums beat to arms, troops appeared along the ramparts

---

* Brigadier General Henry W. Powell, then in command at Niagara. He returned to England after the Revolution and rose to the rank of full general in 1801.

and shovel parties began clearing snow from the embrasures and readying the guns.

Willett, against his desire but under clear advance orders for caution, called retreat. Scaling-ladders were flung into a hollow southeast of Oak Hill, where their fragments were found by pioneer settlers in Oswego's civic phase, which was belated in contrast to its early military history. Willett's party returned to Fort Brewerton.

On reaching their home base at Fort Stanwix, the raiders found they had been engaged in useless toil. While they had been absent on this final Revolutionary raid in the north, word of the peace declaration had been received. Thus the Ontario border war, on the important Oswego sector, ended right where it began—at the "great outpouring" where central New York gives its waters to Lake Ontario.

The two Johnsons who took important parts as Tory leaders in the councils and campaigns centering on Oswego are frequently confused. When old Sir William Johnson died in 1774, the power he had wielded was divided. To his son, Sir John Johnson, went the bulk of his huge fortune, consisting chiefly of land, and the leadership of a considerable body of semi-feudal retainers. To Sir William's nephew, secretary and son-in-law, Guy Johnson, later Sir Guy, went the official leadership of Indian affairs, which had taken on tremendous political and economic importance.

First let us consider Guy Johnson, the nephew and able upstart of the family. Short in both words and stature, he had considerable capabilities which were often nullified by reckless pride. For instance, he had come to the Oswego Council in 1775 at a white heat against the Continentals because his wife had died at the fort there while in flight to Canada as a refugee. But Guy had been well trained by his uncle, the great Sir William, in the ticklish diplomacy needed to handle the Indians.

When Sir William died, Guy was directed by General Gage to take his place in superintending the Indians, a temporary appointment later made permanent. In recognition of his services he received a knighthood. After leading his Loyalist friends from Oswego to Montreal in July 1775 he sailed to England and spent almost a year there before coming back across the Atlantic to New York, where he spent some time in fruitless negotiations.

Although a man of councils rather than battles, he was with the British and Iroquois at the battle of Newtown in 1779. Fleeing to Niagara, he made his base there for the next two years. In 1782 he retired as Indian Superintendent and was succeeded by his brother-in-law. Thereafter Sir Guy made his home in England, trying unsuccessfully to get compensation for his confiscated American estate, Guy Park, near Amsterdam, New York. The estate, still one of the Mohawk Valley's show places, is now owned by the State of New York, supervised by the State Historian and maintained and managed by the Daughters of the American Revolution.

Now for Sir John Johnson, the heir-at-law. Neither Guy nor Sir John could measure up to the stature of Sir William Johnson, but Sir John's inability to fill his father's shoes was accentuated by his nature and manner. He carried himself with more ostentation than his cousin Guy did, although he lacked Guy's abilities. In youth John Johnson was little more than a rich mediocrity with an amorous bent. In his native Mohawk Valley he lorded it with unseemly pride, yet his title as a baronet now appears to have been somewhat clouded. In British law an illegitimate son does not inherit his father's title. John Johnson's father and mother never married. Nevertheless, backed by the Johnson position, he was knighted while his father was alive and inherited the baronetcy at his father's death.

Old Sir William Johnson had been bluff and jolly, never losing the common touch, but the son was always aloof and haughty. He wore this vain pride in spite of an origin most humble. His mother, a bound servant until she became the consort of William Johnson, then a rising fur trader of Irish birth, had her three children baptized in her name only. This fact is convincingly shown by the record book of the Reverend Henry Barclay, Anglican missionary to Fort Hunter, whose manuscript volume is now in the possession of Montgomery County, New York. Burke's *Peerage* misrepresents the case by changing the name of John's mother from Catherine Weissenburg to Mary de Wissenbergh and indicating legal marriage.

Sir John Johnson disliked his Loyalist neighbors John and Walter Butler even though they were his comrades-at-arms and fellow commanders in the grim campaigns of the border war. His hostility to the Butlers may have been due merely to a parvenu resentment against aristocrats. The Butlers of the Mohawk, although they never became as wealthy as the Johnsons, were second only to the Johnsons in land holdings and they could, moreover, boast direct descent from the mighty Anglo-Irish clan of Butlers, two of whom, as Dukes of Ormond, had served as Lords Lieutenant in Ireland. Among Sir John Johnson's neighbors probably only the Butlers were sufficiently familiar with heraldry to know that his title was flawed.

Throughout the Revolution Sir John's Loyalist zeal blazed with a fanaticism not less fierce because his immense fortune hung in the balance. New York State confiscated and sold all his lands. It is true that Britain dealt generously with him in postwar compensation. After the peace he lived in Canada, making his home in Montreal, Lachine, Kingston, or his country house, Mount Johnson on the tract of the Seigneury of Monnoir in the county of Iberville, which had been granted to him by the British government. Sir John died in 1830 at the age of eighty-eight, an unreconstructed Loyalist whose sobered later years somewhat redeemed his wild youth and bloodstained middle age.

## Chapter 8

# Sullivan's Drive on Niagara—1779

---

*They [the Indians] may possibly be engaged by address, secrecy and stratagem to surprise the garrison and the shipping upon the Lakes and put them in our possession.*
—GENERAL WASHINGTON, LETTER TO SULLIVAN

---

STRENGTHENED by French reinforcement and funds after Burgoyne's surrender, the Continental forces could now assume the offensive in the West. The next military campaign in the new state of New York would be aimed at Niagara on Lake Ontario.

Somewhat relieved of seaboard risks by arrival of French reinforcements, Washington, ever a "Westerner" at heart, named Major General John Sullivan of New Hampshire to head a punitive march toward the most distant objective yet attempted by American arms. A cautious, steady soldier, Sullivan had not the dash that commands good fortune, nor the recklessness that deserves ill fortune. In this expedition he reached his highest military reputation, yet missed lasting fame by falling short of his major objective.

From *Butler's Rangers,* a study by the Canadian historian, Cruikshank, comes this description of the American commander: "A striking type of a class of shrewd, pushing, self-reliant men of humble origin which the Revolution had brought to the front. Beginning life as a stable-boy, he became successively a hostler, a tavern-keeper, a lawyer, a member of the Assembly, a delegate in Congress and a general in the Continental Army."

Sullivan's chief antagonist in the Niagara campaign, Colonel John Butler, is described by Cruikshank more intimately as "fat, below the middle stature yet active. . . . Care sat upon his brow. Speaking quickly, he repeated his words when excited. Decision, firmness, courage were undoubted characteristics of the man."

Butler must have smiled at the quaint early idea of Washington's that the western Iroquois could be seduced from the British alliance, made to turn on their allies and seize the shipping on the lakes. Once

109

that mare's nest had been disposed of, Washington and Sullivan prepared the campaign with great care, hoping that it might carry
through 500 miles of wilderness enough strength to overcome and
occupy Fort Niagara.

It was decided to invade the western New York hinterland in
three columns. General Sullivan marched an army from Reading,
Pennsylvania, to Tioga Point (modern Athens) on the Susquehanna.
General James Clinton's division of the New York Continental line
rendezvoused at Canajoharie on the Mohawk. By prodigious toil
his army opened a road through hills and woods to the head of
Otsego Lake, most easterly of the Finger Lakes and a chief source
of the Susquehanna River. In August, a dry month, the resourceful
Clinton had the lake outlet dammed, and so penned enough water
to float his 200 Schenectady-built boats downstream on the freshet
when the dam was broken. His force joined Sullivan's command at
Tioga Point on August 22, a discouragingly late date for the task outlined.

The third invading force has been somewhat neglected by historians. General Brodhead led 600 men from Fort Pitt (Pittsburgh)
in August. They engaged several Mingo and Munsee tribes on the
Alleghany, French Creek and other tributaries of the Ohio, and prevented those peoples from sending reinforcements northward to the
Seneca. Had time permitted Brodhead to join Sullivan as Clinton
had done for a move toward Niagara on schedule, George Washington might have proved in 1779 instead of having to wait two years
for Yorktown to demonstrate that he could plan and push through
a successful long-range offensive campaign.

After Clinton's arrival Sullivan's army numbered 5,000 men. Both
leaders and units had been well picked for staying power. In a sense
this was the most soldierly enterprise yet undertaken by the battling
colonies. Present were veteran regiments and brigades representing
New York, New Jersey, Pennsylvania, New Hampshire and Massachusetts.

Against this seasoned and resourceful force the less numerous defenders could not hold. British weakness was demonstrated at Newtown in the only stand-up battle of the campaign. The enemy units
comprised some British regulars, Loyalist regiments under Colonels
John Butler and Guy and Sir John Johnson, Major Walter N. Butler

and Captain Macdonnell, and Brant's Indians, a total of 1,500 men, but not all of these could be brought into battle at Newtown. While the British had the largest Iroquois force, mostly Seneca, Cayuga, Mohawk and Onondaga, the Americans were aided by Oneida and Tuscarora gathered and inspired by the missionary Samuel Kirkland.

Outnumbered four to one, the king's men, white and red, fortified a picturesque hilltop commanding a bend in the Chemung River. The area is now part of a 200-acre state park known as the Newtown Battlefield Reservation and is reached by a mile-long road leading up a sharp grade from State Route 17 on the run from Binghamton to Elmira. Here on August 29, 1779, Sullivan's men carried the breastwork erected by the Loyalists and Indians and dispersed them after a short but fierce engagement. Under Brant the Iroquois fought more steadfastly than was their wont; indeed, that extraordinary leader had disciplined them into greater military stability than these people had ever known. For a time the battle was waged hotly on those fortified heights, and at one time the Continental attack was almost stalled by unexpected Indian steadiness under fire. But the attackers, too, had been steeled in combat. Sullivan's men were not to be thwarted. After piercing the enemy line, they were then subjected to a sharp counterattack on difficult and rugged ground. The endangered units re-formed their lines in an involved echelon maneuver at the double, charged and shattered the enemy resistance.

The defenders, fearing encirclement, broke and fled to the Narrows at the riverside where many of them were killed by the pursuers. An eyewitness reported that blood streamed down the rocks. During the battle the Seneca village of Kanaweola at the mouth of Newtown Creek beside the Chemung was destroyed.

Victory at Newtown in the Chemung Valley opened the southern gateway to western New York. The Chemung is formed by three rivers: the Tioga, the Cohocton and the Canisteo. The Tioga comes in from northwest Pennsylvania; the Cohocton and Canisteo, which meet at Painted Post, flow from high hills of the so-called Southern Tier of New York. Their upper waters approach closely the great valley of the Genesee, then the homeland of the Seneca, strongest Indian allies of the British. Indeed, the Canisteo was then navigable for bateaux almost to its source in a marsh from which Canaseraga Creek also flows to the Genesee. Newtown Heights therefore was the logical place at which to defend the southern approach to the Genesee Valley, but once that position was carried by superior numbers, a smaller force could hardly make a second determined stand short of the fortress of Niagara itself. All that could be done defensively was to delay Sullivan's march a little here and a little there in the hope that he would dally with punitive measures instead of hastening to his major objective at Niagara.

Sullivan did not disappoint his foe. After the battle beside the Chemung the invaders marched, not by the Canaseraga portage direct to Fort Niagara, but by way of "French Catherine's Town," at the head of Seneca Lake, down the lake's east shore to the Indian village of Kanadesaga (Old Castle), then to Canandaigua and Honeoye, at the head of Conesus Lake, to Groveland. In miniature, Sullivan's progress resembled Sherman's destructive march to the sea. He burned some forty Seneca and Cayuga villages as their frantic populations raced to the protection of Niagara, or into near-by woods. He destroyed apple orchards, plantings of vegetables and 160,000 bushels of corn. As autumn drew on, Niagara's breadbasket had been systematically emptied and its most important Indian allies weakened.

Washington noted that Sullivan's force suffered only forty casualties—killed, wounded, captured and natural deaths. He commented: "Major General Sullivan, for his great perseverance and activity, for his order of march and attack and the whole of his dispositions; the Brigadiers and officers of all ranks, and the whole of the soldiers engaged in the expedition, merit and have the Commander-in-Chief's warmest acknowledgements for their important services upon this occasion."

Throughout the campaign the defenders skulked along the Continentals' moving flanks on the alert for stragglers, seeking to detach and destroy small parties. In that manner was Lieutenant Boyd captured near Little Beardstown for delight of tribesmen at the torture stake. Official figures above, however, reveal how wary these seasoned troops had become. Sullivan's habit of ordering artillery fire before reaching villages, though criticized by some military writers, is generally approved by lay historians as indicating humanitarian motives. These warning shots sent old men, women and children scurrying to safety. Meanwhile the braves were all under arms with the British.

Horror stories trailed this campaign, as indeed they form an after-math of any battle ever waged in any war. Throughout the Revolution, Continental and Loyalist vied in relating these gory accounts, many of them sheer fiction. The prize tidbit is Colonel Butler's claim that after the battle on the Chemung the Americans skinned the legs of their dead enemies from the hips downward to make boot tops or leggings. The Colonel wasn't there at the time; the Americans were not short of leggings and were in too much of a hurry to under-take tanning operations on any large scale. Perhaps they did scalp dead Indians for the sake of claiming reward; both sides did that and worse, as a matter of course, but scalping was a quick job, dead or alive.

The western portion of the Southern Tier abounds with memorials of the expedition. The Boyd-Parker shrine near Geneseo on United States Route 20-A is a small park dedicated to Lieutenant Thomas Boyd and Sergeant Michael Parker. Apparently careless, they were captured by the Seneca on September 14, 1779, and killed slowly at the "Torture Tree," now a gnarled oak more than two centuries old. It is said that they refused to tell the savages the numerical strength and campaign plans of Sullivan's army, which so incensed Joseph Brant that, although a Mason raised up by King George himself, he refused to heed the distress sign of that order as given by one of the doomed men. It is only fair to note that Brant's Masonry had been frequently taken advantage of by non-Masons.

The Yankee column set a slow pace. After all the burning of grain, cutting of trees and wrecking of villages, there was not time enough left for General Sullivan's army, which had hardly been injured at all, to get its heavy artillery to Niagara for the battering of its ex-ceedingly solid wall.

Of course, a quick push on to Niagara might have carried the fort, but Sullivan had to decide whether the post could be held through a famine winter. As it proved, his decision was wise, as winter set in rather quickly. Back in the Chemung country on the way home, the army killed its artillery and cart horses in the need to make haste by bateaux and for lack of fodder. It was impossible to take the patient beasts farther, and to release them to face winter starvation in that snowy region would have been a ghastly cruelty. To this day the village name of Horseheads commemorates that merciful carnage. A desolated countryside, a heap of dead horses, and a broken Iroquois nation—these were accomplished by Sullivan's campaign of 1779, and Niagara, thanks to time and dalliance, had escaped capture.

Back to their log barracks at Niagara proceeded the weary Rangers in their ragged uniforms of dark green cloth trimmed with scarlet and their low, flat caps with brass plates monogrammed "G.R." encircled by the words "Butler's Rangers." Colonel Butler expected Sir John Johnson and 380 men as reinforcements by way of Carleton Island and Oswego. Instead, he found at the fort 5,000 starving Indians who had rushed to Niagara for shelter and sustenance. At last, on October 4, Sir John sailed from Carleton Island and was speeded to Niagara by a terrific gale. Councils were held with the Indians, in order to rally them against the Americans. Some prompt offensive action was needed to restore British prestige in Indian eyes.

Johnson and Butler soon led forces to Oswego, from which point they planned to attack the Oneida in revenge for their aid to Sullivan, but this move was thwarted by a lingering Six Nations loyalty. On October 20 a Ranger scout brought in three Oneida who confessed that their nation had been warned of danger by a Cayuga from Niagara, and that the three of them had been sent to watch the Rangers' movements. There being no chance now for the hoped-for surprise attack, Johnson returned to Carleton Island and the Rangers went back west with Butler to Niagara for a winter on short rations.

Three times strong expeditions had left the Atlantic seaboard to capture Niagara. Those under Braddock in 1755 and under Sullivan in 1779 had failed, one in catastrophe, the other in apparent success. The land route was definitely too long and difficult. Between these expeditions, a third, commanded by Sir William Johnson in 1759, provided a dashing success. Why, then, had the Americans failed to take the easy way followed by Johnson—the water route from the Mohawk to Oswego and west over Lake Ontario? The answer, of course, is sea power. In 1759 the British established control sufficient to ship their troops safely across 160 miles of blue water. Twenty years later the British held the lake and forced the Americans to take the time-killing overland route. There has rarely been a more definite example, on a small and easily comprehended scale, of Admiral Mahan's thesis—the influence of sea power upon history.

A few ships rushed to completion in record time turned what might have been a triumph of strategy into a mere punitive raid, and saved Fort Niagara to the British for another seventeen years.

Before leaving Sullivan's campaign, a word is due about one of the victims who was burned out, Queen Catherine of French Catherine's Town.

French Catherine's Town, among the first of the Seneca villages obliterated, stood near the foot of Seneca Lake in a setting of wild glens and cataracts. It was ruled by "Queen Catherine" Montour, who succeeded to authority after the death of her husband, a Seneca chief. In the rush of settlement after Sullivan's expedition a white man's village was erected on the site and named Havana in 1829. But in the 1890's the name of that thriving manufacturing town was changed to Montour Falls. This substitution was inspired by a romantic tradition of Queen Catherine Montour, a comely and polished woman who spoke French fluently and claimed to be a descendant of Count de Frontenac, Governor of Canada, by an Indian woman. Her family history deserves attention at this point.

In an earlier chapter the reader was introduced in rather macabre circumstances to the French-Indian house of Montour when Joncaire in 1709 had a half-breed British emissary of that name struck down by a hatchet. The circumstance fitly introduces into this narrative the Montours, a family of gifted men and women who moved tragically through the colonial history of New York and Pennsylvania.

The story of the Montours probably begins as early as 1665 and covers at least four generations. Although shadowy in 1709, it is quite well documented after 1744, date of the famous Indian council at Lancaster, Pennsylvania, where white statesmen met those of the Six Nations. Records of official proceedings carry a note describing an unofficial call which the secretary made on the evening of Thursday, June 28, 1744, upon "the celebrated Mrs. Montour" (grandmother of her namesake, "Queen Catherine" Montour, whom Sullivan put to flight) at one of the Seneca cabins, where he talked with her in French.* Witham Marshe, secretary of the Maryland commissioners, describes her as a French lady who through long residence

---

* Witham Marshe, *Lancaster in 1774* (Lancaster, 1884), pp. 27-30.

among the Six Nations had become almost an Indian. She told Marshe she had been born in Canada, that her father had governed the country, and that as a child she had been captured by the Iroquois, taken to a New York colony and brought up with the captors' children. According to her story she was ten years old when captured by the Iroquois, yet had no recollection of a Canadian home. Other lapses were noted in her story, such as placing the Huron-Iroquois wars in her father's administration.

Marshe wrote that Madame Montour was a handsome woman, "genteel and of polite address," presumably about sixty years of age. She had kept in touch with whites through the years by accompanying the chiefs on their missions to colonial governors. Highly placed women in Philadelphia entertained her during her visits there. The "old Madame" retained familiarity with her native tongue by talking much with French fur traders. Two comely married daughters, one of whom was probably Margaret, mother of Catherine and Esther, accompanied her to Lancaster, likewise her handsome small grandson. Her only son was then on the warpath.

Madame's story did not wholly convince Marshe. He decided she was no true daughter of Frontenac or any other French governor of Canada. A certain Monsieur Montour, her probable father and a man of no great distinction, emigrated to Canada about 1665. By an Indian wife he had one son and two daughters.* Marshe reported that Montour was severely wounded by Mohawk near Lake Champlain and that his ten-year-old daughter was captured and adopted by the Iroquois. Her first adult appearance was as interpreter at an Albany conference on August 24, 1711. Fairly well educated, she married Carondowanen or "Big Tree," an Oneida war chief who had named himself "Robert Hunter" in admiration of the New York governor. Big Tree fell in battle with the Catawba in 1729, but not before he and the gifted Madame had traveled widely, since she and Big Tree at one period lived with the Miami at Lake Erie's western end and removed to Pennsylvania about 1727, settling at what is now Montoursville, Lycoming County. Madame died blind and decrepit about 1753 after a truly remarkable life, even though it was no doubt more prosaic than her fancies. She was considered generally untrustworthy by contemporary whites, and the Minister of the Pro-

* *Doc. Rel. to Col. Hist. of N. Y.,* V, 65.

vincial Council of Pennsylvania commented on October 15, 1734, "Her old age only protects her from being punished for such falsehoods."

Montour lore of New York colony and Pennsylvania teems with rude romance, ferocity and impish guile in narrative. One of Madame's children was Margaret Montour, or "French Margaret" as history knows her. She lived on the Susquehanna's eastern branch with her Six Nations husband Katarioniecha. They had five children, one of whom became "Queen Catherine," the fugitive from Sullivan's army in 1779. Catherine's almost equally famous sister, Esther, was erroneously confounded with Catherine by Lossing and other early historians.

Esther still is regarded by Pennsylvania historians as the most diabolical of all the Montours. She was the wife of Echogohund Mousey, who was chosen by the Iroquois to rule the subjugated Delaware with the title of Half-King. At his death she succeeded to his limited powers. Queen Esther held wildwood court at Sheshequin, now Ulster, in Bradford County, Pennsylvania. The death of her son in battle at Exeter transformed her the next day, July 3, 1778, to a raging fury at the Wyoming Massacre, where she led a band of warriors yelling hate and scalping whites. That very autumn, avengers led by Colonel Thomas Hartley burned Sheshequin, giving particular attention to the burning of Esther's "palace," a commodious house which could hardly have been as splendid as fanciful writers of that day had described it. Esther's mother, French Margaret, who fled from that holocaust, died early in the 1800's at the head of Cayuga Lake in a humble cabin—an extremely old woman who had outlived family, fame and an entire historical epoch.

Her celebrated daughter, Catherine, whose career called forth more irresponsible ink than flowed in the case of any other Montour, entered the pagan state of matrimony by marrying Telelemut, who is sometimes described as a member of the Turkey tribe of the Delaware and sometimes as a noted war chief of the Seneca. He might have been both, by reason of adoption, blood brotherhood or official tie in the relations of Iroquois and Delaware who were virtually ruled by an Iroquois "Half-King." Catherine's mate's Anglicized name was Thomas Huston, or Hudson.[*]

---

[*] *Pennsylvania Archives,* 1st Ser., Vol. iii, p. 558.

Conrad Weiser, Pennsylvania's agent and mediator in Indian affairs, mentioned that Catherine had five or six children in 1758. In her later life Queen Catherine lived for many years at the head of Seneca Lake in a village which the Seneca called Sheaquaga, but which the whites knew as French Catherine's Town, for many years before it was razed and burned by Sullivan's men in 1779. The "queen" then fled to the shelter of Niagara where she died a year or two later at a reported age of eighty years.

Queen Catherine is usually credited with three children—Roland, "Stuttering" John and Belle; but whether they were her own or merely adopted is disputed. One Edward Pollard has been designated as their father, but that paternity does not necessarily lift them out of Montour origin. By ancient custom, the lines of Iroquois descent flowed through the mother, and a woman of Catherine's power could have her children fathered outside of marriage if she pleased.

At any rate, however launched into this world and into the British-Seneca alliance, both son Roland and son John fought for the king in the Revolutionary War. Roland, a captain, was wounded and died at Painted Post. John, a lieutenant, stuttered along until 1830, when he died near Geneseo in Ontario County and is buried near the Big Tree, a monster oak near his homestead. By contrast with his adventurous ancestors Stuttering John must have been a mild and quiet character, for he lived to a ripe old age among whites who had overrun the scene. There are still Montours in the land of their ancestors as well as in Canada—handsome brown-red people with a touch of woodland royalty in their dignified speech and graceful gestures. They would have been quite at home with Louis Philippe, later King of France, who visited their country and sketched the family waterfall. Being king, he managed to get the sketch hung in the Louvre.

# Chapter 9

## The Border Turns from War to Peace

*There are who teach only the sweet lessons of peace and safety;*
*But I teach lessons of war and peace to those I love,*
*That they readily meet invasions, when they come.*

—WALT WHITMAN

URING the winter of 1779-1780, General Haldimand, in correspondence with Lord Germain, the Colonial Secretary of State, initiated a plan which opened the north shore of Lake Ontario to trade and settlement in amazingly short time. Passages from Lieutenant Walter Butler's unpublished journal, cited elsewhere in this narrative, reveal the utter loneliness of the north shore before the English applied themselves to developing its trade.

Haldimand warned Lord Germain that if Britain expected to hold the upper country and keep the fur trade, some 1,500 men, adequately provisioned, must be sent in each spring as soon as the rivers and lakes became navigable. The General asked permission to carry on the plan of forming settlements near the principal forts along the border. Extending his system of garrison agriculture, he advocated raising grain and garden stock at Detroit to supply that area and "Machilmackinac." The same plan was practicable at Niagara, he added. There for a time the matter rested.

Late in the doleful autumn of 1779, Sir Guy Johnson, Superintendent of Indian Affairs, came to Niagara and assumed direct charge of the Indian Department. His presence was needed there to hold the wavering Seneca in line after Sullivan's strafing. The Cayuga and loyal Delaware also were downcast by their misfortunes and showed signs of defection. Some Indians sought haven in a few villages that Sullivan's raiders had overlooked. Hunger drove 2,600 others from their scorched earth into frail shelters around Fort Niagara during that cruel winter. The accounts say that snow lay from eight to ten feet deep on the parade ground. Perhaps this is an exaggeration, but we must recall that this location has one of the heaviest snowfalls in all North America.

Eventually, late in the Revolution, the 4,000 Indians dependent on Niagara were gradually drawn away to villages at Buffalo Creek and Katargaras, forty miles from Fort Erie, whither Loyalist refugees from Virginia had also fled.

Meanwhile, John Butler was finally promoted to the rank and pay of a provincial lieutenant colonel and the title by which he is known in history—he had been long a captain and Deputy Superintendent under Superintendent Johnson. Butler had deserved this promotion much sooner than it came.

On May 9, 1780, Sir John Johnson opened a season of retribution by darting south from Crown Point with 300 soldiers and Indians. One hundred and forty-three Loyalists, who had been notified secretly beforehand, joined him. After devastating the settlements near Johnson Hall the party raced back to Canada without loss, though pursued by 1,000 militiamen led by Governor Clinton.

In July, 300 Onondaga and Tuscarora, hitherto pro-Continental, came to Niagara to offer their services because they were angered by American raids. General Cruikshank, the usually reliable military historian of Canada, makes the rather astonishing statement, met with nowhere else, that for the same reason some Oneida from the Fort Stanwix region swung to Brant. Obviously, the ferment in the Indian world was intense for a year or more after Sullivan's campaign.

Early in September General Haldimand decided to send two columns against New York's frontiers, each of 600 men. One was to advance from Crown Point toward Albany, the other from Oswego down the Mohawk River. Like the Burgoyne campaign three years before, this campaign was also planned as a pincers movement to divide the potential strength that the Continental army might bring to bear against Sir Henry Clinton in New York City. Another objective of the grand strategy was either to force the Oneida back into the British connection along with the rest of the Iroquois or hew that rebellious people into impotence.

In accord with this plan Sir John Johnson led the way to Oswego with 150 of his regiment. Colonel Butler was directed to join him with 140 of the Eighth, 80 of the Thirty-fourth Regiment and 200

Rangers. These units were to take from Niagara three cannon—a "grasshopper" and two royals. Haldimand was apprehensive of trouble from disaffected Indians and expressed the hope that Joseph Brant had returned to act as go-between in this raid which developed into one of the most destructive of the entire war.

The Johnson and Butler detachments, starting from their respective posts September 24, rendezvoused at Oswego on October 1. The next day they began a roundabout march to the upper Susquehanna Valley, leaving their boats and reserve provisions at Onondaga Lake. With gun and torch they pushed northward from the Susquehanna down Schoharie Creek to the Mohawk, and westward up the Mohawk along both shores, killing and laying waste night and day. Urged on by Governor Clinton, Continental forces drove forward in an attempted counterattack, but Johnson eluded them by leaving the river and advancing upon Stone Arabia in a dense fog. General Van Rensselaer and the Governor pursued with 1,500 Continentals and a force of Oneida, yet on swept the marauders. Doubling west, they escaped to Onondaga Lake, recovered their boats and returned to Oswego on October 27.

Results were impressive, penalties light. Johnson reported his losses as nine killed, two wounded and fifty-two missing, most of whom reached Carleton Island later. His force had destroyed thirteen gristmills, numerous sawmills, 1,000 houses and as many barns containing 600,000 bushels of grain. For the fertile valley and its patriots, this was the nadir of disaster, but they would not yield.

Meanwhile, on the more constructive side of the war ledger, military need lent force to plans for settlement of Ontario's shores. Colonel Bolton wrote General Haldimand on March 4, 1779, that the country belonging to the Mississaga and the government of Canada on the west side of the Niagara River was an excellent place of residence for Loyalists who had fled New York Province. Military gardens at Oswego and Niagara had already excited the wonderment of citizens of Albany and Montreal because of the great size and fine quality of vegetables produced. It was prophesied that in half a dozen years a successful settlement could be created at Niagara.

Lord Germain approved Haldimand's plan, and on July 7 the General wrote to Colonel Bolton that the land granted by the Mississaga to Sir William Johnson for the Crown, southwest of the river and opposite to the fort, would be reclaimed and divided into lots. It would then be "distributed to such loyalists who could improve them for the maintainance of their families until such time as by peace they shall be restored to their respective homes, should they be inclined to quit their situation at Niagara." The quotation is interesting evidence that in 1780 British commanders did not realize that the Loyalist problem would be an enduring one.

Haldimand directed that the work of reclamation was to be done at government expense. Grants would remain Crown property and tenants would be entitled only to the produce therefrom. Rights of tenancy free of rent would be extended annually at the discretion of the commander in chief. Seed, plows and other agricultural implements were promised without charge. Surplus produce was "to be disposed of to the commanding officer for the use of the troops and not to traders or accidental travelers."

Enamored of this optimistic scheme, Haldimand six days later sent further notice that his "Niagara Plan of edible annex to fortresses," which he described as already going well at Carleton Island, would be extended to other border points on his order, and added, "I hereby enclose instructions for carrying it into execution at Detroit which you will please forward to the commanding officer after having perused them."

By December Colonel Butler could report some progress in husbandry, although winter wheat had arrived too late for planting, so had been stored till the next season. Four or five families who were building houses would require sixty bushels of spring wheat and oats, twelve bushels of buckwheat and a barrel of Indian corn for planting early in the spring.

More important to Colonel Butler were recruits. In January 1781 small parties left Niagara to muster men for the Rangers, and some of these recruiting officers penetrated even to New Jersey. Daring agents won recruits for the Crown openly on the streets of unsuspicious Albany and procured others among the Tories along the Norman's Kill and in the Helderberg Mountains southwest of that old Dutch town. On February 1, Brant led a force from Canada to harass Fort Stanwix. A detachment of raiding hornets buzzed down to burn the deserted fort at Cherry Valley and destroy a settlement at

Bowen's Creek. Raids ran as far as New Jersey to pick up Loyalist reinforcements.

During May five separate scouting parties darted through the Mohawk Valley, one group venturing to the outskirts of Schenectady. Some idea of the American situation can be gleaned from the reports of Colonel Marinus Willett, in command of all American troops in the valley, whose headquarters at Canajoharie was garrisoned by two Continental regiments. He described the militia of the district as reduced from 2,500 to a mere 800. Of the missing 1,700 one-third had been killed or taken prisoners in the various raids, one-third had deserted to the Loyalists and the remaining third had removed from the dangerous ground. In the sixty-three-mile stretch between Schenectady and German Flats there were twenty-four forts, each sheltering from ten to fifty families. Some of these were, of course, merely stone farmhouses, of no great size, to which the neighboring families went when warned that raiders were out in force. Walter D. Edmonds' novel, *Drums Along the Mohawk,* gives a substantially correct picture of these alarms, although by no means accurate in details. By active countermeasures Colonel Willett dispersed some raiding parties in June, but there was no chance to come to grips with the elusive Brant who ranged as far west as Detroit and as far south as Kentucky.

Haldimand wanted even more raids, but at Niagara, in September 1781, Powell endeavored to discourage another raid by saying that both the British troops and the Indians were worn out, while very few people remained in the Mohawk Valley, where they occupied fortified houses inexpedient to attack. Instead, Powell approved a plan prepared by Colonels Johnson and Butler. They recommended that a force be assembled at Oswego and proceed to the south side of Oneida Lake where boats might be left under a guard. The invaders would detach a party to destroy the remaining mills at Canajoharie, and then concentrate against Cobus Kill (Cobleskill). They might even proceed to Duanesburgh, on the patent of James Duane, Patriot leader who became New York City's first mayor after the war. This region had not yet been molested and offered superior possibilities for rapine and slaughter.

General Haldimand approved and the plan went forward. Niagara was called on for thirty-six men of the Eighth Regiment under Lieutenant Coote, 169 Rangers led by Captain Walter N. Butler, and 109 Indians, "the dregs of the tribes," commanded by Captain Tice. Major Ross, who took over command of the expedition, mustered Carleton Island detachments from four regiments, totaling 207 officers and men.

For some months information gleaned from prisoners and deserters had been vague and confusing. To check up, Major Ross sent out a spy from Carleton Island—one John Servos, a former Continental taken prisoner, who had recanted on rebellion and enlisted in Sir John Johnson's regiment. In May 1781, Servos surrendered himself to the trusting Continentals ostensibly as a deserter from the British. Examined by Governor Clinton and a committee at Albany, Servos gave them a false description, as it proved, of Carleton Island which thus remained shrouded in tantalizing mystery. So plausible was Servos, according to Cruikshank's account, that the Albany authorities gave him permission to visit the Mohawk forts, and a pass which admitted him into the Continental lines at New Jersey. These visits accomplished, Servos returned surreptitiously to report to Major Ross and to rejoin his regiment, accompanied by six recruits for Sir John Johnson's Second Battalion. Too, Servos brought word of Mohawk Valley Loyalists who, expecting Sir John to swoop afresh, were secreting provisions for him and his force.

With this information Major Ross impatiently awaited at Oswego the arrival of the Niagara detachment which was delayed by a gale on the lake. That force reached Oswego on October 9 and the column marched next day. On the seventeenth the boats were hidden along a creek tributary to Oneida Lake. Ross, calculating that Willett had some 2,000 men distributed between Schenectady, Schoharie and Canajoharie, pierced between these points straight at Duanesburgh. After a forced night march in cold, wet weather, at the end of eight days of difficult faring they reached a deserted settlement. Warned, the inhabitants had fled during the night. The raiders set fire to farm buildings along a seven-mile stretch, wheeled, marched back and forded the swollen river at Johnstown, dispersing a small force at the fort. But with the militia in full chase the invaders were in a perilous position.

Ross decided to push north through the woods to Carleton Island instead of going west to his boats by the usual route, but kept this intention to himself. Marching through Johnstown village he halted in the fields near Johnson Hall to slaughter cattle and collect provisions. Here the swift-moving Willett caught up with the raiders, but his advance guard of militiamen were too raw to cope with the hard-bitten foe. Later Willett lamented lack of trustworthy Indian allies, for in the game of hide-and-seek Ross's raiders proved superior.

During the evening of October 29, Ross was seeking the trail which led from the German Flats northward to Carleton Island when he found that his Indians, the "dregs," were planning to sneak back to Niagara. Disgusted, he let them go and marched on with his white men, not realizing that the pursuit was again at his heels.

Willett had rushed to German Flats and collected 500 fresh troops including sixty Oneida Indians. Shrewdly guessing that Ross was headed for Carleton Island, Willett gained ground and encamped two miles from the rear guard of Ross's men on the night of the twenty-ninth. The next day he took as prisoners some of Ross's straggling Indians and learned that his foe was just ahead.

Presently Ross heard American riflemen firing in his rear and ordered his exhausted troops to push on and cross East Canada Creek for a last stand. Fording the creek in dense fog, Captain Walter N. Butler, commanding the rear guard, lined the ford with Rangers to delay the Americans' advance until Ross had a chance to establish a defense.

Willett's advance guard came rushing to the opposite bank and plunged into the water. As the fog lightened momentarily there was a volley and dead and wounded Continentals tumbled into the stream. But although the American casualties were more numerous the British loss was more costly. A bullet struck Walter Butler in the head as he stood waving encouragement to his men.

Temporarily relieved by Butler's last stand, Ross had chosen a position in the woods a quarter-mile distant. But Willett did not attack. After an hour's wait, Ross ordered his men to resume the march north. When the firing at the creek had ceased, Willett crossed it to find Butler and three Rangers lying dead. He naturally exulted in the death of Walter Butler and the inhabitants of the Mohawk Valley rejoiced more over his death than they did at the surrender of Cornwallis.

The American leader noted the tremendous endurance of the Loyalists under Ross during their forced retreat. They outstayed both British regulars and Indians. After four days in the wilderness on a ration of only a half-pound of horseflesh a day per man, they marched thirty miles in a day.

In this long pursuit and intermittent skirmishing, Ross lost only ten men, not counting the mutinous Indians sent back to Niagara. Seven days' further march in cold wet weather through dense wilderness brought him to Carleton Island on November 6. The trail was intersected by several streams in flood, passable only by means of rafts. From first to last the expedition cost seventy-four officers and men, two-thirds of whom were returned as missing. Thirteen experienced Rangers later made their way through the woods to Oswego.

The raiding Rangers returned to Niagara for the winter. Progress of the Niagara settlement was briefly sketched in Lieutenant Colonel John Butler's correspondence with the government during the succeeding months. Farmers were already getting themselves established to the point of maintaining their families from first crops, but needed blacksmiths and iron fit for axes, hoes and tools.

On February 23, 1782, Carleton (Lord Dorchester) succeeded Sir Henry Clinton as commander in chief in America. He arrived in New York City on May 5. His policy was conciliating and signified that the war was practically at an end. Slow to give up hope, however, Butler's Rangers continued to guard the frontier and to receive recruits. Nearly 200 of them were detached to Carleton Island, enough to enable Major Ross to occupy Oswego. Mainly because they were in possession at the war's end, the British were able to continue occupation of Oswego to 1796.

Throughout the hostilities Fort Niagara had been an island of congested humanity in an otherwise almost unpeopled wilderness. British remittances had supported the garrison and Indians, and the traders lived off Indian custom. Only sixteen families with a total of sixty-eight persons farmed the adjoining lands. An official survey of Niagara community of August 25, 1783, showed that 236 acres had been cleared. Crops raised during the year comprised 206 bushels of wheat, 46 bushels of oats, 926 bushels of Indian corn and 632 bushels of potatoes. The settlers owned 49 horses, 42 cows, 30 sheep and 103 hogs.

Conversion to peace brought to these frontier husbandmen problems which they proceeded to lay before the authorities with a celerity which seems almost modern. In 1783 the farmers transmitted to Colonel Butler a politely phrased protest signed by Isaac Dolsen, Elijah Phelps, Thomas McMicking and Donal Bee. The communication related that the Haldimand proposals of a year's provisions and the services of a blacksmith had not yet been met. They asked of Brigadier General MacLean formal leases for their farms, setting forth that they had to sell their surplus produce at "ceiling" prices set by the commanding officer of the post. They offered to pay rent to insure more certainty of tenure, as under the conditions they felt insecure and at the government's mercy. To economists this presents an interesting case of rent arising from offer of tenants instead of demands of landlords.

Prospective return of formal peace brought to Loyalist exiles at Niagara little hope of being restored to their former homes. Colonel Butler told General MacLean that none of his people would think of going to law in the former colonies "where they could not expect the shadow of justice, could not re-purchase their estates, and would rather go to Japan than among the Americans."

The Rangers under Butler's command, mostly farmers, wanted to return to the soil. After disbanding, 258 officers and men—with their families a total of 620—agreed to settle on the Niagara tract. For the next quarter-century the names of Ranger veterans recur as legislators, surveyors and town officers in the Dominion. It was the same with their former foes below the line. Many graduates of the hard school of war shone in the activities of civilian life. Fortunately, the Ranger leader, Colonel John Butler, continued to grow in power "as the mainstay of the settlement and an acknowledged authority on all matters concerning it" until his death in 1796. Governor Carleton and Lieutenant-Governor Simcoe depended implicitly upon this transplanted American of the old Irish-Mohawk Valley stock. Many of the Rangers bore arms in the War of 1812, though past the vigor of their youth.

While the Sullivan expedition quite thoroughly scotched the Iroquois, it did not wholly subdue them. A potential Indian menace hung over western New York until "Mad Anthony" Wayne defeated the allied Ohio and Indiana bands at Fallen Timbers on the

Maumee in 1794, whereupon the Iroquois realized the hopelessness of their cause. But the Sullivan expedition held a significance above battle; it brought to the attention of the land-hungry soldiers a rich area which had been walled off from settlement by British compact. After the peace there was a great mass movement of westward emigration.

So the curtain descended slowly on the Revolutionary War on the shores and in the watershed of Lake Ontario. Two new nations had been created, one already an acknowledged sovereign after victory in arms, the other destined to reach the same position by slow and peaceful stages within the elastic framework of the British Empire. In the development toward Federation and Dominion status the Ontario region led the way, as will be related. Meantime it is in order to record the fact that in all probability the American Revolution hastened the evolution of Upper Canada by at least a generation, in providing it with Loyalist settlers, garrison trade, improved shipping on Lake Ontario and a reputation for fertile soil.

COMMODORE

ISAAC CHAUNCEY

MELANCTHON C. WOOLSEY

SIR GEORGE PREVOST

SIR JAMES LUCAS YEO

GENERAL JACOB BROWN GENERAL WINFIELD SCOTT

GENERAL ZEBULON PIKE GENERAL HENRY DEARBORN

# Chapter 10

# The Loyalists and Upper Canada

*Come my tan-faced children,*
*Follow well in order, get your weapons ready;*
*Have you your pistols? Have you your sharp edged axes?*
*Pioneers! O pioneers!*

*All the pulses of the world,*
*Falling in, they beat for us, with the westward movement beat;*
*Holding single or together, steady moving, to the front, all for us,*
*Pioneers! O pioneers!*

—WALT WHITMAN

VICTORY in the Revolution took from Great Britain, as Professor George M. Wrong emphasizes in his *Canada and the American Revolution*, "nearly all the people of her own blood who lived overseas." Britain's population was then only 20,000,000 and elsewhere in the then-youthful overseas British Empire there were less than 1,000,000 whites—100,000 or so in the West Indies, a few in India, none as yet in Australia, New Zealand or South Africa. There were only about 2,000 British in Canada, a good many of whom were not well disposed to the Mother Country, their opinions being of a piece with those of their cousins to the southward.

It seemed incredible that isolated British rule could survive in Canada, the only populated region in North America to maintain a political connection with England. This isolation no doubt was one reason why France for many years maintained more than an academic interest in Canadian affairs. Canada, it seemed at one time, might go French or American but could hardly remain British. But the Revolution itself created a decisive immigration which because of its unwavering loyalty and steady abilities gave staying power to empire. These migrants were Loyalists, detached by the fortunes of war from their American homes and estates, to find new security under the British flag in Nova Scotia, New Brunswick and in Upper Canada, the present province of Ontario.

129

There is no need here to dilate on the sufferings of the Loyalists at the hands of Patriot committees, commanders, armies and mobs. Some of them, described as Tories in other chapters, deserved all the punishment they received. For example, pity is wasted on Sir John Johnson and his fellow raiders, who caused far more damage to poor folk than they ever sustained; and those "blue-eyed Indians" whose depredations and callous cruelty in general exceeded the worst acts of their Indian allies. But other adherents to the king's cause were innocent of overt acts, or at least of serious treachery. Their crimes ran all the way from giving aid and comfort to enemy forces down to mere voicing of opinion contrary to independence.

For a policy that encouraged migration of such able settlers, Britain has Carleton, Lord Dorchester, again to thank for truly imperial foresight. Commanding all British forces from New York after the recall of Sir Henry Clinton, Carleton rendered the Loyalists every assistance. He received with pity these "brave, unfortunate people ... many of them from the very first families ... reduced to a condition that makes one's heart bleed."

Among the 30,000 cases of Loyalists who received financial relief, not all were persons of means, and many once affluent were penniless. There were necessarily many poor folk, even some hundred Negro freedmen. Professor Wrong presents this description of their departure:

"A joint commission supervised the embarking of the exiles and of the British regiments, the harbor of New York was busy with the many ships brought together for the purpose. Almost daily in the summer of 1783 transports left New York, now with a German regiment for Europe, now with a British regiment setting out for England or Scotland or Ireland; now for the West Indies; now with families destined to find sympathy, but also a cheerless outlook in Halifax and other places too thronged with their kind. Some 6,000 embarked in May, the same number in June ... prevailing bitter temper against any loyalists who might remain. ... By November came the final departure of the British. ..."*

This exodus was the culmination of a movement which began in driblets even before Revolutionary warfare started. During hostilities some Loyalists had established themselves in the Maritime Provinces.

---

* *Canada and the American Revolution* (New York: The Macmillan Company), p. 394.

A graphic picture of their hardships on Long Island and the rigors of their first encampments is presented in the novel *Oliver Wiswell,* by Kenneth Roberts. Many who eventually reached Ontario tarried for a time in New Brunswick, but shiploads from New York City are reported as passing through the Gulf and up the St. Lawrence because too many had already gone to Nova Scotia. Those bound for Upper Canada wintered at Sorel on government maintenance and went on in the spring. A number of other routes were followed by Loyalist refugees into Ontario. Some followed the old warpath along Lakes George and Champlain and the Richelieu River; that way went the family from Albany who provided part of the cast of characters for *Bright to the Wanderer,* a recent historical novel of Ontario settlement by Bruce Lancaster.

No doubt most of the Mohawk Valley Loyalists followed the Oswego-Kingston route. At the other end of the lake hundreds crossed at Niagara and settled down alongside Butler's disbanded Rangers. For a dozen years or so they would have the protection of a British garrison at the fort and the enhanced opportunities for better goods and living which always surround a busy trading post. Perhaps for this reason Niagara-on-the-Lake has ever been known for its wealth, charm and culture. Loyalists from the Southern states had the longest journey.

What did they find? An old but sparsely settled country to the east where population hugged the rivers. Inland were small settlements at Kingston, Niagara and Detroit but otherwise a woody wilderness of low elevations, many lakes, plentiful swamps, noble trees and fertile soil under the forest cover. This region had been one of the world's great sources of furs, and even yet many parts of it are huntsmen's and fishermen's paradises. But to some of the new settlers, coming from a seaboard America where white settlements were a century and a half old, the Ontario country seemed hostile and forbidding, its hidden riches being less in evidence than savages, wolves, bears, snakes, cold, fever and ague, and the forbidding gloom of the dense forests.

From Montreal the settlers worked their laborious way upstream in flotillas of a dozen bateaux—a ten or twelve-day journey arduous for unskilled oarsmen, among them former merchants, farmers, soldiers, even a few Hessians.

Each head of a Loyalist family had been provided by the authorities with a "location ticket," giving him the right to a grant of land in a certain area marked off on a surveyor's plan. The exact location was determined by lot. Nearly all wanted water frontage, but this tendency to locate by the waterways was discouraged, since prior claimants to the same land might appear later. An instance of prior settlement would be the area around Fort Frontenac where La Salle's seignory ran for twelve miles along the lake shore. Loyalist settlers on water fronts were allowed only 100 acres; those on inland sites 200 acres. In both cases 50 additional acres were granted for each child. When a son or daughter came of age, he or she was entitled to 200 acres. A commissioned officer might receive as many as 1,000 acres. These grants were too lavish and tended to hamper settlement. Each owner was supposed to cut a road across his property, but this development proved so costly that it was usually avoided. Travel remained handicapped by swamps, fallen trees, shaky bridges or unbridged streams.

Seldom has any pioneering group been better sustained and provided for by a sponsoring government. Settlers on these ample grants received clothing, seed, tools, weapons, tents, boats, domestic animals—a cow for two families. The government promised flour mills, sawmills, churches and church bells. But not all these blessings materialized because of distance, inefficiency, favoritism and, occasionally, graft. There were the usual complaints, delays, and hard-luck stories, and some migrants tended to remain dependent.

The fact that many of the Loyalists had hard money in sight when their claims should be finally settled led to certain condescensions and pretensions unusual on a frontier and hardly conducive to neighborly co-operation—a weakness officially recognized and lamented. This quick social stratification of the new region followed the pattern of the tight social system of the colonial seaboard, of English origin and reinforced by a century or more of American Loyalism. There were few English-born in the new province; in fact, the statistics of migration reveal Yorkers in the majority. "The origins of the present ardently British province of Ontario are in large measure to be found in the State of New York." Not, of course, the New York of either the Sons of Liberty or the Clintons, but the New York of the patroons, manor lords and rich Dutch-English merchants, in its way an extremely aristocratic British province before the great upheaval which swept so many Yorkers into Ontario. In their new home the gentry set the tone, and the poorer majority accepted it, just as they had done previously without protest on their farms and in their shops south of the line.

There were years of hardships the worse to bear because of inexperience and the resentment which comes to those who have seen better days. Those accustomed to town life became embittered in rural isolation. Children grew up without schooling. Drunkenness became a common curse when whisky at sixpence a quart was used as medicine for malaria and employed as a flavoring for the children's porridge. But, in spite of all drawbacks, this strong people had a great hate and a great love to sustain them in labors which must have been well-nigh unending. For in a few years, despite all the handicaps narrated by pessimistic chroniclers, Ontario settlers possessed ample crops and full barns, frame houses in place of log huts, an able clergy, good schools, physicians and growing settlements with sweet, old-country names. Along 500 miles of lake and river frontage homesteads arose on newly cleared land. Although crops failed for two successive years, 1787-1788, and allowances were ended about the same time, the country soon recovered. In 1791 travelers were exclaiming on the vast quantities of food and drink consumed in the better houses and the high level of creature comforts for all.

Upper Canada received a separate government in 1792, with the heady and steady Colonel John Graves Simcoe as governor. No Loyalist could properly complain of General Haldimand's treatment of them, yet enough did so to undermine his prestige. One such complainant wrote, "All our golden promises are vanished in smoke; we have nothing but His Majesty's rotten pork and unbaked beans to subsist on. It is the most inhospitable clime that ever man sat on [sic]." In sober truth Haldimand, himself a Swiss *émigré,* had performed wonders for the dispossessed, yet he never quite comprehended the political aspirations of his people who desired some measure of self-rule and the traditional "rights of Englishmen," without American trimmings. The Crown, more alert than before to symptoms of discontent, soon obliged its Loyalist subjects by giving Upper Canada complete separation from French or Lower Canada.

The Constitutional Act of 1791, championed in Parliament by William Pitt and opposed by Charles James Fox, fixed the government of the new province in a royal Governor appointed by the Crown, a Legislative Council of not less than seven members, chosen for life by the king (in effect by the governor) and a Legislative Assembly of sixteen members elected under property qualifications sufficiently rigid to disfranchise the poorer settlers and pave the way for later oligarchical rule.

The first capital of Upper Canada was Niagara, later Newark (now Niagara-on-the-Lake), across the Niagara River from the old fort. Here Colonel Simcoe opened his first Parliament, but believing a renewal of the American war to be inevitable, he soon removed his capital to York, now named Toronto. There in 1793 the legislature of this infant province outlawed the slave trade years before Great Britain itself did so. No more slaves could be brought into the province, those already there were to be free after nine years, and children of slaves would go free at the age of twenty-five years.

The Mother Country spent $9,000,000 quite promptly on support of exiles and eventually paid the enormous sum of $30,000,000 for all forms of Loyalist relief, including claims for property losses suffered through vandalism and confiscation. The claims inquiry lasted five years, from 1783 to 1788, and as late as 1792 claims were still being met by grants of land. In London a committee of leading American Loyalists, one from each colony, was staggered at finding claims totaling $35,000,000 had been filed by March 1784. The heaviest claimants had migrated to England, but commissioners came to Nova Scotia and New York for hearings which over a four-year period were held at six locations in British North America. Although the commissioners proved both just and diligent, many Loyalist claimants living in remote sections of Canada never received notice. Old soldiers, illiterate persons and those unable to go in person to Niagara or Montreal lost out through misfortune, as the rank and file did through neglect or ignorance. It is estimated that 50,000 or 60,000 Loyalists migrated to present Canada, yet only 3,000 claims were filed. Of these not more than 2,000 could have been of Canadian origin.

Still, one cannot but admire the patience, wisdom and generosity of the British government in this trying situation. Proved claims up to £10,000 were paid in full. Loyalists driven from their American homes received larger proportions of their losses than British owners of American property. Exiles received 90 percent on their proved claims between £10,000 and £30,000, 85 percent on additions up to £50,000, 80 percent on larger sums. Various allowances were also made for income lost during the years of strife. Of the $30,000,000 paid out, about one-third went to Loyalists from New York, and since New Yorkers predominated in the Ontario migration much of that wealth eventually followed them thither. But not all. The richest Loyalists went to London. Among them Beverley Robinson, Frederick Philipse, Jr., and Oliver de Lancey account for nearly $500,000. Loyalists who remained in the United States or who returned here were paid nearly $7,000,000. The Canadian exile who received the largest sum was probably Sir John Johnson with $250,000, which was only a fraction of his loss. He did not retire to the wilderness of Ontario, preferring the already developed region of Lower Canada for his residence.

Less numerous than the Loyalists from the American colonies but immensely influential in Upper Canada were British army officers who after long duty on this side of the water preferred to settle on generous grants in Upper Canada rather than return home. Together with the officers of Loyalist regiments they formed a solid core of martial training and tradition on which a strong militia system was built.

Such were the leaders and founders of Ontario. Soon they would be reinforced by immigrants from Scotland, home of one of the ablest and most tenacious of peoples. A century earlier, at the time of Nicholson's expedition, a story ran through French Canada and lies buried in the *Paris Documents* that the British Crown had given Canada to the Scots to be their heritage forever, if they could take it. Then the Act of Union was still young and the Scots disaffected toward England, as they would show during the risings of 1716 and 1745. Since then the Scots had accepted the inevitable, joined in the proud game of empire-making, and had fought in America in three wars. Now they were coming to possess the land and make it fruitful. As the shore lands of Lake Ontario were taken up, the Scots moved into the interior, cleared the forests and proved anew the riches of the soil. Never as furiously anti-American or pro-British as the United Empire Loyalists, they were a tough and nationally minded people, Canadians from the outset and determined to remain so.

These scattered and differing folk in Upper Canada were united in the belief that Canada could not be conquered; and a considerable portion of them acted as if the United States would never attempt to seize their new domain. Generous as Great Britain showed herself to the victims of the Revolutionary War, she was still blind to the value of Upper Canada and doubtful of her ability to hold it. She was consequently reluctant to invest heavily in its protection. Lord Dorchester expressed grave doubt that Britain would provide an adequate defense of 4,000 to 5,000 infantry, 700 to 800 seamen and ten or twelve ships of 150 tons or more for use on the lakes. Such was the continuing depreciation of Canada in the official British mind that years later one of the influential Barings, of the great banking family, said that Canada was "a lamb held for eventual slaughter" and that providing armament to defend it from conquest by the United States was the "foolishest thing in the world!" Henry Dundas in 1793 thought that if Upper Canada lived and grew, its natural export vent would be down the Mississippi. The noble lord could perceive no possibility that wheat could ever repay transportation for 600 miles from Niagara to Quebec.

While a hungry soldiery remained on the border, grain could be sold. Richard Cartwright, a Loyalist member of the first Legislative Council of Upper Canada and a Judge of the Court of Common Pleas, wrote in 1792:

"As long as the British government shall think proper to hire people to come over here to eat our flour, we shall go on very well and continue to make a figure, but when once we come to export our produce the disadvantages of our remote inland situation will operate in full force . . . and when we go beyond Lake Ontario it will cost as much to bring our rude produce to market as it will be worth and yet it is from such exports alone that we became beneficial to the mother country, who certainly have no intention to make us manufacturers."

Because of the transport difficulties described above, large, boss-capital farming could not prosper, and the oversize Loyalist grants were generally broken up. Thus Ontario developed as a province of small farmers in spite of the feeling of many of its leaders that broad land ownership was the true basis of gentility and social leadership. Aristocracy always needs a steady economic base; in this case wealth could accumulate chiefly from exports. Ontario winter wheat produced unusually good flour, but was not a dependable crop. Up to 1795 only two crops had been large enough to produce an export surplus and 1794 saw a crop failure so serious that Governor Simcoe reported to the Lords of Trade that settlers were being forced to leave the Niagara peninsula.

Lieutenant-Governor Simcoe's correspondence reveals him pushing hard for more British territory—for Vermont, and a boundary line from Lake Ontario to the head of Lake Champlain. To the west he first wanted the United States to end at the Genesee, then at a Presque Isle-Pittsburgh line, then at the Cuyahoga in Ohio and finally at the Miami.

Despite shortages on the spot and indifference among London officials, who seldom would concede that interior Upper Canada was the equal of seaboard Lower Canada, Simcoe persevered—a true empire builder in spirit. He refused to admit that the trade of the lakes would necessarily pass through the United States to Europe instead of down the St. Lawrence. That issue would be settled by waterway development, in which New York and Ontario would each take a hand—New York first with the Western Inland and then with the Erie Canal, Ontario later with the Welland. Both of the latter projects were still far in the future, but in the meantime Governor Simcoe kept heart in his people by assuring them that Upper Canada need not necessarily be sidetracked.

At this period the British people and most of their leaders agreed with Admiral Graves, Commander in Chief of the British naval forces in America, that Upper Canada "is quite a dead weight upon us." The only hope of providing a market for the back country, said the Admiral, was to establish Montreal as a free port like Hamburg, an idea too advanced for his time. The long-range outlook for Upper Canada was extremely gloomy. Obviously it could not look forward to indefinite support from the home country. The inhabitants would have to hustle for themselves. They did.

# Chapter 11

# Land Rush

*As the last dog most commonly catcheth the hare which other dogs have turned and tired before; so such who succeed in dangerous and difficult enterprises, generally reap the benefit of the adventures of those who went before them.*

—THOMAS FULLER

LAKE ONTARIO's southern shore and the western New York lands to the southward were eagerly scanned by prospective settlers. These regions had been closed to whites, first by the Iroquois refusal to sell lands west of the Mohawk confines, next by formal treaty at Fort Stanwix, where in 1768 was established the famous Fort Stanwix line, west of which white settlement was taboo. Nevertheless, penetration went forward by adventurous individuals and speculations undertaken before 1768 lay temptingly dormant but not uprooted.

In New York the Sullivan-Clinton campaign of 1779, which followed the Susquehanna, Genesee and Seneca Valleys, acquainted the soldiery with a tempting country to which many of them returned. So, too, Loyalists troops learned the merits of lands near Niagara on both sides of the present border. Opening of the central New York military tract, bonus lands for New York's Revolutionary War soldiers, stimulated migration enormously.

The land hunger of those at a distance could not be immediately satisfied at the close of the Revolution because of conflicting territorial claims, Indian opposition and resulting title difficulties. Seven states held claims to western lands, and in each case there were conflicting claims. For the Lake Ontario southern shore the claims of Massachusetts and New York were in direct conflict, yet both claims ran far westward. Massachusetts claimed the land and waters to the western ocean, while New York was the leading rival of Virginia in the magnitude of her western claims. New York's claims rested on treaties with the Iroquois, whose acknowledged influence and control had extended over the region between Lake Erie and the Cumberland Mountains—that is, Ohio and a portion of Kentucky. Consequently New York's claims were in conflict with the claims of Virginia, Connecticut and Massachusetts and clouded the title to the Erie panhandle of Pennsylvania.

To New York's credit be it said that she took the first move toward the general cession of contested areas to the Federal Union, whereby a national domain could be set up. This offer was made on March 1, 1781, by New York representatives to the Continental Congress. On that same day Maryland, which had been restively awaiting some such favorable move, finally ratified the Articles of Confederation and completed the first legal union of the Thirteen Colonies. Maryland's obstinacy, rooted in her lack of a hinterland subject to claim, was such that she had declined to commit herself to union with partners better endowed. However, Maryland's representatives interpreted New York's offer as breaking the deadlock, and in fact all seven claimant states within a few years declared themselves well disposed in principle to a settlement. But various complications remained to be worked out by way of adjustments in compensation.

Not until the Hartford treaty of 1786 was the political and economic fate of western New York determined. Then, as her contribution to a general settlement of conflicting claims, New York ceded to Massachusetts ownership of all the lands west of the seventy-seventh parallel of longitude, due north and south through the eighty-second milestone on Mason and Dixon's Line. The north and south line so established in New York is still known as the Pre-emption Line. This cession was subject to two important provisions: (1) Indian title to all the affected lands had to be extinguished by means of direct treaty with the aboriginal owners, and (2) New York reserved a strip a mile and a half deep on the Niagara River, enough to insure a voice in control of Niagara Falls and the portage at that point. Of course, only the ownership would pass; New York expressly reserved all rights of sovereignty and government. The area involved covered upward of 10,000 square miles, and is now occupied by fourteen counties holding more than 2,000,000 population. Of these fourteen counties, four—Wayne, Monroe, Orleans and Niagara—border Lake Ontario and have a total population of 700,000.

It was understood that the Massachusetts fief in New York would be financial only, and that ownership rights would be promptly sold. A start in vending this great domain was made when Oliver Phelps and Nathaniel Gorham of Massachusetts were designated as the successful bidders for Massachusetts' rights. In the Buffalo Indian council of 1788, Phelps and Gorham cleared title to about 1,875,000 acres—forty-five miles from east to west and eighty-four miles from north to south—at a total cost of $300,000, payable on favorable terms in depreciated currency and Massachusetts state bonds. As soon as prompt surveys permitted, thirty to forty townships were sold off on small down payments. Subsequent payments were to be larger in terms of dollars, but it was expected that debtors could pay with the same depreciated dollars and securities in which Phelps and Gorham had agreed to meet their own payments to Massachusetts.

At first the Indians would sell no land west of the Genesee River, holding that the gorge of that stream had been fixed by the Creator as a dividing line between the white and red races. But they were finally persuaded by Phelps to sell a millsite at the Great Falls of the Genesee. It grew under the Phelpsian oratory to include a tract twelve miles wide by twenty-eight miles long running from Lake Ontario to the Indian village of Canawagus. Now known as the "Mill-Seat Tract," it includes a great part of the modern city of Rochester and its thriving environs. Thereafter the Indians called Oliver Phelps by a name which they esteemed complimentary but which in view of his rise and decline now has an ironical twist—"The Great Fall."

Adoption of the Federal Constitution, Hamilton's hard money Treasury policy and the prospect that the Federal government would relieve the states of certain debts, notably the Massachusetts final-settlement notes, all combined to increase the value of bonds and dollars to the ruin of Phelps and Gorham and the serious embarrassment of the first wave of their settlers and minor speculators. Here was proved again the old adage that labor, not land, grows crops. Phelps and Gorham, with an empire of rich land in their possession, could not turn it quickly enough to escape bankruptcy.

Once sales slackened and dollars rose in value, Phelps and Gorham were ruined, along with most of their clients. The State of Massachusetts commenced an action against the firm and its sureties, but compromised, on March 10, 1791, on the reconveyance of all those lands in which the firm had not yet extinguished Indian title. Moreover, Phelps and Gorham were given an extension of time in which to dispose of the remaining one-third at a scale-down price of four shillings on the pound, eighty percent off the original figure. There is no indication that the firm passed any considerable part of this advantage on to those who had purchased from them. Such properties as reverted to them were later dealt off by Oliver Phelps who, after going into seclusion for a time, emerged to make a modest living by small transactions in land parcels which he had once owned en masse. He lies now in a quiet corner of his old domain—the lovely Pioneers Cemetery at Canandaigua, New York, where those who know the story of his rise and fall can muse upon the changing ways of God to man.

Into the Pre-emption Lands now strode a new giant, the great merchant, financier and speculator, Robert Morris of Philadelphia, who, like Atlas, for two years had carried the Revolution on his back. He had been or soon would be repaid for all his Revolutionary advances, and never would be in better shape to undertake a colossal deal in new lands. Two days after Massachusetts renegotiated its contract with Phelps and Gorham, the Bay State agreed to sell to Morris' agent, Samuel Ogden, all of its remaining New York acreage. On May 11, 1791, this vast domain was conveyed to Morris in five separate deeds.

One of the succeeding heavy owners was the Holland Land Company, which apparently was unincorporated. The stay-at-home Hollanders, originally eleven in number but later more than twenty, maintained ownership in various groupings of properties trusteed but they operated through a single general agent in Philadelphia who arranged for surveys and negotiated sales. Purchasers secured deeds, not from the Holland Company or Holland Land Company, as the syndicate was known, but from various groups of owners. There were three main groups. Of the twenty proprietors some held land in only one of the three groups, others in two or all three.

The Dutchmen did a good deal of "unsight unseen" trading among themselves in Holland. Their general agents best known to fame were Paul Busti, Theophile Casenove and John Lincklaen, all well remembered in New York place names. Both owners and agents for many years considered their southerly holdings the more valuable, because of water connections down the Susquehanna to the market at Philadelphia, then the largest city in the country, and access to the sheltered seaports of Chesapeake Bay.

The Holland Purchase, made when Robert Morris the seller was in financial distress and unable to extinguish the Indian title, was accompanied by an agreement that Morris would clear the title with the assistance of the Company as soon as practicable. This was accomplished by a treaty with the Seneca in September 1797 at Geneseo, in which appeared a number of persons notable in the history of the Ontario region:

Jeremiah Wadsworth, as Commissioner of the United States, a founder in the Genesee Valley of the great landowning family which still owns a large tract there and has given New York and the Union a succession of famous legislators and soldiers.

William Shepherd, agent of Massachusetts.

Charles Williamson, Scottish representative of Sir William Pulteney and Associates, an English syndicate whose lands extended from Sodus on Lake Ontario to the Susquehanna watershed in the south, where at Bath, his capital, Williamson quickly built up a settlement. There he had held in 1793 a country fair often described as the first in the United States, with horse races which attracted visitors from Maryland and Virginia, regions where this ardent salesman found buyers for his lands. Sir William Pulteney is said to have expended £500,000 on his project, which eventually paid out. Some of this capital went into the development of Bath, Geneva, Sodus and Charlotte.

In this transaction Williamson was also acting as co-agent for Robert Morris, together with the latter's son, Thomas Morris, who remained in the western country and became an important figure in its land traffic.

The council at Geneseo completed the transfer of Indian title to all lands secured from Massachusetts under the pre-emption right, except for about a dozen Indian reservations, ranging from one square mile to 130 square miles, amounting to 200,000 acres in all.

For thirteen years the pre-emption rights to these Indian reservations remained with the Holland Land Company, which in 1810 sold them to David A. Ogden for fifty cents an acre. By treaty and payment Ogden extinguished Indian title to all the reservations except

Cattaraugus, Allegany and the larger part of Tonawanda, but these transactions were clouded. At Tonawanda the Indians resisted, and refused peaceful possession and legal steps were taken. Ogden's methods were in strong contrast to those of the upright and liberal Holland Company itself.

Present also at the Geneseo council were William Bayard and John Lincklaen as unofficial observers for the Holland Company, and a young surveyor just beginning a twenty-year service which would make him an outstanding man on the Ontario-Niagara frontier. This was Joseph Ellicott, who represented the Hollanders in the basic survey, with Augustus Porter representing the Morris interest. The survey they instituted was notable for its military precision, system and order, although precision was rendered difficult by Indian reservations and some prior deeds.

At first the gridiron system was tried—townships six miles square, divided into sixteen sections, each one and one-half miles square, and each section into twelve lots three-quarters of a mile by one-quarter, or 120 acres. Twenty-four of these checkerboard townships were begun, but the scheme was then abandoned, as settlers desired boundaries suited to the nature of the soil and the slope of land.

The most striking enterprise of the survey was running a meridian line north and south by transit, not compass, across the entire state. North and south boundary lines in this area had previously been run by compass. Since compass north lies somewhat west of true north here, Ellicott's line cut an increasing wedge, like a piece of pie, as it moved north. The Cotringer, Ogden and Craigie tracts lost a considerable area which fell west of the Ellicott line. The Connecticut tract, however, was fully protected from loss by the terms of its deed. At its southern boundary Ellicott broke his meridian, moved due west about two miles and again drove his line north to the lake. To property holders who lost considerable amounts of land by this survey, Morris made some compensation from lands farther east, but could not come within 35,000 to 40,000 acres of offsetting the loss. The discrepancy led to the law courts, without avail to the complainants. Part of the Transit Road, N. Y. 78, is still an important road, due south from Lockport for twenty-five miles. For five miles it also carries the great No. 20 highway around Buffalo at a distance of about ten miles from the water front.

Completion of surveys stimulated speculation. Both Aaron Burr and Alexander Hamilton were contractors for western New York land in 1798. Burr had agreed to pay twelve shillings an acre for land on Tonawanda Bay, Lake Ontario. Although he never paid for it, the Holland Company surrendered his bond, which caused Burr's enemies to say that this favor was in consideration of his efforts as a New York legislator to alter the law so as to permit foreigners to hold real estate. Burr, already showing his dangerous recklessness, challenged Trustee Church to a duel. They exchanged shots, but this time there were no casualties and Church, a good-natured man, apologized. This incident marked the beginning of the Burr scandals.

The turn of the century found these arduous surveys and complicated transactions bearing fruit in actual settlement. In the years between 1781, when New York cleared a path to settlement of state claims, and 1800, when a really serviceable highway was completed, title had been cleared, the British garrisons had departed and a postwar depression had been overcome. The westward movement of settlers revived and increased. On November 26, 1800, Ellicott reported to Busti that sales were brisk and on December 17 wrote that sales for the year exceeded those of the five previous years combined.

An Ellicott handbill of 1800 describes the Lake Ontario lands as rich in soil, pastures, timber and limestone. Western New York is advertised as in water communication with the East and West, with Philadelphia, Baltimore, Pittsburgh and New Orleans. Settlers are invited in by "the Holland Land Company, whose liberality is well known in this country. . . . Those who wish to pay cash will find a liberal discount from the credit price."

All of western New York's chief developers were good advertisers. Oliver Phelps and Robert Morris were promoters and speculators in the grand manner, each of whom attracted settlers and capital from his own region—Phelps from New England, Morris from Pennsylvania. Captain Williamson, developer as well as promoter, cultivated Maryland and Virginia so zealously that planters sold their seaboard land and made the long trek northward with their slaves, as did the Rochesters, Fitzhughs and Roses to the Genesee, Sodus and Geneva areas. Through the influence of these Southern families of wealth and culture Geneva became a seat of education, medical training and

Episcopal tradition influential in the later establishment of Hobart College.

The Holland Land Company's operations were less personal, more massive and institutional in character. Rich absentee owners could wait for profits and did; meantime revenues could be used for developments such as Ellicott's elaborate surveys and highway projects. He scarcely exaggerated in speaking of the Company's "well-known liberality." To maintain a bona fide, industrious settler on his land, the Company would wait patiently until he could pay. There was economic reason for this consideration, since dispossessed settlers would shove off west to Ohio or Indiana, which were beckoning. Evidently convinced that free government would succeed, the Hollanders sought reasonable profits only, content with the difference between the average interest rates of the United States and Europe.

Busti, an Italian, set aside 100 acres in each township for religious purposes. A Catholic, he held out against conveying these tracts entirely to any single denomination. His instructions to his field representative, Ellicott, were most progressive with relation to roads, mills, public buildings and community growth. In all these social advantages northwestern New York received a running start and it still leads the state in community public spirit.

The Company set up its principal field office at Batavia, so named because the owners were then citizens of Napoleon's short-lived Batavian Republic. The phrase "doing a land-office business" is thought to have originated in the subsequent rush. There, twenty-five miles south of Lake Ontario, the settlers held on March 1, 1803, the first town meeting west of the Genesee River. The meeting did its democratic duty by electing thirty citizens to eight offices, including no less than fifteen overseers of highways. A bounty of five dollars was offered for "wolf scalps," half price for whelps, fifty cents for foxes and wildcats. The next year a five-dollar bounty was added for panther scalps.

A quaint measure was passed in town meeting that no one could operate a tavern unless it had a securely enclosed yard to contain "all the sleds, sleighs, wagons, carts and other carriages of the guests"—a means of thwarting the predatory, human and animal.

Batavia became a center of government for the newly set off and enormous county of Genesee. Court was held in the unfinished court-house in 1803. In the first election, held in that year, 182 votes were cast. A year later nearly 250 votes were cast for governor. The village always enjoyed Ellicott's hearty backing; he often said that God would take care of Buffalo but he himself had to look out for Batavia.

It would be pleasant to be able to record that all these settlers throve and that the liberal Dutch bankers profited in proportion. A quick glance over the next twenty years unfortunately reveals no such happy ending. Until the opening of the Erie Canal provided access to markets, the northern lands were plagued by low prices. In 1818 an Orleans County pioneer near the Ontario shore sold his wheat for twenty-five cents a bushel; in 1823, two years before the opening of the canal, thirty-seven and one-half cents was the ruling price throughout the Holland Purchase. Original debts to the Land Company remained unpaid, with heavy arrearages of interest.

The settlers had nothing they could sell at a profit except black salts and potash and perhaps lumber in proximity to Lake Ontario. Gloom beset the pioneers, as they stayed on in their decaying log houses long after they had hoped to replace them with frame buildings, fighting against rising indebtedness and the risk of ultimate dispossession from their land. Distress continued for a few years after the canal was opened, and during those years several agrarian conventions were held in the region to voice the discontent of farmers. But these protests were far less vigorous than those which broke into violence in other parts of New York.

Like so many absentee proprietors, the Dutch bankers lost heart not long before the tide turned, and shortened sail at the wrong time. In 1821 they offered to assign their remaining acreage—about half the original purchase—for a price covering the figure first set and four percent interest. Unable to close, they offered to domestic speculators and bankers all their unsold lands at four shillings an acre, in an effort to close up a protracted business and sidestep litigation. No buyer could be found for so large a holding. The owners had to continue perforce and the final result was somewhat better than they feared.

# Chapter 12

## The War of 1812 Opens

---

*With the nations of Europe in general our friendship and intercourse are undisturbed, and from the governments of the belligerent powers we continue to receive those friendly manifestations which are justly due to an honest neutrality.*
—Thomas Jefferson

*It was criminal folly for Jefferson and his follower, Madison, to neglect to give us a force either of regulars or of well-trained volunteers during the twelve years they had in which to prepare for the struggle that anyone could see was inevitable.*
—Theodore Roosevelt

---

Victory in the Seven Years' War had given Britain a hold on America's western country. In 1763 she had proclaimed that great expanse a permanent Indian reserve and proceeded to enlarge the fur trade, the one profitable industry secured by a costly war. The Quebec Act of 1774 had annexed to an expanded and gigantic Quebec Province the entire Northwest, and thus walled off this rich region from the pioneer Thirteen Colonies, which had battled diplomatically to obtain a foothold in it.

The Revolutionary War's outcome reversed the picture. Then the Mississippi was fixed as the western boundary of United States territory, while to the northward the line was drawn across the middle of the Great Lakes and the St. Lawrence system. But not until 1789 was the United States able to secure a survey of its valuable patrimony on the southern shores of Lakes Ontario and Erie. The surveying engineer, Niff, was directed to report on soundings, locations for shipbuilding, kinds of timber and the quality of land alongshore suitable for settlement. From 1783 to 1789, the loose Articles of Confederation left the new nation far inferior to the British in both diplomacy and commerce. John Adams, our first minister to Great Britain, sought vainly to procure a treaty of commerce and the fulfillment of pledges embodied in the Treaty of Paris. Among these was the cession of

147

British border forts and posts, to be turned over "with all convenient speed." They included Carleton Island (Fort Haldimand), Oswego (Fort Ontario), Niagara, Detroit and Michilimackinac, and other minor posts, depots on the fur routes between Montreal and the far Northwest. These posts had been utilized also by Britain as pivots of control over interior Indian tribes, who had been British allies during the Revolution. As we have seen, possession of Niagara, Oswego and Carleton assured naval supremacy on Lake Ontario and its network of rivers and portages so vital to the fur trade.

Boundary provisions fixed in the Treaty of Paris had dismayed both Governor Haldimand and the traders of Montreal. The Governor expressed apprehension that surrender of the forts to the United States would signal a general bloody Indian uprising. Traders feared financial ruin. American pleas made at London that the British depart forthwith were weakened by the fact that the United States was not ready to take over military responsibility in the Northwest. Britain argued that the Union had failed to comply with the terms of the treaty. American debts owed to British merchants remained unsatisfied and Loyalists were still unable to get justice in American courts.

For ten years, therefore, after 1783, Britain played an opportunist role—"possession is nine points of the law." Her garrisons remained in the border forts on Ontario's south shore and east and west of the lake. European pressure assisted a solution of the American impasse. Britain in 1793 plunged afresh into the wars of Continental Europe, and her resistance to American requests began to weaken. When Mad Anthony Wayne won a final victory over the Northwestern Indian Confederacy and proved American ability to control the Indians, Britain's hands were too full to take on another quarrel, even for the American West. In 1795 she ratified departure from the western forts by June 1, 1796.

Once the British formally agreed to quit, they kept to schedule. Detroit was taken over by American forces on July 11, Oswego on July 15, Niagara on August 19, and Michilimackinac on September 1. That year the pace of westward migration naturally accelerated. Tennessee joined the Union. Although the transfer of flags extended American rule west of Lake Michigan and along Lake Superior, Britain's trade connections and her influence over Indian hunters still continued dominant until after the War of 1812, a stern economic fact which salted the many wounds to American pride.

In addition to the anger aroused by British interference with American shipping and by the impressment of American seamen, a second wave of resentment arose from Indian activities in the Northwest. The tribes were being armed from Canadian sources and it was believed, justly or otherwise, that British influence kept them aroused against the States, a conclusion vehemently denied by sundry British and Canadian historians. In November 1811, Governor William Henry Harrison routed a large force of Indians on Tippecanoe River in Indiana but anti-British feeling did not end with the victory.

An aroused West manifested its resentment when the Twelfth Congress met in extra session November 4, 1811. Henry Clay, a young Virginian who had moved to Lexington, Kentucky, became the fiery leader of the so-called War Hawks, intent upon avenging the honor of the United States which they felt Britain had violated. His faction virtually controlled the session. Chosen Speaker of the House of Representatives, Clay set about making war inevitable by naming War Hawks to strategic posts on committees which advocated military preparation. Divided in sentiment and with no unified will to victory, the United States approached its second war against Britain.

Clay had able support in Congress. With him were Johnson, also from Kentucky, Grundy from Tennessee, the gifted Calhoun of South Carolina, and the forceful Peter Buell Porter, destined to become a major general and Secretary of War. Coming from Connecticut to Canandaigua, New York, in 1795, Porter felt the lure of the Niagara border and in 1810 removed to Black Rock, within the present limits of Buffalo, a few miles from the south shore of Lake Ontario. A clever lawyer, he was a member of Congress from 1809 till 1813. In the Twelfth Congress he became one of Clay's right-hand War Hawks, serving as chairman of a committee which recommended immediate preparation for war against Britain with the taking over of Canada as the chief objective.

Porter's program aimed at complete annexation if possible, but at least the conquest of the Essex and Niagara peninsulas in the Great Lakes triangle. It was emphasized that the international border would be greatly shortened by even partial conquest. From Montreal to Georgian Bay along the Ottawa is only 250 miles as the crow flies, from the foot of Lake Ontario to Georgian Bay, 125 miles, and from the head of Lake Ontario at Hamilton to Georgian Bay only 75 miles. West of the last line is found Ontario's most favorable climate and some of its best land for farming, fruit and tobacco. In War Hawk psychology the War of 1812 was at the very least a war for the conquest of Ontario, if not of all Canada as the extremist Porter declared.

On June 18, 1812, Congress passed the declaration of war against Great Britain. Five days after Congress had cast its fateful ballot, His Majesty's government yielded partially, but the news arrived in America too late. In any case, there would have been no backward step. Britain had not deferred to American feeling on the sorest point—her assumed right of impressment—and that grievance dominated the public sentiment as distinct from the commercial and political interests of sections and classes. The majority, as represented in the Twelfth Congress, wanted war.

On the day war was declared between the United States and Great Britain, Major General Henry Dearborn, senior commanding officer of the United States Army, was in Boston superintending recruiting and work on coast defense in anticipation of hostilities.

As in four past wars, the Canadian border became in Dearborn's plan of campaign the springboard of conflict. Across the St. Lawrence and westward through the lakes, Dearborn's blueprint charted four simultaneous drives upon the British regulars and their supporting Canadian militia in the areas centering upon Montreal, Kingston, Niagara and Detroit. This was practically Amherst's old plan, with Detroit substituted for Quebec, and the whole strategic front shifted westward. It placed the Lake Ontario region squarely in the middle of hostilities, an advantage in view of the considerable American sentiment in Upper Canada. Of the 136,000 white inhabitants of Upper Canada, about four-fifths were of American origin, and of these only one-fourth were Loyalists or of Loyalist descent. It was expected that American invaders would be welcomed by many inhabitants desiring protection from what was glibly termed by the Whigs "the fury and persecution of the Royalists."

Had Dearborn, Secretary of War during Jefferson's two terms, carried out his four-pronged invasion promptly as planned, the onset might have registered a victory for American arms. The English impression of Dearborn, as gathered from a letter written by Augustus J. Foster, His Majesty's Minister at Washington, to the new Foreign Minister, Lord Castlereagh, on April 21, 1812, described the American commander adequately. "The General, who has been lately appointed Commander-in-Chief," wrote Foster, "is a heavy unwieldy-looking man who was a major in the American war and was a prisoner in Canada. He has apparently accepted his appointment with great reluctance, having hesitated until within a few days. His military reputation does not stand very high, nor does that of Mr. Thomas Pinckney, the second Major General."

Although morale on the seaboard was low, the ill equipped and not very numerous soldiery were about as ready as they ever would be. The first northward movement is described in Major Darby Noon's report to General Peter B. Porter from Oswego on July 4, 1812:

"As soon as news of war being declared arrived at this place I immediately repaired to Sackett's Harbor,* and General Brown, who commands that district, ordered me to prepare immediately at Massena, Hamilton, Ogdensburg, Gravelly Point, barracks, etc., to contain about four thousand men. I immediately started to Ogdensburg and the other places and made the necessary arrangements, and no doubt all will be ready in a few days, or as soon as troops can be marched to their respective stations. I have built barracks in the old fort at this place to contain about 700 men, which will probably be as many as will be stationed here.

"P. S. Your brother's vessels are safe at Ogdensburg, and Capt. Wolsey is doing all in his power to collect and arm vessels to carry them up to Sacket's Harbor with the assistance of Genl Brown."

On the same day a list of opposing troops in Upper Canada showed units of the Royal Artillery, Tenth Royal Veteran Battalion, Forty-first Regiment and Royal Newfoundland Regiment, a total of 1,658 officers and men.

The general roster of troops in Lower Canada was larger—5,489

---

* In common usage, Sackets Harbor. When Theodore Roosevelt was President he caused a postal order to be issued restoring the original name of "Sackett's." Since his tenure, however, the public has gone back to eliminating the "t" and the possessive apostrophe. It is often called merely "the Harbor," as occasionally in this text.

officers and men divided among the following units: Royal Artillery, Royal Artillery Drivers, Royal Engineers, Tenth Royal Veterans, First Battalion, Eighth Regiment, Forty-first Foot, Forty-ninth Foot, One Hundredth Foot, One Hundred and Third Foot, Canadian Fencibles, Glengarry Light Infantry and Canadian Voltigeurs.

These figures reveal that the forces available for defense were too small to meet widespread attacks all along the border and that if Dearborn had launched promptly his four simultaneous attacks as planned, the chief British forces might have been hopelessly extended or they might even have been concentrated in the east to hold Montreal, leaving points farther west practically undefended.

Almost the first action of the war came at Sackets Harbor, an attack practically neglected by history although the later action of 1813 in the same sector is well known and frequently described. In the opening skirmish, the British, firing the first gun on the Ontario border, "broke nothing but the Sabbath" as the "York Staters" gleefully related later, and sailed away to return to fight another day. This abortive engagement sounds the *opéra bouffe* note characteristic of the War of 1812 on Lake Ontario in so many of its aspects.

Hero of this brief encounter was Melancthon Taylor Woolsey, gallant son of a dashing Revolutionary War officer. In 1808 as a lieutenant fresh from foreign service on the *Constitution,* "Old Ironsides," he began a naval career on the Great Lakes that was to last more than seventeen years. Establishing his headquarters at Oswego some months before the start of the War of 1812, Woolsey built the brig *Oneida,* which became a timber drogher after the war and was still in service in 1828. Late in the spring of 1812, Woolsey transferred his headquarters to Sackets Harbor and brought the *Oneida,* nucleus of Commodore Chauncey's future war fleet, to the docks in building along "Shiphouse Point."

Through efforts of Brigadier General Jacob Jennings Brown, "the Quaker soldier," the New York militia had been partly armed and somewhat drilled for a number of months before war was declared. Brown was a local worthy, residing five miles from the lake at Brownville on the Black River. To protect Sackets Harbor, a strategic position near the foot of the lake, Brown and his fellow officers arranged to summon the militia by firing artillery signals when the alarm was given. On the morning of July 19, 1812, a warning cannon shot boomed from the Harbor to be repeated by local ordnance. These pieces were Revolutionary War relics, located in a few scattered inland settlements, for the whole region had been virgin forest until the late 1790's. The alarm sounded at dawn as British ships approached the harbor. Immediately, the militia, packed in farm wagons drawn by lumbering spans, or posting astride fat plow horses, rushed motley-armed to Sackets for defense.

Knowing the slow *Oneida* could never escape by flight, Woolsey anchored her near the shore, unloaded her guns and placed them in a battery on the bank. When the British squadron of six vessels led by a flagship, the *Royal George* of twenty-two guns, reached the harbor in a light breeze, Woolsey's improvised shore battery was poised to rake the entrance. The militia were ranged on the adjoining plateau fronting the lake. This plateau, still part of Madison Barracks, is marked today as the first battleground of the War of 1812.*

On the plateau, which terminates in a low sheer bluff facing the open lake, stood a tiny fort which housed in 1812 the only large cannon then at the Harbor, a long thirty-two. This piece the farmer militia nicknamed "the Old Sow." The British had sent Old Sow to the Colonies in 1689 and surrendered it to Ethan Allen at Ticonderoga. Hauled through the New England forests, it was employed at Dorchester Heights by General Knox in the siege of Boston. And at Sackets Harbor in 1812 Old Sow belched the first American cannonade in the War of 1812. It stands today mounted on a square stone pedestal in the public square of Turin, New York, on State Route Number 12.

Commodore Earle, awkward upholder of Royal Navy tradition, sent a boat toward the American shore demanding surrender. When Woolsey refused, the boat returned to the flagship which fired a shot that fell short of the bluff. Old Sow responded after a fashion worthy of record in the annals of American inventiveness. Only twenty-four-pound cannonballs were available but her wide maw was made for thirty-two-pound shot. To fill the gap the gun crew wrapped the balls in pieces of old carpet contributed by the patriotic

---

* Colonel Lewis Cass had fought a slight battle at the Canard River below Sandwich on July 16, in which several soldiers were killed or wounded. Apparently this was the first actual bloodshed of the War of 1812.

women of the small village, which was hard put to it to find enough carpet. Alas, the carpeted projectile fell short.

A battle of sorts went on for two hours before an increasing crowd which gathered from the countryside and thronged the plateau. Most of the shots from the British ships fell short of the bluff. Woolsey's "shore battery" pounded the smaller ships which were within range and inflicted some damage. Finally a thirty-two-pound shot launched from a British ship fell beyond the bluff. Some militiamen rushed it to Old Sow while a sergeant bawled, "We've ketched 'em out now, boys. Let's send it back!" The return shot, Old Sow's first chance for a good bead, tore away a mast from the *Royal George* and injured some of the crew. Earle, his ship thus damaged by his own ammunition, gave the signal for the ships to withdraw to Kingston.

The Harbor had been saved by a bold young lieutenant who made the most of small resources. But this auspicious opening was soon forgotten in the surrender of Detroit on August 16, by an elderly general, William Hull, who believed the worst of his own forces and the best of the enemy. Thereupon the struggle for control of the Lower Lakes of Erie and Ontario took on added significance. The Upper Lakes were lost to the United States; could the Lower Lakes be held? If not, the war in the West would end almost inevitably in British victory.

A communication from General Porter on the Niagara frontier, dated August 30, 1812, to Governor Tompkins of New York, reveals the bewildered state of the public mind following Hull's surrender. The general wrote:

"Yesterday a number of men were shot at Fort George in view of our troops. They are supposed to be the unfortunate fellows who joined General Hull in Canada and were surrendered at Detroit, and for whose protection provision should have been made in the capitulation at the expense of the life of every man in the garrison. . . . The public mind in this quarter is wrought up almost to a state of madness. Jealousy and distrust prevail toward the general officers, occasioned . . . principally by the surrender of Detroit, which among the common people is almost universally ascribed to treachery."*

General Porter added that the military circles at Niagara and vicin-

* Tompkins' Papers, New York State Library, Vol. VIII, pp. 96-102.

ity were amused daily with "news" of the approach of heavy ordnance, flying artillery and regular troops to reinforce the frontier,
but none had arrived. They reached Utica, he wrote, then "danced
backward and forward in the interior of the State without being of
service anywhere." The Genesee River, Sodus, Oswego and the brig
at Sackets Harbor were all alternately to be defended whenever a
British ship passed from one end of Ontario to the other. "This
miserable and timid system of defence must be abandoned, or the
nation is ruined and disgraced. Make a bold push at any one point
and you will find your enemy, give them as much business as they
can attend to at Niagara and at Ogdensburg, and you will not see
them groping about the marshes at Sodus to pillage the miserable
huts of the poor inhabitants."

A man of bolder kidney than Hull commanded in northern New
York, albeit a new recruit to the art of war, General Jacob Brown.
Foreseeing the second clash with Great Britain, he had been urging
the Albany authorities for several years to build roads through the
North Country for the movement of war supplies. Brown maintained
stoutly that reliance upon the water route for this purpose was not
enough, and the event proved him right. Given his commission in
1811, he was assigned only militia forces with which to guard, during the summer of 1812, the 300 miles of frontier from Oswego to
St. Regis. He spent weeks in reconnoitering the shores of the St.
Lawrence and training his raw troops. This ambitious general spent
his spare moments studying military tactics from textbooks, and in
this respect improved on most of his fellow militia officers who
neither knew nor tried to learn the military art.

On orders from Washington, Lieutenant Woolsey, hero of the
Sackets defense, set about adding to the Ontario war fleet. The
quickest way was to steal the other fellow's ships. While Brown
prowled on land, Woolsey busied himself on the water, purloining
the enemy's small shipping to be employed as gunboats until the
Americans could build their own. He took a British schooner
named the *Julia,* with Lieutenant Henry Wells and a crew of thirty
men aboard her, and started her toward Ogdensburg on the St.
Lawrence. On the way the *Moira,* of fourteen guns, and the *Gloucester,* with ten, challenged her passage. With her long thirty-two and
her two sixes the *Julia* drove them off and reached her destination.

Meanwhile, Brown proceeded to Ogdensburg for the purpose of harassing enemy shipping on the St. Lawrence. Though the lower lake and near-by reaches of the river held many enemy ships at the time and the water route was risky, he elected to go that way, for the land route lay through almost impassable timber. In a rude flotilla which sailed cautiously and hugged the shore, 400 men with artillery and baggage made the trip without loss.

Following the capture of the *Julia,* Woolsey experienced no more luck building up a navy by larceny, because enemy vessels were now on the alert and traveled in convoys, so he bought five schooners for conversion to war use. Of these the *Hamilton* had an armament of ten guns. The remaining four vessels, *Governor Tompkins, Growler, Conquest* and *Pert,* carried only eleven pieces among them.

On September 1, 1812, Commodore Isaac Chauncey was appointed to naval command on all the lakes with the exception of Champlain. On paper the appointment seemed excellent. He was descended from Charles Chauncy, second President of Harvard College, but a personal whim caused him to insert an "e" in the second syllable of his surname. This crotchet suggests a bold fellow indeed. Follower of the sea from his teens, he had performed brilliantly and with great daring in the Mediterranean. His service aboard the *Constitution,* when that dependable vessel and her sisters of Preble's fleet crushed Tripoli, won high praise. Chauncey advanced to master-commandant in 1804 and to captain in 1806, the highest statutory rank in the American Navy in that period. President Madison and Secretary of the Navy Paul Hamilton held him in high esteem as one of the Navy's ablest officers and picked him above all others to command on Ontario and Erie. Summoned to confer with his chiefs, Chauncey presented an elaborate program which they warmly approved.

Chauncey arrived at Sackets Harbor in October. From the beginning he revealed power as an organizer. Ship's carpenters and more than a hundred officers and seamen had been sent up to the lake in advance. With the shipwrights had come Henry Eckford. All lovers of yesterday's billowing sails are aware of his amazing shipbuilding career on Lake Ontario and the Atlantic seaboard, but among landsmen on the border the impression holds that Eckford was a sort of happy accident. Rather, he was a picked man sent to the fresh-water battle front on his salt-water record.

A native of Scotland, Eckford was studying ship-designing in the yards of his uncle John Black in Quebec at the age of sixteen. In 1800 he owned yards on the Long Island side of the East River near the Brooklyn Navy Yard. Because of the dense forests sprawling near navigable waters, American shipping could be built then for $35 a ton, as against $50 in England and $60 in France. Congress enacted protective legislation that further benefited Yankee ship-builders.

Eckford showed marked originality from the outset and main-tained it to the end of his career, which came in Turkey in 1832, after a life of busy creativeness in which he greatly advanced the art of shipbuilding. His designs carried a slicing in the traditional size of stern frames and important changes in details of rigging. It was his habit to question captains after voyages regarding the behavior of their vessels in various winds and weathers, and to use this informa-tion in the design of his next ship.

When the United States Navy decided to build warcraft on Lake Ontario, Eckford was summoned to take charge of the construction at Sackets Harbor. There to keep the refloated *Oneida* company as a competent warship, the keel of the *Madison* was laid.

This vessel, soon to be Chauncey's flagship on Ontario, was built in forty-five working days from near-by timber. Nearly everything else for the square-rigger, designed to mount twenty-four 32-pound carronades, had to be hauled northward from New York City over wretched roads. Small items that could be handled at the portages were boated through the Mohawk-Oneida inland waterway but dan-ger from prowling British craft lurked in the final stage of the journey, the thirty miles along the lake shore from Oswego to Sackets Harbor. Notwithstanding these difficulties, the *Madison* was finished during 1812 although not outfitted until the following spring.

After Eckford hit his stride he produced for Chauncey one war-craft—either brig, square-rigger, schooner, corvette or sloop—every six weeks. He worked his men through all the daylight hours seven days a week. There were no unions, no strikes and almost no hint of dissension. Eckford was a leader whom men followed gladly, and this was war. Right at hand stood the oak for keel, ribs and plank-ing, pine for living quarters and decks, and lightweight cedar for fillers and upper works.

Axmen tramped into the woods before dawn. Chips would fly from a white oak tree blazed for the keel. When it crashed, a dozen men would pounce on it to lop off the limbs. Fifty men, seventy— a hundred if Eckford were lucky that week in the continual come-and-go—would adze the timber where it fell. Horses and oxen, lashed and goaded to the limit of their strength, would haul the squared timber to the shipyard immediately.

For seasoning? No. With a war to win, Eckford knew there was no time to waste. Slap! the timber went onto the keelblocks. Over the timbers swarmed shipwrights, dissecting and reshaping them into stem, frames, aprons, shelfpieces and the myriad other joints, hinges and vertebrae of a good ship's skeleton. Back in the new-made clear-ing, neighbor trees felled in their turn would be split into plank in saw pits shoveled out around their roots. The next day they would be hauled to the shipyard and spiked to the ribs of the new craft.

Had Chauncey's daring equaled Eckford's production, the United States must have won on Lake Ontario as signally as it did on Erie. No sooner did Chauncey ask for another ship "to balance power" in the building race, than Eckford laid it—speaking figuratively—in the commander's big lap. In an average forty days of working time, what had been a tree would slide down the ways as part of the finished hulk of one more warcraft. Green-timbered, these ships were doomed to early decay, of course. There would be no postwar use for them, but Eckford was not serving commerce. He served—or sought to serve—war.

While Eckford's workmen toiled at a building program which it was hoped would clear the lake of British shipping within a year, General Brown's force harassed British shipping downstream in the St. Lawrence. His resources were slender enough. In fact, shortages ruled all the frontier, as this excerpt from a letter from Major Gen-eral Stephen Van Rensselaer at Buffalo to Governor Tompkins at the time discloses:

"We are here, as indeed at all our posts, lamentably deficient in ordnance. The situation of Ogdensburg, and the necessity of supplying it with heavy ordnance, I have before stated to Your Excellency in my letter by express from that place. Every consideration connected with the success of any operation in this quarter urges me to solicit the earliest possible supply of heavy ordnance and some skilful engineers and artillerists. Without such aid and supplies I can hardly conceive how it will be possible for us to achieve anything of importance or even to defend our posts in case of attack from the enemy."

Nevertheless, Brown mustered enough ordnance and aroused enough fighting spirit among his men stationed at Ogdensburg to repel a British attacking party of double their number who came in boats from the Canadian shore to take the town. After a spirited skirmish in which little blood was spilled, the enemy retired.

Chauncey planned for Sackets a model naval station, including a neat navy yard with naval hospital, naval school and ropewalk, fit for the fleet of more than twenty vessels which he had in mind to construct without delay. He bought four more schooners through the autumn, christening them respectively the *Asp, Scourge, Ontario* and *Fair American,* but they were little used until the following year. The *Oneida,* rolling like a fat pig in the Ontario wash, and the attendant schooners previously mentioned did some prowling that fall. At that time Earle, the opposing commander, had twice as many ships available, but his men were ill-trained by comparison with Chauncey's original force. The Canadian "water militia," willing but raw and with officers of indifferent caliber, needed seasoning, which they soon received.

Chauncey first appeared on the lake aboard his flagship *Oneida* on November 8. Six schooners, in general charge of the never-say-die Woolsey, trailed along like a flock of chicks after an old hen. Chauncey found H.M.S. *Royal George* off False Duck Islands the next day and pursued her to cover under the batteries of Kingston.

The short but hot action which followed inspired hopes south of the border that in Chauncey the nation had found an intrepid naval leader. Lacking force enough to capture Kingston, on the site of the old French Fort Frontenac, he concentrated on the *Royal George,* while two of his gunboats, the *Hamilton* and *Tompkins,* chased Canadian merchantmen out in the lake and did not return until after the battle had been joined. Chauncey sent the *Conquest, Growler, Pert* and *Julia* ahead to begin the attack while the *Oneida* lumbered after.

Then misfortune began. On the *Pert* a gun burst at the third broadside, causing the death of her commander, Sailing Master Arundel. The remaining gunboats continued to engage the shore batteries while the *Oneida* closed with the *Royal George* and began firing. The British flagship, which carried double the American force, sheared her cables and made for a wharf protected by a detachment of steady British regulars. This prompt action saved the vessels. Dusk was falling and Chauncey's squadron had no choice but to beat out into the lake against a fresh head wind. The next day in squally weather the American squadron returned to Sackets Harbor. No decision had been scored in spite of an auspicious start.

Cruising continued in inclement conditions until the middle of November. Again the *Oneida,* on the prowl alone, found the *Royal George* which refused to give battle and scudded for Kingston. Chauncey then tried blockading Kingston with four of his schooners until late in the month, when navigation closed. The new *Madison* was launched on November 26, as ice was forming in the lake.

At the western end of the lake, also, the early promise of "bright, victorious war" broke down into smudgy stalemate. The Queenston operations, which also closed indecisively with the ebb of November, dampened spirits along the entire southern shore. An "invasion" of the Niagara peninsula proved to be as abortive as Hull's unfortunate move from Detroit. Generals Stephen Van Rennselaer and Alexander Smyth assembled 5,000 men on the American side of the Niagara, sent a detachment across and captured the heights above the Canadian village. At the critical moment the two commanders quarreled and the New York state militia refused to leave their boundary line. British forces, rallied by Generals Brock and Sheaffe, recaptured Queenston Heights on October 13. Nine hundred Americans were taken prisoners, but the British suffered a heavy loss in the death of their determined and vigilant General Brock. By order of General Van Rensselaer, the Americans fired a salute on the day of his funeral.

On October 20, in a letter to General Dearborn, Van Rensselaer announced he had turned over the command to Smyth. He gave as his reason his mortification over the defection of the militia which "had changed triumph into defeat." On the same date Smyth was writing the Secretary of War from "near Buffalo" that he was now in command, prepared "to enter Canada and leave the rest to heaven. . . . Give me here a clear stage, men and money, and I will retrieve your affairs or perish."

Smyth's grandiloquent proclamations then brought more thousands of militiamen from far and near to waste their time from November 27 until the end of the month in what was scarcely even a gesture of invasion. From Buffalo, Josiah Robinson wrote Colonel Solomon Van Rensselaer, kinsman of the retired General Van Rensselaer:

"The troops were again ordered to embark, the American flag was raised with everything ready for a descent, when lo! the coward appeared, and the remainder cannot be described but by the fallen countenances of the officers and the fury of the privates."

This one fainthearted attempt of Smyth's to cross the river, after indifferent preparation, was easily repelled by a force of 400 Canadians.

To the complaint of a committee of Buffalo citizens, sent him upon the heels of the fiasco, Smyth replied with apologies. "The affair at Queenstown is a caution against relying on crowds who go to the bank of Niagara to look on a battle as on a theatrical exhibition." Soon afterward General Smyth was relieved of his command.

A bleak northern winter closed down on an ebbing first war year that held little encouragement for York Staters. On the naval side of the ledger there was equal dissatisfaction in Canada. Soon the official shears were snipping off the heads of incompetents. Earle's indifferent services terminated with the close of navigation; it was announced that Sir James Yeo would be sent from England to succeed him.

In the United States, Secretary of War William Eustis resigned in December in answer to public clamor. Eustis, a Massachusetts man, had taken the portfolio in 1807 and had continued under Madison. In the months before the outbreak of the war his office force mustered eight clerks. The War Department did its poor best to prepare the army, meeting with curses for its "inefficiency" from critics of all stripes, including Clay of the War Hawks. After the resignation of

Eustis, James Monroe, Secretary of State, took over the War Department in addition to his other duties, until Eustis' successor should be named.

A severe winter hampered Chauncey's preparations at Sackets Harbor. January found the post cut off from needed munitions and stores required from New York and Albany. Interior water supply routes were, of course, frozen. Improved roads, urged by General Brown and M. James LeRay de Chaumont, famous French émigré who lived near the lake, were started to connect the North Country with downstate, now that war had emphasized the need for them.

Chauncey's chief lack was trained sailors. The British government could move its seamen where it pleased, but American sailors in 1812 enlisted for service only in particular ships. Those on the seaboard were not at all enamored of the idea of serving on the Great Lakes where there was little or no prize money in prospect. Early in January, however, some crew detachments volunteered to follow their officers to Sackets Harbor and thereafter a small but steady stream of salt-water tars moved toward fresh water. Chauncey proved energetic in recruiting. Snowshoes, or sleighs or sleds over rough country roads, brought more shipwrights to join Eckford's gangs after the New Year. Work began on equipping the *Madison,* a 593-ton ship. The keel of the *General Pike* was laid. A small dispatch sloop, *Lady of the Lake,* was built. Work was started on the *Goliath,* Chauncey's largest ship, of 875 tons, twenty-eight long 24's and quarters for a crew of 300 men.

At frozen Kingston on the Canadian shore, Sir George Prevost, having dismissed the sluggish Earle a second time, ordered two 24-gun ships to be built, one in Kingston and the other at the dockyards at York.

In January, President Madison named a picturesque figure to replace Eustis as Secretary of War. John Armstrong, soldier and diplomat, had been aide-de-camp to Gates in the Revolution. Encamped on the lower Hudson in the later days of that war, he had composed the caustic *Newburg Letters* calling on Congress to meet arrears in soldiers' pay. After he married Alida Livingston, sister to Chancellor Robert R. Livingston, Armstrong figured importantly with the Livingstons and DeWitt Clinton in New York politics. Armstrong had resigned from the United States Senate in 1804 to succeed Livingston as Minister to France. Returning from Paris at the outbreak of the War of 1812, he was made a brigadier general, built defenses for New York City and stimulated recruiting. Summoned to Washington, he took over the War portfolio in Madison's cabinet on February 5, 1813.

Despite reverses and stalemates in 1812 the American army still set as its objective the conquest of Canada. The plan for 1813 called for the forces to advance on three fronts. The Army of the North, commanded by General Wade Hampton of South Carolina and stationed along Champlain's southern shore, was poised to invade Lower Canada. The Army of the Center, 7,000 effectives, theoretically occupied the entire Ontario region from Champlain to Buffalo. In reality it was split in half, General Wilkinson commanding the eastern end and General Dearborn the western. The third unit, the Army of the West, comprised some 8,000 men commanded by Generals Harrison and Winchester.

In the early spring there was a series of raids back and forth across the St. Lawrence, just below Lake Ontario, forays in which Americans came off second best. Soon after a British raid on Ogdensburg early in February, Major Benjamin Forsyth led a small body of American riflemen and volunteers across the river at Elizabethtown. They returned with fifty-two prisoners and some stores, not having lost a man. In reprisal, early on February 21 the British crossed the river with 1,200 men. At daylight they attacked in two columns with 600 of the crack Glengarry Light Infantry headed by Captain Macdonell and an equal number of militia under Colonel Fraser. The American defenders, though aided by militia called out by Colonel Benedict, were outnumbered. They maintained the contest for an hour, at the loss of some twenty killed and wounded, inflicting twice that loss upon the invaders, including five officers. They then retreated in good order while the British, steady despite their losses, took over the town of Ogdensburg.

Spring preparations at Sackets Harbor, while adequate enough in shipbuilding, were deficient in safeguarding the town and yards against seizure. General Brown, his term of service expired, had retired to his business affairs, but the government had arranged with him that in case of an attack by the enemy he should come to the rescue, an arrangement that subsequently proved fortunate for American arms but which reads oddly today. Lieutenant Colonel Backus, in charge at the Harbor, had only 250 dragoons and 200 invalids in his feeble garrison. The other regular troops had been withdrawn in preparation for a foray against Fort George. The sole reserves were the raw militia of the countryside. As a grotesque addition to all-round carelessness, General Wilkinson early dismantled nearly all the shore batteries the better to prepare an expected expedition along the lake. The Harbor could have put up only weak resistance if an attack had come before April.

Meanwhile the nineteenth-century Cincinnatus, "Quaker" Brown of Brownville, conducted his store, ran his mills, and sold his real estate against the day when the summons to defense would start his real career as one of the handful of worth-while generals revealed on the border in this weirdest of wars.

At Sackets Harbor that spring was another historic figure, Zebulon Montgomery Pike, soldier and explorer. In 1806 he had discovered the Rocky Mountain peak which bears his name. Appointed a brigadier general early in the war, in 1813 he was entrusted with preparations for a fateful expedition, that against York.

In sanctioning this undertaking Secretary Armstrong allowed Dearborn and Chauncey to persuade him to attack York, instead of following his original decision to move on Kingston. This shift toward the West probably was influenced by the presence in and around York of a considerable population of American immigrants not sympathetic to Britain and eager to assist the American conquest of Canada. Kingston, by contrast, was altogether "royal and loyal."

The contending fleets were about equal in numerical strength. Chauncey with nearly 1,000 seamen outmanned Yeo by about ten percent. His guns also outranged those of the British, though they were not quite their equal in number and fire power. The Americans could fire at one discharge 694 pounds of long-gun metal and 536 pounds of carronade metal, while Yeo's long guns could throw only 180 pounds, though his carronades could muster 1,194 pounds. This unequal distribution of metal was so far in Chauncey's favor that if he had employed it in a well-supported sortie on Kingston, he might have captured the enemy's base.

The land forces were well prepared for the expedition. Fresh

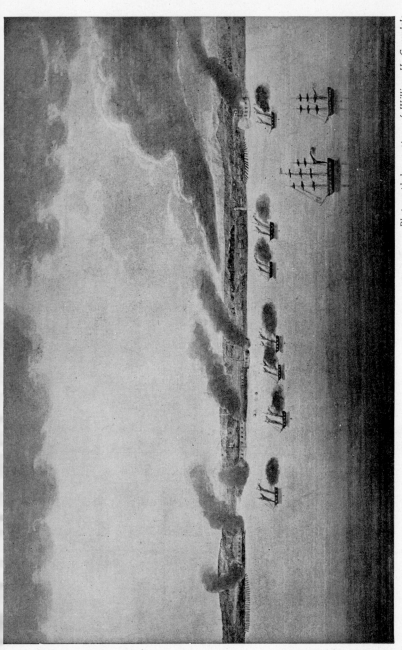

CAPTURE OF FORT GEORGE, MAY 1813

Drawn during the battle by an officer of Commodore Chauncey's flagship *Madison*.

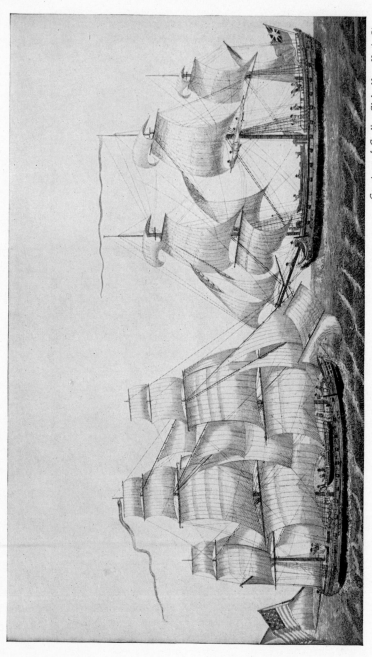

A SCENE ON LAKE ONTARIO

Commodore Chauncey's sloop of war *General Pike* and Sir James Yeo's sloop of war *Wolf* preparing for action, September 28, 1813.

levies of militia, arriving daily at Sackets Harbor, were trained assiduously by Pike, a Regular Army man who knew how to handle sensitive militiamen. Popular with all ranks, he soon whipped his farm boys into soldierly shape.

Their objective, York, was the capital of Upper Canada and served as the depot from which the British supplied western posts with military stores. The Americans aimed to seize these stores and also to destroy a warship nearing completion at the York docks. Following the York attack, a descent was planned on Fort George.

Shortly after his selection to lead the land forces in the attack on York, Pike wrote his father on April 24 a letter strangely prophetic of his imminent doom:

"I embark tomorrow in the fleet at Sackets Harbor, at the head of a column of 1500 choice troops, on a secret expedition. If success attends my steps, honour and glory await my name; if defeat, still shall it be said that we died like brave men, and conferred honour, even in death, on the American name.

"Should I be the happy mortal destined to turn the scale of war, will you not rejoice my father? May heaven be propitious and smile on the cause of my country! But if we are destined to fall, may my fall be like Wolfe's—to sleep in the arms of victory."

On April 25 Chauncey's fleet moved up the lake with Dearborn and Pike and some 1,700 soldiers aboard tightly packed vessels. The Commodore led in the flagship *Madison*, followed by the sluggish *Oneida* and the schooners *Hamilton, Scourge, Tompkins, Conquest, Growler, Julia, Asp, Pert, Ontario, Lady of the Lake*, the transport *Raven* and the *American*, a schooner commanded by Lieutenant Wolcott F. Chauncey, brother of the Commodore.

To withstand this force York was garrisoned by about 700 British regulars and militia, 500 Indians, a body of Grenadiers and a unit of the famous Glengarry Fencibles—the whole under command of Major General Sir Roger Sheaffe.

The defenders were alert early on April 27 when the fleet hove in sight. The new twenty-four-gun ship was nearly completed and the *Gloucester*, a ten-gun brig, was in port. Guns of both vessels opened fire as the American schooners, firing their long pieces, beat up to the shore. Pike was permitted to carry out his own tactical plan for landing on this dangerous Ontario beachhead—an open space at the ruins of Toronto, former site of an old trading post about two miles above the town.

Sheaffe had brought almost his full garrison to oppose the landing. He stationed his Indians in thickets on the lake shore. Some of his regulars were drawn up in the open, others concealed by a wood. At eight o'clock in the morning Forsyth's riflemen in bateaux led the way to the shore followed by Pike and his staff in their boat with Major King's regiment behind. In good order the advance guard swarmed up the bank and put the Grenadiers and Indians to flight. The Grenadiers essayed a countercharge which failed. As they attempted to form again at a distance, reinforcements were pouring from the fleet. The British fell back to their garrison. The entire American army was ashore two hours after debarkation began, a successful amphibious operation on no mean scale for that period.

Pike led the invading force forward while Chauncey's vessels exchanged shots with the two British ships in port and with the shore batteries. Silencing a pair of enemy batteries on the way, Pike then halted his column on suspicion that the retreating British had some trick in reserve. Lieutenant Riddle went forward to investigate while the General questioned a wounded British soldier. While he was sitting on a stump in a fringe of woods talking to the prisoner a terrific explosion occurred near by. The magazine containing 500 barrels of powder had been fired, bringing death or wounds to 260 Americans, nearly one-sixth of the attacking army. Canadian losses at this tragic spot numbered forty, the bulk of the defenders having retreated. Pike, struck in the breast by a great stone, gasped that his back and ribs were broken. Colonel Pearce of the Sixteenth Infantry took over command.

Pike was removed to the *Pert* and given all possible medical attention, but it was seen at once that his wound was mortal. A British royal standard, left behind by Sheaffe in his haste to depart, was brought to the stricken leader. Making signs for the enemy flag to be placed under his head, he died.

Pike had had a persistent premonition of early death. He had written some years before to his wife: "If I fall far from my friends and from you, my Clara, remember that 'the choicest tears which are ever shed, are those which bedew the unburied head of a soldier.' . . .

Let these maxims be present in the mind of our young son as he rises to manhood. 1. Preserve your honour free from blemish. 2. Be always ready to die for your country." Thus perished at the early age of thirty-four one of America's most competent young generals, while the "old blunderers" continued to mishandle their troops.

In this war it is commonplace to find commanders behaving as if preordained to defeat and apparently unable to take advantage of circumstances. Sheaffe's destruction of the magazine, which had been blown up somewhat prematurely, proved highly damaging to the Americans, yet the British commander did not seize that favorable opportunity for a counterattack. Instead, determined to save his regular troops, he marched them off toward the town. Nor did Sheaffe attempt a defense of the town. He merely marched on toward Kingston with his precious regulars.

As we shall see, testimony regarding the subsequent surrender and occupation are somewhat mixed, but there is no question that the Americans won an easy victory with considerable booty.

American losses afloat and ashore totaled 306, including fifty-two killed. The British loss in killed and wounded was 180, and 290 taken prisoners. The new twenty-four-gun ship was burned, her guns taken away, and the *Gloucester* was sailed back to Sackets Harbor as an addition to Chauncey's fleet. Many military and naval stores had been destroyed or otherwise disposed of, but a greater quantity was taken to the Harbor. General Dearborn's report says that two blockhouses and several sheds in the naval yard were destroyed, but expressly denies responsibility for damage to any other buildings, public or private.

Bad weather kept the fleet at York for several days, during which time Pike's body was embalmed. The hero's body was later buried in the magazine of tiny Fort Tompkins on the plateau of Sackets Harbor "with all the stately pomp of military honor amidst the regrets of every good man." At Dearborn's command, Captain Nicholson of Maryland, Pike's protégé who was killed at his side, was laid in the same grave with him. Today the dust of the romantic young general lies in the graveyard of Madison Barracks.

In a way the occupation of York gave the visitors more trouble than the conquest, for while the place was in their hands the Parliament Houses of Upper Canada were burned in a fire of unknown origin which has given rise to one of the persistent myths of border history. The tale is frequently repeated that the burning was a deliberate act of vandalism by the invaders and that in retaliation for this destruction the British subsequently burned the White House and other public buildings of Washington. In an effort to lay this ghost, events during the occupation are here presented in some detail.

Misunderstandings stem back to the explosion of the magazine. This tragic burst was no accident, but its timing went awry, apparently because the Canadian militia were not fully advised of Sheaffe's comprehensive plan of demolition. Negotiations for the surrender were being conducted by Colonel Chewitt and Major Allan of the Canadian militia when word came that the British were trying to burn some of their ships. Major Allan was then seized as a prisoner, and the proceedings were delayed until the following day. General Sheaffe stands convicted of a gross breach of good faith and military practice in ordering or even countenancing demolition during negotiations for surrender.

That night, Forsyth's riflemen were assigned the difficult duty of patrolling a frontier community at fever heat. Apparently these militiamen did some minor looting and winked at vandalism by irresponsible Canadians. Upon complaints of citizens, however, General Dearborn took prompt steps. He changed and enlarged the guard, selecting his best Regulars for that duty, offered to give every household individual protection and proclaimed that the authority of the civil magistrates would be upheld.

The negotiations for surrender were resumed the next day. The Reverend John Strachan, self-appointed spokesman for York's townsmen, came to Dearborn and Chauncey in angry mood and succeeded in arousing the usually calm Dearborn, who accused Strachan of making false statements of conditions. After these verbosities fresh articles of capitulation were swiftly ratified. All public stores were surrendered to the victors. The Canadian militia were paroled and permission given to remove sick and wounded. Civil officers were to retain their posts. Surgeons attending the wounded were not to be considered as prisoners of war. Sanctity of private property was guaranteed. In view of all that had happened Dearborn's terms were both light and liberal, and are so acknowledged by Canadian sources.

As the American army continued to occupy York for several days, rising unrest manifested itself among the "lower orders" of the community and particularly among homesteaders from the United States who streamed into town from the back country in the exultant hope that the surrender of York marked the end of Canada.

The whole situation was ripe for trouble when on Friday, April 30, 1813, the Parliament Houses were found ablaze. No contemporary evidence has been adduced that American soldiers set the fires. Major Allan, Colonel Chewitt and Judge Powell, while complaining of other things, never charged the Americans with this outrage. Not even the Reverend Mr. Strachan alleged it.

The first American officer to report the blaze was Major Grafton who saw "a column of smoke arising at 200 or 300 paces." Spurring his horse, he dashed forward and saw flames bursting from a low one-story building. No other American soldier was in sight at the time.

Canadian evidence also fails to support the statement that American soldiers fired the Parliament Houses. Instead, Canadian sources testify to the appreciation felt by leading citizens for the manner in which the victors administered affairs during their short occupancy of the town. Chief Justice Scott wrote a letter to General Dearborn commending him for his "humane and honorable conduct." The militant cleric Strachan joined with other prominent citizens in signing a statement condoning some violation of private property by American soldiers before the guard of regulars was posted. The statement read: "After . . . we had time to reflect we must acknowledge that they behaved much better than we expected, and if it had not been for the misconduct of the troops at Ogdensburg, many of them told us that there would have been little or no depredations committed here."

Several instances demonstrate how early bitterness was ameliorated. Excellent service by American regulars detailed to guard the town was later recognized by the British in a significant manner. Captain Pelham, who commanded the American Twenty-first Regiment at York, was captured at Chrystler's Field and paroled in recognition of his conduct of the guard at York. Before leaving York, General Dearborn donated some of the captured supplies to the poor, although he was offered payment. He also paid a generous price for an old privately owned vessel. Both Dearborn and Chauncey avoided the role of domineering conquerors.

Historical myths die hard, and are frequently not worth the labor of killing. But the relations of Canada and America have become so much a model of peaceful statecraft and good neighborliness that misinformation on the occupation of York ought to be swept aside. In brief, the whole operation was a decisive success for American arms and a credit to both the American commanders and the Canadian community in one of the most difficult administrative situations arising throughout the entire war.

# Chapter 13

## Seesaw on Ontario

---

*Fold him in his country's stars,*
*Roll the drum and fire the volley!*
*What to him are all our wars,*
*What but death be-mocking folly?*
*Lay him low, lay him low*
*In the clover or the snow!*
*What cares he? He cannot know:*
*Lay him low!*

—George H. Baker

---

FOLLOWING hard upon the York occupation which ended by American withdrawal on May 2, came action at both ends of the lake. An American assault on Fort George led off but the British were only two days behind in waging a second attempt upon Sackets Harbor.

After conveying troops and stores for a fortnight Chauncey's ships moved to the attack on Fort George. It was defended by Major General John Vincent with about 1,800 Regulars, 600 militia and about 100 Indians. The Americans mustered 4,500 men under General Dearborn, though fortunately he left the general conduct of operations to Lieutenant Colonel Winfield Scott, destined to emerge from the war as one of the few stars on either side. On May 26, Chauncey reconnoitered the near-by shores, took soundings and laid buoys to direct the smaller vessels which because of shallow water were to do the fighting. At three o'clock the next morning the fleet moved in. The heavy land artillery was aboard the *Madison*. The *Oneida, Lady of the Lake* and a number of bateaux captured at York were jammed with troops. While the *Julia, Growler* and *Ontario* silenced a battery near the lighthouse, landing troops were boated farther along the lake where militia manned a battery of one long twenty-four pounder. The *Conquest* and *Tompkins* moved forward under fire to drive off the artillerymen who spiked the gun and fled.

171

General Dearborn had been confined to his bunk with illness, but he was on the deck of the *Madison* with General Morgan Lewis to watch the attack. The landing craft and their troops, under Scott and Lieutenant Oliver Hazard Perry, future hero of Erie, rushed in. From behind them the *Hamilton, Scourge* and *Asp* rained grape with destructive effect upon the British. The care with which Chauncey had prepared the landing and the effectiveness of the barrage laid down ahead of the onrushing boats are revealed in the loss figures. American casualties were only sixty-five, one-fifth those of the defending British, who had the advantage in position. As the schooners continued firing with precision, the ranks of the outnumbered British regulars broke. In retreat they blew up the fort. While the regulars made their retreat in good order, some 500 Canadian militia surrendered. This sharp victory gave the Americans temporary possession of the entire Niagara frontier, and opened the way to effective naval action on Lake Erie.

While Chauncey's squadron was engaged at Ontario's western end, Sir James Lucas Yeo finished equipping the *Wolfe,* a formidable ship of 637 tons, carrying 220 men and twenty-four guns capable of hurling a broadside of 392 pounds. This addition gave the British a temporary superiority which they promptly sought to stabilize by destroying the *General Pike,* next American vessel scheduled for completion. Sir George Prevost and Yeo, now commanders in chief of Canadian land and water forces respectively, moved at once on Sackets Harbor where the *General Pike,* newly pierced for 28 long twenty-fours, lay helpless on the stocks. Success in this bold move would have assured supremacy on the lake for the rest of the year.

As these two British officers were soon to be at loggerheads, their personalities require analysis. Yeo was a dogged but uninspiring sailor who had risen fast on sheer good luck in the West Indies, but through excessive caution on Lake Ontario he wrecked a most promising career. On the contrary, Governor Sir George Prevost, an eccentric character, was all for action, even if the fleet was not ready. Eventually Yeo brought charges of gross neglect of duty against Prevost, who died under the strain before he could be court-martialed. Only twice did Sir George appear in battle, at Sackets Harbor in 1813 and at Plattsburg in 1814, and both efforts proved disasters for his cause. Within two years after Prevost's death, Yeo himself died at thirty-six, a blighted man. Prevost and Yeo ended by destroying each other. But for the moment which we are describing, before Sackets Harbor, the two saw eye to eye, though none too sharply.

On May 27 the *Wolfe* led forth from Kingston the *Moira, Royal George, Prince Regent, Simcoe* and *Seneca* with many gunboats, barges and bateaux bobbing in their wake. On the next day the fleet sighted and attacked a flotilla of nineteen boats conveying troops from Oswego to the Harbor under command of Lieutenant Aspinwall. Though then only five miles from the goal, Prevost and Yeo chose to take up the chase of the lame ducks. This diversion proved costly to the British, for it gave the small defending forces a chance to prepare a belated resistance.

The Oswego boats led the British fleet a merry chase, but twelve of them were driven ashore and seventy men captured. Aspinwall succeeded in reaching the Harbor with 100 men, bringing the number of regulars there to 500. But some small observation boats had seen the British fleet putting out from Kingston and scurried back to Sackets. Alarm guns brought General Brown hurrying from his home eight miles away and summoned the militia. Six hundred of them, most of whom had never smelled powder except when hunting, assembled during May 28. With this undependable increment, the defense force now mustered about 1,000 men. Although Prevost's landing force was about the same size, it was of better quality, for he had far more regulars. General Brown had improved the time afforded by the enemy's delay. At the only available landing point he had a breastwork constructed and on the bluff above he had a battery set up. Throughout the night his troops slept on their arms while he personally reconnoitered the shores.

At dawn on May 29 boatloads of the foe, led by the impetuous Prevost, swarmed toward the shore. Close to the water's edge Brown's militia were sheltered by breastworks, while behind them were aligned Regular Army units and Colonel Mills's Albany Volunteers, proved and dependable. This second line, deployed near the barracks and public buildings, mustered a scant 500 men but it was spotted with some light artillery.

As the enemy's boats advanced, the militia at first held unexpectedly steady and discharged an effective volley. But when the disciplined redcoats came on again, the militia broke for the rear.

While the British debarked unmolested, the American Captain McKnitt, working desperately, rallied about a hundred of the scampering militia to join the secondary defense. This second line fell back in good order upon some log huts, from which cover they poured a destructive fire that halted the British march.

At this critical moment with the battle apparently at a stalemate General Brown, who had been harassing the invaders, had an inspiration that turned the day. Seeing some of the disbanded militia unconcernedly watching the battle at a distance, he hurried over and gave them a tongue-lashing that soon had some of them in tears and others "fighting mad." Forming them into line, he marched this slim reserve through a strip of woodland to emerge at a point in full view of the enemy who saw the unexpected maneuver as an encircling movement.

Brown's ruse, intended merely to give the British the impression that fresh reinforcements had arrived, proved unexpectedly successful. Seeing this column approaching and not knowing its strength, Prevost turned from hot to cold and was conquered by his own doubt when he should have won. After a volley from the advancing "reinforcements" had stung his flanks, Sir George ordered a retreat. The withdrawal degenerated into a desperate rush back to the boats. The British even left their dead and wounded behind. Piling into their ships and barges, the now thoroughly disorganized invaders returned to Kingston.

American losses in this strange engagement were only twenty-three killed and 114 wounded, while the enemy lost fifty-two killed and 211 wounded, most of the latter being taken prisoners. Among the American killed were two Regular Army colonels—Mills and Backus. The Americans, too, suffered a serious and unnecessary loss in material. During the battle Lieutenant Chauncey, mistakenly believing that the Americans were in full retreat, set fire to well-filled storehouses which were totally destroyed. A little later steps were taken to destroy the *Pike* and the *Duke of Gloucester,* chief prize taken at York, that they might not fall into British hands, but the flames were extinguished before grave harm was done to the vessels.

Brown's victory was rewarded by appointment to the rank of

brigadier general in the Regular Army, prelude to promotion to major general in the following January.

Chauncey, having heard of the *Wolfe's* appearance, moved down the lake and arrived at Sackets Harbor two days after the second attempt of the Britons to secure that important base. Instead of moving at once against the discomfited enemy, he continued to lurk in the harbor until the *Pike* should be finished "to restore the balance of power."

Both timid commanders preferred winning the building race to winning battles. The summer campaign on Ontario settled down to cautious sailing and all-out construction. When Chauncey wanted to fight, having the advantage in tonnage and armament, Yeo usually dodged battle. Then, with the conditions reversed, Chauncey proved the coy commander. They played at war as weary old men play at chess, not to overwhelm the adversary, but to prove their skill and pass the time untroubled. Since the two never risked a desperate encounter, Chauncey won on points: that is to say, he was sufficiently "top dog" to co-operate effectively with the land forces for about two-thirds of the time.

Events on Lake Champlain and the St. Lawrence, too remote to be described here, encouraged Yeo to action and the newly commissioned *Wolfe* gave him a theoretical superiority sufficient to overawe Chauncey and keep him in port. On June 3, Yeo sailed from Kingston aboard the *Wolfe* to lead his pack through wind-whipped waters to the head of the lake to intercept, with the help of a land force, supplies consigned to the Americans. On June 8 he attacked a small American supply camp near Forty Mile Creek. Fire from the *Beresford, Sydney Smith* and the gunboats drove the garrison inland. Their provisions, equipment and bateaux were taken, and the British occupied the post.

Yeo continued to use his undisputed freedom of action to harass the south-shore stations. On June 13 he captured a pair of schooners and some boats bringing supplies to the Americans. Three days later a provision depot on the Genesee River was taken. On June 19 a party of British soldiers put ashore at Great Sodus Bay and took off several hundred barrels of flour. Yeo returned to anchor at Kingston on June 27.

Meantime the American force at the western end of the lake, after their easy capture of Fort George, had suffered reverses. On withdrawing from the fort, the British under Colonel Vincent had retired to Burlington Heights near modern Hamilton. From this position a most effective sortie was made upon the American camp at Stony Creek, which resulted in the capture of stores and prisoners, including two American generals, Chandler and Winder, and the consequent withdrawal of the American army to Queenston.

It was late in June that Laura Secord emerged as a Canadian heroine whose fame is now generously applauded throughout the Dominion. She was born in Great Barrington, Massachusetts, in 1775 and accompanied her father to Canada in 1793. She was a resident of Queenston, where her husband had been wounded and her house plundered. They then removed to the village of St. David's. The story told of her runs briefly as follows: With the Americans in possession of the frontier she learned the plans of the commander and determined to forestall them. The task involved evading the American guards who were posted ten miles back in the country. Rising before dawn on June 24, Mrs. Secord walked nineteen miles over difficult country to reach at nightfall a camp of Indians. These were British allies, but taking her for a foe they greeted her with savage yells. A chief who understood English accompanied her to the near-by camp of Lieutenant James Fitzgibbon, of the Forty-ninth Regiment, at Beaver Dams. To him she gave the information that a force of Americans was then on its way to surprise and annihilate his command.

Like many another myth of heroic women in American wars—Barbara Frietchie, Molly Pitcher and a host of others—the saga of Laura Secord is, to use the Scots phrase, "not proven." Among the John Askin Papers one letter from Charles Askin, an excellent Canadian witness present at the battle, gives a quite different story of the way in which the Canadians were warned of the American attack. But however Fitzgibbon received advance information of the American raid, he was able to lay a trap for the stalking Americans, a trap which bagged the entire detachment of 550 men and a fieldpiece.

General Dearborn, too old for active service, had been ill throughout the campaign. He was removed from command by Secretary

Armstrong on July 6, and the next day departed from Fort George, leaving the command to Brigadier General John P. Boyd. Boyd succeeded to a diminished and dispirited force, while the defenders of the peninsula had gained so many regulars, militia and Indians that the American commander was instructed to avoid an engagement.

In July neither naval squadron put out in force on Lake Ontario, though early in the month Yeo, in a "pussy cat cruise," sought to surprise Sackets Harbor a third time. The post was on the alert, however, and the British squadron scuttled back to Kingston.

By July 21 the *General Pike* was launched, and again Chauncey had Yeo one down in the seesaw contest for superiority in ships and fire power. The American fleet now numbered fourteen vessels, as follows: ships, *Pike* and *Madison;* brig, *Oneida;* schooners, *Hamilton, Scourge, Conquest, Tompkins, Julia, Growler, Ontario, Fair American, Pert, Asp* and *Lady of the Lake.* The captured *Duke of Gloucester* had not yet been reconditioned. The totals were: tonnage 2,576; crew 980; and broadside metal 1,399 pounds. The *Lady,* however, was a mere dispatch boat, while the *Scourge* and *Hamilton* were lost before Chauncey and Yeo came into collision. Deducting these, Chauncey was left with eleven vessels of 2,265 tonnage, with 865 men and ninety-two guns flinging a broadside of 1,230 pounds.

Yeo mustered in opposition his famous "Slippery Six," ships of eel-like elusiveness. These swift vessels were the full-rigged *Wolfe* and *Royal George,* the brigs *Melville* and *Moira* and the schooners *Beresford* and *Sydney Smith.* The six totaled 2,091 tons, mustered 770 men in the crews and fired a broadside of 1,374 pounds. Total armament gave Chauncey 112 guns to Yeo's 92, with the Americans excelling in fire range. The *Pike* with her 15 long twenty-fours in battery was superior to any one of Yeo's six, and the *Pike, Madison* and *Oneida* were potentially more than a match for the four heaviest opponents. But the *Oneida* was a slug and hard to maneuver, not Eckford-built.

With the launching of the *Pike* on July 21 Chauncey immediately took the initiative. On the quarter-deck of the newly christened ship he led the American squadron up the lake, reaching Niagara on July 27. There Colonel Scott and some of his regulars were taken aboard for a second assault on York, which had recovered quickly from the earlier attack. Eleven transports in the harbor and on the ways were destroyed, five cannon, ammunition and some stores were carried off, and the barracks burned.

On August 3, Scott's raiders were carried back to Niagara, from which point more than a hundred officers and seamen were dispatched to join Perry on Lake Erie. This withdrawal left the squadron shorthanded, so General Boyd lent Chauncey the services of 150 militia. Militiamen at sea are perhaps the last word in futility. Fifty from the *Growler* and *Julia* were soon lost by capture.

Taking advantage again of Chauncey's operation to the westward, Yeo sailed saucily with his squadron from sheltering Kingston on August 2. Five days later the two commanders, perhaps to their mutual consternation, came within sight of each other's fleets for the first time. The Americans were anchored off Fort Niagara, when the British appeared six miles up windward in the northwest. Through the day the ships maneuvered in light winds, ostensibly to attack, but as usual neither would clinch for action. As if to penalize Chauncey for delaying while superior in armament, a gale that night careened the *Hamilton* and *Scourge,* heavy guns broke loose, longboats foundered and all but sixteen of the crew were drowned. This disaster again reduced Chauncey's fleet to equality with Yeo's. Nearly all of a third day was similarly wasted until seven of the evening, when—possibly because of impatient winds—the squadrons reached firing range of each other, but only shot-holes through the sails resulted from this imprudence. Yeo finally cut off and captured the *Growler* and *Julia* a number of hours later. Chauncey sailed to Sackets Harbor for supplies, restocking on August 13 and sailing up the lake again that evening.

Both Chauncey and Yeo tried to make their subordinates act with the prudence they themselves always displayed. Yeo did his best to keep Barclay in check. It was probably fortunate that Chauncey could not see Perry go into action on Lake Erie on September 10, 1813. Certainly, if Commodore Perry had heeded the admonitions to caution that streamed from the desk of his chief at Sackets Harbor, he would have missed his chance to report, "We have met the enemy and they are ours."

Through these fruitless days and weeks, Henry Eckford had been busy at the Harbor fashioning more ships of war for the overcautious Chauncey. A minor poet of the period wrote:

> "Hank Eckford, he
> Made a Ship of a tree
> As fast as you could see—O!—
> His bag of tricks
> Chased the 'Slippery Six'
> From under the pants of Yeo!"

Had Eckford's ships been well and boldly fought by Chauncey, the American squadron should have won full supremacy. Perhaps Eckford's finest ship of that year was the *Sylph,* of fourteen guns. White oak in her keel, red cedar in the covering board, she was launched in mid-August. Handier than the brigs, or the three-masted square-rigged ships, the *Sylph* on cruise was a lovely sight.

Commodore Chauncey reported glowingly on Eckford's work: "His exertions here were unexampled. The *Madison* was built in forty-five working days in a country where everything was transported over terrible wilderness roads except the timber. The *General Pike* would have been launched in forty days, except from the circumstances of my being obliged to send Mr. Eckford with thirty-five of his best workmen to Black Rock where he rebuilt and fitted for war five commercial vessels in less than thirty days, returned to this place and launched the *General Pike* in sixty-two days from the time her keel was laid. The *Sylph,* a schooner of 340 tons, was built in twenty-one days."

The *Sylph* and her crew of seventy men were ready for action ten days after her launching on August 18, despite a shortage of bolt rope for her sails, which was remedied by taking old running rigging from the *Madison.* She was equipped with ten guns at first, later fourteen, and still later was marked for conversion to a brig of twenty-eight guns.

Twenty-four days off the launching ways, the *Sylph,* then in the lake's western bight, engaged in another of the irritating running "fights" known to posterity as the "Burlington Races" when, on September 11, she saved the disabled *Tompkins* from capture. Later she helped to capture a fleet of transports. Next year she drove the brig *Magnet* ashore near Niagara.

Following Dearborn's resignation, General James Wilkinson, native of Maryland, succeeded to command on the border. In the Revolution he had advanced from a captaincy to a brevet commission as brigadier general in 1777. After a stormy, romantic and often questionable career in varied fields he was commissioned a major general at Mobile and ordered north to succeed Dearborn.

At Niagara, Wilkinson's force comprised 8,000 regulars besides a detachment destined for Harrison in the West. General Wade Hampton, another Southern officer with whom Wilkinson had already clashed, took charge of the Army of the North, some 4,000 men centered at Plattsburg.

Secretary of War Armstrong sent on from Washington a revised plan which had been discussed in the Cabinet. Wilkinson was to descend the St. Lawrence, pass the British posts, join Hampton and lead their merged forces upon Montreal where, in Wilkinson's grandiose words, "their artillery, bayonets and swords must secure them a triumph or provide for them honourable graves." When Secretary Armstrong came to the Harbor early in September, he found Wilkinson and Hampton already quarreling over details. The indecision arising from their disputes handicapped the campaign from the start, but Armstrong could not escape responsibility, since he must have known that Wilkinson and Hampton had long been at odds.

Grenadier Island, lying between Sackets Harbor and Kingston, was selected as the rendezvous for American troops from Ontario posts. Wilkinson left Fort George for the island with the main body of his troops on October 2, and by October 22 had assembled there 7,000 men. Two days later the army embarked. For once secrecy prevailed and the enemy had to guess. This time the British believed Kingston was the Americans' objective and concentrated defense forces there.

Brigadier General Brown was ordered to proceed to French Creek on the upper St. Lawrence. There Brown's brigade repulsed a naval sortie from Kingston. At a point below Fort Prescott a messenger was sent to Hampton at Plattsburg ordering his co-operation with the on-coming Wilkinson.

By November 7 the British were aware that Montreal, not Kingston, was the Americans' objective and hurried troops along the shore to oppose further advance. These measures proved insufficient although they gave rise to hot skirmishes. By the evening of November 9 the American army arrived at the Yellow House near the Long Sault rapid where camp was made. Marching in advance the next morning, Brown's troops repulsed land and water attacks. Following Brown came a larger force under General Boyd.

The defenders elected to fight on the morning of November 11, about 10:00 A.M. Of the Americans Boyd's brigade and those of Generals Covington and Swartwout were massed some distance behind Brown, when word came that the enemy was approaching on the flank. Wilkinson ordered Boyd to face about to counterattack the oncoming Britons. Meanwhile British galleys began firing on the rear of the American flotilla in the river. To repulse the Forty-ninth British Regiment and the Glengarry Fencibles, Colonel Ripley led his Twenty-first U. S. Infantry into Chrystler's Field, after which the battle has been named. As Ripley assailed the enemy's left flank, Covington charged the right flank with initial promise of success, but fell from his horse mortally wounded by a sharpshooter's bullet fired from the Chrystler house. This loss, and accurate British artillery fire, threw the brigade into confusion. Fighting continued fitfully but without decision for two hours, after which the British retired to their camp while the Americans returned to their boats.

Brown's brigade did not learn of this indecisive engagement in time to be involved in it. Marching on to the foot of the rapids, it had waited there for the arrival of the main force which was supposed to be on its heels.

Both armies claimed victory at Chrystler's Field. One estimate puts the loss of the Americans in killed and wounded at 339, of whom 102 were killed; the British losses about the same.

Still free to advance and to that extent undamaged by losses in the drawn battle, Wilkinson proceeded down the river and joined Brown's advance near Barnhart. There he received a letter from General Hampton that ended all hope of taking Montreal. Hampton wrote that he could not keep the appointed rendezvous. The usual explanation is that the South Carolinian had got himself into a box. On September 21, Hampton had descended the Chateaugay River in an invasion threat of his own. His purpose was to divert British attention from Wilkinson's movements, but it did not "jell." Prevost, believing Hampton's movement to be a main thrust upon Montreal, massed his forces to stop it just beyond the boundary, which Hampton reached October 21. His further progress was obstructed by abatis and ambuscades of enemy regulars, militia and Indian allies. After some skirmishing Hampton retreated to a former position, the Four Corners, arriving October 31. There he wrote to Wilkinson the letter which upset the campaign.

While Wilkinson's forlorn "invasion" of the Dominion was in progress, equally indecisive action prevailed on Ontario's waters. On September 11 an "engagement" occurred near the mouth of the Genesee River. Chauncey describes it as a running fight of three and a half hours, with Yeo finally escaping into Amherst Bay. Yet the fleets remained at long range instead of closing. The Americans suffered no losses; the British had one midshipman and three seamen killed and seven wounded. Yeo reported:

"At sunset a breeze sprang up from the westward, when I steered for the False Duck Islands, under which the enemy could not keep the weather-gage, but be obliged to meet us on equal terms. This, however, he carefully avoided doing."

What Sir James means by this harrying of words is that he steered not for but away from the enemy.

The squadrons came in closer contact on September 28 in York Bay. With the fleets a league apart, the British formed on the port tack with their heavier vessels ahead. Chauncey's vessels edged down toward them on the same tack, the *Pike, Tompkins, Madison* and *Sylph* in order, towing schooners, followed by the *Oneida* and two more schooners. After a series of maneuvers the weight of the British fire fell on the *Pike, Asp* and *Tompkins,* and shot away the foremast of the *Tompkins.*

The *Pike* damaged Yeo's flagship *Wolfe* so severely that Sir James again turned, crowded on all sail and fled past his own ships, which forthwith followed him, their withdrawal being ably covered by the *Royal George* under Captain W. H. Mulcaster, described by leading authorities as the ablest British naval officer on the lake during the entire war.

The best that Chauncey could claim from the issue was another partial victory. If the Commodore had ordered the *Madison, Pike* and *Sylph* to cast off their tows, they could have run in close enough to do real damage. The *Pike,* encumbered by towing the *Asp,* could not come to grips with the *Royal George.* If all three had cast loose, there might have been a real victory.

Chauncey's culminating blunder was failure to chase the fleeing enemy. The *Pike* and the *Sylph* were faster than any of Yeo's ships. The British at last were in a roadstead from which they could not easily escape. Chauncey, always apprehensive, feared on this occasion a gale that would beach both fleets.

To be sure, a gale did arrive to whip to fury Ontario's waters, but not until the next day. Then the storm lasted three days. Thereafter Chauncey kept Yeo blockaded in Kingston and had his small schooners converted into transports to convey units of Harrison's troops from the mouth of the Genesee to Sackets Harbor. Transport of troops and stores went on until November 29 when navigation closed.

As the year which had opened so favorably drew toward its melancholy close there occurred an event shameful in American annals and certain to bring British reprisals. When the British recovered the back country of the Niagara peninsula, Fort George had been left in American hands under the command of Brigadier General George McClure, with a small force of militiamen whose terms of service had nearly expired. By December 10 he had only a handful of defenders left. When it was learned that the British were again on the march against the feeble post, an officers' council agreed it was useless to hold out.

McClure barely had time to escape with what men he had left before the British appeared. He blew up the fort, which was legitimate enough. In addition he performed an act of vandalism which was to have serious repercussions in the following year. Below the fort stood Newark, an attractive village, now called Niagara-on-the-Lake. McClure, just before quitting the scene, notified the inhabitants to retire with their effects and applied the torch to their homes, which were almost wholly destroyed.

American authorities at Washington were horrified when the news reached them. They immediately sent an official disavowal to Sir George Prevost, describing McClure's action as being "unauthorized by the American government and abhorrent to every American feeling." Though the Governor General responded with frigid courtesy, it was inevitable that reprisals for the outrage would follow in due course. This wanton destruction at Newark, rather than the earlier accidental burning at York, kindled the spirit of revenge which inspired the burning of the public buildings at Washington, D. C., by General Ross in 1814.

# Chapter 14

## Invasions Repelled

*The desolation of countries and the slaughter of men are losses that never fail to be repaired, and at the end of a few centuries every vestige of them is repaired. . . . But the discoveries of great men never leave us; they are immortal, they contain those eternal truths which survive the shock of empires . . . it is to them we owe all that we now have; they are for all times and all ages.*

—HENRY THOMAS BUCKLE

THE ebbing of 1813 had seen a cat-and-dog fight in Congress over the futile and hesitant conduct of the war. Threats were uttered that New England, where white-hot opposition to war still ruled, would secede from the Union.

Wilkinson, who had tried, with some justice, to make General Wade Hampton the scapegoat for their failure in 1813, submitted a new plan to divide Upper and Lower Canada, but Secretary of War Armstrong drew still another design from his capacious Pandora's box. As a preliminary, Jacob Brown, who became a major general in January 1814, was instructed to return to Sackets Harbor from French Mills with his 2,000 troops and artillery. This task, no light assignment for the bleaker months in that latitude, Brown successfully discharged before the spring breakup.

Meantime on both sides of the lake more ships were being built. Weary at last of wasting the sailspread of his heavier vessels in hauling slow schooners, Chauncey reconverted those former merchantmen into troop transports. The *Sylph* had amply proved herself; during the winter she was brig-rigged and rearmed. Chips continued to fly in the forest where Henry Eckford drove on his axmen. During February two 22-gun brigs, the *Jefferson* and the *Jones,* were on the ways and the keel of the new frigate *Superior* laid.

Four hundred ship carpenters worked under Eckford throughout the winter, but until Brown's troops arrived from French Mills they were in constant fear of a surprise attack from Kingston. The fleet was, of course, frozen in but had been moored in positions from which its guns could be served for defense after the manner of shore batteries.

After the *Superior* was well under way a British navy deserter came from Kingston to inform Chauncey that his rival commander, Yeo, was building two enormous frigates. Though the *Superior* had been planned to carry fifty guns, she was promptly enlarged to accommodate sixty-two. As finally equipped, however, the *Superior*—largest craft in Chauncey's navy up to that time—carried fifty-eight guns, totaling a potential of 1,050 pounds broadside metal. The ship's tonnage was 1,580; she carried a crew of 500.

Work progressed, too, on the *Jones,* a brig of 500 tons to be manned by a crew of 160. That spring saw also the start of another frigate, the *Mohawk,* only a little smaller than the *Superior.* Of 1,350 tons, she was to be manned by a crew of 350 and armed with forty-two guns, flinging a broadside of 554 pounds.

Chauncey went to Washington in December with spy reports that the British at Kingston had been reinforced by 500 men and were laying keels for new ships. On his return late in February he was gratified to find his three new ships "in a great state of forwardness; the largest has all her ribs up and the two smaller ones all planked and nearly half caulked, and will be ready to launch before the ice breaks up. . . . The roads are dreadful, and if the present mild weather continues we shall experience difficulty in getting in our stores."

During this mild and sickly winter all hands were plagued by disease and shortages. Neither guns nor men for the three new ships could arrive until spring. The expected raid from Kingston came at last—an abortive attempt by a small force to blow up the *Superior,* but the defenders were alert. One-third of the working force were ill in the bunks every day and about one-sixth died before navigation opened. The *Madison,* said James Fenimore Cooper, buried one-fifth of her crew that winter. Discipline wore thin under these trials. Bickering among the men compelled constant watchfulness on the part of their chiefs. On one occasion a nervous sentinel shot and killed a shipwright whose working mates thereupon struck in a body. Nevertheless, an amazing amount of work was done by these sorely tried shipwrights and sailors, and for this the unquenchable ardor of Henry Eckford must be credited.

On February 28, Secretary of War Armstrong sent a communication to Major General Brown covering his matured plan for 1814. To prevent Prevost from re-establishing British strength on Lake Erie in the spring, Armstrong wrote, his line at Kingston or Montreal must be weakened. The most feasible maneuver was one Armstrong had planned to have Pike undertake in 1812-1813: "to cross the river or head of the lake on the ice and attempt Kingston by a *coup de main*. This is not, however, to be attempted but under . . . a combination of practical roads, good weather, large detachments (made westerly) on the part of the enemy, and a full and hearty cooperation on the part of our own naval commander."

Armstrong enclosed a second letter with injunctions that the General let nobody but Chauncey into the secret of his real objective. The second letter also provided for a diversion by assigning Colonel Scott, in nomination as a brigadier, to the Niagara frontier with a force calculated to lure the enemy westward from Kingston. Also, Brown was instructed to convey to Batavia with a minimum of delay a brigade from French Mills "where other and more detailed orders await you."

With this oddly assorted stack of conflicting orders in his hands, Quaker Brown no doubt wrinkled his heavy brows. The attack on Kingston, over the ice of a lake which seldom freezes over, never came to pass and the British headquarters remained uncaptured throughout the war.

Chauncey's spy news from Kingston proved well founded. British shipwrights, however, could not hit the Eckford pace and Yeo's monster would not be completed until navigation had nearly closed. Meanwhile, the two new British frigates proceeded handily toward their launching, and Sir James still had his Slippery Six. Of these the transformed schooners *Sydney Smith* and *Beresford* were converted into brigs, to accompany the original *Melville* and *Moira*. Next, anticipating modern advertisers who rename old products, he rechristened the sextet. The *Wolfe, Royal George, Melville, Moira, Beresford* and *Sydney Smith* now became respectively the *Montreal, Niagara, Star, Charwell, Netly* and *Magnet*. Some of these vessels were rearmed.

When the two new British frigates *Prince Regent* and *Princess Charlotte* were launched, Yeo's squadron mustered eight vessels of 4,756 total tonnage and combined crews of 1,620. The *Prince Regent,* new giant of the fleet, had a crew of 485 and mounted fifty-eight guns shooting a broadside of 872 pounds. The *Princess Charlotte,* of 1,215 tons, carried 315 men; her armament comprised forty-two guns. The total broadside metal fired by the entire fleet was 2,874 pounds distributed from the muzzles of 209 guns.

As against this rejuvenated force Chauncey presented the same number of vessels—eight—with 5,941 total tonnage and 1,870 crew personnel distributed through the four ships and four brigs. The concerted broadside discharge was 3,352 pounds, 478 pounds more than Yeo's ships, Chauncey having 228 guns, nineteen more than Sir James. Both commanders used in addition small vessels not included in the cruising forces. Chauncey had his converted schooners, Sir James a large number of smaller craft. Chauncey's roster showed 2,321 men, and with light armament of the satellite troopships could hurl a broadside of 4,188 pounds.

On paper the American fleet was stronger in the proportion of six to four. Yet, on March 29, Chauncey reported to Washington that he was apprehensive. Because of untimely thaws a large portion of the heavy guns which had left New York in the early part of February were still on the road between New York and Albany in April, and then had to travel from Oswego some fifty miles eastward. That post, with no guns mounted, lay at the enemy's mercy. The Commodore noted that with the Niagara frontier now in enemy hands no guns could be expected from Lake Erie.

The *Jefferson* slid into Ontario's waters on April 7, the *Jones* three days later, the *Superior* on May 2. Across the lake Yeo's *Prince Regent* and *Princess Charlotte* were launched on April 15. Behind in guns and outfitting, Chauncey feared Sackets Harbor had been chosen for attack. His information gave Yeo twelve to fourteen gunboats and 3,000 troops ready to embark, while the defenders could muster only 1,000 men under the newly arrived General Gaines, besides the sailors and marines.

Across the lake at Kingston, Yeo and Governor Prevost were ready with a plan, but it left Sackets out and established as a first objective the old and decayed port of Oswego. Oswego had been battered consistently since the French wars. In this spring of 1814 what was left of it had been garrisoned, impromptu, by about 300 men of a light artillery regiment commanded by Lieutenant Colonel Mitchell and some thirty sailors under Lieutenant Pearce of the navy.

It was entirely due to the foresight of General Brown that Mitchell was on the spot and able to make a defense of Oswego. Brown believed Oswego needed a garrison because large stores of provisions, ordnance and naval equipment destined for Sackets Harbor were at Oswego Falls, only twelve miles up the Oswego River. At Batavia, on his way to the Niagara frontier with 2,000 men, Brown detached Mitchell and his small force, ordering them to garrison the old fort.

Covering the 150 miles to Oswego in four and a half days of forced marching, Mitchell found the fortifications badly decayed. Not a single piece of ordnance was in prime shape. The old barracks were, however, fairly habitable. Hasty entrenchments were thrown up, and the little force pulled itself together for combat. Only four mounted guns could be readied for firing, but in addition two dismounted ones were hurriedly restored to position.

On May 3, Yeo's eight ships, accompanied by a covey of transports bobbing in the raw winds of early spring, made for Oswego expecting to find it wholly abandoned. In addition to the crews, there were more than 1,000 soldiers aboard under Lieutenant General Sir Gordon Drummond.

The schooner *Growler,* recently recaptured, lay in the threatened harbor. As the British approached on May 5, her commander sank her with a load of seven guns which had been destined for Sackets Harbor.

The fort's few but well-served guns banged away at thirteen British gunboats to such purpose that the British flotilla retired but returned to more serious attack the next day. Then the weak shore batteries were engaged by the *Princess Charlotte, Montreal* and *Niagara,* while the *Charwell* and *Star* showered grape into the woods to clear them of phantom militia, for by then the British idea of the strength of American resistance had, as usual, become greatly exaggerated.

Oswego's revamped guns bit as well as barked. While the British troops debarked for shore, two long twenty-fours, a long twelve and a long six from the crumbling walls raked the *Montreal,* cutting her hull, masts and rigging and finally setting her afire. She returned the fire fruitlessly while covering the landing of 800 troops under Lieutenant Colonel Fischer and sailors under Captain Mulcaster. The assault wave came steadily up a long hill under fire, sustaining gallantly a loss of ninety-five men killed and wounded, nearly a third of the total American force engaged. The Americans, skillfully handled, lost only six men killed, thirty-eight wounded and twenty-five prisoners.

Mitchell then drew his small but sturdy force back to Oswego Falls, prepared for a desperate defense of the stores, but the British had received enough punishment. As in so many of Prevost's stratagems, the issue was not pressed to a firm conclusion. Only the remnant of Mitchell's force, about 200 men, stood between him and total capture of all military stores in the area. The British lingered at Oswego long enough to raise the sunken *Growler,* bail her out and patch her speedily to join their fleet with her vital gun cargo. Yeo's seamen then carried off a small amount of ordnance stores and flour and burned the barracks. The British withdrawal was so complete that the Americans were able to reoccupy the port without firing a single shot.

Yeo returned in wan triumph to Kingston, emerging on May 19 to set up a blockade of Sackets Harbor, particularly inconvenient for Chauncey because guns for the *Superior* and cables for the two new frigates had not yet arrived. Lighter-weight equipment could be conveyed overland, but the heavier pieces required lake transportation part of the way and Yeo's fleet now stood guard offshore.

In his emergency, as if in answer to prayer, the resourceful Captain Woolsey reappeared, hero of the initial skirmish at Sackets Harbor in 1812, first engagement in this curious war. Volunteering to get this heavy equipment to the Harbor, Woolsey decided to risk water transportation along the lake from Oswego to Stony Creek and thence have it carried overland to the Harbor, three miles farther on. Success would mean that Chauncey could finish equipping his new vessels and regain command of the lake on the basis of comparative armaments if not of normal action.

At sunset of May 28, Captain Woolsey left Oswego with a string of nineteen bateaux carrying a precious cargo of twenty-one long 32's, ten long 24's, three 42-pound carronades, and ten cables.

One of the cables was a huge rope twenty-two inches in circumference, weighing 9,600 pounds. Sturdy oarsmen pulled the heavy-laden boats throughout the night. At dawn they were off the Big Salmon inlet, eight miles from Sackets Harbor. Eighteen boats were hidden in Big Sandy Creek but one laggard, carrying two long 24's and one cable, was captured by the British.

Yeo sent 180 men in two flatboats, equipped with small arms and light artillery, up the creek in quest of the others at dawn of May 30. Woolsey expected this search and countered by sending Major Appling to form an ambush downstream with 120 riflemen and some Indians. Their close-range volley routed the British with heavy loss, eighteen men being killed and fifty wounded.

Most of the supplies were then loaded into ox carts and transported to Sackets Harbor. However the giant cable proved too cumbersome to handle by wagon. The stout shoulders of men served where wheels and oxen failed. A hundred huskies from Colonel Stark's militia regiment, reinforced by relays of "bush" farmers, shouldered the cable. A long sinuous line of burden-bearers, they marched with the cable on their shoulders along the winding trail through the woods. While the garrison cheered, the sweating packmen entered the port and carried the cable straight to the waiting ship. Today a stone on a country road memorializes the "Rope Job," as it came to be known, one of those homely feats of strength and endurance which live forever in the traditions of a locality.

By spring Secretary Armstrong's January plans had been enlarged. General Brown's army was to cross the Niagara to storm Burlington Heights and later, in conjunction with Chauncey's fleet, to attack the British posts on the Niagara peninsula. Meanwhile General Izard, commanding the Army of the North, was expected to control the passage of the St. Lawrence Rapids with his armed boats and to cut enemy communications between Kingston and Montreal.

Shortly after Brown's move from French Mills back to Sackets, the Twenty-first went with the Quaker General to the Niagara frontier. On April 15 Ripley received promotion to brigadier general and on May 4 he took leave of the regiment he had personally trained. Brown's division then consisted of two brigades commanded respectively by Ripley and Winfield Scott.

From May 4 to July 3 these troops were put through rigid instruction planned by Scott, who was the only trained soldier of the trio. On July 3 Brown's troops began the passage of the turbulent Niagara to invade Upper Canada. Brown was properly pessimistic over the chance of gaining support from either the Ontario or Erie fleets, as Chauncey had made no move to assist this third invasion of Canada, which was unfortunately aimed at one of its most easily defended points.

The Governor of Canada, Sir George Prevost, was also planning an invasion by way of Lake Champlain with Plattsburg as its immediate objective. The Canadian forces had now been reinforced by some of Wellington's veterans of the Peninsular campaigns. Special attention had been given to militia training by British officers. The army had a large fleet to co-operate with it for the reduction of Plattsburg.

So, with the arrival of summer, military preparations seethed from the head of Lake Ontario, where Brown stood poised to invade Canada, eastward to the middle St. Lawrence, where Prevost with 11,000 men and a big fleet mounted his counterthreat of invasion.

Yeo's blockade of Sackets Harbor was raised on June 6, but Chauncey lacked equipment enough to allow him to sally forth in full strength. Six weeks were frittered away in minor clashes, before Chauncey sailed, fully ready, on July 31. He paraded to the head of the lake, left the *Jefferson, Sylph* and *Oneida* to watch some small enemy craft in the Niagara, and returned with the four larger vessels to blockade Yeo's larger ships in Kingston Harbor. It was another gesture in the dull game between two naval arithmeticians, but this time Chauncey's indecisive movements had serious results because he had pledged naval assistance in the invasion of the Niagara peninsula.

Brown opened his campaign daringly and scored an initial success. Crossing the Niagara River on July 3, he easily captured Fort Erie which surrendered that afternoon. No doubt its defenders overestimated the American forces, which numbered rather less than 3,500 men fit for duty. To oppose them the British General Riall had hastily rallied about 2,100 men at Chippawa, three-quarters of whom were British regulars. They took a strong position behind the Chippawa River, but their commander was not in a situation where he could risk a last-ditch fight because his reserves were so light. His regulars in line at Chippawa were half of the total force Riall had

SOUTHEAST VIEW OF SACKETS HARBOR, 1815

Copied from an original engraving by W. Strickland.

*Photograph by courtesy of the A. W. Mellon Educational and Charitable Trust*

HENRY ECKFORD, BY ROBERT FULTON

available to hold the entire line around the western end of the lake and to garrison York, Burlington Bay and Newark.

On the morning of July 4, Winfield Scott, on the threshold of his military maturity, led the American advance to the plain, where he posted his brigade with its right on the river and its front protected by a ravine. An entire day was spent in arranging troops. Quaker Brown somewhat doubted whether the enemy would stand firm and give battle. Time was on his side for reinforcements of New York and Pennsylvania militia were being brought up by General Porter. While these fresh but unseasoned troops were moving in the British advanced in battle order, as Riall endeavored to force the issue while the opposing numbers were somewhat equal. Scott soon brought his 1,300 well-trained men into action. In the center the two lines poured volleys into each other at sixty paces; on both flanks they fought hand to hand. Porter's militiamen gave way, but while reserves were marching to their rescue Scott's brigade gained mastery of the plain, and the British retreated toward Fort George. A contemporary account in the *Analectic Magazine,* an aged and long defunct magazine of the period, describes this "picture battle" as if it had been play instead of war:

"One of the most brilliant spectacles that could well be conceived. The day was clear and bright; the sun still high in the heavens. The plain was such as might have been selected for a parade or a tournament; the troops on both sides, though not numerous, admirably disciplined; the Generals leading on their columns in person, the glitter of the arms in the sun, and the precision and exactness of every movement, were all calculated to carry the mind back to ancient story or poetry; to the plains of Latium or Troy, and all those recollections which fill the imagination with images of personal heroism and romantic valour in this field beside the Chippeway, a deep, still stream which runs into the Niagara, nearly at right angles, three miles above the falls."*

In this stubborn and dramatic battle, one of those rare occasions when equal bodies of well-trained regulars met in broad daylight on

---

* This passage, probably written by Washington Irving, sometime editor of the *Analectic,* occurs in a biographical sketch of Major General Winfield S. Scott, Vol. IV, pp. 478-479, New Series, December 1814.

the open field at close range, American musketry and artillery fire showed superiority. Riall reported 515 casualties not including Indians; but the Americans had only 297. Of the two bodies of regulars who fought it out toe to toe, the British lost 137 killed and 305 wounded; the Americans forty-eight killed and 227 wounded. At last the Americans had met and whipped a British redcoat line without benefit of cover or guile. This gave the army, in Winfield Scott's opinion, a character and pride it had never before possessed.

Proceeding to Queenston, General Brown awaited the reinforcements and supplies which Commodore Chauncey should have been ferrying to him. Bitter messages passed between the two commanders. On July 13, Brown wrote: "I do not doubt my ability to meet the enemy in the field and to march in any direction over his country, your fleet carrying for me the necessary supplies. We can threaten Forts George and Niagara, and carry Burlington Heights and York, and proceed direct to Kingston and carry that place. For God's sake let me see you; Sir James will not fight."*

To which Chauncey pettishly replied: "I shall afford every assistance in my power to cooperate with the army whenever it can be done without losing sight of the great object for the attainment of which this fleet has been created—the capture or destruction of the enemy's fleet. But I shall not be diverted from my efforts to effectuate it by any sinister attempt to render us subordinate to, or an appendage of, the army."

Ever since their founding the American Army and Navy have been jealous of each other, but usually war dampens this chronic hostility and permits the two services to work together for victory. Chauncey's attitude seems grotesque, even treasonable. In attempted justification of his stupid course he wrote the Navy Department on August 10 following: "I told General Brown that I should not visit the head of the lake unless the enemy's fleet did so."

To Chauncey's refusal to follow the charted co-operation may be justly charged the failure in 1814 of the Washington plan for the invasion of Canada by way of the Niagara peninsula.

On July 25 occurred the savage battle of Niagara, or Lundy's Lane,

---

* These sample letters in the bitter Brown-Chauncey controversy were selected by Theodore Roosevelt for his *Naval History of the War of 1812* (New York: G. P. Putnam's Sons, 1882) from the many which appear in Volume VII of *Niles' Register,* which in this period served as the nearest approach to a Congressional Record.

a heavy butcher's bill exacted largely because of Chauncey's failure to appear. At Lundy's Lane as at Chippawa, Scott's brigade led off, but Ripley's brigade and the militia soon moved into savage enemy fire. British batteries, well located on the heights, were stormed and taken by an heroic advance under Colonel Miller, but the Americans found it impossible to remove the guns before the British surged back in a hot rally. Both Generals Brown and Scott were wounded. Retiring, Brown left Ripley in charge after scoring a tactical victory, though by no means a conclusive one. Ripley, judging it inadvisable to hold his ground, quit the field, which angered Brown, though some authorities consider Ripley justified in this precaution. Brown, with his gift for phrases, analyzed Ripley neatly, saying that the latter dreaded responsibility more than danger and had more physical than mental courage.

Though the contending forces numbered less than 3,000 men each, Niagara remains to this day a famous battle in both American and Canadian history. Both armies lost about the same number of total casualties: 860 for the Americans, 878 for the British. The Americans under Ripley fell back to Fort Erie, and the British in turn began their long siege of the Niagara bastion, mournful end for an ambitious campaign that might have succeeded. As General Sherman said in similar circumstances after Shiloh, both armies had had enough of fighting for a while.

Meanwhile, through most of the summer of 1814, Chauncey's fleet remained off Kingston blockading Yeo. His Lieutenant Gregory, with Midshipman Hart and six men, scouted Kingston harbor on August 25. The lieutenant was wounded and captured, the midshipman killed. At last, on September 21, Chauncey could spare ships for an Army task, transporting General Izard and 3,000 men from Sackets Harbor to the Genesee. Then the inveterate blockader bottled up Kingston until the new two-decker in the yards there was nearly completed, whereupon, considering himself again outbuilt, Chauncey led his fleet off again to the Harbor.

On the British side army and navy worked well together. To aid Drummond, Yeo transported reinforcing troops from Kingston, and even from Prescott on the St. Lawrence, to the siege of Fort Erie, which was in full force by August 3, with some 5,000 British engaged. This "fort," really an unfinished redoubt augmented swiftly by

American efforts into a fortified camp, was situated opposite Black Rock about 100 yards from the lake shore on a plateau of considerable height.

Late in July, Secretary of War Armstrong, learning that the British were sending strong reinforcements from Montreal to Kingston, had directed General Izard to transfer the bulk of his force from Plattsburg to Sackets Harbor, there to join with General Gaines's army. Izard was also to threaten Prescott and Kingston, and send a portion of his force to the aid of General Brown. Here, to Izard's ill fortune in history, occurred another of Armstrong's miscalculations. Subtracting 4,000 men from the north, for the Lake Ontario transfer, would leave only 2,000 troops to man the defenses at Plattsburg. Izard saw the folly of this move but had no choice other than to obey orders. He took his troops, now the border's most effective army, through virgin forests in bad weather some 400 miles to Batavia in twenty-nine days, only to find that Drummond had retreated from Fort Erie six days earlier.

Izard then crossed into Canada but Drummond remained behind his defenses at Fort George. For the Americans to by-pass the fort seemed foolhardy, for the British now mustered 30,000 regular troops in Canada while the Americans had only 10,000 regulars between Plattsburg and Detroit. Izard, of necessity inactive until it was time to go into winter quarters, distributed his troops among Buffalo, Black Rock and Batavia. Thus the third "invasion" of Canada ended in another stalemate, largely because of faulty calculations and non-co-operating commanders, plus determined and cohesive Canadian defense on the Niagara frontier.

On Lake Champlain, Macdonough's fleet saved a dangerous situation, but within the moccasin-shaped shore line of Ontario, the wary Yeo did not again venture from the shelter of Kingston Harbor until October 15. This time he sailed boldly to the Niagara frontier and remained there to assist British troop movements until the close of navigation about November 21.

Throughout both countries raged savage criticism of those in authority. English-speaking Canadians of Ontario derided the vacillations of Governor Prevost, though he continued to be popular with the merchants and habitants of French Quebec who were little interested in the war. South of the border public clamor mounted for the removal of Chauncey from naval command. Also there was a rising cry for the official scalp of Armstrong.

In the ebbing days of August, when Ross and Cockburn occupied Washington and burned the Capitol and other buildings, mass anger leaped to flame against Secretary of War Armstrong, who resigned and thereafter conducted a bitter campaign of criticism against General Izard, who in turn resigned.

Public pressure against Commodore Chauncey became so fierce that President Madison yielded and ordered Commodore Decatur to relieve him, but this change was not carried out and careful Isaac remained. His later career was undistinguished, but included some excellent assignments right up to the time of his death when he was serving as President of the Board of Navy Commissioners. Obviously, Chauncey had a way of finding good berths despite his aimless record on the waters of Ontario.

Toward the end of 1814, Chauncey even found the means of outweighing the enemy. In the *New Orleans,* Eckford planned a crowning exploit in "heft" and gunnery potential. Apparently the idea was to cow the enemy by her enormous size. The *New Orleans* was a three-decker, longer and wider than Nelson's *Victory.* Her keel was laid about the time the war officially ended but months were required for news of the Peace of Ghent to cross the Atlantic and reach Sackets Harbor over the forest trails. So, through the winter of 1814-1815, shipwrights continued to slam this dreadnought together from freshly sawed logs. Her dimensions were 187 feet on the keel, 30 feet deep in the hold, 3,000 tons burden. Pierced for 120 guns and the largest wooden ship ever built for Ontario's waters, she was ready for calking in ninety days from the laying of her keel.

In casting up the naval account for the year, British material losses were the heavier. A fourteen-gun brig had been burned by her crew, a ten-gun schooner was burned on the stocks, and three gunboats, three cutters and a gig had been captured. American losses included a schooner loaded with seven guns, a boat laden with two guns, and a gig captured and four guns destroyed at Oswego. The British naval operations cost in killed, wounded, and prisoners about 300 men in the Ontario operations for the year, against American losses of 80. Even so Chauncey knew that he had been outgeneraled by the youthful Yeo, and confessed as much to the Secretary of the Navy in a letter of August 10.

What was obviously needed, in the progress of the two years' aquatic game of hide-and-seek, was a combined land-and-sea assault on Sackets Harbor or Kingston, main fortresses of either foe. The British showed more dash. They made two sorties against the Harbor, and on the second occasion had really carried the position when Prevost's timidity spoiled the victory. Never once, however, was an American land force conveyed across the lake to attack Kingston.

Yeo, like Chauncey, was an excellent organizer. Many British writers have contended that his crews outmatched his opponent's in experience and fighting potentials. He was handicapped by nearness to an unstable superior, Governor Prevost; and probably he did not place enough confidence in the intangibles which have so often extended British sea power—fighting spirit backed by an immense prestige. Clearly Chauncey was overfearful; yet Yeo seldom made his opponent pay the price of fear.

With the respective armies in winter quarters and the fleets at rest in ice-locked harbors, the winter of 1814-1815 opened on Lake Ontario with the dreariness common to that region of low temperatures. At Sackets Harbor, under gray skies or blue, resounded the clang of hammers, rasp of saws and oaths of Eckford's men readying "Old Never-wet" for expected renewal of the fray. Across at Kingston these sounds were re-echoed by Yeo's shipwrights as they toiled on. Before the new vessels could be launched, however, the war ended.

Henry Eckford acquired a large fortune through his shipbuilding drive during the war. Returning to New York City, however, he suffered heavily from luckless stock investments. His death at Constantinople on November 12, 1832, closed a brilliant last phase as chief director of Turkey's dockyards. The Ottoman sultan is quoted as saying: "America must be GREAT, if it could spare such men as Eckford."

Fear of a third British attack mounted in Sackets Harbor during the closing months of the war. Colonel Washington Irving, aide-de-camp to Governor Daniel D. Tompkins, visited the Harbor on October 5, 1814, with orders to reinforce the militia there. General

Oliver Collins, commanding officer, called the North Country yeomen en masse. With nearly 3,000 reinforcements, in some houses twenty or thirty men were wedged into a single room.

The treaty of amity between the United States and Britain, both disposed at last to live and let live, had been signed at Ghent on the day before Christmas 1814 and ratified at Washington on February 18, 1815.

Peace, when it arrived at last, was complete to a degree of demilitarization never yet attempted on a geographic scale so vast. No new fortifications would be erected; no more fleets, flotillas, navies, navy yards. Existing military locations could be maintained. The only naval vessels allowable were craft of small tonnage needed to regulate and protect commerce and fisheries, enforce customs collection and train naval cadets and reserves. It was hardly expected that this thrifty but quixotic arrangement would endure, yet it has endured against occasional heavy strains, an example to all nations.

When the war was over, and men saw the folly of it, they hardly knew what to call this bloodletting between neighbors of like language and basic concords. It had begun as a war for the conquest of Canada, which failing, no better name could be found for the affair than a mere designation in time, the War of 1812, rather an anomaly since the war took three years, not one. The term Second War for Independence has more dignity and is gaining favor. The war, however named, cost the United States less than 2,000 killed in battle, with perhaps ten times as many dead of wounds and disease. British costs and losses no doubt were heavier, because they were fighting at a distance. It was unmistakably a cheap war, and satisfactory if measured in lessons learned at low cost. No doubt the young republic and Canada both would have paid more to prove that neither could be conquered in whole or part.

No doubt Lake Ontario history would be more exciting if the fleets of Chauncey and Yeo and the armies of Brown and Prevost had met and destroyed each other. Stay-at-homes like bloodletting, and posterity acclaims wastage wrought in the name of glory. History can find little enough to praise in those commanders who barged, boated and maneuvered safely through three years, during which the god of battles decided to resign as far as the border of the United States and Canada is concerned. The leaders seldom gained their objectives, but they did gain time during which some blazing issues died down of themselves. It is difficult to believe that two determined nations, each intent upon damaging the other to fullest possible extent, could actually punish each other so lightly in three years of trying, or that these nations could end the conflict as cheerfully disposed to each other and as serenely inclined to accept the lessons of war on that small stage as a guide to their larger amicable destiny.

Great Britain, a gamecock nation which always requires two lessons where one should serve all purposes of normal enlightenment, decided there was nothing very much she could do henceforth about the United States of America. The blessed Treaty of Ghent inaugurated an enduring peace, the living symbol of which is the unfortified frontier where the existing military posts are only archaic fortifications or ruins restored and maintained to impress upon succeeding generations their romantic stories of wars forever dead and gone.

# Chapter 15

## Erie Canal—"The Big Ditch"

*This solemnity, at this place, on the first arrival of vessels from Lake Erie, is intended to indicate and commemorate the navigable communication which has been accomplished between our Mediterranean Seas and the Atlantic Ocean, in about eight years, to the extent of more than 425 miles, by the wisdom, public spirit, and energy of the people of New York; and may the God of heavens and the earth smile most propitiously on this work, and render it subservient to the best interests of the human race.*

—GOVERNOR DeWITT CLINTON

ONE of the first author-travelers to use the new Hudson River steamboat of Robert Fulton in 1807 was Christopher Schultz, who described his progress in *Travels on an Inland Voyage,* copiously drawn upon by Dunbar in his encyclopedic *History of Travel in America.* Using the swift *Clermont* for the first leg of his jaunt from New York City to Black Rock near Buffalo, Schultz made the trip in the remarkably fast time of fifteen days. Dunbar works out his schedule as follows:

| | Miles | Method | Days |
|---|---|---|---|
| New York to Albany | 160 | Steamboat | 1½ |
| Albany to Schenectady | 15 | Turnpike | 1½ |
| Schenectady to Utica | 104 | 5 ton keel-boat | 5 |
| Utica to Oswego | 104 | 5 ton keel-boat | 3 |
| Oswego to Lewiston | 172 | Lake sailing boat | 3 |
| Lewiston to Black Rock | 17 | Mud Road | 1½ |

This schedule shows the sharp contrast between the speed of water travel and the slowness of highway travel on the atrocious roads of the period. For freight transport the waterways had even greater advantages in both speed and expense. But while natural waterways sufficed for light Indian trade, improved waterways were needed for the heavier and bulkier commodities of white civilization. The demand for canals rose loud and clear; the American sage, Franklin, viewing his native land from canalized Europe, pronounced them America's greatest need. As soon as public attention became concentrated on the subject the advantage of using the lakes and rivers of central New York for canal purposes became apparent to those who knew the geography of the Ontario-Erie region, scene of the nation's most serviceable and durable canal system.

Need of a canal to Lake Erie was felt a hundred years and more before the Erie Canal was built. Cadwallader Colden, Surveyor General of New York and later Lieutenant Governor, in 1724 gave the idea official cognizance. In 1777 Gouverneur Morris was talking of tapping Lake Erie as a postwar development, for it was perceived that to hold the West better transport would be needed. With Britain holding the northern waterway and Spain the outlet of the Mississippi, General George Washington noted with concern in 1783 that "the western settlers ... stand as it were upon a pivot. The touch of a feather would turn them any way."

With shrewd engineering eye George Washington read the water map of New York and the Great Lakes. In 1783 he wrote to the Marquis de Chastellux: "I have lately made a tour through the Lakes George and Champlain, as far as Crown Point. Thence returning to Schenectady, I proceeded up the Mohawk River to Fort Schuyler (formerly Fort Stanwix), crossed over to Wood Creek, which empties into the Oneida Lake, and affords the water communication with Ontario. I then traversed the country to the head of the eastern branch of the Susquehanna, and viewed the Lake Otsego, and the portage between that Lake and the Mohawk River at Canajoharie. Prompted by these actual observations, I could not help taking a more extensive view of the vast inland navigation of these United States, from maps and the information of others; and could not but be struck with the immense extent and importance of it, and with the goodness of that Providence which has dealt its favors to us with so profuse a hand. Would to God we may have wisdom enough to improve them. I shall not rest contented, till I have explored the western country, and traversed those lines, or a great part of them, which have given bounds to a new empire."*

Washington never found time for a journey to the Northwest and in retirement at Mount Vernon he so far lost his earlier vision that he drew plans for a canal connecting Lake Erie with Chesapeake Bay by way of the Muskingum, Ohio, Monongahela and Potomac.

Hardly had the Revolution broken the Iroquois hold than Colonel Christopher Colles was sent by New York on an exploratory survey. Then came Elkanah Watson, young in years but widely traveled and a student of European canals, having been set to that task by the farsighted Benjamin Franklin. Watson's *Journals,* only part of which have as yet been published, show a prompt grasp of the possibility of founding the "full trade of Lake Ontario and that of the Great Lake above, from Alexandria and Quebec to Albany and New York." Forestalled once by lack of capital, Watson returned to New York to found the Bank of Albany in 1792, gain the confidence of rich Dutchmen and establish the Western Inland Lock Navigation Company, chartered in 1794. This company, by means of small locks and other minor works, operated between Schenectady and Lakes Ontario and Seneca with enough success to earn and pay dividends for a number of years. Its success was short-lived, however, perhaps because its founder fell out with his backers. Although Watson was the first of New York's canal operators, and defended his claim to that fame ably in well-turned pamphlets, he never seriously considered the possibility of connecting the Mohawk-Hudson directly with Lake Erie.

The influential Clinton family became early indoctrinated with the value of New York waterways when its founder, Colonel Charles Clinton, went on Bradstreet's expedition for the destruction of Fort Frontenac on the northeast shore of Lake Ontario in 1758. His son, General James Clinton, gained unusual experience of New York's rivers in the campaign of 1779, in both the Mohawk and Susquehanna Valleys. James's brother George, the first Governor of New York and later Vice-President, was always a "Westerner" in politics,

---

* Letter of October 12, 1783, as it apears in *The Writings of Washington* edited by Jared Sparks (Boston, 1835), VIII, 488-489. Another version, identical except for old-fashioned spelling and punctuation, appears on pages 391-392 of *Travels in North America, 1780, '81, '82* (New York, 1827), by François Jean, Chevalier de Chastellux, later Marquis, Major General in the French forces on American service.

favoring all means of access to the undeveloped hinterland. James Clinton's son DeWitt, twice Governor, brought this sequence of interest to a triumphant conclusion in the Erie Canal, at first officially called the Grand Canal.

The act to secure that paramount objective passed the New York legislature in 1817. On October 22, 1819, the section from Rome to Utica was opened, and on October 25, 1825, Clinton's "Big Ditch" was opened along its entire length with protracted ceremonial. Before it was finished, Canada started the Welland Canal connecting Lakes Erie and Ontario, but that task was not completed until 1831, so that for six years the Erie had a monopoly on communications with the rapidly growing West.

The Erie cost $7,000,000—perhaps $35,000,000 at present value— and was the largest engineering work constructed by any government in the world up to that time. To this cost the nation contributed not a dollar; the Virginians, then in the saddle at Washington, followed Jefferson's lead in declaring the project "little short of madness." This daring enterprise, undertaken by a state of only 1,300,000 population, covered about 600 miles of territory, of which 360 miles lay through frontier wilderness. From tidewater at Troy to Lake Erie it conquered 571 feet of altitude by means of eighty-two locks. The ditch was forty feet wide and four feet deep.

At two points, Little Falls and Lockport, its channel had to be blasted and cut through solid limestone; in the Montezuma Marshes, where the problem was too much water instead of too much rock, hundreds of workmen fell ill and many died. The contractors lacked both experience and engineering science, yet they brought their respective sections accurately together at proper levels and with adequate feeders from reliable reservoirs. Most impressive were the watertight stone aqueducts which carried the canal across Schoharie Creek and the gorge of the Genesee River at Rochester, for which work skillful stonemasons were recruited in all parts of the nation and even in Europe.

As water poured into the canal, section by section, the public rushed to behold the new internal river. "You might see the people running across the fields, climbing trees and crowding the banks to gaze upon the welcome sight. A boat had been prepared at Rome, and as the waters came down the canal, this new Argo floated triumphantly along the Hellespont of the West."*

The Rome section at the old Oneida carry was the first opened by the shrewd governor, who ordered the construction to proceed from the middle toward both ends. Thus the easiest work was done first, and public opinion at both extremities pushed for quick completion.

Launching of a canal boat at Rochester in 1823 aroused more excitement than the launching "of the proudest ship from a seaport. To behold a vessel committed to the water 400 miles inland, in a place which ten years since was a wilderness, and reflect that it was to navigate a stream erected by the hand of man, two hundred and fifty miles in length ... excites emotions of no uncommon kind."†

Although Rochester had been squeamish about the canal's effect on her future, the city did itself proud at the formal opening. On October 26, 1825, guns mounted along the shallow waterway from Buffalo eastward boomed in succession at one-minute intervals, the signal reaching Manhattan in an hour and twenty minutes. It was then returned in the same manner to Buffalo, having traveled a distance of over 1,000 miles in less than three hours.

Following the *Seneca Chief,* which carried eastward Governor DeWitt Clinton and other dignitaries, came the tugboat *Noah's Ark,* laden with motley contributions from the awakening West. These exhibits included two Indian boys in barbaric regalia, a bear, a pair of eagles, two fawns and various other animals and birds. The tug carried also "two highly finished kegs" of Lake Erie water to be poured later into the Atlantic at New York Harbor to symbolize the mating of the waters.

At two o'clock of the afternoon of October 27 the two boats arrived at Rochester, where eight companies of militia drawn up at the aqueduct fired a volley of welcome. The *Young Lion of the West,* a sentinel craft stationed to protect the entrance to the aqueduct, hailed the approaching boats:

"Who comes there?"

"Your brethren of the West from the waters of the Great Lakes."

---

* From a contemporary letter dated Utica, N. Y., October 22, 1819, so described and published in the *History of Travel in America* (ed. 1937), p. 780.

† *Ibid.,* p. 782.

"By what means have they been diverted from their natural course?"

"By the channel of the Grand Erie Canal."

"By whose authority and by whom was a work of such magnitude accomplished?"

"By the authority and enterprise of the patriotic people of the State of New York."

"All right! Pass."

As the *Young Lion* sidled to the edge, *Seneca Chief* and the *Ark* entered the aqueduct. A program of oratory, parade and church service was topped off with a Gargantuan dinner at Christopher's Mansion House.

Never did an engineering work produce speedier economic and political results. "The six great states that grew up promptly in the Middle West turned their faces definitely East."* New York City within the decade of Erie construction grew from third American city to first in wealth and population, and with the economic weight of the Midlands behind it has never since been surpassed. Forever laid to rest was the dream of Captain Williamson and others who believed that the commerce of western New York would drain southeast to the Chesapeake by means of the Susquehanna or southwest to Pittsburgh and the Ohio down the Allegheny. Northwestern lands boomed because they had access to the Erie; those too far away to benefit by it suffered in the competition for settlers and markets. Ontario immediately and, in diminishing degree, for a long time to come, would feel the pull of the economic current exerted by the great artificial waterway of the Erie Canal, outlet for grain that had been stifling the slim home market. A boom in land values began which lasted for twelve years.

The Erie Canal route ran from eight to twenty-five miles south of the Lake Ontario southern shore. Immediate shore development suffered in consequence. Intervening lands benefited, the population of the whole region increased, but the canal, not Lake Ontario, became the artery attracting trade and enterprise. For instance, Rochester at the falls of the Genesee became the metropolis instead of Charlotte eight miles north where the Genesee enters Lake Ontario.

---

* F. P. Kimball, *New York—The Canal State* (Albany, 1937), p. 13.

A less costly project had been proposed which would have benefited the lake shore of Ontario far more than the Erie. This was the relatively simple plan of connecting the Hudson with Lake Ontario by means of a canal through the Mohawk-Lake Oneida-Oswego route, already well established on a primitive bateau basis as we have seen, and then building in wholly American territory a canal around Niagara Falls into Lake Erie. But this would have routed commerce through an international waterway swept only a few years before by almost continuous naval warfare. The War of 1812 and the raids of Yeo could not be so easily or quickly forgotten, and the unfortified frontier was still an experiment without prestige.

Lake Erie steamboats soon adjusted their schedule to the canal schedule for the inside route which took settlers west and brought their produce east without leaving the United States. By the time the Welland Canal was opened in 1831, eastern merchants as far south as Baltimore were shipping their goods by the Erie to Buffalo, Cleveland, Detroit, Toronto and Pittsburgh. But New York City always retained the edge, because the products of a hinterland of vast extent could be carried there most cheaply. Transportation had proved itself to be king in this country of magnificent distances.

For twelve years the constructive forces released in the lake plains by the Erie Canal caused a crescendo of speculation. Then in 1837 came a crash the like of which has never yet been matched for agricultural distress. More land had been cleared than could be profitably used, more capital had been sunk in land and in public improvements than could be paid for or served with interest payments. On the fringes of the New West, land values dropped from dollars an acre to cents an acre; in the Ontario region, by then quite well settled and no longer a raw frontier, land went down half to three-quarters in price. No relief came from the government of a republic too young to cope with economic cycles even in a halfhearted way. Those dispossessed by pressure of mortgage debt salvaged what they could and struck out for the West.

But agriculture, like nature, abhors a vacuum. European immigration was now on the way. Into the homesteads of the Lake Ontario region left vacant by first and second generation Yankees who were off to the cheaper lands of the new states of Michigan and Wisconsin, came the sturdy, patient sons and daughters of Europe, seeking not only to better their economic condition but also to expand their personalities as citizens of a democratic republic.

An example is the coming of the Prussians in the early 1840's. Soon they comprised one-third of the population of Buffalo and were active in all branches of its business. Others became farmers throughout a considerable part of the Ontario countryside. A contemporary newspaper account says:

"In Niagara county there are three villages or colonies of Prussians; the first came into the county in 1843, purchased and located upon 4,000 acres of land in the northern and central parts of Wheatfield. During the same year another village was founded on the Tonawanda Creek, at the mouth of the Cayuga Creek, called Martinsville; and a third has been added on the Shawnee road leading from Lockport to Niagara Falls, called Wallnow. The three villages are all in the town of Wheatfield; their aggregate population is nearly 2,000. They are refugees from religious persecution; their religious faith is purely Lutheran with the Augsburg Confession as their standard. They are not Communists or Fourierites, their lands being held in severalty, and yet there is among them a system of mutual aid and common interest that grows out of their position and religious organization. The poor among them have small tracts of land set apart for their use, and have the privilege of purchasing upon long credits. They brought with them their ministers, schoolmasters and mechanics; the excellent indications, meeting and schoolhouses marked their advent; industry and thrift are the general aspect of their settlements."

In 1816 there were only 331 people in Rochester, yet by 1840 it had become a wheat-shipping and milling center with 40,000 inhabitants, the "most sudden" growing town in America. An English traveler of artistic bent, Captain Basil Hall, saw it rising. "Hammers were clattering, axes ringing, machinery creaking. I cannot say how many churches, court houses, jails and hotels I counted creeping upward. Here and there we saw great warehouses, unfinished but half-filled with goods and furnished with hoisting cranes ready to fish up the huge pyramids of flour, barrels, bales and boxes lying in the streets." Along the route of the Erie, "ports" multiplied—Lockport, Gasport, Middleport, Brockport, Spencerport, Fairport, Port Byron,

Weedsport—and to some degree each showed the enterprise which stirred the newly crowned "Flour City."

Improved land increased from 5,700,000 acres in 1821 to 9,560,000 acres in 1835, already nearly half of what it was a century later. By 1846, says Whitford, shipments to tidewater on New York canals exceeded the whole export trade of the state and came to about half of the combined trade of the Union. Whitford's basis of measurement is not quite clear in the foregoing, but enough trade flowed through the "big ditch" to energize the whole state, because the general level of prosperity produced taxes for internal improvements in the Southern Tier beyond the Erie's immediate range. For farm wagons over ordinary roads canal influence extended only about thirty miles, but as roads were improved this rose to fifty miles for wheat and other staples. "Thus in a few brief years," as Kimball says in his *New York—The Canal State,* "New York had been lifted out of a primitive and disorganized condition into a thriving, unified and growing commonwealth,"* ready to play a constructive role in the development of the new western states.

Soon the Erie became crowded. In 1835 the state began deepening the channel from four to seven feet, but a panic soon set in, public works became unpopular and the project was not completed in all sections until the beginning of the Civil War. Thereafter during the period of active railroad construction the canal fell into disrepair. Tolls were eliminated in 1882. Locks were lengthened to 220 feet in 1884. Six years later, deepening to nine feet was decided upon but political scandal intervened and the effort fell through.

Down to 1904 barges were still being hauled by horses on a towpath in hopeless competition against railroads alongside. The time handicap was somewhat reduced by the building of a new barge canal chiefly on the old Erie route and levels and by the introduction of power towing. This bigger and better artery was opened in 1918, but water transport—even on this enlarged "ditch"—never recovered fully the prestige it enjoyed before the railroads arrived with their new standards of speed.

The transition from canal to rail, from tow-mules to locomotives, was part of the change in our national economy from agricultural to industrial dominion which has been the commanding feature of our

---

* F. P. Kimball, *New York—The Canal State* (Albany, 1937), p. 22.

progress. As grain ceased to be the chief staple and as other ports, among them Buffalo and Oswego, took over the flour trade, Rochester enjoyed a graceful interlude in which it became known as the "Flower City" by reason of its nurseries and commercial gardens. The rich soil, equable temperatures and well-spaced rains of the lakeshore region led to flower, vegetable, fruit and tree culture which have given beauty and prosperity to the American scene. Among the pioneer leaders in these developments were the old-country folk whose coming has been described—notably the Germans, who, now well acclimated themselves, proceeded to acclimate plants with their accustomed thoroughness in husbandry.

That phase, too, passed. Industry swung toward manufacturing. And now, since the chief railroads had followed the canal system along the easiest level, the factories arose, not on the Lake Ontario shore but along the arterial route south of it. Oswego and the lesser places on the lake marked time, while Rochester proceeded, as told later in this volume, to swing into industrial development of noble scope and arresting variety.

## Chapter 16

## Rough Road to Federation

*As I sat alone, by blue Ontario's shore,*
*As I mused of these mighty days, and of peace return'd,*
*    and the dead that return no more,*
*A Phantom, gigantic, superb, with stern visage, accosted me;*
Chant me the poem, *it said*, that comes from the soul of America—
    chant me the carol of victory;
And strike up the marches of Libertad—marches more powerful yet;
And sing me before you go, the song of the throes of Democracy.
                                        —WALT WHITMAN

JUST as growing pains attended transition of the Thirteen Colonies to self-rule by democratic processes, the course of Upper and Lower Canadas toward unification and self-government was long, trying and often painful. In a period distinguished for intolerance between Christian creeds Canada was half Catholic, half Protestant. Political strife between the "haves" and "have-nots," between the crystallizing aristocracy and the pushing masses, became part of the atmosphere in both provinces. Popular discontent smoldered to flare at last in armed uprisings. At York friction grew between a reactionary ruling oligarchy and an increasingly demanding electorate. In Quebec and Montreal the English socially patronized the French who in turn resented the presence of the conquerors of New France. Imperious early English army governors with no skill in statecraft further muddled affairs. Canada was a house divided, geographically and politically.

Ontario was peopled by a picturesque and complex horde of humanity. Loyalist refugees from the States, British and European immigrants, Yankees and Yorkers swarmed in by the thousands. Their very differences made them difficult for the new domain to digest. Many Loyalists, especially those from leading Colonial families, although impoverished, had the brains and background to re-establish their financial position and to make themselves leaders. One such

211

was Jonathan Sewell, able and industrious Tory. Appointed Speaker of Lower Canada's Assembly in 1809, he served in that post for thirty years. Also he sat as Chief Justice over the Governor's Council of the Upper Province. The ermine did not deter him from playing in politics while on the bench, which caused resentment among the French. As a result, legislation was passed removing the power of judges to dabble in politics—openly, at least!

At first most of the small tradesmen and hired laborers in the new communities were immigrants from Britain or the continent of Europe. Later many New England Yankees left their stony farms to go to the richer lands along Lake Ontario's north shore, and to set up as tradesmen and artificers.

The outbreak of the War of 1812 interrupted emigration from the United States, but not long after peace returned some 10,000 emigrants were annually crossing the boundary into Canada. These were mostly small farmers and laborers. Such folk shifting from one European country to another would have remained humble and submissive to the caste system, but in North America they grew ambitious to rise and eager for political recognition. In the United States and Canada these folk movements early developed bonds of blood and sentiment between the two populations which continued basically undisturbed in spite of misunderstandings and superficial quarrels which often had their origin abroad. The two countries were gradually evolving responsible governments different but by no means antagonistic. Canada in her struggle for unification and dominion status did much to round out the education of Downing Street which the American Revolution had begun.

In 1815, however, when as a postwar measure Britain sent penniless families to Canada to avoid supporting them at home, the picture was different. Ontario's problem then as now was to fill her immense territory with worthy settlers. The dumping of improvidents from overseas who were ill-fitted to wrest livings from the soil added a social stratum below that of the competent laborers to the thinly distributed population along the lake shore, where the British ideal of upper-class rule was in conflict with economics and geography.

Political life centering at York soon became a parade of snobbery and sycophancy. Soldier governors, veterans of Waterloo, were sent from England to head a government whose chief officials held life tenure at high salaries. Periodically a governor and his retinue were replaced. Bureaucrats too numerous for their duties fawned upon successive governors, bent the knee before rank and pomp, ignored tradesmen and tried to ignore the popularly elected Assembly whose members were considered rough, uncouth fellows. Harsh procedures ruled a supine public; in 1798 a man was hanged for a £4 forgery. At York only the upper chamber or the Legislative Council named by the governor counted. This Council assumed without legal warrant the authority of a British Cabinet. Absentee control grew up through gubernatorial appointments of men living in England to serve as Canada's higher officers. Britishers usually enjoyed the emoluments of these sinecures but the working berths were filled by Canadians, all appointed for life by the governor as administrators and staff members, judges, militia officers and collectors of revenue.

A resident clique of leading families was thus protected by official favor from the specter of future jobless days. Safe for life, they took care not to nip the hand that fed them, and in a narrow atmosphere of intense loyalty and complete financial security they intermarried freely. By its foes this Upper Canadian oligarchy was called the "Family Compact," a term borrowed from French history where it signified a partnership of French and Spanish royalty.

While the Family Compact held fast, London's "concession" of popular government for the Canadians meant little. Far from the center of authority, the clique did about as it pleased. To reach York then involved a week or more of wearisome travel from Montreal or New York City. In the summer, postage of four shillings and sixpence might take a letter to London in about a month. The rest of the year mail required four months in transit from York to the Home Office. A governor so remote from the seat of power had to make his own decisions instead of conferring with his chief. As the martinet governors usually restricted their acquaintance to the ruling clique their decisions were usually narrow and arbitrary, out of line with popular sentiment and based only upon advice of the "good people" involved in the Family Compact.

For example, Sir Peregrine Maitland, who lorded it in York from 1819 to 1829, held that only gentlemen were fit to share in government. Tradesmen and brewers were taboo. His political creed upheld a cultivated minority ruling over a vulgar, ill-educated and

smelly majority. Since the objectionable masses were not worth edu-
cating, on the chance that they might develop responsible leaders,
Maitland heartily aided the Family Compact group in suppressing
any popular movement toward liberalization and reform.

The Church of England entrenched itself legally as the endowed
church of York and Upper Canada. In a day when things temporal
and spiritual were not usually divided, religion appeared as an arm
of government and often its head as well. In 1791 religion was endowed under the Canada Act. For every seven acres of land freshly
surveyed an additional acre was reserved for support of the Protestant
clergy. Ontario was overwhelmingly Protestant, but Methodists,
Baptists, Presbyterians and members of other dissenting sects considerably outnumbered the Episcopalian communicants. In law each
sect had claim to the forested Clergy Reserves which by 1825 totaled
2,000,000 idle acres in Upper Canada. But these dissenters' claims
were not recognized in York!

Intrusion of this bitterly contested issue recalls to this narrative a
masterful figure whom the reader met previously as the stubborn
champion of the little community of York after its capture by the
Americans early in the War of 1812. Since then the Reverend John
Strachan had become the Rector of York and was on his way to a
bishopric, bestowed in 1839, which gave him ecclesiastical authority
over Upper Canada. Zealous for Canada's interests as he saw them,
Strachan had a despotic will and an intolerant static quality of mind
that rejected violently all ideas not his own unless they stemmed from
royalty or hierarchy.

As chief adviser to the pompous Maitland, Strachan maintained
that the Church of England alone was entitled to income from the
Clergy Reserves. The court at York supported his contention, and
the Church began to squeeze the Dissenters. In 1824 the Legislative
Council for Upper Canada actually rejected an Assembly measure
authorizing Methodist clergymen to perform the marriage ceremony,
a prohibition which lasted for seven years.

Called to Maitland's council in 1818, Strachan soon grew into the
Compact's most uncompromising leader. On the record he was too
impetuous and belligerent, but his sincerity was absolute. Firmly
convinced that democracy was loosed upon a luckless world by Satan,
he pointed to the United States as a horrible example. Any act that

might put even the thinnest wedge between the pulpit and the secular government he denounced and opposed.

This champion of cassocked force visited England in 1827 and returned with a charter for a university, King's College at York, to be endowed by the state with himself as president. The new university was to put an Anglican stamp on its graduates just as Oxford and Cambridge did in England. Like them, King's College was to train youth for future political leadership. Since only about one-tenth of Upper Canada's scattered population then adhered to the Church of England, dissenting sects howled disapproval.

Another Scot, born in 1795, brought quite another set of ideas to Ontario, ideas born of discontent with things as they were. In 1824, four years after arriving in Canada, William Lyon Mackenzie was editing *The Colonial Advocate* in York and savagely attacking the entrenched Compact system led by Tory Strachan. In 1826 a youthful group of hotheads headed by Maitland's secretary wrecked Mackenzie's printing office and threw his fonts of type into the bay. Mackenzie collected damages and continued his fulminations.

A monument memorializing General Brock was then under erection at Niagara. According to custom, newspapers had been placed beneath it. Governor Maitland childishly ordered that fourteen feet of the structure already reared should be torn down to remove from the base a copy of Mackenzie's journal that lay with the others!

Mackenzie's radical movement was part of a widespread revolt against inequality and authoritarian government. In the United States, Andrew Jackson's election as President, as the champion of the frontiersman, culminated a long dissatisfaction against entrenched wealth and prestige. In England continual agitation finally brought the passage, in 1832, of the famous Reform Bill, which extended the suffrage privilege. The same democratic wave swept Mackenzie into office as an Assemblyman from the province's foremost county, York. From the floor of the Assembly he attacked the government on a wide variety of grievances. In 1830 he was re-elected, to the dismay of Sir John Colborne, the new governor who had entered office when Maitland was transferred to govern quieter Nova Scotia.

Although the Assembly sometimes resented the arbitrary treatment it received from the Compact-controlled Upper House and might conceivably have welcomed a radical, the fact is that Assemblyman Mackenzie made himself unpopular with his fellow legislators through his truculence and lack of tact. His colleagues tossed him out of office for alleged libel. Twice again his angry constituents returned him and each time he was promptly ousted. Then the Assembly highhandedly disfranchised York County for persisting in returning a member deemed unfit.

In 1832 Mackenzie packed up his political troubles and sailed to England to discuss them with other radicals. There he induced Lord Goderich of the Colonial Office to dismiss from their posts some of his bitterest foes at home, and returned to York to some extent a victor.

In 1834 "dirty little York" became the city of Toronto, and its jubilant citizens chose gamecock Mackenzie as the municipality's first mayor. The ruling set at Governor's House was first taken aback, then grew more resentful and vindictive.

Upper Canada's political forces now shaped swiftly into three groups: Compact standpatters, Mackenzie radicals and middle-of-the-roaders. The Compact clique denounced as anarchistic the tenets of Mackenzie followers, whose list of wants sounds mild enough today. The radicals urged that the Legislature control all provincial revenue excepting hereditary dues, called for an independent judiciary, demanded a housecleaning in the legislative council to end governor-appointees' blocking of Assembly measures, and insisted on a policy of religious equality and responsible government.

The third group, the moderates, eventually supplied the men and legal machinery which definitely started Canada toward her present stable, responsible, broad-gauged form of government. Leaders included the Baldwins, lawyers of Irish extraction who practiced well the art of compromise in clean politics. Allied with them were the Bidwells, father and son; Marshall Spring Bidwell rather than Mackenzie was elected to the speakership when the reformers took over Assembly control in 1828. Egerton Ryerson, Methodist leader from the States, was another strong man who fought the Church of England over the Clergy Reserves and for recognition of the rights of dissenters. These were men of more position and substance than the small farmers and laborers who made up the rank and file of Mackenzie's radical followers, yet the benighted Compact group had never admitted them to partnership.

Robert Baldwin's plan to end the despotic sway of the Family Compact envisioned a Canadian political scene modeled upon England's. It included a cabinet continuing only while supported by the popularly elected chamber.

Accession of Victoria to the throne very soon came to be of utmost significance to Canada's fortunes. It brought an end at last to reaction, sloth and misunderstanding at the source of governing authority. The young Victoria's able ministers immediately sought to deal openly and fairly with grievances from overseas instead of continuing to govern aloofly behind militarized façades and social exclusiveness.

At last the Crown had ministers with common sense enough to inquire into reasons for Colonial aches and irks. Lord Melbourne determined to find out why British colonies were seeking to pull away from Britain's skirts, freshly laundered as these skirts were by the Reform Bill of 1832.

But by autumn 1837 and before the new leaven had time to work, Mackenzie was persuaded that the hour for successful rebellion had arrived. Radicals with whom he had hobnobbed on his trip to England had counseled direct action. He had exchanged views with Louis Joseph Papineau, the famous malcontent leader in Lower Canada. Convinced that a coup in Upper Canada, timed with Papineau's meditated stroke in Quebec province, would win Toronto and all Upper Canada, Mackenzie determined either to set up a provisional government or lead his province into the United States. Eagerly he awaited word from the east that the Papineau forces had marched.

Papineau's abortive trial at arms was launched in mid-November 1837. In Toronto Mackenzie then sent out his summons. On the morning of December 5 a few hundred men armed with muskets and pikes started southward from Montgomery's tavern in Yonge Street a few miles from Toronto. The mob straggled toward the city, which Mackenzie had promised would be seized along with the governor.

A will-o'-the-wisp danced at the head of that sorry procession as Mackenzie led his dupes toward never-never land. Through the years he had lost much of his original support. Most of the folk who followed the little man on the appointed day were irresponsibles whom posterity would describe as "the lunatic fringe." Cooler heads than theirs had determined to win through to democratic privilege, without disorder, by quiet and lawful means.

Mackenzie started his march with about 800 men. He thought thousands more would join the ranks before the goal was reached. But when the city's bells began ringing and the marchers learned that the government was alert to the demonstration, numbers of rebel farmers left the ranks. A ruse delayed them, a false flag of truce, while the government's troops constructed defenses. In a night battle both sides retired after an initial volley. They seemed to have become suddenly dazed by their temerity in firing at all. A few men were killed, others wounded.

Mackenzie's control waned. His assistants wasted a day quarreling over plans. Then 1,100 Loyalist troops, having overcome their scruples, shelled the rebels who were gathered in a woodlot. They fled in terror and the rebellion ended then and there. Some of Mackenzie's lowly followers were hanged after treason trials later.

With a few adherents, the editor escaped to Buffalo where he was wined, dined and lauded. He received assurances, largely from Irish-American sources, that he would have plenty of fighting Yankees with arms, ammunition and food when he started his next foray against York.

It was heady wine for a zealot. Under the unctuous promises of his new friends, Mackenzie recovered his delusions of grandeur. With twenty-five men he crossed the Niagara River to Navy Island some two miles above the Falls on the Canadian side. There he proclaimed a provisional government and offered a reward for the capture of Bond Head. He recruited many Yankee followers and soon had 800 to 1,000 supporters under his command. Ill-advised but earnest musket fire was exchanged between his men and Canadian troops marshaled on the opposite mainland.

A small American-owned steamer, the *Caroline,* brought supplies from Buffalo to the rebels. On December 29 Colonel Allan MacNab, Loyalist, ordered the seizure of the *Caroline* at Fort Schlosser, killed an American in the scuffle, set the boat ablaze and sent her rocketing over the Falls. Mass meetings of protest were held throughout the United States, calling upon Washington "to provide for the protection of our shores against invasion by subjects of a foreign power." For the next five years the *Caroline* incident was diplomatic touch-and-go between the two nations. On January 5, 1838, President Van Buren issued a proclamation forbidding Americans to aid Canada's rebels, and sent troops under General Scott to the Border to maintain order. Congress, on January 30, 1838, appropriated $625,000 to safeguard the northern frontier and provided for calling out the militia and other war measures. Nevertheless, the so-called Patriots' War brought forth ugly reprisals. On the night of February 19 hotheads intent on a foray into Canada stole 400 stand of arms from the state arsenal at Watertown. To balk a threatened thrust at Kingston two militia companies were posted at Cape Vincent. During that year the British steamer *Sir Robert Peel* was burned in American waters, and British soldiers at Brockville on the St. Lawrence fired upon the American vessel *Telegraph*.

Another outbreak occurred on the St. Lawrence a few miles below the lake. "Admiral Bill" Johnston got together a fleet of small boats on the American side and carried a force of 200 men under a Polish refugee named von Schultz across the river to attack Prescott. Von Schultz caught the Canadian defenders by surprise, captured the Windmill, a stone tower near the town, and held it for two days before regulars and Canadian volunteers brought him to surrender.

Of this abortive battle Harry F. Landon writes: "Then the exploits of 'Admiral Bill' Johnston, commander of the fleet of rowboats which was the Patriot Navy, and his daughter, Kate, the 'Queen of the Thousand Isles,' were the talk of the borderland. We catch, too, something of the tenseness the people of Ogdensburg must have felt on that November day when they crowded the waterfront and watched with straining eyes the battle that raged about the tall, stone windmill across the river from whose tower floated the two starred flag of the 'Republic of Canada.' "*

Von Schultz, although defended at his trial by John A. Macdonald, who later became a great Canadian statesman, was convicted and hanged, along with eleven other ringleaders, and a few more were banished to Van Diemen's Land, or Tasmania. But Bill Johnston, probably the man most responsible for the raid into Canada, got back safely to the American shore, hid out for a time in the famous Slave's Cave, later noted as the last American station on the Underground Railroad, and he finally got off scot-free. In later years, rounding out a career as a fake and filibuster, Johnston became well known as the teller of the tallest tales on the border.

* *The North Country* (Indianapolis, 1932), I, 301.

Arrested on January 30, 1838, by Federal authorities, the chieftain Mackenzie, after remaining at liberty on moderate bail for sixteen months, finally served out his sentence of eleven months in the Rochester jail for violation of neutrality laws. Canada forgave both Mackenzie and Papineau, and in 1849 prodigal "Mac" returned from self-imposed exile in the United States. Re-elected to the Union parliament, Mackenzie lived out the remainder of his career quietly. His life of hardship, yearning and indispensable service ended in 1861. By that time, Toronto, place of his earlier triumphs and subsequent discomfiture, had become a proud, expanding city. Long gone by then was the Family Compact and its cynical philosophy. The little Scot had failed to bring in freedom—but it had come without him. Upper Canada used William Lyon Mackenzie while traveling toward union and democracy at her own gait, refusing to be hurried by his hectic program of revolt.

As a sequence to Papineau's collapsed revolt in Lower Canada, Lord Melbourne in London caused the provincial constitution to be suspended. Lower Canada then reverted to its status prior to the Constitutional Act of 1791. This meant that representative government would be laid aside while a Crown-appointed governor and his council took over—an arbitrary gesture intended to clear ground for a calm, deliberate study of the Canadian outbreaks.

Melbourne chose a master to diagnose the ills of Canada. John George Lambton, Earl of Durham, was a rich mine owner of radical sympathies. He had helped to frame the famous British Reform Bill of 1832. On Durham's return from Russia, where he served as ambassador, he was induced to accept a more onerous post with greater responsibilities than had been previously laid upon any man named to govern in Canada. Durham was named governor in chief of all six British-American provinces. Newfoundland, lonely and aloof as it still remains, was quietly loyal and stood apart from the others. Prince Edward Island presented no real problem. New Brunswick and Nova Scotia had offered to help in crushing the two rebellions. Upper and Lower Canada and their relations with the United States presented a trying situation in which Lord Durham was expected to foster harmony between warring Canadians, revive loyalty to the Crown, and promote peace on the American border.

Though physically doomed and doubtless aware of it, Durham

made a decisive start. On arriving at Quebec in 1838, he dismissed the executive council named under the suspended constitution, ignored the "Chateau clique" which resembled in misrule the Family Compact in Upper Canada, and conciliated the popular party. Committees were named to investigate the administration of Crown lands, the status of popular education and municipal government in the provinces. Traveling widely, he observed the differences between residents of the upper and lower provinces, and studied means to adjust and heal them. Crossing the Niagara River, he made a friendly dinner speech that soothed relations made raw by Bond Head's diatribes against the United States.

Before returning to Quebec to begin framing there an elaborate report on his findings and conclusions, he issued in August 1838 an ordinance banishing eight rebels to Bermuda. It provided that if these men or sixteen other rebels, including the fugitive Papineau, should return to Canada without permission, they would be summarily executed. This minor action precipitated the end of his regime; under English common law Durham had no authority to decree or threaten death without trial. When Melbourne refused to back up his unfortunate ordinance, Durham mailed his resignation and sailed for England on November 1, 1838. Though chagrined, the imperturbable invalid continued to work for Canada. In February 1839 he submitted to the Crown his memorable *Report on the Affairs of British North America,* a paper immensely influential in liberalizing Britain's colonial policy. Lord Durham upheld reform contentions by drawing a somber picture of government as he found it operating in Toronto and Quebec. Public-lands transactions were described as riddled with fraud, public education was farcically scant, local government existed only in name, while the British Colonial Office looked with indifference upon these ills.

Lord Durham advocated a division of powers in which the British government would control foreign relations, regulate commerce, determine ruling constitutions and dispose of public lands, while all other authority should be vested in the colony. Though Tories considered these concessions to be perilous, not only these but all of the functions recommended for reservation to the Crown are now administered by the Dominion government.

Among other recommendations in the report were that all Crown revenues apart from public land moneys be held in the colonial treasury to defray costs of a permanent civil list, that cabinets be responsible to majorities of elected lower houses, and that Upper Canada and Lower Canada be unified under one government.

Lord Durham had not remained long enough in the vast Ontario region to form more than a hazy view of its difficulties in development. Perhaps for that reason an observation crept into the report that was less than fair to Canada. Durham saw in the United States "a well-ordered society with good roads, schools, prosperous farms and industries, activity, bustle, wealth; in contrast with lack of hope and enterprise in Canada." But the States in the half-century since their adoption of the Federal Union had been releasing popular enthusiasms and individual energies which in Canada were still buried by archaic institutions and social norms unfitted to the New World. The United States had then 16,000,000 inhabitants against Upper Canada's 400,000. Railroads had not supplanted rude frontier roads and canal diggers had yet to skirt completely the St. Lawrence rapids.

Durham glimpsed truly, however, immense opportunities ahead for Canadians when released from stupid and officious rule. "Lack of hope and enterprise," he had himself written down as a cause of apathy. It was given him not merely to diagnose the disease but to prescribe a remedy. Broadening of popular liberties, he held, would quicken the national initiative. The brave spirit who wrote that famous report would be quite at home today in bustling Toronto, business center of a land he loved so well "with its spacious harbors and vast inland seas, its many long, deep rivers, its fertile soil, inexhaustible forests and wealth in minerals."

"Canada has been the death of him," said John Stuart Mill when Durham died in July 1840. Perhaps the feverish pace of his last dutiful days hastened the end, but he was a sufferer from tuberculosis before he accepted the Canadian assignment. His last words were: "I would fain hope I have not lived altogether in vain. Whatever the Tories may say, the Canadians will one day do justice to my memory." No great man ever wrote for himself a more modest epitaph.

A competent successor, Charles Poulett Thomson, English candle manufacturer, arrived in October 1839 to administer the affairs of British North America. Thomson had been a friend of Durham's and believed fervently in his theories of colonial administration.

Still sitting unwanted at Toronto was the Assembly elected after Bond Head's plea to oust "disloyal republicans." In the capital of Upper Canada Thomson found chaos. Factions warred over the issue of national separation from Britain. Annual deficits paralyzed credit and property values were shredded. That ancient problem of Clergy Reserves developed more thorns as it grew older. Immigrants tarried, gazed, shook tousled heads and rambled on into the United States. The amazed Thomson remonstrated: "But Upper Canada is the finest country I ever knew." Veterans of the Family Council grew uneasy as their influence waned.

Thomson met his legislature at York on December 3, 1839. Under his tactful handling, Tories passed a bill parceling the church lands among the religious bodies in numerical ratio, despite the ire of die-hard Strachan, who held out for Episcopalian monopoly to the last.

The victory established Thomson's ability as a diplomat. In return for Tory support he arranged to float a fat loan for public works, the burden of cost to be shared by the two Canadas since both provinces would benefit. Meanwhile a movement for the Union which Lord Durham had proposed gained headway. The legislative session closed in February 1840. Tories were voting with radicals in favor of Union. The Family Compact dissolved of its own weight after nearly fifty years of reactionary control.

Following this signal triumph in his brilliant three months' campaign, Thomson received a peerage as Baron Sydenham. The new lord needed all possible prestige to defend his action on the Clergy Reserves in London, where the stubborn Strachan had carried his case. The cleric won. Distribution of church lands to all religious sects pro rata was disallowed, and the Church of England kept all funds and titles for a further twelve years of furious religious strife.

A second irritation developed. In his proposed Act of Union, Sydenham had incorporated legislation to remove existing restrictions which hampered communities in managing their own affairs. Specifically, he sought to relieve a local government of the need to petition provincial legislators for the right to pave thoroughfares, build bridges, establish schools and the like. Centralization of authority in such matters had long been the rule, for the Family Compact, thriving through handling of revenues, had never permitted a system of local taxation. A last-ditch alliance of the oligarchs and what would now be termed "pressure groups" succeeded in getting the London government to delete from the Act of Union Sydenham's sensible bill to allow communities to handle their own local affairs. Sydenham was so irked by this that he meditated resigning his post.

In England's Parliament the Act of Union was otherwise mauled and mangled but pulled through with Peel's support against opposition led by the Duke of Wellington, who contended that Union would bring French domination in Canada. Oddly enough, many French Canadians disliked Union for the opposite reason, the fear that it would diminish their autonomy.

Union government as provided by Parliament in London comprised a Governor, Legislative Council and Assembly. Governor and Council members—twenty or more in number and serving life terms—were to be named by the Crown. The Assembly of eighty-four members was to be chosen by popular vote, half from Lower Canada and half from Upper Canada, a concession to the latter, which had by far the smaller population. Records were to be kept in English with privilege of translation into French, while either English or French speech would be permitted in official debate. Britain would continue its control of customs duties, but measures involving Crown lands and religion were to be referred to the provincial government. Internal Canadian revenues were to be consolidated, the Crown relinquishing both hereditary and territorial claims in exchange for a permanent civil list of £75,000. Legislation dealing with taxation and allocation of public moneys was to stem from the Governor's desk, but the Assembly would discuss all fiscal measures. The Union assumed the debts of both provinces.

The Act of Union was passed on July 23, 1840, but did not go into effect until early the following year. When they joined on schedule, Lower Canada had 600,000 people, Upper Canada 400,000. This balance, however, was soon reversed, and by 1850 the English province, now Ontario, was the more populous. The obvious explanation was immigration. Few French families came to Lower Canada after the restless era of exploration and initial settling, but the Ontario region received large numbers of settlers who left Europe following the revolutionary outbreaks of the period.

Union came into legal existence on February 10, 1841, after a noisy referendum. Fists, boots and clubs swung through both prov-

MANSION OF JAMES LERAY DE CHAUMONT, FRENCH
NOBLEMAN, AT LERAYSVILLE, N. Y.
One of America's best Georgian houses.

HOME OF VINCENT LERAY DE CHAUMONT, FRENCH EMIGRÉ, AT
CAPE VINCENT, N. Y.
The village was named for him.

MAMMOTH ELECTRIC GENERATING STATION ON LAKE SHORE AT
OSWEGO, N. Y.

*Upper left*: Buildings of Oswego State Teachers College with campus
stretching shoreward.

inces, but the English faction voted or fought sufficiently to win ratification finally by a substantial majority of the whole oddly assorted population, the French being generally opposed. The London-named Council contained five from Ontario and three from Lower Canada. In reality Sydenham was his own Prime Minister. He said of his council: "They are here for me to consult and for no other purpose. I will govern as I think right and not as they fancy." Not yet was Canada to be governed by Canadians, but merely by an able and liberal Englishman who knew how to manage Canadians for their own welfare.

Again "the little grey city of Kingston" on Lake Ontario's northeast shore became a capital, as in Simcoe's day it had been briefly; but now it was the capital not of a new frontier province, but of two United Provinces of Canada, with a million souls. Quebec lay too far eastward and was too sullenly French. Toronto sprawled too far westward and was too noisily English. A new crop of parliamentarians jammed Kingston's limited lodgings. Robert Baldwin, Liberal, and Hippolyte Lafontaine, who would become Canada's first Prime Minister, shared progressive political opinions. Baldwin resigned when Sydenham would not endorse his plan to group French and English Liberals as a majority by means of which government would be carried on by party after the English custom.

Ever a driver, Sydenham forced through the Kingston legislative mill more self-government for communities, and curbs on petty jobberies. Criminal laws were reformed and immigrants' settlement was better regulated. Sound foundations were laid for Canada's economic future. Laws were passed for completion of the Welland Canal, setting up lighthouses, improvement of St. Lawrence navigation and for building highways and bridges. Competent engineering attention to needs of navigation on Lake Ontario dates from this period. Her Majesty's government guaranteed a loan of £1,500,000 for public works. Annual appropriations of $200,000 were set up to establish a common-school system for which a chief superintendent was to be named for United Canada with assistants in each of the two provinces. Sydenham wished also to establish a national bank to issue notes, but private banks crushed that proposal.

Enormous as these achievements were, Sydenham's tenure of office, like the Earl of Durham's, was short. On August 28, 1841, Lord

Sydenham wrote a properly enthusiastic summary of his record in office. A few days later, while exercising, he fell from his horse and suffered a fractured leg which developed infection. Nervously run down by overwork, he failed to rally and died on September 19, 1841, happy in the delusion that he had solved Canada's problem. True, he had partially solved it by replacing confusion with order. However, he had either missed the great essential or had not sensed its importance. What Canada needed, wanted and would eventually get was responsibility of government to the people. Though he had followed Durham's lead as clearly as was given him to see the course, Sydenham had not met, analyzed and isolated the element required to guarantee progress in a New World pattern.

Specifically what Ontario reformers wanted most at the moment was the British type of parliamentary control, executive responsibility through a party cabinet responsible to an elected legislature. As governor Sydenham would not accept this view, and honestly believed that its adoption would loosen Britain's hold on Canada. Analysis of his administration reveals that his conception of colonial government remained that of beneficent but autocratic power lodged in a Crown representative, for whom an elected assembly would be no more than a rubber stamp. Like most strong rulers of his era, this benefactor of Ontario could not bring himself to trust the people.

Lord Sydenham's dust lies under the floor of St. George's Church in Kingston, and over it might well be engraved, "Here lies one who ruled justly a land in sore need of justice until he came."

The next to govern Britain's North American holdings was Sir Charles Bagot, a mild Tory who had been British minister to the United States after the War of 1812. In 1817, Acting Secretary of State Rush at Washington signed the famous Rush-Bagot treaty of enduring friendship. Under its terms the nations agreed to limit ships of war and their armaments on border waterways, a provision immensely helpful in safeguarding peace.

Bagot began his duties in January 1842. He had inherited an inflammable political mixture made up of hot Tories, lukewarm Tories who called themselves Liberals, and mild democrats and home-rulers of the sort Bagot called "radicalissimus." Wary of kindling a bonfire with some chance spark of indiscretion, he spent some months in Lower Canada listening to French grievances and believed he had found a way toward harmony. In September 1842 he met the Legislature at Kingston and proposed that Lafontaine, the Quebec leader, and two of his compatriots in the assembly join the Governor's Council. Lafontaine declined. He and Baldwin, in accord, controlled a Liberal majority in the assembly and thought they could force Bagot to grant cabinet government on the British model.

Bagot faced a dilemma. To yield to the French would arouse Tory ire in both London and Kingston. To assume dictatorship would be futile against an Assembly majority which controlled appropriations and legislation. He determined to plunge toward progress and, braving reactionary wrath abroad and at home, he asked Lafontaine to co-operate with Baldwin in forming a ministry. By means of Bagot's reluctant but daring decision, Canada acquired a cabinet at last, headed by a French Canadian. At his back was a safe working Liberal majority of French and English in the Assembly. By Ontario's shore in gray-stoned Kingston, once the wildwood fortress of Frontenac, a people's victory had been won that would benefit all future British colonial policy. To Bagot it meant political martyrdom, self-chosen in advance.

Wholesale excoriation followed Bagot's act of decision. Old Family Compact newspapers shrieked that he had tossed the British to the talons of the French rabble. They dubbed him a radical, an apostate, an old woman. Tories taunted Lafontaine as an ex-rebel who had fled Canada with Papineau.

Bagot found comfort in the truth that he had reconciled Lower Canada to the Union idea. But the strain of crisis and conflict sapped his strength. On November 18 he wrote the Colonial Secretary's office that he was likely to die at his post, and die he did at Kingston on May 19, 1843. Too late to bring Sir Charles comfort on this earth, Britain's Secretary of State for the Colonies approved his courageous sponsoring of a more unified government.

Bagot's successor, Sir Charles Theophilus Metcalfe, had been born in India, and at twenty-six he entered upon a brilliant career there in the course of which he decisively stamped out both the slave trade and sutteeism, the custom of widows burning themselves atop their husbands' funeral pyres. After ruling Hindus with a firm hand for thirty-seven years, he retired and sailed to England in 1838. There Sir Charles espoused the Liberal cause, endorsed free trade and favored vote by ballot and widening of the franchise privilege.

This extraordinary person was about to stand for Parliament as a Liberal when he was induced to continue in colonial affairs. After experience in Jamaica he was sent on to Canada to succeed the dying Bagot, and reached Kingston by way of the United States in January 1843. Apparently Sir Charles had left his new-found Liberalism in England and reverted to despotic Indian practice. He scowled in disapproval at a Cabinet claiming power after the English model, and asserted that he had been sent to Canada to rule, not to advise.

With that, the pendulum swung backward and what Bagot had painfully erected seemed lost. Troubles developed swiftly between the new, arrogant, "rule or ruin" governor and his refractory counselors. Lafontaine refused to truckle to him. On November 26, 1843, the Liberal ministry resigned in protest against appointments made by the governor without ministerial approval.

In April 1844 the government was transferred to Montreal. Kingston lacked sufficient accommodations and conservatively refused to grow to desirable capital size. Montreal, a political hotbed, had a population of 40,000, about equally divided in religion, language and political opinion. There Metcalfe with difficulty formed a cabinet headed by William Henry Draper, but on September 23 Metcalfe dissolved his parliament with an appeal to the Canadian electorate in which he savagely raked the Liberals.

In the new election thus precipitated, the governor saw himself as St. George fighting a dragon body "of disloyal men who wished to break the tie with Britain." Even Ryerson, the Methodist leader, swallowed his beliefs and yielded to Metcalfe. Metcalfe won the election by a small margin and was rewarded with a barony. In Lower Canada the French raged against him, and on second thought the Tories of both provinces began to question the wisdom of his brusque denial of self-government. Metcalfe's victory was a hollow one. Wasted and half-blinded with cancer, he returned to England in the autumn of 1845. Within nine months he was in his grave.

A certain young lawyer, newly elected from Kingston as a Tory, had studiously refrained from endorsing Metcalfe's dictatorial views. Even at the modest outset of his memorable career, John Alexander Macdonald believed Canada had the right to govern herself. Brought to Canada from Glasgow in 1820 when he was five years old and

reared at Kingston, the immigrant lad lived to become a chief architect of modern Ontario and Canada. In his young manhood the
future master of political federation and material progress saw clearly
the path toward growth. Later, with shrewdness and vigor, he followed courses which, though cynically devious at times, won him
place among the Dominion's immortals.

In England the political whirligig brought to the post of Prime
Minister Lord John Russell, a friend to Canada, with Earl Grey as
Colonial Secretary. Now was written "finis" to Britain's outmoded
colonial system as applied to Canada. Grey, believing in Canadians'
ability to govern themselves, replaced Cathcart with James Bruce,
Earl of Elgin. It was soon evident that he had arrived at an opportune time for Canada.

The elections of January 1848 swept into office the Liberals, now
self-styled Reformers. Again Lafontaine became Premier, with Baldwin as his English colleague. Together they practiced a moderate
Liberalism. Now, after the stormy years of former regimes, Elgin's
ministers were invested with real power and harmony reigned between them and the Governor's House.

When Sir Edmund Head succeeded Lord Elgin, he entered upon a
governor general's post whose duties functioned from a democratic
base. No longer could the representative of the Crown assume an
open lead in politics. Rule by cabinet directly responsible to the electorate had become a securely established principle beyond challenge.
Where to lodge this responsible government of the people, where to
sit, plan and legislate for Canada's good, had become an acute problem. As a permanent capital Kingston had proved too small, Montreal too disorderly. Toronto was then too English and too far west.
Quebec was too French and too far east. A trial was made of having
Parliament sit at Toronto four years and then four years in Quebec
while government offices remained in Montreal, but this proved to
be an awkward arrangement and both Toronto and Quebec were held
to be too vulnerable in event of war.

At last Queen Victoria was asked to choose a permanent capital
site. Taking counsel of those who knew the country, she selected
Ottawa in Upper Canada, just across the Ottawa River from Lower
Canada. The eminent historian Goldwin Smith described the community as "a lumber-village, nearest to the North Pole," but Ottawa

has since become a solid, dignified and impressive capital city.

With removal of the Canadian capital from Lake Ontario's shore, the political development is less appropriate to this book, but Macdonald's leading role in federation and his career in general have meaning for his home region.

During these two administrations some momentous questions between the United States and Britain were decided amicably. Among these was the determination of the international boundary after long negotiations between Baron Ashburton and Daniel Webster, the American Secretary of State, in 1842. The boundary through Lake Ontario offered no considerable difficulties, but there were problems in Maine and elsewhere. Between them, Webster and Ashburton settled the boundary which now runs from the Bay of Fundy to the borders of Manitoba. A later negotiation amicably settled a serious controversy over the boundary line to the Pacific.

When Parliament first met at Ottawa in 1866 some threatening events were in the making. Ever since the United States plunged into civil war in 1861, there had been friction between America and Britain. English newspapers complained of "Canadian apathy" toward defense at a time when American military power was expanding. Although the two governments remained at peace, some unsettled veterans of the Civil War, especially groups of blustering Irishmen, whipped up a strong anti-British feeling that flared into violence on the border in 1866. Between 1866 and 1871 the Fenian Movement gathered together bands of these men to try several abortive but disturbing "invasions" of Canada.

Canada, too, was in an expanding mood. Union had joined together Upper and Lower Canada, or Ontario and Quebec as we know them today, but had left out Nova Scotia, New Brunswick, Prince Edward Island and Newfoundland. A movement to bring them in came to a head in the 1864 session at Quebec. On October 10 of that year delegates met at Quebec from all six provinces, where Macdonald of Kingston gave promise of future greatness by inducing valuable concessions to the principle of federal authority. Parliament considered these resolutions in January 1865. Both houses ratified strongly, but difficulty arose in the unrepresented provinces, so the indispensable Macdonald was sent to London. Newfoundland did not approve the federation proposal and never did come in, but the other three provinces eventually accepted the plan for federation.

These preliminaries to Canada's modern and larger phase embraced a rechristening of the realm significant in its implications. The original draft of the vast setup employed the proud phrase "Kingdom of Canada." Framing the empowering act, the powers in London substituted the word "Dominion." No slap at Canada was implied, nor any rebuke for assumed presumptuousness. What the Lords feared was possible resentment in the United States, were the word "kingdom" allowed to stand.

The British North America Act of March 29, 1867, provided for four provinces: Ontario, Quebec, Nova Scotia and New Brunswick. Ontario and Quebec were to be represented by twenty-four senators each, the other provinces by twelve each. Commons had 181 members—eighty-two for Ontario, sixty-five for Quebec, nineteen for Nova Scotia and fifteen for New Brunswick. Every male British subject of twenty-one years or more was allowed to vote, if he was a householder.

Federation was proclaimed at Ottawa on July 1, 1867. The first day of July has since then been observed as a public holiday in Canada. Macdonald headed the first Dominion cabinet.

Strong, bold and resourceful in Canada's movement toward federation was George Brown, a fighting Scot and Liberal leader who helped his father found the famous newspaper, the Toronto *Globe,* which in 1943 celebrated its hundredth milestone as the *Globe and Mail.* Puritanical in outlook and fearless in attack, Brown had long fought from Toronto the political purposes of Macdonald, another notable Ontarian. However, ardent Federalist Brown threw his strength to Macdonald for the grouping of the provinces. Then he resumed his onslaughts upon Sir John's political philosophy. Brown was murdered in 1880 by a printer he had dismissed.

With Federation won, Macdonald began his long, able leadership in the larger frame of Dominion affairs. He proved to be a master empire-builder, bringing two alien peoples together to work for the growth and glory of Canada. The Kingston lawyer grew large in statesmanship, and facile in the uglier, practical field of politics. He foresaw the opportunities ahead for the vast, raw country.

An imperative problem lay in the West, where wild lands were fur-trading preserves of the Hudson's Bay Company. Appeals to London resulted in the company's title being extinguished in 1869, opening the north country to settlement and mineral development.

Through the years Macdonald the idealist became a practical politician to the point of cynicism. In 1873 he lost the confidence of the House of Commons after a public scandal and retired as Prime Minister. This enforced retirement followed disclosure that Macdonald and another had accepted in the government's behalf some $400,000 with which to carry an election. No personal taint was involved, and the fate of the Canadian Pacific Railway had been at stake.

Macdonald was a private member for five years. The government remained unimaginative and resourceless, while Sir John from "obscurity" urged a novel program for encouragement of small, diversified industries to balance the lopsided pursuit of agriculture throughout the Dominion. In the 1878 elections Macdonald was returned to power over Alexander Mackenzie by a large majority. He remained Prime Minister through the thirteen remaining years of his life.

Sir John's course met the economic needs of a young country. He was never sure of Ontario, his own stamping ground and the most thickly populated of the provinces. So for the 1882 election Macdonald outwitted his Liberal foes by gerrymandering Ontario constituencies. Ruthlessly, Sir John juggled boundaries and ridings with such skill that he won the election that year and the succeeding elections in 1887. Again in 1891 he was successful, the Conservatives being backed by manufacturers and business interests. But, old and worn, he broke under the strain. He died at Ottawa on June 6, 1891, after a stroke of paralysis.

Sir Wilfrid Laurier, while condemning Macdonald's cold-blooded political methods, pronounced him "Canada's foremost citizen and statesman" and condensed the reasons for his great rival's supremacy into these words:

"He had the supreme art of governing men. The fact that he could congregate together elements the most heterogeneous and blend them into one compact party, and to the end of his life keep them steadily under his hand, is perhaps unprecedented."

In the judgment of leading Canadian and American historians the Canada of today and the Ontario which is the heart of Canada's industry and transportation are in no small part creations of Sir John Alexander Macdonald, sometime of the sturdy gray city of Kingston whose roots go back to the great Frontenac.

# Part III

## SHORE JOURNEY

## Chapter 17

# The Eastern Corner and Oswego

*Three leagues from Choüégen [Oswego] I sent three Wampum belts to notify the Nontagué [Onondaga] Chiefs to meet me. . . . On the arrival of the Nontagués at my tent, they told me, on the part of the Commandant at Choüégen, that as I was passing his place on public business, I must fire the first salute and lower my flag. . . . On the day of our departure it was the same tune. This I would not do; therefore no salute on the one side or the other. . . . I reproached the Nontagués with their weakness. . . . They answered—You're right, Father, but you know we have to use every sort of management here. . . .*
*—Report of the Voyage of M. de la Chauvignerie,*
*Interpreter of the Five Iroquois Nations*

THE uninformed traveler traversing long stretches of the "York State" portion of Lake Ontario's shore line would gain the idea that the Empire State was more agrarian than industrial. It is, of course, important in both ways, but agriculture would never have given the state its present dominant position.

In the first years after the Revolution the state was only seventh in population. Land and water transportation development and harnessing water power started the process which makes the state today lead the Union in population, though its area is but twenty-ninth among the forty-eight states. In value of agricultural products New York ranks seventh. It produces some fourteen percent of the nation's manufactured products, operates eighteen percent of all our manufacturing establishments and employs about twelve percent of all the industrial workers in the United States.

Yet the stranger boating from Cape Vincent, New York—where the St. Lawrence River begins—westward along the south shore of the lake would swiftly assume that York State was mostly given over to orchards and farms. Except for Oswego and Rochester, the shore would present an almost unbroken succession of rural and resort scenes.

Cape Vincent guards the New York side of the St. Lawrence outlet. Clayton and Alexandria Bay are the trading and transportation centers for the Thousand Islands Region, with Clayton the American terminus for the leading ferry to Kingston, which provides the hurried traveler with an easy way of sampling the unique beauties of that crowded journey. Another ferry route—Cape Vincent to Kingston—is broken by a seven-mile drive across Wolfe Island.

Off Clayton is Rock Island Light, the final refuge for one of America's most controversial characters. William (Bill) Johnston was born at Three Rivers in Lower Canada in 1782. His family removed to Ontario Province two years later. In 1812 he was a grocer near Kingston connected with a military company. Arrested for insubordination he broke from jail and fled to the York State shore to begin his career of reprisals against Britain. As a spy for America he once robbed the British mail of official dispatches which he delivered to Sackets Harbor. Following the Battle of the Windmill, Johnston was captured on November 17, 1838, and jailed in Auburn. Escaping, he was retaken and imprisoned in Albany. Another jailbreak ushered in a merry chase by civil officers. These Johnston successfully dodged. His lurid and not always believable tales highlighted his past. Although he was a scoundrel from youth to old age, the government appointed him keeper of Rock Island Light in the St. Lawrence waters. Its ray lighted the spot off Wells Island where the British steamer *Sir Robert Peel* was boarded and burned in the night of May 29, 1838, by the men painted like Indians whom Johnston led.

Cape Vincent's founders, the LeRays de Chaumont, planned the community as a commercial rival to Kingston, directly across the wide headwaters of the St. Lawrence, but this part of their vision was never realized. Cape Vincent is still small, lovely and peaceful, a resort in the quiet, respectable manner of the Thousand Islands, with a healthy reputation among fishermen for proximity to muskellunge, largemouthed bass and lake trout.

During the 1830's Cape Vincent enjoyed more trade than small Buffalo, yet in 1943 it cleared barely more than fifty tons of foodstuff and 75,000 tons of wood, paper and pulpwood. Its failure to develop industrially is perhaps typical of a dozen small ports on either side of the lake. But Cape Vincent finds a profitable business in its tourists.

Cape Vincent village was a noted center for French émigrés. It takes its name from Vincent, son of James Donatien LeRay de Chaumont, a French nobleman whose father had put much of his fortune into the American cause during the Revolution, both by generous loans and by assisting Benjamin Franklin with abundant hospitality at Passy. The son came to America in 1785 to present claims for reimbursement which Congress settled in 1790. Another of our envoys to France, Gouverneur Morris, interested LeRay de Chaumont in the North Country. To his surprise Morris discovered that the French nobles, instead of resenting trees as most American frontiersmen did, were entranced with the prospect of having their American châteaux surrounded by the forest. In 1802 LeRay bought thousands of acres in the present Jefferson and Lewis Counties. His family arrived from France six years later. LeRay developed his holdings by building mills and furnaces. Agriculture he encouraged by promoting improved methods and importing blooded animals from France. His pillared house at LeRaysville, built in 1822 and still standing in the Pine Plains military reservation, has been described as one of the best Georgian houses in America. It is a queer turn of fate which brought this once-French property into a military program destined to rescue the native land of its former owner.

The LeRaysville home and the mansion he built for his son Vincent at Cape Vincent are both show places of the region. Vincent's house is still a private home.

A third and more famous structure of French origin was the Cup and Saucer House which was burned in 1867. Its name arose from its quaint shape—octagonal with a rounded roof and cupola. All living and sleeping rooms were on the first floor. The upper floor contained only two large rooms intended to house the banished Emperor Napoleon Bonaparte by the French émigrés who flocked to the side of the hospitable Count de Chaumont when they were forced to flee from France. The émigré group included some notable persons but the LeRays de Chaumont suffered greatly in pocket from the excess of hospitality extended to impoverished compatriots.

A daughter of the LeRays, Thérèse de Gouvelle, brought with her in 1816 the talented Madame la Baronne de Ferriet, whose name lives on in Deferiet, a village now given over to the manufacture of paper. Her grand house, the Hermitage, burned in 1840, was a pleasant stopover for Joseph Bonaparte, Prince Charles Lucien and others. But this mannered lady strongly disapproved of Joseph's nephew, Prince Lucien Murat, bad boy of the transplanted aristocrats, whom she considered a disgrace to France because of his gaming, quarreling and drinking.

Vincent LeRay maintained a sales office at Cape Vincent to dispose of acreage that his father opened to settlement as successive clearings were sheared from the forest and townships were set up. Land which in 1792 had been valued at from two to three dollars an acre sold in 1800 for a dollar an acre profit. This increase brought on general selling and speculation as others followed the LeRay lead.

In all important respects this admirable French family greatly affected the development of the region. The family policy was consistently helpful to settlers in the matters of prices, deeds, assistance in hard times and avoidance of foreclosures. It would be pleasant to record that this considerate attitude brought its just reward, but fortune turned. Completion of the Erie Canal depressed North Country land prices and stopped sales as more arable and open western lands opened to settlement. Migrating New Englanders passed through the North Country and kept going. Practically all the various French plans, whether for settlements or speculation, were blasted. LeRay was forced to seek advantage of the insolvent act and to turn over the following holdings to his son Vincent, in trust for his creditors:

| | | | |
|---|---|---|---|
| In Franklin County | 30,758 | acres valued at | $ 22,500 |
| In St. Lawrence County | 78,947 | acres valued at | 106,000 |
| In Jefferson County | 143,500 | acres valued at | 574,000 |
| In Lewis County | 100,000 | acres valued at | 133,000 |
| Total | 348,205 | | $835,500 |

Hough's *History of Jefferson County* says that 18,000 LeRay acres in that county were then subject to settlers' contracts, and contained three gristmills, three sawmills and various clearings with buildings. At LeRaysville the family gristmill and storehouses were valued at $26,000. There were other valuable LeRay properties in Otsego County, New York, in Pennsylvania and in France.* Steady-going son Vincent so managed affairs that he satisfied all American claims

* Franklin B. Hough, M. D., *History of Jefferson County* (Albany, 1854), p. 60.

in full, and let us hope he had something left over to reward this sterling French family for its pioneer work in developing one of Lake Ontario's fairest corners. Time and again New York history reveals losses by big landlords with creative programs.

Fortunately the LeRay prestige and leadership survived this financial shock. It is to James LeRay that this part of New York owes its early start in raising blooded livestock. The Jefferson County Agricultural Society was formed in 1817 with LeRay as president and Jacob Brown as first vice-president.

The first cattle show and fair of the Jefferson County Society occurred at Watertown in 1818, with Governor Clinton and General Stephen Van Rensselaer as guests. At Albany in 1832 LeRay was chosen President of the pioneer State Agricultural Society which aimed "to improve the condition of agriculture, horticulture and other household arts." In 1833 the Jefferson County Society memorialized the Legislature to encourage the formation of county societies, and LeRay's name led the list of sponsors.

The family name of nobility, Chaumont, lives in the village and bay of Chaumont, also in the slang name for Lake Ontario whitefish or ciscoes, which are still locally known as "Chaumont currency." For forty years after the close of the War of 1812, Chaumont shipped barreled ciscoes to all parts of the country, and on that shore the fish often passed as legal tender.

The headlands guarding Chaumont Bay were the rendezvous where Montcalm's fleet picked up his advance force under De Villiers, which had been harrying the approaches to Oswego. Searchers on Point Peninsula may still trace outlines of a fortification which in its day was a considerable post protected by a stockade of short timbers. Here 500 soldiers and boatmen were encamped in the grim year of 1756, when Oswego fell easy prey to the French marshal.

A more famous Frenchman came to the North Country in Chaumont's wake, not to build up the country, but for speculation, vacation and romantic love. This visitor was Joseph Bonaparte, favorite brother of Napoleon, former King of Naples and of Spain. Settled in exile at Bordentown, New Jersey, Joseph acquired a large tract of lake-studded forest land that at points touched Lake Ontario. Jour-

neying with his retinue by stagecoach over the new, rude roads from
his New Jersey estate, he aroused a local poet to this effusion:

> "Here he forgot La Granja's glades,
>    Escurial's dark and gloomy dome,
> And sweet Sorrento's deathless shades
>    In his far-off secluded home:
>
> "Brother of him whose charmed sword
>    Clove or created kingdoms fair,
> Whose faith in him was as the word
>    Writ in the Memlook's scimiter."*

Joseph Bonaparte bought from James LeRay de Chaumont 150,000
acres of land for $120,000 worth of diamonds and real estate. This
tall timber transaction, covering four townships, bred in some Gallic
minds a dream of another wholesale aristocratic French settlement
in America. By legislative act in Albany during 1825, Count de Sur-
villiers (the name Joseph Bonaparte used in America) was authorized
to hold lands in New York State "without his promising or expecting
to become a citizen."

Although an ardent huntsman, Joseph did not come north to explore his lands for several years. The town of Diana, formed from
Watson in 1830, was named in deference to his wishes in honor of
the pagan goddess of the chase. Four times he paid summer visits
to his holdings, flinging largesse in a prodigal way which endeared
him to the populace, who considered their "Joe Nap" a true democrat
as well as a good spender. He had roads cut to Lake Bonaparte, a
body of water of 1,200 acres he owned in Lewis County. On the
high ground of his property he had a new log house erected and a
summerhouse at the outlet of the lake where the village of Alpina
now stands. He built another house at Natural Bridge in Jefferson
County, with walls bored for gunsights commanding the Utica trail
in case his European enemies came prowling. Always Joseph, during
his years in America, took pains to keep his erstwhile royal self well
guarded. His lady fair, a Quakeress from New Jersey, had a daugh-

---

* This poem, from the pen of Caleb Lyon, poet of Lyonsdale, New York, appeared
near the mid-1800's under the title of "Bonaparte Lake" in the Louisville *Journal* and
was extensively reprinted in the press throughout the United States.

ter who lived most of her life at near-by Oxbow. It is said that Joseph's granddaughter was accepted by Napoleon III and the Empress Eugénie at the imperial court, and became a lady in waiting to Her Majesty.

North Country folk often repeat Joe Nap's words in his reported refusal of the throne of Mexico: "I have been happier on this little lake . . . than I ever was in Spain or probably ever would be in Mexico."

In 1835 John La Farge bought for $80,000 Survilliers' remaining interests in Lewis and Jefferson Counties, after Joseph had sold some other parcels, mainly to Frenchmen. The tracts were then swiftly settled by New Englanders. After Joseph's sale to La Farge, the unfinished house at the lake outlet rotted, the log house on the hill was lost by fire and the house at Natural Bridge was torn down by an unimaginative buyer to incorporate the material in another structure used as a general store. Bonaparte's intentions toward the North Country never seem to have been as serious as those of LeRay and some other Frenchmen interested in Lake Ontario lands.

While most of the French nobles were easy spenders, John La Farge earned the hatred of his tenants. The last of his homes—the great stone house built in 1833 a mile south of LeRaysville—was rated the finest residence in the North Country in its day. After only four years of family use it was abandoned, and for a time served as an early Catholic seminary in the state. That project failed because of the remoteness of the site. Today only one ruined wing of the house remains, but the La Farge family continues creative in the fine arts.

Another ambitious Gallic enterprise in this region was the French company organized to handle the Chassanis Tract of Castorland, Lewis County. This holding of 210,000 acres, containing valuable timber and water-power sites, was sold on April 12, 1793, by William Constable to Peter Chassanis of Paris for £25,000. Rodolphe Tillier, agent of Chassanis, was instructed to "solicit from the State the opening of roads and canals with headquarters at Castorland." No measure toward canalizing the northern counties was proposed, however, until 1825, when two surveys were run from the Erie to the headwaters of Black River and thence to Ogdensburg. The ruins of some of the well-masoned locks of this Black River canal are still to be seen.

The Black, draining the wet western side of the Adirondacks, is now a mighty power stream. It enters the lake at Dexter, an industrial village. Rather quaintly, Dexter claims the first Civil War monument erected after the close of the conflict.

Immediately above Dexter is Brownville, founded by Quaker brothers, of whom Jacob rose to deserved military fame. General Brown's excellent house still stands, but his grave is in Washington, where he died in 1828. This inconvenient fact paralyzes efforts to make Brownville a shrine to the memory of this noble man. For a time Brownville seemed likely to become the big town of the region. Now it has only a few small paper mills, and its neighbor, Watertown, has left it far behind.

In 1799 Henry Coffeen and Zachariah Butterfield visited the future site of Watertown, the "Garland City," and bought its heavily timbered lands for their farms. In 1800 they trekked in with their families from Schuyler, Oneida County, and wasting little time in preliminary agriculture, founded the village of Watertown. Today, with 33,323 population, Watertown is a summer gateway to the Thousand Islands and the Adirondacks, in addition to being the section's leading trading and industrial center.

The Black River bisects the city and, with its 112 feet of falls within the corporate limits, provides power for some sixty industries. Manufactures include paper, air brakes, plumbing supplies, thermometers and surgical instruments. The factories stem from original sawmills and gristmills run by rude water wheels.

The world's first sleeping cars were built in the late 1850's almost simultaneously by Theodore Woodruff of Watertown and Webster Wagner, ticket agent at Palatine Bridge, New York. Subsequent deals merged these models with the later Pullman sleeping car, whose backers read the future aright. With a little better foresight Watertown might have made a fortune in sleeping cars.

Another Watertown idea panned out supremely well. The Woolworth Building, Public Square and Arsenal Street, carries a tablet about a local boy who made good in a very big way. In 1878 Frank W. Woolworth, a clerk in a general store on that site, secured permission to pile a table with stock leftovers topped by a sign "ANY ARTICLE 5¢." Everybody bought. Sure of his big idea, Woolworth opened a store in Utica the next year, and followed with one in Pennsylvania. Both the Woolworth chain and Woolworth himself kept growing. Literally, he invented a system of distributing cheap merchandise which has greatly affected the national economy.

Arsenal Street, named for the arsenal erected there before the War of 1812, leads from Watertown to Sackets Harbor, eleven miles westward. That way went ammunition for Chauncey's fleets and Brown's armies.

Along the broken shore line stretch a succession of bays and promontories that provided lookouts during the War of 1812 when strict watch was kept for expected forays from Kingston. Such names as Grenadier Island and Guffin's Bay possess historic significance scarcely indicated by their present quiet. On a calm summer Sunday from the white-steepled church at Sackets a bell resounds across rippling blue waters, but he who dodges church to go boating may not see a human being on the shore for miles at a stretch, unless it is the season for a fish run. Sackets Harbor, still a military post, occupies many pages in this record. Its founder was Augustus Sacket, a lawyer born in New York City in 1769. In 1801, having purchased land in the town of Houndsfield, he began the settlement. Planning to ease the hardships of pioneering with the fees of public office, he became first collector and first judge of his own settlement. But it proved too quiet for Judge Sacket, who sold his property in 1809 and departed, only to return in 1820 for a second pull of seven years. He died in 1827 at Albany—"came out minus fortune," as his biographer says. The Augustus Sacket home built in 1801 stands on Main Street in the village.

Madison Barracks occupies the east village line of Sackets Harbor. This United States Army post accommodates forty-five officers and 1,040 enlisted men in rows of brick and stone barracks and officers' dwellings. The solid structures frame an oval parade ground. As at Niagara, Uncle Sam picked for his purposes a pleasant waterside location more appreciated by the troops in summer than in winter.

Both Grant and Pershing did tours of duty at Madison Barracks. Grant brought his bride there after their honeymoon in the autumn of 1848, stayed about six months, then went to Detroit for two years and returned to Sackets in the spring of 1851 for a year's stay. Twenty years later, as President, he visited the Harbor and was joyously received.

The most influential of Sackets' citizens in more recent times were the successive heads of the Camp family, who owned the newspaper and had their fingers in all regional projects. The best known of the later Camps was Walter, a famous Yale athlete, sports writer and father of the thriving idea of All-American football elevens.

Here at Sackets in March 1817 was launched the 170-ton steamship *Ontario,* the first American steamship built on the Great Lakes. Although launched later than the Canadian *Frontenac* of Kingston, the *Ontario* beat her rival to the honor of taking the first long voyage.

Sackets Harbor still figures commercially as a port with controlling depth nine feet, project depth twelve feet. Her 1940 navigation season opened May 28 and closed October 7.

South of Watertown and Sackets Harbor dairy farms thrive on the prime pasturage bestowed by dependable rainfall. Here a west wind brings moisture even when no rain falls. The shore begins to show vistas of amusement parks and recreation grounds. The lakeside village of Henderson Harbor is noted for its bass fishing. There hotels, rambling inns and cottages overlook Horse Island in Henderson Bay. During the War of 1812 American sharpshooters were detailed for duty in the village and successfully balked British attempts to reach the mainland from Horse Island.

An anonymous poet of this indented shore has given us this treasure:

"Green are thy waters—green as bottle glass;
  Behold them streched thar!
Fine muscolunges and Oswego bass
  Is often catch'd thar;
Onst the red Indian here took delights,
  Fish'd, fit and bled—
Now the inhabitants is mostly whites,
  And nary red."

Among other lakeside resorts are Port Ontario and Selkirk Shores State Park. Then comes the long sweep past Mexico Bay and Sandy Creek.

In the town of Mexico, where Big Sandy Creek enters the lake, are remains of quite extensive fortifications, apparently too massive to have been made by the rather small Indian nations known to have resided there, and too ancient to belong to the white phase whose records, fairly complete, reveal no such extensive settlements and works. In 1802 the Reverend John Taylor, a Congregational missionary, visited, measured and sketched these works, also others near Watertown. His observations, which threw the good man "in a wilderness of conjecture" and will do the same for any reader, have been preserved in the *Documentary History of New York*.

From its simple beginnings as an open-air fur market in an untenanted wilderness, Oswego has been a pivot for water-borne commerce. In early days the nation that held Oswego bestrode a trade route practicable for light colonial merchandise all the way from Manhattan to Niagara. Oswego was the first, and for many years the only, British port on the Great Lakes.

In May 1725, when M. de Longueuil* reconnoitered the location for the French army, he found plenty of British trading activity but no trading post built as yet.

From Oswego De Longueuil proceeded to the chief Onondaga village, addressed the Iroquois chiefs in council and secured their consent to two French vessels on Ontario and recognition of the French right to erect the "stone house" fort or citadel at Niagara, which was finished in 1726. It was to balance this fortification at Niagara that the British pressed for equivalent rights at Oswego.

In the same year Governor Burnet with Iroquois consent dispatched workmen to build "a stone house of strength" at Oswego, and soon hurried forward three officers with sixty soldiers to prevent interruption from the French. A French account, written while the little fort christened Fort Oswego was being built, notes that seventy English and Dutch traders' cabins had already arisen on the shore.

Governor Burnet figured that building Fort Oswego was a master stroke to check the French advance, keep the Iroquois under John Bull's hand and promote barter with Indians from the West. It is likewise approved by history as a coup of fateful influence toward the final ousting of French sovereignty from mid-America.

In 1740 Acting Governor Clarke had to call upon the colonial

---

* The Barony de Longueuil, which dates from 1657, is described as the sole existing hereditary title of the French regime in Canada. At one time its boundaries included 250 square miles.

Assembly to renovate the fort, which had fallen into disrepair. He wrote, "The peace and happiness of the plantations, and the trade of England, if not the very being of His Majesty's dominions on this continent, depend on the holding of Oswego." The Assembly voted £600 ($1,500 in New York currency at that time) to erect a stone wall around "the trading-house at Oswego"—a circumlocution to save Iroquois pride—with a bastion or blockhouse in each corner.

About that time (1743) John Bartram, a pioneer naturalist from Pennsylvania, journeyed for scientific observations to Lake Ontario's south shore.* While botanizing at Oswego he observed a graveyard near the castle, or trading place, which reminded him "that the neighborhood of this Lake is esteemed unhealthful." From a trader he bought some dried beef and a gallon of rum, and left for Oswego Falls where they tried to sleep the night with indifferent success. "The Indian squaws got very drunk, and made a sad noise till morning."

Bartram described the fort, or "trading castle," as built of stone enclosed by a stone wall almost twenty feet high and 120 paces around. The big squared stones of the wall were oddly soft; he carved his name on one with his knife. The community held some seventy log cabins, half in a row near the river, the others standing irregularly opposite them. The officer in command at the castle was at great pains to protect the Indians from rapacious white traders, especially traders getting red men drunk to cheat them.

At the outbreak of King George's War in 1744 many traders, fearing Indian attacks from Canada, fled Oswego but the bolder spirits remained. The Peace of Aix-la-Chapelle restored Oswego's trade, and some shrewd French traders also came to Oswego, as they could buy English goods cheaper than French. Official French resentment at this "black market" operation was expressed by Abbé Picquet, head of the colony of Catholic Iroquois at Fort La Présentation (later Ogdensburg). Choueguen, he wrote, was a post pernicious to France, but he had to admit that the British and Dutch traders at Oswego sold goods to the Indians at a fourth of the price in furs that the French charged the red men at Niagara!

During these uneasy years, from the peace of 1748 to the next war,

---

* *Observations on the Inhabitants, Climate, Soil, Rivers, Productions, Animals, and other Matters worthy of notice, made by Mr. John Bartram, in his Travels from Pennsylvania to Onondaga, Oswego and Lake Ontario in Canada, 1751.*

the tiny Oswego fort never held more than a single company of regular soldiers as a garrison. In 1755, however, a second fort, known as Fort Ontario and still standing, was rushed through to completion, across the river from the old fort.

A little girl named Ann MacVicar, daughter of a Scots officer of the Fifty-fifth Regiment, played in the gardens of Fort Ontario when that durable pentagon was still young. To this precocious child, who as Mrs. Grant became one of Scotland's leading novelists, Oswego was then a dream of beauty clad in pure colors; at least so it seemed when she wrote reminiscently of the scene fifty years later in the *Memoirs of an American Lady,* which was published in 1808. The American Lady was "Aunt" Schuyler, widow of Colonel Philip Schuyler and aunt of the Revolutionary general of the same name. At her home on the Flats north of Albany, Mrs. Schuyler lavished hospitality which Ann MacVicar and her mother shared for a considerable period while Lieutenant MacVicar did frontier duty. Because of that kindness Aunt Schuyler lives forever in a delightful literary frame which also encloses a picture of old Oswego.

All was then peaceful on Ontario's shores. After drilling, the soldiers cultivated gardens in the wilderness and proudly showed their vegetables. The lake sparkled; meadows were deep in luxuriant grasses and wild flowers. Nuts and berries filled the woods; the parade ground, most remarkably, was red with strawberries. There was no need to hunt game; instead, it seemed as if game came to the hunter. Indians brought saddles of venison to the garrison to sell at a shilling each. Salmon by the thousands ascended the river, fins flashing in sunlight as they leaped the falls. "There was no need of doctors then; everybody was healthy. There used to be two or three years at a time without a funeral. There were no lawyers then, and no need of them; everybody was honest. Ah what happy times! What a beautiful, beautiful country!"

Old Oswego could excite the poetic fancy too. Alexander Wilson, ornithologist, walked from Philadelphia to Niagara via Oswego in 1804. One result of that journey was the long poem entitled "The Foresters," where Oswego is introduced thus:

> "Mark yon bleak hill where rolling billows break,
> Just where the River joins the spacious Lake."

High on the hill's brow the poet discerned, "deserted and forlorn," old Fort Oswego where winds howled to the restless surge below. The lone sentry of aforetime "heard a foe in every whooping owl." Wilson paints a picture of huts that straggled to the left of the harbor "where boats and ships their crowded masts uprear." Next comes a picture of vanished trading days:

> "But time and war have banished all their trains,
> And nought but potash, salt and rum remains.
> The boisterous boatman, drunk but twice a day,
> Begs of the landlord: but forgets to pay;
> Pledges his salt, a cask for every quart,
> Pleased thus for poison with his pay to part.
> From morn to night here noise and riot reign;
> From night to morn 'tis noise and roar again."

One of Oswego's prideful literary connections is with J. Fenimore Cooper, pioneer American historical novelist, on duty there in 1808 when Lieutenant Woolsey was in command. In *The Pathfinder* Cooper described "Station Island," of high strategic worth, otherwise unidentified but thought to be Carleton Island, a British base during the Revolution.

Not until the Stars and Stripes had been raised tardily to supplant the Union Jack did the weathered port seriously undertake to establish a stable community as distinct from transients—soldiers, sailors, traders and trappers. In 1796, when the old fort at Oswego unfurled its third flag, the Stars and Stripes, Neil McMullin arrived, bringing with him by canal and portage a house frame from Kingston, New York. This house was set up six years before the first sawmill was established in Oswego. If the transportation feat seems incredible, let it be recalled that in 1723 Cadwallader Colden, as truthful a man as ever saw New York, mentions the exportation of house frames ready to set up. No doubt McMullin's house traveled knocked-down.

Until the Erie Canal took the trade away, up to 30,000 barrels of Salina, or Syracuse, salt passed through Oswego each year on its way west to the salt-hungry prairies and frontier. One of Pittsburgh's early fortunes, that of General O'Hara, arose from Salina salt routed through Lake Ontario and the Niagara Portage, to Erie, Pennsylvania, then either by flatboat or wagon to Pittsburgh. From that point it found markets down the Ohio and Mississippi.

From 1819 until the 1850's schooners, brigs and sloops were built in considerable numbers. A boom in flour-milling, brewing, distilling and starch manufacture at Oswego followed the entry of cheap western farm products after the Welland Canal was opened. A traveler who thought the Oswego of his day worth a long count listed forty-two industrial establishments in 1835:

"Flouring mills with 29 runs of stone which manufactured in 1834 about 100,000 barrels of flour, one tannery, a morocco factory, one cotton factory having 1,500 spindles, a machine shop, two sawmills which sawed in 1834 about 3,000,000 feet of Canada red cedar for shingles, posts and railroad ties; 3 cabinet shops, 3 hat factories, one furnace, a stove foundry, 2 wagon shops, 2 watchmakers, one scythe and ax factory."*

This route naturally suffered through the opening of the Erie Canal, after which Oswego lost trade and Rochester gained the commercial leadership of Lake Ontario's southern shore. But other shifts in transportation facilities helped Oswego. Better connections between the Erie Canal and Lake Ontario were provided by the Oswego Canal, opened in 1838. The federal government undertook the improvement of Oswego Harbor by a series of breakwaters which, with various other federal and state works, have since made Oswego one of the safest harbors and most efficient canal terminals in the world.

An echo of the waning border troubles of the Patriots' War came in the incident of the British steamer *Great Britain* at Oswego on June 6, 1840. From that port a heavy trunk was smuggled aboard the craft. Laden with explosives, it promptly blew up, causing some casualties and starting a blaze which was soon extinguished. A pair of Canadian refugees, Lett and Defoe, taken into custody, confessed to a plan to burn the ship in the hope of renewing strain between the United States and Canada. They had placed in the trunk powder, turpentine, copal and nitre and a time fuse. Lett figured in the Cobourg Conspiracy described later; also in the daring escape of nine so-called Patriots from Fort Henry at Kingston and their rough crossing to Oswego by canoe.

---

* *An Industrial and Commercial Survey of Oswego and Vicinity* as prepared by the Oswego Chamber of Commerce, July 1942.

Oswego was still building ships in this period. The Navy launched there in 1844 the revenue cutter *Jefferson,* built of iron by Pittsburgh contractors on a novel design, steam-propelled by screw wheels astern for work in shallow waters as a threat to smugglers.

She mounted sixteen guns with one long 68-pounder swung on a pivot. Apparently not a success for the purpose planned, the *Jefferson* soon passed down the St. Lawrence for duty on the high seas.

Today the city, quadrupled in size since 1835, makes shades, shade cloth, Venetian blinds, foundry and machine work, matches, textiles, cardboard boxes, paper and paper bags, electric power and gas, food products, milling, dairy feeds. The principal products received and shipped are pulp, pulpwood, sugar, zinc, steel, scrap iron, sand, iron ore, soybeans, cement and copper; and these tonnages tend to increase. The cargoes of 650 vessels in 1941 were physically transferred in the Port of Oswego.

Transformation of the Erie Canal into the present New York State Barge Canal was completed in 1918. In fitting the waterway for steam and electric-propelled boats of more than 2,000-ton capacity, the eastern section of the "big ditch" was discarded and the Mohawk canalized. This brought a wide and deep waterway as far west as Rome portage. Similar treatment for the Oswego River and its connecting lake and river system, at a cost of $175,000,000, speeded Oswego shipping schedules. With good luck the 194 miles of canal between Oswego and Albany can be covered in a day and a half, and New York City—383 miles from Oswego—can be reached in another day. A Detroit motorized freighter regularly plies this route from its home port to Newark, New Jersey, in five and a half days, carrying soda ash and returning with soap. Diesel-electric boats, shallow-hulled and equipped with stacks that "duck down" at the bridges, even carry cargoes from Lake Superior to New York Harbor without transshipments. In 1939 the total barge tonnage was 4,689,037 tons, of which the Oswego branch furnished more than one-fourth.

Oswego Harbor is the most easterly United States lake port with canal and rail connections to the Atlantic seaboard. Thanks to massive breakwaters, the largest lake vessels can dock there without summoning pilots or tugs. Port facilities include a state grain elevator with storage for 1,000,000 bushels, and a freight warehouse with floor space of 12,000 square feet. Within the inner harbor is the terminus of the Barge Canal. Oswego Lock, modeled after the terminal lock of the Kiel Canal in Germany, is the only one in the United States which is operated on the siphon principle.

Just as competing Rochester proudly called itself "the Flour City," so Oswego was "the Starch City." Milling and processing close to the grain fields in the West and Northwest hurt both cities, but Oswego continues some activities in that line, though at a reduced pace.

Oswego is served by three railroad systems, the New York Central, the Delaware, Lackawanna & Western and the New York, Ontario & Western. The Central has three lines serving the Oswego area: a connection to the main line at Syracuse direct from Oswego; and lines east and west of Oswego paralleling the shore of the lake, east to the international boundary line and on to Montreal and Quebec; and west to the Niagara River and Buffalo. The Delaware, Lackawanna & Western and the New York, Ontario & Western are important to Oswego as the principal roads having access to the anthracite coal fields of Pennsylvania.

The city is definitely on the rise. Though in 1931 and 1932 business was generally subnormal, this port went ahead. Apparently the trend of thrifty commerce is toward Lake Ontario. Enlargement of the Welland Canal and development of harbors along Ontario's shores bore fruit even in bitter times. Employment of the all-water route now available to the entire Great Lakes system is working out particularly for Ontario's benefit as an eastern trade funnel.

Important to all shippers in the Great Lakes section is the spring opening of navigation. Ontario's southern shores are consistently free of ice some time before Buffalo's harbor opens. Yet Ontario enjoys a local seasonal priority. Her merchant craft can go to work each springtime a fortnight or more—sometimes a full month—before shipping in the ports of her sister lakes has freed itself from the ice. This advantage is most marked where the pull of the St. Lawrence current swings the ice floes to the north, leaving Oswego Harbor clear.

United States Weather Bureau records and annual reports covering the years from 1920 to 1924 give the following table, showing the dates when navigation opened in the spring:

*Ice Conditions*

| Season | At Oswego | At Buffalo | Welland Canal open to Navigation |
|---|---|---|---|
| 1920 | March 30—Harbor open | April 13—End of Lake Erie packed with ice although harbor reported open April 3 | April 19 |
| 1921 | No ice in Lake Ontario after early March | No ice in Lake Erie except small fields after early March | April 15 |
| 1922 | March 7 — Harbor open for lake navigation | April 1—Four steamers left port. Navigation reported open April 11 | April 17 |
| 1923 | March 29—Harbor free from ice. April 3 — Lake became free from ice | April 24—Harbor still closed by ice. Navigation opened April 9 but later suspended | April 17 |
| 1924 | April 1—No ice in lake or harbor | April 8—Ice field shows little change but is breaking up in places | April 16 |

Another factor that will increasingly benefit both Oswego and the whole south shore is the pool of available electric power. To the current provided by well-harnessed waterways has been added that of the Central New York Power Corporation's steam-generating plant in the West Harbor area. The plant, erected in 1939-1940, cost $17,000,000 and has 160,000 kilowatt hours' capacity at present, with more to come. Annual coal consumption is about 6,000,000 tons. Technical-minded visitors come to see one of the world's most efficient power-generating units, capable of producing one kilowatt hour of electricity for each 0.85 pounds of coal consumed. Two reasons are given for building this huge steam plant where it is: plenty of cold water for cooling the installations and good transportation from the coal fields.

The first unit of the great steam-generating plant started operating in September 1940, the second unit in June 1941. Eventually there will be five units. The current production rate for war purposes actually tops the 160,000 kwh normal capacity of the two units. The owning corporation—one of the so-called "Carlisle Powers"—also operates hydroelectric plants on the Oswego River within the city limits, under power rights obtained under long-term lease from Oswego City. Surplus current from both steam and hydroelectric sources is sent to other communities in central New York through a superpower hookup whose potentialities will be important in postwar development.

The United States Military Reservation, garrisoned by infantry units, contains old Fort Ontario, pentagonal in shape. No doubt this old fort and historic site will someday be as well known and as popular as old Fort Niagara. The present battalion post was laid out in 1905. During World War I the fort was used as a base hospital. World War II found the reservation employed first as an Army training camp, next as a clearing station for European refugees.

On the western edge of the city, its campus sweeping grandly down to Lake Ontario, stands Oswego State Teachers College, heir to a fine tradition in public education. At its entrance is a bronze statue of the founder, Edward Austin Sheldon, who established Oswego's first free school, called the "ragged school," in 1848, and in 1861 founded the Oswego Primary Training School, which became the State Normal Training School in 1866. Recently New York's State Normal Schools were changed to Teachers Colleges and empowered to grant degrees. Five hundred students are usually in attendance, and special attention is given to training teachers in branches connected with industrial design, management and service.

The "Oswego Movement," which Dr. Sheldon built up on the Pestalozzi base, became a strong influence on American education. His gifted daughter, Mrs. Mary Sheldon Barnes, one of the first women to graduate from a coeducational college, the University of Michigan, became the author of Sheldon's *General History,* for years a leading textbook.

Another educator was Oswego-born Dr. Mary Walker, an unusual woman who according to popular rumor wore pants by grace of a special act of Congress soon after the Civil War. One of the first feminine physicians in the United States, she served as a nurse with the Union Army. A hater of tobacco, Dr. Walker used sometimes to stalk through city streets clad in frock coat, striped trousers and silk hat, and knock glowing cigars from the lips of masculine smokers.

What a quandary the little doctor would be in today if she met a woman in slacks smoking cigarettes! In 1897 she founded a feminist colony which she called "Adamless Eden." Her eccentric performances may have been inspired by sex antagonism or staged for advertising purposes, but at any rate she triumphed—women do wear trousers, or slacks, and who cares?

Oswego today is a city with a past, present and future. A substantial historical society, a good newspaper, and a federal government somewhat alive to the stabilizing effects of history help to keep the past alive. All hands look out for the present. Nature, Uncle Sam and the State of New York seem to have provided well for a future. With any growth in Lake Ontario commerce, Oswego seems certain to find levels of prosperity and influence.

## Chapter 18

# West to Niagara

*The thoughts are strange that crowd into my brain,*
*While I look upward unto thee. It would seem*
*As if God poured thee from his hollow hand,*
*And hung his bow upon thine awful front;*
*And spoke in that loud voice, which seemed to him*
*Who dwelt in Patmos for his Saviour's sake,*
*The sound of many waters; and had bade*
*Thy flood to chronicle the ages back,*
*And notch His centuries in the eternal rock.*

*Deep calleth unto deep.*
　　　　　　　　　　　　　　　—JOHN A. C. BRAINARD

AFTER Oswego, as one moves westward, he comes into a region definitely more modern. Both Oswego and Niagara are eighteenth-century, but Rochester and nearly everything else on the south shore, except for a few memories grouped around Irondequoit, are quite definitely nineteenth-century. Settlement was held east of the Fort Stanwix line until the Revolution broke the Iroquois hold, and even then migration favored the inland regions more than the lake shore, where lands required considerable drainage. The broad Montezuma Marshes in eastern Wayne County, not yet entirely drained but yielding banner crops of celery in the reclaimed area, formed a barrier which the Great Western Turnpike avoided by following the hills to the southward. Lands which are now recognized as part of one of earth's choicest garden spots went begging.

The south shore is principally rural, with small fruits as the chief crops. Then several miles inland, where the lake's effect on the climate is diminished, garden truck is grown in tremendous quantities. The glacial drumlins and foothills farther inland contain New York's heaviest stand of apple orchards. Ranking second to Washington with nearly 17,000,000 bushels to its credit, New York grows apples in many sections, but the southern portions of these Lake

255

Ontario counties, all of which are underlaid with limestone, are heavy producers of the old standbys—McIntosh, Baldwin, Northern Spy and Greening. Except in the Rochester industrial complex, the odds are that factory smoke anywhere along the south shore means food processing—canning, preserving, the making of jellies and all sorts of delicacies.

To this fertile area Lake Ontario was once the open door; now most visitors approach from the south where the Erie Canal and New York Central Railroad have developed thriving centers. For twenty miles west of Oswego there is no good road immediately paralleling the shore and Fairhaven State Park of 600 acres has only a dirt road to bring in the thousands of camping parties who use the pine woods. A lighthouse at this point serves notice of the bend in the shore and marks the inlet.

A westward run from Maple View to Rochester on U. S. Highway 104, paralleling the lake shore at three to four miles distance, bisects the small-fruits belt. Motorists throng this route in "May blossom time" and again when fruits are ready for sale. This is the Ridge Road. A narrow glacial moraine formed a well-drained base, first for an Iroquois road, then for a pioneer wagon track. After the Revolution it became a noted turnpike for western travelers until the Erie Canal took over. More than three-quarters of a century passed before "the horseless carriage," first visioned in America by a man born beside this very road, brought renewed popularity to the old highway. In its western reaches toward Niagara the Ridge Road is known as "the Honeymoon Trail." A few miles to the south it is paralleled by the "Million Dollar Highway." Love and dollars!

Westward from Oswego the story is mainly utilitarian. Except for landings of unopposed expeditions, this coast was little used for war. But its contributions to peaceful agriculture have been substantial. The Sheldon Pear was developed in Wayne County in 1815, Hill's Chili Peach at Chili, Monroe County, in 1810 and the Northern Spy apple in Ontario County in 1800.

Near Wolcott cherry, peach, pear, plum and apple orchards thrive. Sour cherries are plucked early in July, with pickers living in barns and makeshift shelters. From cherry time on, the village canneries hum. Main-line canneries handle vegetables as well as fruit, with sauerkraut and its juice as staples.

THE UPPER FALLS OF THE GENESEE AT ROCHESTER FROM THE
EAST BANKS LOOKING NORTHWEST

A lithograph of about 1836.

GORGE OF THE GENESEE SHOWING PLATT STREET BRIDGE

**EASTMAN KODAK COMPANY**

View of the Camera Works Building, with the tower of the Kodak Office showing in the background.

**UNIVERSITY OF ROCHESTER**

Aerial View of School of Medicine and Dentistry, University of Rochester.

So scarce is the seasonal labor for orchards and truck gardens that caravans of Negroes and Mexicans come in from the South, camp out in makeshift shelters and depart in the fall. Often employers withhold the bulk of pickers' earnings until each crop is cleaned up in order to prevent workers from moving on to the next job.

Sodus Bay retains its reputation for good fishing. Resort, a summer colony on its east shore, is a chief starting point for boat trips. Through August and September the bay carries a brave show of American lotus—great white blossoms nearly six inches in diameter rising two feet above green pads that float on the bay's surface. Because the Sodus lotus is rare elsewhere and of unknown origin, the bed is zealously protected by the State Conservation Department.

The complex indentation of the shores of Sodus Bay made it a favorite shelter for sailing vessels and bateau expeditions. La Salle no doubt stopped here, as did all of the Johnsons and Butlers at one time or another. It was on Chauncey's calling list, too. His rival, Sir James Yeo, descended upon Sodus Point on June 10, 1813, looted the place and burned all but one building. Sodus was part of the enormous Pulteney holdings, which were managed by Captain Charles Williamson. A romantic but not well-authenticated tale, lately repeated in Carl Carmer's novel *Genesee Fever,* narrates that in 1795 Captain Williamson met by appointment a British officer whom he had known in England, on the shore near Sodus. There he was urged to join a plot to help the British take advantage of Indian unrest to recover western New York, in which the British still held the fortresses of Niagara and Oswego. It is said that Williamson spurned the offer. No clear evidence of this intrigue has been found.

A Shaker setlement held extensive lands near Sodus Point from 1823 to 1836, when they sold out to the promoters of the proposed Sodus Canal to join Lake Ontario with the Erie Canal. This public improvement had great merit, since it would provide freight movement and water transport from north to south. But the scheme was soon dropped, and a Fourierist group took over, which in turn dwindled away. Other religious and economic communities of various kinds flourished farther south along the canal, but not many of the experiments were tried near the lake shore. A stock farm now occupies 1,600 acres of the old Shaker farm.

Pultneyville, named for the British baronet, Sir William Pulteney, who never visited his Western appanage, lies at the mouth of Salmon Creek. Of old, the shelter of the estuary brought Indians and traders together in a woodland market place, and a trail led to the Seneca River at the head of Seneca Lake. Denonville halted there on his Western expedition. For a long time it was a port of entry but its commercial eminence is of the past.

Some account has already been given of Irondequoit Valley geography and history from the early French period on through the life of the Joncaire trading post, Fort des Sables, on the western shore of Irondequoit Bay. Long after that settlement had been forgotten the approximate site was eventually developed as the Sea Breeze summer resort hotel. A railroad ten miles long—described as the shortest railroad in the country—connected the hotel with Rochester. Its proprietors are said to have perpetuated the Sea Breeze far beyond its appointed time in order to benefit by exchanging passes with other railroads.

Rochester so far overshadows all the other cities of the south shore that it deserves a chapter to itself. For the present we will pass by it, clinging close to the shore of the lake and crossing only the northern fringes of the city. Two tongues of Rochester reach northward to the lake, separated from each other by the town of Irondequoit, whose voters have refused to be absorbed into the metropolis.

The more easterly of the two tongues extending north from the center of Rochester widens out near the lake and the tip contains the 500-acre rolling, wooded Durand-Eastman Park with two miles of shore. A mile of sandy beach is floodlighted for night bathing. On the other tongue, just west of the river's mouth, is Ontario Beach Park, used chiefly for bathing.

Near the lake Rochester has little new residential development, not as much as the towns of Irondequoit and Greece which border on it. The two city strips include, beside the parks, the mouth of the Genesee River, docks, railroads, a number of factories, some large religious institutions and the old village of Charlotte, said to have been named for Charlotte, Countess of Bath, wife of Sir William Pulteney. Charlotte village was annexed to Rochester in 1916; in 1931 the harbor was deepened, piers were built and a terminal building erected. But Rochester's lake front is not impressive commercially. A double breakwater protects the entrance to the Genesee River, and a beautiful ivy-clad lighthouse built of sandstone and brick in 1822 recalls the days of sail when the bar at the river entrance was a real danger.

West of Rochester the Ridge Road or Honeymoon Trail rolls on through the fruit belt. The shore bulges northward somewhat west of Rochester and more roads interlace the area between the Ridge Road and the shore. This whole stretch of seventy-five miles is without a deep harbor. Of the creeks flowing into the lake the longest, Eighteen Mile Creek, has been dammed near Burt to form a lake two miles long.

From out on Lake Ontario the shore offers vistas of farmlands with an occasional village. Beyond Point Breeze, guarded by fashionable Oak Orchard-on-the Lake with its lighthouse, lies another rural stretch. Beyond Thirty-Mile Point lighthouse are Somerset Lake Road and Olcott with another lighthouse, then Wilson Harbor and more fruit country.

For three months in the summer Olcott is a strident village and beach resort. Clothes are scant, music mechanical and loud. Crowds, large, gay and noisy, come swarming in from the larger towns and villages to the south, of which Lockport is the nearest.

Altogether the fruit belt is at its best a few miles inland, where the trading villages are located. Clarkson is noted as the birthplace of George B. Selden of Selden Patent fame. Childs offers the visitor plenty of cobblestone architecture, a church and several near-by residences. No doubt most of the stones for these curious houses, usually commodious and conventional enough inside, came from the lake shore instead of the land. At many points along the shore the beach is deep with cobbles, from gravel to dornick size, rolled in by Ontario surges. A good guess is that the cobblestones of the Ontario shore and fruit-belt houses are mostly rounded limestones and sandstones.

In Gaines, an apple hamlet, linger memories of General Edmund P. Gaines, who held Fort Erie for nine days against Drummond's siege during the War of 1812. As a young cavalry lieutenant, Gaines led the pursuit of Aaron Burr and captured the former Vice-President on the Tombigbee River after failure of the 1806 Burr conspiracy for the invasion of Mexico.

Niagara County, jutting into Lake Ontario as New York's northwest corner, is first-rate peach country. John Bartram in his book

*Travels from Pensilvania to . . . Lake Ontario,* published in 1751, reports peaches, plums and grapes growing in Indian villages. The first commercial orchard in western New York was planted on Grand Island in the Niagara River in 1827 by a New Englander, Lewis F. Allen. He brought the trees from the Hudson Valley via the Erie Canal. The island produced vast quantities of peaches from native trees but "the yellows"—a parasitic disease—drove the early peach industry to Niagara County where it has flourished ever since.

Approaching Niagara Falls, the Honeymoon Trail touches the 6,000-acre Tuscarora Indian Reservation, occupied by 400 Indians.

At Lewiston village one can see the results of long erosion on the walls of the gorge. A village of the Attawandaronk Indians was found on the site by a Franciscan missionary in 1626. The Indian village was later destroyed by the Seneca and no inhabitants returned and the Americans who finally settled there named their village after Governor Morgan Lewis. The town was burned by the British in 1813 but promptly rebuilt.

One of the historic spots in Lewiston is the old Frontier House, built on Center Street in 1824. It is noted as the inn where James Fenimore Cooper is said to have written *The Spy.* The character Betty Flanagan in that novel is identified as Mrs. Thomas Hustler, wife of the landlord, and she is one of several New York barmaids credited with inventing the cocktail.

While this corner of the lake lies close to tremendous power developments, it remains entirely rural. In 1893 William J. Love, a Tennessee promoter, planned Model City on 30,000 acres between the Ridge Road and the lake, but the project failed in the "hard times" period. Uncle Sam's Ordnance Department took 7,000 acres on the same location, and built a huge plant for TNT production; but it soon closed down, cleared away the buildings and resold the land.

Two routes lead out of Lewiston, an international bridge to Queenston, Ontario, and a road up the east bank of the river to Niagara Falls. Midway is Niagara University. Near by is Devil's Hole, the scene of a deadly massacre. In 1763 John Stedman, keeper of the portage, and a wagon train with twenty-four men were ambushed there by the Seneca. Only Stedman and two others escaped to give the alarm. A detachment of British soldiers hurrying from Lewiston to save the remnant of Stedman's party blundered into the same ambush and lost seventy-five men. Stedman was not frightened away and as soon as the portage was opened took up his duties again.

The traveler at Niagara Falls on the American side views a scene startlingly different from the lonely wilderness waterfall described by Father Louis Hennepin in 1678. While Niagara Falls appear under the name of Ongiara in Sanson's Map of Canada published in 1657, Father Hennepin is the first white man known to have seen them, although illiterate voyageurs may have done so earlier. A member of La Salle's party in 1678, Hennepin described the spectacle as "A vast and prodigious cadence of water which falls down after a surprizing and astonishing manner, insomuch that the Universe does not afford its Parallel. . . . The Waters which fall from this vast height do foam and Boil after the Most hideous manner imaginable, making an outrageous Noise, more terrible than that of Thunder; for when the wind blows from off the South, their dismal roaring may be heard above fifteen leagues off."

The seven-mile portage around the Falls formed the sole break in an otherwise open waterway from the St. Lawrence to the Upper Lakes. In 1745 and 1750 the French built two forts near the Falls to support Fort Niagara and to guard the portage at its upper end. On the British approach in 1759, Chabert Joncaire, French master of the portage, burned the forts and fled across the river.

Under the British, John Stedman had received authority over the Niagara portage and he carried goods over it on the east side of the river until 1791. The road across the river from Lewiston to Chippawa Creek was completed in 1788-1789 but government goods were still sent by Lewiston and Fort Schlosser until his contract expired. Stedman grew rich on his monopoly, and developed a splendid farm which amazed all visitors by its high production and many varieties of livestock. His goats, pastured on the island between the American and Canadian Falls to protect them from bears and wolves, gave Goat Island its name.

Under the Jay Treaty Indians are permitted to cross the border without hindrance, taking along their family possessions. To refresh white memories, a Tuscarora chief each year leads a march of several hundred of his people across the bridge into Canada, where they hold exercises commemorating peace between nations.

New York State took care to reserve the eastern shore of the Niagara River when it turned over western New York lands to Massachusetts in the post-Revolutionary settlement, hence they were not affected by the early orgies of speculation. About 1806 Augustus Porter from Canandaigua bought the land immediately surrounding the Falls at auction for $18 an acre, took charge of the portage, and founded a family prominent in war and politics. Porter named the embryo city Manchester, for England's smoky industrial city. The British burned Manchester and Fort Schlosser, built by Captain Joseph Schlosser, a German officer in the English army, in 1813. Porter rebuilt the place and with the opening of the Erie Canal began to urge industrial development. The digging of a canal around the Falls for power purposes only was begun in 1853 and finished eight years later at a cost of $1,000,000. No use was made of it until 1875.

In 1877 the canal property was auctioned. Jacob F. Schoellkopf bid it in for $76,000 and spent a lifetime developing Niagara power. The first Niagara generator dates from 1881. Power lines pierced through to Buffalo in 1896 and to Syracuse in 1905. During World War I, Schoellkopf's descendants merged their holdings with the Niagara Falls Power Company. Niagara power now serves a population of 2,500,000 persons in western and central New York and is the mainstay of superpower hookups which, in emergency, can be effective in New York City and New England. More than 450,000 horsepower of electric current now generated at Niagara Falls help to produce abrasives, flour, paper, machinery, foundry materials, aluminum, calcium, silicon, graphite, carbide and ferroalloys in local plants. On both sides of the river total horsepower generated is now 1,500,000. For several of the newer industries, such as aluminum and artificial abrasives, Niagara's volts make possible the intense yet easily controlled heats of the electric furnace.

Today the American city christened for the cataract has a population of 90,000 and the Ontario city of the same name across the river has about a quarter as many. More than a million and a half visitors come annually to these cities to watch Niagara's blue-green waters plunge over the lip of the ledge to the boiling maelstrom in the channel below. To preserve the profitable spectacle a British-American treaty limits power diversion of river water to 20,000 cubic feet a second on the American shore, 36,000 on the Canadian side.

The geological explanation of Niagara Falls is fairly simple. When the Ice Age thawed, the river was plunging straight into Lake Ontario over the shorn edge of a dolomite or crystalline lime-and-magnesia formation. In time the mad waters at the cataract's foot eroded the underlying soft shale. Blocks of dolomite broke off, enforcing recession of the Falls' crest and slowly creating the Gorge. Erosion of limestone and shale move the Falls gradually upstream at the rate of two and one-fifth feet a year on the Canadian side and two-thirds of a foot on the American side. The difference is explained by the present position of the Falls on a curve of which the American shore is the inner arc. It is estimated that a retreat of two miles upstream will bring the Falls to softer stone and reduce their height by perhaps half. Unless modern science in the meantime can devise means of compelling the Falls to stay put, they will end as a whirlpool in Lake Erie. Engineers are now considering steps to hold them, but Providence may take a more decisive hand in the matter.

The Falls now stand twenty-two miles from the river's head in Lake Erie and fourteen miles from its mouth in Lake Ontario. In its brief course of thirty-six miles the Niagara descends about 330 feet. The current is swift for two miles from Lake Erie, then slows down appreciably as the rocky channel broadens. Below Grand Island the river is two and a half miles wide. Fifteen miles from parent Erie the channel narrows again at the point where the rapids begin. The waters fairly dash down the last fifty-five-foot descent to the brink.

The river here is almost a mile wide. The American Fall is now more than 1,000 feet wide and 167 feet high. The Canadian or Horseshoe Fall is more than three times as wide but somewhat lower. Fifteen million cubic feet of water per minute—about a cubic mile per week—storm over the cataracts' worn ledges. About nine-tenths of the total amount boils over the Horseshoe Fall.

Below the Falls the river contracts between high rock walls, becoming from 1,000 to 1,250 feet wide. Two miles farther on it is barely 800 feet wide, and at the Whirlpool is but 250 feet wide. Within seven miles the lower rapids slide down more than 100 feet, but at Lewiston the stream widens and becomes smoother. In the Whirlpool Rapids the flow is squeezed into a 300-foot channel which forces the stream into convex form, with the center twenty feet higher than the edges. That central wave is a tremendous unleashed force, and few who trifle with it escape. Those who do are born lucky and never try it a second time.

The great Whirlpool itself, farther downstream, is a maelstrom through which race at mad rate the slowly gathered waters of Superior, Huron, Michigan, Erie and the multitude of smaller lakes. A sealed bottle cast into Green Bay—in fact, any piece of durable debris—has a good chance to reach that mighty eddy, course around it and then be cast out to resume its journey to the sea. Cedar-clothed cliffs rise to a height of 200 feet above the Whirlpool, high enough to dwarf the spectacle to the point where angry waves and rings of water seem mere ripples in size. Yet occasionally a stout swimmer braves these terrors and survives.

The Indians have a tradition that the Falls demand two human victims yearly, but this is too conservative a figure to satisfy the big white brother. Many lives have been lost in foolhardy attempts to cross the river above Goat Island. Both successful and unlucky attempts have been made by "stunt" performers to plunge over the Falls and shoot the rapids in barrels, special boats, tinkered life preservers, freak balls of rubber and the like.

The picaresque gentry who live by gambling with death to amuse the crowds have been risking their lives at the Falls ever since the days of pathfinding. Sam Patch, a New Jersey leaper who in 1829 tackled Niagara, survived two 95-foot jumps off a Goat Island ledge, but was killed leaping into the Genesee soon afterward. Best remembered are the exploits of Blondin in 1859 and 1860. This French tightrope walker catfooted across Niagara several times. As a climax he trod the swaying tightrope with a passenger on his back.

During the earlier 1880's several hardy men in sealed barrels successfully shot the rapids. William J. Kendall, a stalwart Boston policeman and headline hunter, resolved to reveal these fleeting champions as sissies. In August 1886 he hurtled through protected only by a cork life preserver. But Captain Matthew Webb, greatest swimmer of his day, lost his life in the whirlpool.

The next high-spot performer was Steve Brodie, reputed to have leaped without damage from Brooklyn Bridge. Brodie jumped into the Niagara in September 1889, cased in a suit of India rubber thickly padded and reinforced by steel bands. Surviving, he lived sumptuously for a while, a hero to his audiences. Then he dropped from sight, but "he came a Brodie" remains in our language to denote a sudden drop or failure.

For a long time men monopolized the effort to win sudden fame at the Falls, but finally Mrs. Annie Edson Taylor, a schoolmistress, came along. In October 1901 she rolled over the Falls with neatness and success. Not all the women barrel-shooters have been so lucky.

A little later there came to Watertown a small, dapper Englishman named Bobby Leach. After telling everyone he met for ten years that he was going over the Falls in a steel barrel of his own invention, he actually did so in July 1911. Then he spent twenty-three weeks recuperating in a hospital—said he couldn't remember a thing after he started to drop. Years afterward he slipped on a banana peel and was killed.

Jean Laussier probably enjoyed himself more than anyone else who has negotiated the Falls. In July 1928 he sat himself down in a viselike, though cushioned, metal apparatus set in a big rubber ball, had a roaring trip and emerged smiling and unhurt.

Captain Klaus Larsen in 1910 tried to get through the Rapids in a motorboat, failed and was rescued from death by the famous William "Red" Hill, who pulled 150 people, dead or alive, from Niagara. Hill himself ran the Rapids in barrels, twice.

Mrs. Martha Wagenfuehrer of Niagara Falls took her pet dog through the Whirlpool Rapids in a barrel, but only the dog survived.

Lincoln Beechey flew a small airplane under the Falls Bridge in 1911, after which the stunt was banned, but on January 26, 1941, an unidentified aviator flew under all of Niagara's bridges.

These are only a few of the daredevil stunts called forth by the challenge of the swift waters and steep cliffs. Sizable books have been written on this theme alone. They represent an epoch that has passed, and may never be resumed, just as the Gorge railroad and the great hotels had their day and vanished. But Niagara roars on alike for lovers, poets, painters, daredevils and fakes. Although diminished by withdrawals of water by power canals, the great cataract remains unique, beautiful and masterful, still worthy of the reverence accorded it in Indian lore as the noblest work of the Great White Father, who in Seneca myth calls his worthy sons out of its mists and up the face of the cataract to the Happy Hunting Grounds where all is well with man forever.

# Chapter 19

## Rochester—Utility with Grace

---

*I went forth hastily and lo! I met a hundred men,*
*The worker with the chisel and the worker with the pen;*
*The restless toilers after good, who sow and never reap,*
*And one who maketh music for their souls that may not sleep.*

       \*       \*       \*       \*       \*       \*

*And 'tis not wholly mine or theirs I think of through the day,*
*But the great eternal thing we make together, I and they;*
*Far in the sunset I behold a city that man owns,*
*Made fair with all their nobler toil, built of my common stones.*
                —ARTHUR O'SHAUGHNESSY

---

ROCHESTER, the metropolis of Lake Ontario's south shore, is the third largest city in the Empire State. In 1940 its population numbered 325,000. More than most industrial cities it unites workaday vigor with suave beauty. The vines that drape factory walls and the trim lawns and flower gardens in front of them show that Rochester today is truly the "Flower City," instead of the "Flour City" of a century ago.

The city's beginnings were raw enough, as a local historian, Howard L. Osgood, confessed in a paper before the Rochester Historical Society on April 13, 1894. He began: "A distinction must be made between the first settlers within the present limits of our city and those who actually established it as a settlement. The first white settler on the site of Rochester was undoubtedly Ebenezer Allan, a man whose repute appears to have been wholly disrepute, and therefore is best when unknown. Before 1812, a few settlers lived near the Genesee Falls, but they certainly made no effort to establish a village, and had no influence upon the events here chronicled."*

While Osgood spelled the first pioneer's name "Allan," other chroniclers use the "e" rendering of the surname "Allen." Despite the man's scandalous ways which still distress respectable citizens, histo-

---

* Published with similar material in *Rochester, the Semi-Centennial Souvenir* (Rochester, Express Printing Company, 1884).

266

rians keep harking back to this backwoods rip who set up at the Falls of the Genesee before the godly arrived. "Indian" Allen owed his nickname to his liking for the Indian way of life and particularly for Indian women. Sundry of these he took to wife either seriatim or in company, and yet he retained the affection of a white wife. Neither in location nor polygamous bent was Rochester's first white settler far removed from the beginnings of Mormonism, although Allen could take his wives straight, without benefit of religious revelation.

Octogenarian Lyman Barker Langworthy's opinion of Allen's character and activities is no more flattering than Osgood's. Langworthy wrote:

"That part of the city on the west side of the river was purchased of Phelps and Gorham, owners of nearly half of Western New York, about 1791 by seven purchasers. P. & G. had given in 1789 a mill lot of one hundred acres to Indian Allen, on condition he should build a mill for the convenience of new settlers. Allen was a vilanous scamp, a coldblooded murderer and Tory in the revolutionary war, and led many Indian massacres."*

Another annalist of Rochester, George C. Bragdon, locates precisely the site where Allen built a sawmill and gristmill. At that time there was a cascading waterfall of twelve feet where the Canal aqueduct stands, and the conveyance to Allen extended from this fall equal distances up and down the river on the west side, and westward far enough to make the hundred acres approximately square.†

Allen wasted no time; Genesee water began on November 13, 1789, to turn the wheel of the nondescript gristmill he had flung together on the river's west shore where Aqueduct and Graves Streets now cross. He was aided by a few settlers and his Iroquois friends and relatives by marriage. Allen and his workers celebrated the raising of the mill with a spree, after which the first of Rochester's many millers settled down to grinding up to ten bushels of grain a day. Allen sold out in 1792. He moved up the Genesee to Mount Morris, New York, with white and Indian wives. Benjamin Burton, who bought Allen out, sold the millsite to Samuel Ogden of New York

---

* *Desultory Notes and Reminiscences of the City of Rochester: Its early history, remarkable men and events, strange revelations, of the murders, mysteries and miseries, casualties, curiosities and progress of this young and growing city, for the last fifty years* (Rochester, 1868).

† *Notable men of Rochester and Vicinity* (Dwight J. Stoddard, Publisher, 1902) notes more details of the sale to Allen (p. xxii).

City, who in turn conveyed the property to Captain Charles Williamson, Sir William Pulteney's agent, in 1794. A spring freshet finally swept Allen's mill to ruin. The wreckage burned later.

After "Indian" Allen left Genesee Falls, the place declined for a time, then began to grow in size, grace and godliness, but regeneration took some time. Dens of rattlesnakes abounded in the cliffs along the Gorge. Swarms of raccoons riddled the first crops of corn. But not all was grief and varmints—the salmon swarmed in from the lake and could be scooped up.

Captain Williamson induced well-to-do persons and families from Maryland and Virginia to buy western New York lands. The Allen hundred acres went in 1803 to three buyers, Nathaniel Rochester, William Fitzhugh and Charles Carroll, for $17.50 an acre. It was 1811 before they subdivided it into village lots.

Amid these mixed trials and blessings, Josiah Fish from Vermont found growing custom for log houses which, as the settlement's first contractor, he built to order. This Yankee's profession indicated a growing, thriving community where newcomers were too busy to build cabins for themselves or for one another on the "bee" system.

An early industry was the making of potash. In 1812 a mail delivery was established between Rochester and Canandaigua and the first bridge was erected over the river at $12,000 cost. The first pioneer trader at Charlotte was Erastus Spaulding; his vessel was captured by the British during the war. A growing trade between the settlement and Montreal was based on staves, potash and flour. In 1814 the hamlet had some twenty houses and a variety of small businesses. During that year two new flour mills were erected by enterprising newcomers, and others were built in the next few years.

Village incorporation came in 1817, when the population was approaching 1,000. The corporate limits then comprised 655 acres, 430 on the west shore of the river only. The village saw the first real boom then. Many new settlers arrived and a number of new buildings were erected. Also in that year occurred Rochester's initial Fourth of July celebration, the highlight of which was a sham battle.

After sixteen years as an absentee owner, Colonel Rochester finally succumbed to the charms of the Genesee, and in 1818 moved to the village. He found things going ahead. A wheat trade had developed. The steamboat *Ontario,* chugging from Sackets Harbor to

Lewiston on the Niagara River, stopped at the port of the Genesee for the flour products of the "Old Red Mill," which had been erected in 1814 by Hervey and Elisha Ely and Josiah Bissell, Jr. Twenty-six thousand barrels were exported to the Canadian market in the year of the Colonel's arrival. He decided to remain in a town with a future rather than a past, and his neighbors liked him so well that they took his fine English surname for their city.

By 1822, Thomas Hart Rochester, the Colonel's enterprising sixth child, had completed a bigger and better mill at the site of "Indian" Allen's first ramshackle structure. The original millstones were saved and are now on display at the courthouse. Bragdon says that clearance for the Erie Canal aqueduct swept away "Indian" Allen's original power site. The aqueduct, more than 800 feet long, was built of New Jerusalem sandstone, but soon proved inadequate in size and was rebuilt of granite on a larger plan.

By 1834 there were 12,000 residents. Millers and merchants clamored for a city charter, and obtained it. With an annual output of 300,000 barrels, Genesee flour sifted throughout the world for fifty years. About 1878 thirty-one mills were in operation and the total output had increased to a million barrels a year. Flour milling kept moving west to the wheat fields in order to save freight charges. Though the municipal seal still retains the legend "The Flour City," one by one Rochester's mills closed.

Expanding nurseries changed the popular publicity tag to "The Flower City." The horticultural development from a seed business started in the famous Arcade built in 1828 by Abelard Reynolds. Hiram Sibley, a pioneer industrialist, who founded one of western New York's great fortunes, was once a seedsman. George Ellwanger in 1839 bought eight acres in Mount Hope Avenue, the nucleus of the Mount Hope Nurseries, which had 600 acres under cultivation by 1884. Ellwanger effected a partnership with Patrick Barry in 1840, and the firm established nurseries in Toronto and Columbus, Ohio. They supplied California's early orchards. Their trees are growing today in China, India, New Zealand, Australia and Arabia, and even in Emperor Hirohito's Imperial Gardens in the Tokyo palace grounds.

There was James Vick, too, who once set type by hand with Horace Greeley of the New York *Tribune*. Settling in Rochester to work as a compositor and later an editor and publisher, Vick started as a side line a seed business which still flourishes. In 1894 there were in Rochester a dozen seed and nursery firms. This concentration on growing things has given Rochester a charming dress of flowers, shrubs and trees, both on homesites and in public parks. The park system includes a total area of 1,777 acres. Highland Park, partly donated by Ellwanger and Barry, contains nearly 400 varieties of lilac, a feature matched only by England's Kew Gardens and the Arnold Arboretum near Boston. Rochester's May lilac festivals are internationally famous. The aster, however, is Rochester's official flower—trust this city to have one!

Pioneer dissatisfaction with the slovenly footwear usually to be had encouraged Abner Wakelee, a cobbler, to set up a shop in Rochester. From this small beginning a large shoe-manufacturing business developed there. In 1931, one of the best years, the city's big shops produced $11,587,932 worth of shoes, employing 3,610 workers who earned $3,194,110 in wages. Now, however, the peak seems to have been passed. Rochester shoemakers invented many useful devices. There was, for instance, Jesse W. Hatch's sewing machine for uppers, which previously had to be hand-pegged. This machine was a step toward mass production of ready-made shoes.

Rochester has manufactured clothes almost as long as it has made shoes. One Jehiel Barnard—his shears have been preserved—cut and sewed together in 1813 the first suit fashioned in the village. By 1875 there were seventy custom tailors. Mass production brought in big factories. By 1940 Rochester plants had run up their production of men's clothing beyond the $30,000,000 mark.

In education, Rochester is many-sided and progressive. An admirable public-school system is fortified by many parochial and private schools. The Rochester Athenaeum and Mechanic's Institute, teaching the practical arts by which the city lives industrially, has been recently rechristened the Rochester Institute of Technology. Colgate-Rochester Divinity School is a merger of the divinity studies of the two former Baptist colleges now gone secular and grown into universities, Colgate at Hamilton, New York, and the University of Rochester.

The university started life in 1850 with sixty students taught by a faculty of five. In 1900, as the result of a movement led by Susan B. Anthony, women were admitted on the same conditions as men students. Through nearly a century of existence it has had only four presidents, a fact reassuring to its local supporters who sought for their funds an institutional harbor remote from political influence. That situation is known to have led George Eastman into selecting the University of Rochester as custodian of funds for various enterprises. Eastman made the first of a series of gifts in 1904. The Memorial Art Gallery was given to the university in 1912, which in 1919 also received the Eastman School of Music and Eastman Theater. That large and beautiful structure, part of a great experiment not yet ended, proved difficult to handle. A lively account of its rise and decline will be found in Edward Hungerford's *Pathway of Empire* (New York, 1935).* The university's famous school of medicine and dentistry dates from 1926, the River Campus from 1930. The College for Women is in quite another part of the city—Prince Street and University Avenue, the site of the old college campus.

Largely responsible for the university's growth was George Eastman, of whose character and career his contemporaries usually spoke in superlatives. President Nicholas Murray Butler of Columbia University described him as "a literally stupendous factor in the education of the modern world," and E. R. A. Seligman, the distinguished economist, said of the founder of Eastman Kodak: "There has been a distinct aesthetic side in all his accomplishments, in his vocation as well as in his avocations."

These comments upon the career and achievements of George Eastman indicate that he bore wealth graciously and used it constructively. His supreme excellence is that he knew how to dispose of funds modestly for creative social purposes. As the world enriched him, he was careful to enrich the world in return.

Eastman was born in 1854 at Waterville, Oneida County, one of those delightful villages in central New York where the New England influence is strong. For a time this youth followed the Horatio Alger pattern of the period: Boy moved with his family to Rochester in 1860; left school at fourteen to help support widowed mother; saved something regularly out of three-dollar weekly pay. Loved

---

* See pp. 175ff.

even then a wide range of recreation—a picnic, a ball game, music—but had little time for them then. In his immature soul rankled a single hatred—he hated and feared poverty.

So away with the long, long thoughts of boyhood and on to work. On scant pay as insurance clerk and bank clerk, young George Eastman saved $5,000 by his twenty-sixth year. His single indulgence was photography, then still in its clumsy infancy of huge cameras, dark rooms in attics, and heavy glass plates which the photographer had to coat by hand as needed.

The sum of his still-nebulous ambition was to go into business for himself. What field to enter with his $5,000? Chance and a vacation trip to Mackinac Island decided him. With his other baggage, he lugged along a weighty camera, tripod, glass plates and chemicals for sensitizing and developing them, and a tent which he used as a "dark room." There he sweated with his plates, nitrate of silver and collodion. The best thing developed there was not a photograph but the germ of an idea for coating dry plates mechanically.

The nucleus of Eastman's zooming fortune was the dry plate. Five years later came the first crude film as a substitute for plates, and before 1890 appeared his pathfinder Kodak, a clumsy camera by today's standards, but opening for a wide public what was in effect a new art. Eastman film, transparent and flexible, pleased photo-snappers in all lands, but further developments of profound social meaning were around the corner.

Into Eastman's life at this time came Thomas A. Edison. Deep in problems connected with motion pictures, the Wizard of Menlo Park needed a workable medium for running long series of photographic images. He sent a remittance of $2.50 to the Eastman factory and an order for experimental materials, and received a roll of Kodak film which solved his problem. Eastman's film made up in long rolls provided the necessary continuity for successful moving-picture presentation. Within a few years the movies grew into a tremendously popular amusement. In due course "the films" gained sound tracks and the talking picture entered the theater.

Even midway of this development, George Eastman was a rich man and money rolled in faster and faster. Although Eastman Kodak Company prospered enormously from motion pictures, it never forgot the needs of the amateurs for whom the Eastman service was first designed. From black-and-white photography amateurs were led into taking motion pictures in 1923 and into color photography in 1928.

In addition Eastman pioneered photography in the fields of the X ray and of astronomy. Photographing the heavens is a gigantic task in which the leading observatories of the world ceaselessly cooperate, each covering a certain segment of the sky. Knowledge from this source concerning the heavenly bodies and the behavior of light is steadily accumulating in a way that would delight the soul of George Eastman.

While George Eastman's lifework was directly beneficial to society, and the great company he founded is one of the nation's industrial pillars, it is in his philanthropies that this unusual man stands revealed. The fortune he gave away was colossal—in all some $72,-000,000. The wisdom and taste shown in its disposition is quite as remarkable as the sum itself.

Quiet Mr. Eastman disclaimed praise for generosity, and declared that he was merely distributing excess money which he could not personally use. As the money came in, it went out on two errands—first, the business and cultural development of Rochester, and second, carefully chosen philanthropies for the general welfare of humanity. The first was in the nature of a friendly gift to neighbors and associates in the community where he had prospered, the second a social dividend to the larger public which had rewarded his efforts.

For Rochester, Eastman provided the beautiful River Campus, most of the University of Rochester's impressive buildings, the Eastman Theater, part of the School of Music, and the Chamber of Commerce building. For the larger public, millions went to points at home and abroad in support of technical education, medical and dental research, Negro education and the promotion of international good will. Advancing medicine and the elevation of musical standards were perhaps the two causes nearest to his heart and, thanks to him, Rochester excels in both these directions.

A master organizer in practical affairs, the founder of Eastman Kodak Company left his company strong the world over, with thirteen plants employing 35,000 persons.

On the personal side this unassuming bachelor was no doubt a lonely man. Although lauded for his achievements by scientific, political and business leaders of his country, decorated by France, Italy and Poland, awarded the Progress Medal by the Royal Photographic Society of Great Britain, he remained plain George Eastman to Rochester and disliked having his neighbors make a fuss over him. Once he tried to hide a large gift to the Massachusetts Institute of Technology by having it listed as from Mr. Smith, but, alas, checks are not anonymous and the secret leaked out. For recreation he who had in boyhood grudged the time to see a ball game in his later life hunted big game in Africa and Alaska.

Finally Eastman developed an incurable illness. After all his gifts to medicine, those arts could not heal him. He braced himself to receive a long deserved tribute when in 1931 he was honor guest at a dinner given in New York by the Society of the Genesee, but he was nearing the end of his strength. George Eastman died alone, as he had lived alone. On a spring day in 1932 he was found dead by his own hand. He left a clipped, precise note of explanation, a single line, crisp and orderly as his life had been. It read: "My work is done; why wait?"

He was wrong. His work goes on. It proceeds in laboratories and surgeries, in motion-picture theaters and on production lots, in the pictures of amateur and professional photographers, in manufacturing plants and wherever an American military plane takes a camera aloft. But these are remote activities. In Rochester his work goes on in the daily round of production, in cultural and recreational activities and in the very soul of the unique, efficient and superior city which he helped to build.

His ashes rest in a bronze urn in a pleasant little memorial garden at the Lake Avenue entrance to Kodak Park, one of his Rochester factories.

Bausch & Lomb, an optical company, though smaller than Eastman Kodak, is equally commanding in its line. The founder was John Jacob Bausch, a native of Germany who brought to Rochester skill acquired in the Old Country, began making spectacles by hand, and opened a shop in 1853. Henry Lomb put in his small capital and the two fought their way up to eminence. Bausch was the founder of a large family, important both in the family business and in Rochester's expanding social consciousness. Lomb, a Civil War captain who never married, founded the Mechanics' Institute in 1885. In 1903 he gave the money to found the Rochester Dental Clinic. The Lomb Memorial Tower is a feature of the Plaza facing the works on St. Paul Street, and the Bausch Memorial Bridge crosses the Genesee River at Bausch Street.

From that bridge one looks down 105 feet into the gorge of the Genesee, where the glass furnaces of the company are located. Here, after several years of difficult experiments, was cast the first optical glass in America by William Bausch, son of the founder. This triumph led to American independence of European importations and has had immense military and naval significance.

An elder son, Edward Bausch, early applied himself to the improvement and wider distribution of microscopes, and eventually brought high-grade instruments within the price range of school laboratories. Toward the close of his distinguished and useful career, he became the chief donor of the new building of the Rochester Museum of Arts and Sciences, opened in 1942 as the nation's most modern museum devoted to the history of material culture.

The able and progressive director of that impressive museum, Dr. Arthur C. Parker, had been working along on a reduced budget in an old building at Edgerton Park when one day Mr. Bausch called to ask, in his quiet way, "What would you do if you had half a million dollars for a new building?" Swallowing hard, the director reached into a drawer, pulled out a set of plans and replied, "This would be a good place to start, Mr. Bausch." This case is often instanced in Rochester of the way big things are done there—the idea is born, is thought through and matured, people talk about it and presently the money is found to materialize the dream.

The founder of the remarkable Bausch & Lomb business was always afraid the company would grow too big. His son says the old gentleman used to come into the office, look around and say, "Do you really need all these people?" A master craftsman himself, he found it difficult to realize that the Machine Age had arrived in optics. His firm now makes 15,000 to 20,000 kinds of optical instruments and lenses, all the way from ordinary spectacles to complicated instruments for gunnery and navigation. In World War I it was said that the Navy would have lost its eyes if Bausch & Lomb had been destroyed; the dependence of the government on this one firm was even greater in World War II. Certainly the Navy moved into Bausch & Lomb early, and very strict precautions to safeguard secrecy prevailed there at all stages.

A good many of Rochester's other sizable industries also stem from precise craftsmanship, such as the Taylor Utility Company which began with thermometer manufacture by George Taylor and David Kendall in 1853. General Motors discovered Rochester through the youthful efforts of Halbleib Brothers, in self-starters—whence came Delco Appliance—and then, recognizing Rochester's penchant for making small, fine things, it established its Rochester Products Division to manufacture precision items for motorcars. But the industrial strength of Rochester is far from being confined to big names or a few lines; there are a thousand industries, big and small, in the city.

However, Rochester missed a chance to become the Detroit of America. George B. Selden, patent attorney from near-by Clarkson, was certainly the first man in the United States, if not in the world, to conceive and describe a road vehicle driven by an internal-combustion engine. This is evident from his patent application of 1877 which he kept alive until 1895 when the patent was granted. Under the patent, royalties were collected from nearly all automobile manufacturers down to 1903. In deciding lawsuits brought by Henry Ford, the Federal Court of Appeals ruled that, while Selden's patent was good, it did not apply because the art had swept so far beyond the original Selden concept of thirty years before. Mr. Selden took his defeat philosophically, saying that he had entered into his automobile project to make a little money and received from it about $200,000, which was more than he had expected. If Selden had built the vehicle of his imagination any time before 1892, when the Duryea brothers started work on the first American gasoline car, which was later completed by J. Frank Duryea, no doubt he would have won his suit, and his fame today would be far greater than it is. America pays off on performance, not on ideas.

This chapter began with "Indian" Allen; let it close with Sam Patch, another odd figure in the annals of this beautiful, strait-laced, creative city. Sam the waterfall leaper has been dead 115 years, but his name and fame endure. And such are the follies of mankind that Sam Patch lore may outlast that of George Eastman.

Chronicler Langworthy testifies that Sam Patch "was endowed with a very feeble mind and low grade of intelligence; he loved the ardent, and resorted to the original device of jumping from great heights to raise the means to gratify his ruling passion, and by a very unintentional exploit, immortalized his feat and his name, and will be read of and quoted, and illustrated, when Webster, Calhoun, Douglass and Sumner, *et omne genus* are lost in the bottomless pit of oblivion. Yea, ten thousand years hence . . . his name and exploit will 'point a paragraph and adorn a tale' . . . with the caption of Sam's motto some things can be done as well as others."

Sam made the "big time" with his already noticed 100-foot leap into Niagara Gorge at the foot of the American Falls. In Rochester he pasted up placards that he would jump down the Genesee Falls on November 8, 1829. True to his promise, he and a tame bear leaped and came up safely, to the great satisfaction of all the beholders. Taking the bear along in this jump was a true Sam Patch touch, but the animal's escape alive suggests that the scene was the lowest of the three falls in the city, Middle Falls, a mere twenty-five footer. Anyway, Sam was just warming up.

Exhilarated by the large collection and by the "ardent" aftermath of its investment, Sam conceived a real show for the good people of Rochester. Five days after his first jump an enormous throng massed on the river's shores to see Sam leap from a twenty-foot scaffold on the brink of the Upper Falls, a total descent of more than 100 feet. Sam appeared on the dot, prompt but slightly inebriated, tossed off a last drink, tipsily mounted the scaffold, and after a half hour of antic speech and caper, took the plunge, feet first after his fashion. The jump was nothing for Sam sober, but too much for Sam drunk. "A hush equal to the primeval chaos existed for near ten minutes, when spontaneously every mouth proclaimed, 'he is lost—he is dead.'" Thus wrote Langworthy years after an event that awed all beholders.

So overwrought was the populace by this spectacle that many broke arms and legs scrambling up and down the rocks, while many others suffered from ailments due to exposure on that "raw, severe, suicidal day in November."

Sam's death is attributed to his losing balance and striking on his side, with a force estimated at more than 4,000 pounds. Yet the tale is still repeated that he came up under the rocks and "played possum" till night, when he left for parts unknown. Wagers were laid on his assumed survival. With the arrival of spring, however, his body was found at the river's mouth and received burial in the Charlotte cemetery.

Luckless Sam Patch lived on in frontier song and story. One colored print issued some fifty years later represented him leaping cloud-high from the Genesee westward to Niagara Falls as he grinned down at a mass of gaping faces, his public faithful to the last.

In what other American city could a Patch find such a waterfall in the center of the town? Rochester's physical setting is unique among American cities. It stretches twelve miles along the picturesque "Casconchigon—the river of many falls," which, despite taming here and there, has three large waterfalls within the city limits—the largest with a perpendicular drop of nearly 100 feet, the second with eighty-five. The aqueduct which carried the Erie Canal over the Genesee is 850 feet long with a trough forty-five feet wide. In the spectacular gorge are factory groups at some points, parks at others. White water rushes past the Rundel Library, then the river is lost under the bridge which carries Main Street through the business district.

Main Street, on and near the river crossing, is not what it used to be in terms of mercantile leadership, since stores of the better grade moved east toward fashionable outlying areas and decay gnaws at old structures. Whither the business district is drifting is a conundrum which real-estate interests have guessed wrong many times. Perhaps the resulting disappointments explain a current feeling that Rochester has reached its peak in population, enterprise, fortune.

It is a mistaken feeling. This city has both the tangibles and intangibles to command a share in any advance the nation makes. It still disregards too much its port facilities on Lake Ontario which may well pace the city's next upswing. When ships can leave Rochester for any port in the world, via a deepened lakes-to-ocean St. Lawrence waterway, Rochester should hum as it did in response to the Erie Canal. Railroads and highways give Rochester first call on cargoes originating many miles to the southward. Meantime, Rochester can be counted on to show the rest of the nation a city which fills the eye with joy and the soul with hope in the abundant future of well-organized urban living.

# Chapter 20

# The Canadian Shores

*I made me great works; I builded me houses; I planted me vineyards: I made me gardens and orchards, and I planted trees in them of all kind of fruits.*

—ECCLESIASTES 2:4-5

THE small end of Lake Ontario is the subpeninsula of Niagara, twenty to thirty miles broad between widening Lake Erie on the south and narrowing Lake Ontario on the north. Across the peninsula, like a flattened letter S, runs the Welland Canal, which opens on Lake Ontario at Port Dalhousie, twelve miles west from Niagara or at the new opening, Port Weller, three miles east of Dalhousie. Welland County, containing two-thirds of the canal's length and the Canadian Niagara Falls, has a population of nearly 93,000. Manufacturing has developed at each of the three points where the canal is crossed by a trunk-line railroad. For instance, the city of Welland now has about fifty establishments with an annual output valued at $26,000,000.

Welland Canal traffic is growing and is of true international character. Of the 13,000,000 tons floated through it in 1940-1941, 9,000,000 tons originated in the United States. Tonnage which passed through both the St. Lawrence and Welland, up or down, totaled 2,700,000 tons in 1941, which is a fair measure of Lake Ontario's value as a through waterway. Seven million other tons passed through the Welland in the same period and either ended the journey at a Lake Ontario port or went on to Albany and New York or way points on the New York Barge Canal.

Lincoln County occupies the northeastern corner of Niagara Peninsula, with St. Catharines as county seat. The name commemorates Catharine Askin Robertson, daughter of John Askin, well-to-do merchant of Mackinac and Detroit, by an Indian mother. By her second marriage, Mrs. Robertson became the wife of Robert Hamilton, merchant of Queenston and all-around leader of the region. William Hamilton Merritt, chief promoter of the Welland Canal, is often described as founder of the city.

Located where chief railways cross the Welland, St. Catharines is a thriving commercial city of 30,000, nearly half of Lincoln County's total population. Vessel clearances there are few and the city lives principally by manufacturing and marketing. It is the seat of Bishop Ridley College (Church of England) with a student body of some 300 boys. Local hydroelectric systems with Niagara power activate nearly a hundred industrial plants which produce around $23,000,000 worth of goods. More than 700,000 horsepower are generated in the district, chiefly at near-by Queenston. Market-wise, the stone fruits predominate—cherries, peaches, plums.

As an annual attraction for tourists—in peacetime—St. Catharines features "May Blossom Time." Under ordinary conditions the Canadian Henley regatta is another prominent feature of St. Catharines' summer. Her mineral springs are advertised as relieving victims of rheumatism—"the Mt. Clemens of Canada."

Just as William H. Merritt founded St. Catharines, so his son, Thomas Rodman Merritt, founded Merriton, another rail and canal crossing. These worthies were son and grandson respectively of Thomas Merritt, a New England Loyalist who reached the Niagara country by way of New Brunswick. He served as cavalry officer in two wars, then for eighteen years as sheriff of Lincoln County. Thus three generations made history and geography.

Lincoln County also contains the delightful but rather sleepy villages of Queenston—opposite Lewiston, New York—and Niagara-on-the-Lake (older Newark) across from Old Fort Niagara.

Compared with the antiquity of Fort Niagara, this is all new country. Less than 160 years ago dense forests stood on these shores. They were first settled by the Loyalist families who sought shelter at Old Fort Niagara during the border war and were placed on near-by lands as tenants of the Crown. Niagara is the cradle of Upper Canada, scene of its first Parliament of only seven members. Today with St. Mark's Church and partially restored Fort George, it is still one of Canada's historic shrines.

It is related that when Lieutenant Governor Simcoe arrived in 1792 he contrived a Government House out of a warehouse, Navy Hall, but nevertheless managed to open his Parliament with colorful ceremony. Present were his own regiment, the Queen's Rangers, in green uniforms, and a redcoat company of the Fifth British Regiment of Foot, boated up from the Kingston garrison.

Simcoe's chief at Quebec was the sagacious but aging Guy Carleton, Lord Dorchester, of Revolutionary fame. The two did not always see eye to eye. But during Simcoe's five years in office the population of Upper Canada rose from 12,000 to 35,000. His habit of taking long views is revealed by his hesitation between locating the new capital on the Thames at what is now London or at York, the final choice. Both sites, as the years have shown, possess advantages over old Newark which continues as Niagara-on-the-Lake, proud of a past which includes Upper Canada's first newspaper and public library.

Queenston and Niagara were once busy ports with regular sail and steamship schedules to Hamilton, Toronto, Kingston and Montreal. Queenston doubled with Lewiston on the American side as a chief beneficiary of the Niagara portage for freight and passengers, while Niagara prospered as a shipbuilding center. Some of the famous ships built there will be mentioned later. As chief take-off for the Toronto run, Niagara's interest in the spring break-up developed into a sporting event. The first boat into port received remission of port dues, but this was nothing compared to pride in performance. Captain Hugh Richardson usually won, even if he had to land his passengers on the ice just inside the harbor while the docks were still encrusted.

The first ship on the lake to be specially equipped to conquer ice was the *Chief Justice Robinson,* built in 1842 by the Niagara Dock Company and commanded by Captain Hugh Richardson, Jr. Her prow was designed like a double-furrowed plow to throw the ice away from the ship. For ten years she maintained winter service between Niagara and Toronto, although at the latter place she could proceed no farther in winter than the outer end of Queen's Wharf. Often frozen in, and once driven ashore, the *Robinson* always pulled out somehow.

The Welland Canal reduced shipping at Queenston and Niagara, drawing trade to Port Dalhousie which is now the port for the Toronto-Niagara Falls route, with busses used between the falls and Port Dalhousie. The Muir yards at Dalhousie built goodly ships over many years and maintain drydock service. In turn Dalhousie has been outflanked by Port Weller, the New Welland's opening to deep water three miles to the eastward.

Although fruit is grown abundantly in most parts of the Niagara Peninsula, and St. Catharines is a considerable fruit market and canning center, the famed Canadian fruit belt is at its best in the thirty-mile stretch from Jordan to Hamilton. The leading market and cannery towns are Beamsville and Grimsby with Hamilton as chief concentration point.

The Canadian fruit belt as a whole includes the entire western end of Lake Ontario on both the north and south shores of the Lake's western end. Its area, including the apple-growing background, is often described as larger than the whole of England. The comparison is pertinent because England is the heaviest buyer of Canadian fruit, particularly of apples, which in the Lake Ontario region can be grown successfully over an area nearly 300 miles long. For grape, peach and pear culture the favored area is less extensive, with the Canada south shore in better position for the smaller fruits.

While the Ontario fruit belt extends on both sides of the border, its economic significance is far greater in Canada than in the United States, because many other regions in the United States are well adapted to horticulture, while Canada depends principally upon this particular region. Since the Ontario region is Canada's main source of small fruits, it has a strong domestic market for its wares, with only minor competition from Nova Scotia and British Columbia. On top of that, it has the great British market with the tariff advantage of Empire trade agreements. The Ontario fruit belt, consequently, is an important part of the total Canadian economy.

The most highly favored south-shore belt is seldom more than seven miles in width, between the lake shore and the Niagara Escarpment, behind which rise the Helderleigh Hills. Small fruits edge the lake, with apples in favor on the higher reaches. In general the orchards seem to be better managed on the western half of the Niagara Peninsula than on its eastern portion, perhaps because nearness to the Hamilton market gives better returns to the growers within easy reach. Here the land seems to be blessed with a cozy prosperity smiling from closely knit small holdings. There are long stretches of weedless orchards and scrupulously clean villages which fairly shine with respectable contentment. Their industries are chiefly connected with food processing and fruit preserving. While these family businesses are small they are quite numerous. Grimsby, for instance, has sixteen establishments which do a million-dollar-a-year business and also a noted beach well developed for recreation.

For so young a country trans-Niagara Canada wears a most convincing air of stability. Its brick and stone houses are built to last and are usually set in spacious grounds. The characteristic Ontario farmhouse has a spruce windbreak, a long driveway and a good-sized field between it and the highway. Because of high land values and the horticultural influence, this tendency to aloofness is less marked in the fruit country than elsewhere. Yet even here Old Country pride in land ownership reveals itself in ample lawns, good landscaping and lovely gardens.

La Salle, the great French pathfinder, brought his string of canoes to beach inside a picturesque harbor at the western end of Lake Ontario in September 1669. He soon departed and the important site now occupied by Hamilton received little further attention for more than a century. Robert Land, who arrived in 1778, is named as the first settler. Loyalists fleeing from New York discovered the richness of the soil and settled down to rebuild their fortunes. Looking lakeward now from Mount Hamilton over the top of the sturdy brick-and-stone modern city, the imaginative eye can still see afar off on the blue water the crowded boats of the Loyalist refugees.

Among those who struggled ashore, made camp and cleared the forest were many of questing blood who followed the Royal Standard faithfully from Scotland to the Thirteen Colonies and then on to this far shore. Stuarts, Harveys, McKinstrys, Buchanans and Mc-Nabs established families of distinction. Strong and persistent Loyalist pride is symbolized in the memorial to the founders which stands in the Wentworth County House grounds in Prince's Square. Not till 1813, however, was the townsite surveyed by George Hamilton and christened for his father, the Honorable Robert Hamilton.

A glance at the map will indicate both the advantages and disadvantages of this site at the western end of the lake—forty-nine miles from the Niagara River and forty-three miles from Toronto Bay. For east-west trade and travel the site was superbly located, but not so favorably placed in relation to other points of the compass. Lusty York would soon arise to overshadow it to the north and northeast. For a long time the inland reaches had few settlers. At Brantford, twenty miles west, the New York Iroquois, as a reward for their loyalty during the Revolutionary War, received an extensive reservation. This settlement held back somewhat the surrounding area, simply because Indians had fewer wants and so generated less trade than white settlers. But Hamilton possessed sheltered Lake Geneva and Burlington Bay, beside which the settlement took root on a narrow foothold between the water and the Niagara limestone escarpment, here called "the Mountain" and the most impressive elevation close to any Lake Ontario shore. Lake Geneva has been developed as an inner harbor.

With Loyalist blood pulsing in every vein it was inevitable that Hamilton's sons would serve Britain and Canada with fierce devotion in the War of 1812. Still visible are traces of earthworks erected by General Vincent at the battlefield on Burlington Heights, now a public park. Here was fought the battle of Stoney Creek in June, 1813, where the American invaders were thrown back. This engagement has deep historic significance; never were American arms so close to turning the corner of the lake and driving toward Georgian Bay in the effort to cut off from the rest of Canada its warmest, most southerly region.

In all directions from the head of the lake stretch highly fertile lands lying in a climate mellowed by lake airs. Easy of access from both north and south shores, Hamilton naturally has become the great market and shipping point for the fruit and vegetable trade. Market days in Hamilton are something to remember. Its public market, said to be the world's largest, is crowded from mid-May to mid-October with sellers and buyers of seasonal fruits and vegetables. Vast quantities of berries, cherries, peaches, plums, pears, apples and grapes are shipped from here to all parts of Canada and, normally, to Great Britain and other parts of the Empire. When autumn fruits begin to be shipped in and out of the city, the Hamilton market becomes a colorful sight admired by tourists, well patronized by townspeople and stimulating to the whole business community.

Although Hamilton first made headway as a market town, its place as the second city of Ontario has been won by its early financial and industrial initiative. During the 1830's threshing machines were made in Hamilton and also Canada's first friction sulphur matches. Other "firsts" are claimed in various fields of transportation by land and water. Whether Hamilton or Toronto constructed the first Canadian-built railroad locomotive is in dispute between the two cities. The evidence indicates that Toronto's "first" was home-built throughout, while Hamilton's may have embodied some importations. It was constructed for one of western Ontario's earliest railways, from Niagara to Windsor, begun in 1847.

McMaster University (Baptist) was founded in 1887 in Toronto, removed to Westdale, Hamilton, in 1930, where it occupies a sightly campus of ninety acres. The university enjoys income from the estate of the Hon. William McMaster, a Scots-Irish immigrant who rose to be president of the Canadian Bank of Commerce.

The city registered a rapid growth soon after 1898 when hydro-electric power was brought in from DeCew Falls, thirty-five miles to the southeast. Hamilton's own John Patterson is credited with solving then-difficult problems of transmission of electric power over long distances.

From these beginnings arose the present city of 180,000, "the Birmingham of Canada," which is a center of the Dominion's thriving iron and steel industry. Some 62,000 men and women were employed industrially in about 3,000 establishments during 1942, and as Hamilton has been a stronghold of Canadian war industry, this figure has since increased. Normally, Hamilton's manufactures are worth $200,000,000 a year. Hamilton has 1700 acres in 42 parks.

The present century has seen sixty United States concerns, including a number of world-known trade names, establish branch factories in Hamilton. The best known of these industrial offshoots of the States are International Harvester and Westinghouse Company.

Deepening the new Welland Ship Canal connecting Lakes Ontario and Erie has strongly aided commercial Hamilton because of its nearness to the Canal's Ontario outlet at Port Dalhousie. When Welland's locks were lengthened to 800 feet with accompanying deepening and widening, corresponding work in the Burlington Channel, connecting Lake Ontario with Hamilton Harbor, gave Hamilton an advantage for steamers moving to and from the Upper Lakes. Through these channels the largest freighters now bring coal, ore and other cargoes direct to the docks of Hamilton's largest manufacturing establishments. Hamilton lies a little nearer to the Welland than Toronto, and ships plying between Hamilton and the Welland enjoy shelter from southwest winds—a point of some moment in connection with early spring and late autumn storms.

The Loyalist tradition persists strongly in modern Hamilton. One sees the adjective "Royal" liberally applied to public buildings and business establishments. Most striking of these is the Royal Connaught Hotel, a swank and serviceable establishment which may have invented Canadian bacon, that tasty smoked tenderloin of pork which, as served there, approaches perfection. Canada takes pigs seriously, pays a dollar per head bonus on Grade-A porkers and fifty cents on Grade-B, so neither the packers nor the hotels are likely to run out of this choice brand which Americans so easily learn to like. Tea at the Royal Connaught is a rite requiring ample time. The many well-dressed persons who are to be seen there show daily that Hamilton is the home of a prosperous and leisurely society. The popularity of yachting and a fringe of fine summer houses around Burlington Bay are further evidence that this community has both time and money to spend on the graces of life.

Each of the three counties occupying Canada's portion of Lake Ontario's southern shore is more or less industrialized and consequently well populated. In addition, horticulture packs rural population more closely together than other types of agriculture. Nearly 375,000 people live in Welland, Lincoln and Wentworth counties, the last of which includes Hamilton. But when the western corner of the lake has been turned, industries are less numerous and the country is less well adapted to fruit growing. As a result, the counties northeast of Hamilton, except York, which includes Toronto, and Ontario, which includes Oshawa, are thinly populated.

The first two counties beyond Hamilton are Halton County with only 28,000 inhabitants and Peel with 25,000. Then east of York and Ontario counties come Northumberland with 31,000, Prince Edward (the Quinte Peninsula) with 19,000, Lennox with 11,000 and finally Frontenac, which includes Kingston, with 53,000. Progress from west to east beyond Oshawa is a gradual retreat from industry and horticulture. At the northeast corner of the lake the fertility of the back country is noticeably less than that of western Ontario. Travel from the western end of the lake to the eastern is also a transition from plow to ax, from pruning hook to fishing rod, from prairies to lakes, from pigs to fish, from metal industries to woodworking shops, from big business to small, until Belleville and Kingston are reached.

Along the way are many tidy and prosperous places. Burlington and Dundas are now quite definitely part of Hamilton's suburban area. Bronte thrives as a strawberry center. Oakville lies midway between Hamilton and Toronto, but is within the orbit of Toronto, which, like all huge cities, reduces its smaller neighbors to the position of satellites. Oakville builds boats and processes metals, and Port Credit still does commercial fishing; both provide many summer resorts with fine facilities for golf, fishing and yachting. Yet it was along these now well-manicured beaches that Walter Butler in 1779 found the worst going of his entire journey—high swells, heavy squalls, cold northwest winds, but plenty of salmon running.

The coldness of Lake Ontario's waters along this popular shore even in midsummer is something to reckon with. The chilly winds from the Northwest, the inflow of waters from the north and the great depth of the lake itself—700 to 775 feet in most offshore readings—combine to keep water temperatures well down even close to land. On this account Toronto's aquatic marathons are cruel tests of physical stamina and many exhausted swimmers have to be pulled from the water on the way to the finish line.

Toronto deserves a chapter to itself and will have it. Its outskirts stretch along the lake as far as Scarborough with its clay bluffs descending to the lake and near-by Pine Wood Creek.

Port Union, Frenchman Bay and Whitby Harbor are all rich in adventurous history, for they were centers of the fur trade in the far-off French and Indian days and later of the lumber trade.

The town of Whitby, inland a few miles on the railroad, is of much later origin.

Oshawa—"crossing a stream"—is the thriving seat of General Motors of Canada. Like the Michigan cities of Flint and Pontiac, Oshawa first manufactured horse-drawn vehicles. Its famous McLaughlin Carriage factories early became affiliated with the Buick Motor Company and later with the General Motors Corporation.

From the standpoint of production, Oshawa is part of the Michigan motorland transferred to Canada, even down to international unionism. This is one more testimony to the truth that the Dominion and the Republic grow more like and are more closely knit together, "for better, for worse," with every passing day.

On the shore of Durham County lie Bowmanville, Port Granby, Newcastle and Port Hope. Bowmanville has a good harbor, builds pianos and furniture. Port Hope used to be a boom-and-sawmill port in the lumber days, and great things were expected of it, but for forty years it has grown little and holds its own today principally because of its residential and resort charm. Lumber, grain and flour are the staple commodities of trade, while Trinity College Institute (Anglican) is a famous school. The Right Reverend Charles H. Brent, first Episcopal bishop of the Philippines and later bishop of western New York, began his notable career in Port Hope.

Cobourg, midway between Toronto and Kingston, has an excellent artificial harbor developed as the Canadian terminus of the Lake Ontario coal trade. Coal mined in the Pennsylvania hills is carried to Rochester by several railroads. From the docks of Rochester car ferries transport the loaded cars to Cobourg where they are passed over directly to the Canadian railroads.

With a population of 6,000, Cobourg is considerably more than a coal port, since its industries produce about $3,000,000 worth of goods a year. It has car works and breweries and also a thriving resort trade. Ten miles northward lies Rice Lake, famous for muskellunge and bass, and historically a seat of the Mississaga Indians, an eastern branch of the Ojibwa, or Chippewa, who arrived late in Indian history but are still on the ground as guides and woodsmen.

Formerly Cobourg was the seat of Victoria College, an independent Methodist institution, now affiliated with the University of Toronto. Vanished too is Cobourg's early name of Hardscrabble.

Early settlers in this region had more than ordinary culture and literary ability, and the annals of the northern shore are consequently of unusual breadth and depth. Their influence still lingers, and is apparent in such recent fiction as the *Jalna* series of novels by Mazo de la Roche, with setting and characters inspired by the scenery and sturdy individuals of this part of the lake shore.

Material for fiction seems to be endless hereabouts, with the rich

WINTER SCENE OF NIAGARA FALLS

*Courtesy of the Toronto Convention and Tourist Association*

QUEENSTON GENERATING STATION BELOW THE RAPIDS OF THE
NIAGARA RIVER

The operating head of water utilized at full load is 294 feet, and the total capacity is about 525,000 horsepower. Length of powerhouse is 590 feet.

**ELEVATORS OF TORONTO ELEVATOR LIMITED**
Capacity 2,000,000 bushels.

**MOUNTAINS OF COAL IN TORONTO HARBOR**

background of tales from the back country around Cobourg. It is still peopled by family stocks of several distinct English, Irish and Scottish groups of settlers who established themselves under unusual conditions and leadership. These groups had not yet become a cohesive society when the revolutionary movement of 1837—the year the town was founded—struck the community, and Cobourg consequently seethed with turmoil. The same difficulty appeared at many points along the lake, but in Cobourg it was intensified until it finally resulted in the plot which earned the rather fearsome title of "the Cobourg Conspiracy."

Before the conspiracy came to a head, in August 1839, Cobourg had experienced in acute form the chronic disorder of the time. While the Mackenzie reformers in that vicinity were persistent and noisy—and quite properly so as long as their course remained straight and their practices peaceful—they were always outnumbered by the Tory opposition. The Cobourg country militia turned out loyally to rescue Toronto from Mackenzie, but their services were not required and so they did not finish their march to the relief of the capital. In Cobourg and its vicinity there were the usual street fights, burning of opposition newspapers and disruption of public meetings. In these skirmishes the reformers, patriots or rebels—the same men, under different labels—were usually worsted. In the end they were driven under cover, but they emerged after Lord Durham's famous report indicated that the Family Compact was not without responsibility for the existing unrest. Local historians report feeling against the reformers ran so high that Catholics and Orangemen (Protestant Irish) made common cause there in opposition to reform, and apparently not even Lord Durham's report could cool down the Conservatives.

As in most undercover movements, the quality of the leadership soon deteriorated and as moderate men withdrew and abandoned the cause, desperate characters took control. What had been a movement to redress grievances degenerated at many points into a system of organized robbery and piracy.

Bill Johnston does not figure in the Cobourg affair, but a ruffian almost as famous does—Benjamin Lett. Lett seems to have been with Johnston when the gang seized and burned the steamer *Sir Robert Peel,* off Wells Island, Johnston's favorite hangout. He is also described as one of the party which escaped from military jail at

Kingston by paddling thirty-six miles across the lake in a canoe. But while Lett was one of the bullies of the Cobourg Conspiracy, its leader was a man of somewhat higher stamp—Samuel P. Hart, whose newspaper office had been burned by a Tory mob.

Hart matured his plot at Oswego, where he recruited followers and took over the schooner *Guernsey*. With the help of some sailors, more or less disaffected also, Hart ran the ship across the lake to the vicinity of Cobourg. They disembarked and he led the way to the home of a farmer named Ash, known to be sympathetic to the cause. Hart had planned to rob a rich farmer who lived near by and then go on to Cobourg and rob the bank owned by Robert Henry. As a side line the bloodthirsty Lett wanted to murder two prominent Family Compact leaders, the Boultons, and various other worthy citizens. The conspirators sent out a summons for the faithful to assemble, but few responded, and those who did appear were seized with qualms when they discovered that Hart was only after loot and bloodshed. While they discussed the sanguinary plans several plotters grew lukewarm and quietly decamped. One of them, Henry J. Moon, sought out the authorities, confessed everything and returned to the Ash homestead to serve as the "finger man." He was followed by a posse which surrounded the house and captured the remnants of Hart's gang. The only one to escape was Lett, who fled to the States and later died there.

As for Hart, he was let off with seven months' imprisonment, no doubt because Lord Durham's logic was beginning to seep into the public mind. He was actually defended in court by D'Arcy Boulton, one of the conspiracy's intended victims. Apparently the jury thought the misguided Hart had some reason to seek compensation in Cobourg for his burned newspaper office.

Hart had been part of—or at least had knowledge of—more important plots that had fortunately been thwarted: to burn all British shipping and fire the "enemy" fleet. He belonged to the Patriot Hunters' Lodges which existed on both sides of the border, held secret meetings and had codes and signals known only to the initiated. But apparently he was not high in the councils of that subversive movement, for his arrest seemed to have no effect on their program of intrigue and sabotage, which continued for several years after he was unmasked.

The other conspirators escaped with even less punishment. Thus ended the Cobourg Conspiracy, a tremendous thing in its time and place and cited here in some detail as an extreme example of the disturbances which racked the whole border intermittently for five years after the Revolution of 1837.

Along the remainder of the Northumberland County coast are spaced the villages of Grafton, Colborne and Brighton. Largest of these is Brighton, which benefits from the Murray Canal connecting Presque Isle harbor with the Bay of Quinte and the Trent system. Here we are approaching the part of the coast with the most varied contours and scenery—the deeply indented Quinte Peninsula which comprises Prince Edward County, and the beautiful Bay of Quinte which lies between the peninsula and the mainland.

At the northwestern entrance to the peninsula stands Trenton, whose twenty-one industries are turning out $53,000,000 worth of products annually. Located at the head of the bay, it is the outlet for the Trent River and the canal system of that name which runs northwest along a bewildering succession of rivers, lakes and creeks, through Lake Simcoe and on by way of the Severn River to Georgian Bay. Champlain came this way from Georgian Bay for his discovery of Lake Ontario. The Dominion has spent $20,000,000 on this mazy waterway. No doubt it will someday be enlarged into a chief carrier, of standard breadth and depth, but at present both its capacity and the cargoes routed through it are limited. In 1940 the Trent system carried only 24,000 tons, most of which no doubt were floated between Trenton and Peterboro, a thriving milling and manufacturing center about twenty miles north of the lake.

At Peterboro stands an unusual hydraulic lift lock—really a pair of locks in one of which the vessel remains stationary while the entire lock in which it floats is lifted more than sixty feet by means of rising water in the other lock. Peterboro is famous for its canoes and no wonder, for this long stretch of waterways is perhaps as pleasant and safe a course for canoes as can be found anywhere. At Peterboro tourists and fishermen outfit and secure Indian guides for their expeditions into the famous Kawartha Lakes and the wilder reaches stretching northward toward huge Algonquin Park.

Trenton is the gateway to the Quinte Peninsula, which is roughly twenty miles by ten but deeply indented and connected with the mainland at its northwest corner. The sand dunes on the peninsula can be reached by steamer, or by motor from either Wellington or Picton, the county seat. These place names commemorating the Iron Duke and the greatest of his lieutenants, Sir John Picton, indicate the comparative youth of these communities. Early settlers passed by the region in favor of the more open and fertile lands to the west, just as Americans by-passed the southern New York and northern Pennsylvania uplands, with the result that limited frontiers moved eastward long after the Northwest had been settled. Land-seekers were not easily attracted by the sand which gave the region its name, derived from a corrupted Iroquois word for sandy flat.

At Big Sandy Bay the dunes march inland at the rate of about 150 feet a year. They do their traveling in winter and late spring when drifting snow assists the flow and melting helps to wash the sand forward. In summer the white sands and blue waters attract vacationers, but as no large cities are near by the shore is seldom crowded. These dazzling white shores seem lonely beyond all others perhaps because they are bare of vegetation. But if one is weary of crowds and likes open sky, earth and water, the dunes are ideal.

On a considerable elevation not far from the village of Picton stands a fair-sized body of water known as the Lake-on-the-Mountain. It drains only a tiny area, by no means enough to compensate for the evaporation from its surface, and it is frequently described as having no tributary whatever. As far as anyone can see there is no connection with surrounding Lake Ontario, and there seems to be no underground connection either—at least the natives swear that the levels of the small lake are not affected by the rise and fall of water levels in Lake Ontario. This phenomenon is likely to stump anyone who leaves the dry sands of the Ontario shore, drives up the steep slope and finds this little tree-surrounded lake serenely aloft by itself. What force gathers that amount of water and pushes it up to that height has never been convincingly explained—not, at least, to this inquiring tourist. One explanation, which seems to be remarkable beyond belief, is that the Lake-on-the-Mountain occupies a volcanic tube and that its underground water connections are with distant Lake Erie, which is about as high above Lake Ontario as this small lake. It is said that the Lake-on-the-Mountain falls and rises with Lake Erie rather than with Lake Ontario, but as Erie and Ontario tend to go up or down together, it would take elaborate and accurate measurements to establish that fact. They never have been made, and may never be made. But if such a natural pipe line for Erie water exists it must follow the Canadian shore instead of cutting across Lake Ontario. Either that, or it goes under Lake Ontario at something like a depth of 800 feet below the surface of that deep body of water. Here is a mystery that may never be solved.

The peninsula can be left behind by bridge to Belleville, a thriving manufacturing city with good transportation to St. Lawrence and Lake Ontario cities by water, railroad and highway. Occupying a middle position on the Bay of Quinte, Belleville has grown into the metropolis of that lovely and diversified region. Since 1900 its population has risen from 10,000 to 18,000. Its wholesalers handle large quantities of cheese and farm produce grown in the highly fertile surrounding district. Many of the farms are on the peninsula, which is by no means all drifting sand, although the dunes are what one goes there to see.

Industrially, Belleville lives chiefly by making cement, cheese, whisky and lumber. Nine sizable industries annually produce $9,000,000 in manufactures. There are a large institution for the deaf and dumb, a convent school and a business college there. But Belleville is primarily a business town. When her affluent citizens relax for the summer, they go to Mississaga Point across the bay. Captain John W. Meyers named the Belleville location Meyers Creek when he set up his mill there in 1794, but Lieutenant-Governor Gore requested that it be named for his wife, Lady Arabella.

The Bay of Quinte region, particularly the northern arm stretching toward Deseronto and Nappanee, is now arousing archaeological interest as a probable motherland of the Iroquois, whence the New York Nations migrated across Lake Ontario. Thence came Dekanawida, father of the Iroquois Confederacy. French missionaries had a mission near Trenton from 1668 to 1680, by which time the Mississaga were present.

Between commerce and sport the waters of Quinte are seldom vacant during the open season. The fishing is excellent. The mainland shores and those of Amherst Island, which partially blocks the entrance to the bay, offer excellent duck-shooting. Duck Island and False Duck Island, which extend off Point Traverse, the southeasterly point of the peninsula, and help to screen the St. Lawrence outlet, came honestly by their names. The island barrier here provides the quiet water and good feeding thoroughly appreciated by waterfowl. For those sportsmen who can be happy without mountains this region and its northward extension have everything else to offer.

Between Amherst and Wolfe Islands runs the ship channel to Kingston, a historic port and naval base, located on the mainland at the entrance of the Rideau River and Canal. Wolfe Island screens the approaches both to east and west, providing shelter for a deep harbor accessible both from Lake Ontario on the west and the St. Lawrence River on the east. Keen French eyes bent on empire selected this strategic position, and to this day it remains a place of strength and militant tradition.

Like Oswego, Kingston reveals the storied past wrestling with the dynamic present, but of the two Kingston contains more and sightlier vestiges of dangerous days. In the past its military and naval glories far outshone its other activities, even those of its brief flowering as capital of Upper Canada. To this day, trade lags well behind education and the military activities in this picturesque city of 27,000 on Cataraqui Bay.

Of all Ontario's cities, the seed of Kingston was sown earliest. In 1673, La Salle, with immense energy and personal sacrifice, established there the fortified trading post long known as Fort Frontenac. For both France and England this site became the naval base from which their vessels swept the lake. Colonel Bradstreet's raid in 1758 destroyed both post and shipping and two years later, following the capitulation of Canada, Britain entered into possession.

Because of their concentration on seaboard trade and disregard of interior regions, the British let the Ontario posts decline. When Walter Butler reconnoitered the north shore for General Haldimand in 1779, he found it difficult to enter the harbor and did not consider the settlement itself worthy of notice. He wrote, under date of March 16: "Off very early—much ice formed in night—wind ahead and partly off shore, which drove the ice in the lake. Rowed till 9 o'clock. The weather calm—rowed across a deep bay. Continued rowing till the mouth of Caderonque Bay—wind coming fair sailed into Caderonque Harbour. I am told vesels can't sail out of C. Harbor to the lake but with a N. or N.E. wind, an E. & S.E. and S. wind are fair winds for ships once clear of the river to Niag."

During the Revolutionary War the British used Cataraqui as a military and naval base and it was after 1781 that the place began to take on a substantial aspect. Then the sturdy gray stone houses, which are typical of Kingston today, began to supersede the wooden houses of French habitants and traders. Unlike transitory French power in America, as typified by the flimsy shelters of the voyageurs, the stone houses of the conqueror race seem fit to stand for centuries.

In 1783 Loyalists emigrating from the States founded Bath, twenty miles west of Kingston, a small village with deep roots, an enduring settlement rather than a garrison town. Loyalists led by Captain Michael Grasse came to Cataraqui in the same year, which was also marked by a survey of the townsite and the first work on the Fort Henry site.

Joseph Hadfield, author of *An Englishman in America,** encountered many boatloads of Loyalists moving into this region when he ascended the St. Lawrence in 1785. They were traveling, four or five families together, in large bateaux, sharp-pointed and flat-bottomed except at the ends. In addition to passengers, these vessels could carry two tons of merchandise and were loaded deep with provisions and household effects. At the rapids the passengers disembarked and sometimes had to carry cargo around while the boats were pulled upstream. Many losses were incurred through inexperience. Hadfield wrote feelingly of the sufferings the Loyalists underwent in this migration. The new Loyalist settlers found a small community grouped around the still-evident ruins of the old French fort, a second structure built by the great Frontenac in 1695.

After the abandonment of Carleton Island, the ancient and well-sheltered settlement near the site of old Fort Frontenac was selected as the chief military and naval depot. However, Kingston did not receive its ultra-British name until 1792, when the Lieutenant Governor of the infant province of Upper Canada, Colonel John Graves Simcoe, met the Executive Council in the town.

Throughout the city grim gray walls, towers and bastions link the peace of the present with memories of a war-torn past. Fort Henry, which the Americans in 1812 never quite dared to assault, has been modernized and is rated as chief element in the third

---

* Edited by Douglas S. Robertson (Toronto: Hunter-Rose Company, Ltd., 1933), pp. 50ff.

strongest defense system in Canada, following Halifax and Quebec. The Fort Frontenac Barracks standing today were erected in 1821 on the former French site. Garrison troops of the Royal Canadian Horse Artillery parade daily over the buried foundation of old Fort Frontenac. With Fort Frontenac and Fort Henry, Fort Frederick, the Royal Military College and three military hospitals, Kingston has a martial air which is especially keen in wartime.

Indeed, wherever one strolls he encounters reminders of the city's unique and colorful past. A cairn in City Park marks the starting point for the first survey of Upper Canada or Ontario Province, a tremendous task begun soon after the Loyalists arrived. Memorials of preceding conflicts abound, and the city contains buried and half-buried fortifications as reminders of faithful garrisons long gone to dust and of fleets built there to control Lake Ontario.

Following the War of 1812, in which Kingston was a key fortress and the chief British naval base on the lake, the city began its long-delayed commercial rise. Like its south-shore prototype, Oswego, Kingston had a staple activity in transferring cargoes from ships to barges and vice versa. The St. Lawrence River canals handled 3,600,-000 tons of freight up and down in 1941, and of this a considerable part was transshipped at Kingston.

Just as Oswego has interior waterways at its command, so Kingston has the Rideau Canal connecting the port with the Ottawa River at the Dominion's capital city, but while the Rideau touches the Land of a Thousand Lakes, a beautiful recreation area, it is a puny water-way in comparison with New York's Barge Canal. The Rideau canal system suffers apparently from two causes—lack of cargoes and government neglect. While $20,000,000 was being spent on the Trent system, the Rideau had to put up with a beggarly $4,500,000. But perhaps this relatively small sum is justified by the fact that the Rideau carried only 1,300 tons of freight. Its chief and almost its only source of cargoes no doubt was lumber. Since the canal connects the splendid Ottawa River with the Great Lakes system, further development may take place.

Kingston's spacious harbor, shipyards and dry docks are already much used and will no doubt expand as the St. Lawrence is improved for navigation. Vessel entries and a lively tourist trade to the Thousand Islands pull many travelers to Kingston. Probably no lovelier ferry ride exists than that between Kingston and the American ports of Clayton and Alexandria Bay. For steady year-round work, in nine sizable and several smaller establishments, Kingston manufactures locomotives, textiles, tiles, brooms, paper boxes, moldings, pianos, steam and marine engines, ships, boats and a variety of chemicals to a value of $53,000,000 a year. Large mines of feldspar and mica are located near by.

A Dominion government dry dock, leased by the Kingston Ship-building Company, is more than 350 feet long with an entrance width of 55 feet and a depth of 14.7 feet at low water. Sailing out of Kingston and registered there in 1941 were 103 vessels totaling 158,000 tons.

The public buildings, including large Anglican and Catholic cathedrals, are mostly built of limestone along the lines of classical architecture. Unfortunately not all are of the same type of classic, but the effect is impressive. Vestige of an era gone forever is a double gate, the sole remnant saved from the ancient French fort which is set in the massive stone walls of Fort Frontenac. The most pictur-esque reminder of the past is the round West Ditch Tower of Fort Frederick, on the grounds of the Military College. Fort Frederick is architecturally the most impressive of the three guardian forts and lends grim dignity to the Royal Military College reservation. Founded in 1876, the Royal Military College, often called the Woolwich of Canada, has indeed won its spurs. From this notable institution have gone forth a steady stream of well-trained youths to defend Empire and Dominion in two World Wars.

Kingston's only daily newspaper, the *Whig-Standard,* goes back in direct line, by merger and purchase, to the Kingston *Gazette* which was founded on September 25, 1806, by young Stephen Miles. The founder was still a minor, so he invented the firm of Moore and Kendall to cover his operations. By another line the *Whig-Standard* is also descended from the *British Whig,* founded in 1834 by Edward John Barber, which in 1849 became the first daily newspaper pub-lished in Ontario.

Incorporated in 1838, the city three years later was chosen capital of United Canada, as related earlier. In that year Queens University, third largest university in Canada, was founded by Royal Charter.

For at least one major sport Kingston is a world center. The growing popularity of ice hockey in Canada and in northern cities of the United States found lively expression on February 12, 1944, when an International Hockey Hall of Fame was organized in Kingston. It is claimed this game, born in England, was introduced to Canada at Kingston under rules so thoroughly revamped that the Kingston event amounted to a rebirth. Another version credits McGill University at Montreal with priority on rules.

The United States adopted hockey, the Canadian national sport, as avidly as Canada adopted baseball. Because of larger urban populations south of the border, American teams outnumber the Canadian teams in both major professional leagues. Toronto and Montreal are the only two Canadian cities in the ace International Hockey League, but Ontario remains a training and recruiting ground for professional hockey players. Many of her stars are lured away to the States by high salaries. Probably Canada, because of better ice, will always lead in amateur hockey, for swift, sure skating is what hockey requires, plus the ability to take the physical punishment involved in collisions at top speed, euphemistically called "body checks."

A good deal has been made by André Siegfried and others of the continuing Americanization of Canada by the heavy pull of commerce, travel and opinion exercised by a United States grown so rich, populous and influential in the past century. No doubt the sheer economic weight of the United States on this continent does tend to draw Canadians generally toward the American way of life. But in the Lake Ontario region, where the Canadian shores are more populous and dominant in national affairs than are the American shores, examples of the reverse trend are not infrequent. Probably more Americans in the Lake Ontario region listen to Canadian broadcasts than vice versa. At any rate New York followed avidly Ontario's lead on hockey and is gradually working up some enthusiasm for rugby and association football. Those sports are first cousins of standard American football as now played by both college and professional teams, but curiously enough Ontario shows little interest in the American game. The influence seems to come not from the United States but from Canada, as the spread of hockey shows.

Eighteen miles east of Kingston and before the St. Lawrence narrows itself at Wells Island is Gananoque, which works in copper and steel, yet manages a resort trade also. This little city "where rocks rise out of the water" seems likely to grow.

An excellent recreational project at Lake Ontario's eastern gateway is the St. Lawrence Islands Park, which consists chiefly of thirteen islands in the eighty-mile stretch of river between Kingston and Morrisburg. With a mainland reservation, this park safeguards for the people and their posterity an entry into one of Nature's loveliest wonderlands—the Thousand Islands. No doubt in time most of those scenic isles on both sides of the international border will pass into public possession to preserve their beauties against destruction by ice and current or by predatory men.

In general, it can be said that while Canadians visit the States on business, Americans visit Ontario chiefly for recreation. It follows that while Canadians are influenced more by business methods south of the line, Americans are more influenced by those noncommercial elements of Canadian life to which they are attracted while on tour. Sport is one of these elements, but by no means the only one. Indeed, Americans usually return from Ontario highly appreciative of her energy, culture, stability and all-round decency of behavior, public and private.

## Chapter 21

# Toronto—Self-Made City

*We must be free or die, who speak the tongue*
*That Shakespeare spoke, the faith and morals hold*
*Which Milton held.—In everything we are sprung*
*Of earth's first blood, have titles manifold.*
— WILLIAM WORDSWORTH

RESIDENTS of growing metropolitan Toronto are well aware that change rules this earth. Their vistas alter swiftly as new skyscrapers are reared, and even the excavations show that things are not as they were. Where Toronto's finest buildings stand was once deep water. Lauder Avenue, one of Toronto's pleasant residential streets, runs along the crest of a low hill which slopes up from the water front. In prehistoric times this elevation, two miles inland from the present beach, was the shore of Lake Ontario. The ridge begins at the lake shore about four miles east of the city and continues west far beyond the city. At Hamilton on Lake Ontario's western tip it joins the Niagara escarpment which runs parallel with the lake, and extends on northwest through the province, outcropping in Georgian Bay as Manitoulin Island.

These contours signify that Lake Ontario, smallest of the Great Lakes, was at one time considerably larger and deeper than it is at present. The geologic change accounts for the succession of fine beaches which line the shore, but limits harbors to river estuaries requiring steady and often extensive engineering work to meet modern demands of shipping for depth of water and dock developments. For this reason, in the early stages of white settlement, the unimproved Toronto Bay was inconvenient for large vessels, but the shore there was a popular spot for canoes or small boats to rendezvous. Toronto Bay was a natural starting point for land journeys westward. Through the deep forests bordering the lake's north shore the Indians opened a trail from Ontario to Georgian Bay which

300

wound across country to Lake Simcoe and the Severn River, thence to the Bay of Thirty Thousand Islands on Huron.

The name "Toronto" was a transference. First applied in the seventeenth century to the Huron country, it was shifted naturally to the white man's Rouillé, "the place of meeting." The aborigines' "To-ron-to" was easier to pronounce than the fort's name and so was commonly used. When white settlers at last built their cabins on the site they continued to use the name.

The first cargo discharged at the present Port of Toronto in 1749 came there on an armed French vessel of some fifty tons, its hold jammed with supplies and traders' goods, invoiced to one M. Varran, keeper of Fort Rouillé, which the restless French had newly established on the old Indian meeting site. The fort, referred to subsequently by itinerant traders as the Fort at Toronto, was the ordinary trading post of its day enclosed by a strong if rude stockade. Canadian National Exhibition grounds now occupy its site. For seven years a brisk traffic was carried on there. In the few years intervening before the French burned Fort Rouillé to save it from the British in 1756, customers for the post occupied a series of Indian villages along the shore. The braves hunted and quickly bartered their furs for the rum, beads, blankets, weapons and gimcracks dear to them. Port Credit, some twelve miles west of Toronto, was then a populous trading center for thousands of Indians and "breeds." Natural food supplies were plentiful. Up to twenty-five years ago, it is said that along that shore salmon crowded the rivers at spawning time.

On deserting the post the French removed their effects, burned Fort Rouillé and made the long trek overland to Niagara. Never again would a French fortress command the entrance to Toronto.

As years passed after French evacuation and the destruction of Fort Rouillé, a few squatters and itinerant traders straggled to and from the site. They lived from hand to mouth, by trap and gun rather than by cultivation of the land. Nobody troubled to establish law and order. Along the lake the place was called either "To-ron-to" or "the Fort," usually "Toronto" by Indians and "the Fort" by whites.

Lieutenant Walter N. Butler, the Tory leader, on a north shore journey to spy out the shore for the high command in 1779, had trouble navigating the coast in this vicinity and wrote this graphic entry in his unpublished Journal of March 12.

"Set off at 7 o'clock—wind N.W. Too much off land to sail—rowed till 11 o'clock—put into river called DuCredit 17 miles from our last station—Sand low and a good beach except the points which are bluff. Two Mississaugoes informed me a number of them lived up this river, gave them bread, put off at 12 rowed to the bottom of bay at Toronto, hoisted sail—found the wind too high to go around *long point* forming the basin or bay below *Toronto* continued sailing down the bay to the carrying place—unloaded the boat—hauled her over and loaded again in an hour and a half—rowed to the beginning of the high lands—camped on the beach—the bay of Toronto filled with all sorts of wild fowl—saw on the N. side several wigwams—Canoes turned up on the shore."*

Butler's report makes it clear that there was no white settlement on Toronto Bay in 1779. Responsibility for starting a British town there and for giving it a new name goes to the first governor of Upper Canada, Colonel Simcoe. The provisional capital of the province was first established at Niagara. But neither Simcoe nor Lord Dorchester could see wisdom in maintaining a capital located as Niagara was on an enemy frontier. At Lord Dorchester's order, Simcoe spent some time in the spring of 1793 examining the north shore of the lake for a suitable site. In May he decided that Toronto Bay had the proper qualifications.

Two months later a company of troops landed and set up their camp. They were followed, in about ten days, by Mrs. Simcoe, who soon selected a suitable site for the two-roomed tent which the Colonel had bought from the estate of the explorer, Captain Cook. This canvas house was the nucleus of the new community. Colonel Simcoe soon had surveyors lay out a plan for the town. He himself christened it York in honor of the Duke of York's victory over the French. As York, the town went through its early development, and it was not until 1834 that the name Toronto was restored.

Through Simcoe's agency York was chosen as a capital before it was a town. In its early years its streets were quagmires in wet weather. Mosquitoes bred in its swampy creek and malaria hung over the town. Little lumber was available and the earliest houses were built of logs. Three years after the town was established, Sim-

---

* By permission of the Public Archives of Canada and the courtesy of Harvey Chalmers II, of Amsterdam, N. Y., author of *West to the Setting Sun*.

coe began construction of brick Parliament Houses and in 1797 the capital was actually moved. The town was still little more than a collection of crude huts in the center of mud and desolation.

Partly burned in the War of 1812, still deep in dirt and mire, York had a long way to rise when the Loyalists took control. But rise it did. Roads were built. The creek was improved with dikes and sluices. On the Humber and the Don fine mills were set up. By 1817 the civilian population already amounted to about 1,200.

By the time the town of York gave place to the city of Toronto in 1834 the population had multiplied to nearly 11,000. The city was full of bustling life and many improvements had been made. It was considered a large, handsome, well-laid-out city. Even Charles Dickens admitted as much, when he saw it in 1842.

Pace of growth continued rapid by Canadian standards. In 1861, Toronto numbered 44,821 persons, and twenty years later there were 86,415. Swinging into the 1900's, the "Boston of Canada," to employ a phrase from a day now outgrown, had doubled again.

The reasons for this swift, startling metamorphosis from seeds to substance were two: first, the natural advantages; second, types of incoming population qualified to make the most of them. After the War of 1812 the character of the population had changed. Simcoe's United Loyalists had cleansed or swept away the original mass of nondescripts. Responsibility, thrift and sturdy loyalty took command. The modern city is ultra-British in sympathy and tone, but it has the driving force which characterizes its big U. S. neighbor, Detroit. It is by no means merely accident that Toronto leads all rivals as the metropolis of Ontario, a huge province of 407,262 square miles.

Inland, what the early occasional visitors saw only as grass and timber has proved to be immensely rich. Southern Ontario contains more than sixty percent of the population of the province and produces nearly half the total of Canada's manufactured products. Its mineral wealth, in contrast to the silver and gold of the more northerly districts around the towns of Cobalt and Timmins, is chiefly nonmetallic—natural gas, salt, ornamental stone, road material, cement and lime. Mining of gypsum, feldspar, graphite, talc and lead is also carried on. But the wealth of the Lake Ontario shore is the indestructible might of a strong, shrewd population occupying a fertile area favorable for trade and manufacturing.

For a time a harbor some three and a half square miles in extent, with a narrow entrance at the west end, was still oversize for shipping, but by 1900 the city had outgrown its shores and stretched along the lake front for eight miles. This was but a start for greater things to come in the first forty-four years of the present century.

In this region water provided the first transportation. Nearly a hundred years ago logs cut in winter were sent swimming down swift currents of the Don and Humber Rivers to form rafts to be sailed or towed to Quebec for transshipment to England. Later the timber, brought in by rail, was slid into Toronto Bay between Queen's Wharf and Spadina Avenue. As the forest fringe receded northward under steady shearing, ports on Georgian Bay took over and Toronto's once wide timber business became localized. Vast inland forests in Ontario are still untapped, but most of the near-by timber supply is used in the home market. Indeed, for some kinds of wood the Toronto area now depends upon British Columbia. A timber terminal with unloading cranes has been built on harbor lands fronting the ship channel to receive timber brought around from the Pacific Coast via the Panama Canal and the St. Lawrence.

Railroads and steamships brought faster transportation and greater carrying capacities at an opportune time for Toronto. While it was only one of several good harbors on the northern shore of Lake Ontario, it was the one best located and adapted for rail purposes, and a logical terminus for a direct rail route from navigable water to the North Country. As a junction point between rail and water transportation the city soon outstripped the other Ontario ports, leaping far ahead of Kingston, which is too close to Montreal for marketing independence.

Once started, railroad construction came with amazing speed. As in the United States the first locomotives used in Canada were imported, but in 1853 Canada's first completely home-built locomotive, the "Toronto," was manufactured in that city by the well-known firm of James Good on Sherburne Street. Toronto has never lost the leadership in heavy manufacturing that the building of this locomotive symbolized. Equally it has kept its place as a rail center. Two hundred trains now roll in and out of Toronto every day.

Adequate development of Toronto's railway opportunities has helped develop both the province of Ontario and the whole Dominion. The province is the bridge between Canada East and Canada West, and Toronto is the keystone of the Ontario bridge. In the Dominion's official words: "Canada, nearly 4,000 miles in length from east to west, with the main topographic barriers running in a north-south direction and a relatively small population of 11,419,895 (preliminary count of population from the census of 1941) thinly distributed along the southern strip of this vast area, presents unusual difficulties from the standpoint of transportation. To such a country ... cheap transportation is a necessity of life."* And to meet this critical need for unifying communications, Toronto inevitably developed not only as a railroad center, but also as a focus for postal, telegraph, telephone and radio systems.

The city is listed as a Canadian pioneer in electric street railways. As of 1940, the municipally owned Toronto Transportation Company controlled and operated 214.91 track miles, with gross earnings of $12,043,163 "against operating expenses of $6,898,237; fare passengers carried, 173,639,820; service given by 3,194 employes who received $4,817,205 in salaries and wages."

Of the whole gigantic rail development of Canada, in which public funds and credit have been used fully, Toronto has become the principal focus, particularly in its spacious port development where steel rails and ships meet amid superb facilities.

Toronto's growth as a port is a shining example of intelligent public control guiding private interests into effective co-operation. The port and harbor system represents an investment of $40,000,000. Along the ten-mile water front the improved wharves and docks have handled 4,000,000 tons of cargo in a year.

This magnificent development is less than forty years old. In 1911 the city of Toronto transferred control of Ashbridge's Bay and Marsh and its own water-front properties to the Harbour Commissioners. As usual business shied away at the start; only three industries were established in the district during the first two years. Additional marshlands containing three square miles have since been drained to form two other port areas—Eastern Harbor Terminals and Central Harbor Terminals, both equipped with railroad tracks, concrete wharves, industrial and warehouse buildings, and public utilities of

---

* *The Canada Year Book 1942*, published by authority of the Honourable James A. McKinnon, M.P., Minister of Trade and Commerce, p. 574.

all kinds needed by ships, cargoes and transport workers. By the end of 1933 there were more than seventy businesses flourishing in these areas, most of which had come in since 1922 when commercial revival after a postwar slump found Toronto ready with ample locations. Toronto folk proclaim that their city was the first on the Great Lakes to plan and provide improved modern harbor facilities on so vast a scale.

Back of this harbor development stood the experience and resources gained by Toronto as Canada's best located distributing center, the Chicago of the Dominion as contrasted with Montreal, which resembles New York City in salt-water shipping and financial position. Toronto's confidence in its future rests on the substantial fact that ten percent of Canada's total population reside within a ten-mile radius of the city's heart. Another million persons live within a second circle of 250 miles, and one-third of Canada's entire buying power is concentrated within 100 miles of Toronto's downtown district. Not even New York City has so large a proportion of a nation's buying power concentrated as tightly around it. In addition, the city's industries are diversified, with a good balance between light and heavy manufacturing and between wholesale and retail trade. Any transportation improvement serving the Toronto district was soundly based and from that base wider and wider areas could be tapped.

Right up to World War II engineering work continued along the water front. By 1939 these results could be chalked up: a commission railway thirty miles long tied together the two great systems, the Canadian National Railways and the Canadian Pacific Railways. Fourteen miles of wide paved streets served the harbor areas. A temporary bulkhead wall 4,200 feet long had been built and adjoining it to the south stretched fifty-three and a half acres of unimproved dock sites. Harbour Commissioners had worked out plans for new piers, wharves and slips to equip future purchasers or long-term lessees. All their plans now await postwar fulfillment, for which Toronto stands well prepared. On the harbor program are a combined airplane and seaplane base on Toronto Island, the Malton Airport—a massive development which would have delighted progressives like Simcoe, Drummond and Macdonald.

Although not as open as Oswego and Rochester on the American side of the lake, Toronto harbor is less icebound than any other large

Canadian harbor on the lake. Inside the port Toronto's ice is seldom heavy enough, even during the deep winter months, to keep ships berthed there from being moved. This convenience gains both traffic and repair work for Toronto's harbor because it saves time in preparing ships for the initial voyage of the season. Carriers from Toronto usually start the season with full cargoes, and vessels arriving at Toronto are quite certain of at least a 90-percent return cargo, normally of iron and steel products which provide most of the heavy freight originating in the Toronto region.

Wartime visitors are impressed by the swarming factories everywhere rumbling at top speed. Today these great shops are manufacturing munitions and engines of war. Enlarged and multiplied by these special demands, when they turn once more to the production of peacetime civilian goods, they will play an augmented part in the industrial life of the Dominion. Within Toronto there are now some 2,500 shops, employing more than 150,000 men and women. Plans are already well formed for converting the production of these plants smoothly and rapidly to peacetime needs.

Business and industry in Toronto take on more and more an international flavor. F. D. Tolchard, general manager of the Board of Trade of the city, reports that approximately 400 United States and British companies operate plants in Toronto. Scores of well-known American companies have located their Canadian divisions in the city so that it produces a variety of goods from tooth paste to aircraft, from bowling balls to hydraulic brakes.

From the tiny mills on the Don and Humber in the dirty little York of 1834 to the great factories of modern Toronto is an industrial advance which few communities can match. The city's progress as the social, intellectual and artistic center of a region has been as rapid and as sweeping as its commercial development. The modern city, with its parks, its great buildings such as the Canadian Bank of Commerce, its university, its museums, its hockey arena, its symphony orchestra, its hotels such as the Royal York, is well equipped not merely to produce and handle goods but to offer a full and rounded life to its 850,000 residents and the thousands who visit it. The mud of York has proved rich ground.

A fair part of Toronto's social and intellectual development stems directly from little York. In the winter of 1830-1831 a group in the town founded the Mechanics' Institute and scheduled regular meetings and lectures after the manner of similar organizations in England and Scotland. The membership was in no way restricted to mechanics and included many of the leading business and professional men of the community. For some years it met in the Masonic Hall on Colborne Street. Finally, after several moves, and nearly ten years of money-raising, in 1861 the Institute moved into its own building. Besides sponsoring lectures on a wide variety of highly educational subjects, even including astronomy and biology, the Institute offered a library and reading room and some recreational facilities.

The old Mechanics' Institute finally died but its spirit went marching on. The city arranged to take over the building and what remained of its collection of books to form a public library. In 1884 the new library had its formal opening, the beginning of Toronto's present library system.

Meanwhile, supplementing the Mechanics' Institute as a center of social and intellectual life was St. Lawrence Hall. Built of stone in ornate Corinthian style, the hall had a seating capacity of about a thousand, but considerably more sometimes crowded in. From 1851 on, it was a social center of many uses. Primarily it was an auditorium. Lectures of the Mechanics' Institute were sometimes held here. Speakers fought out the slavery issue, explained biology and the proper raising of children, argued for woman suffrage and blue laws for Sunday.

It was used for plays and entertainments of all sorts and especially for concerts. Some of these were by local artists, including the Toronto brass band, but more commonly foreign talent was in demand. Patti sang there in the summer of 1851. Jenny Lind, who sang there that same fall, filled the hall at three dollars a ticket and gave another performance the next day to accommodate those who were turned away from the first performance. In 1857 Handel's *Messiah* was given its first performance in Toronto with a splendid group of local and imported singers.

The hall was often taken over for banquets, balls and festivals by organizations, fraternal orders, one of the National Societies, the Fire Companies or the like. Some of these affairs were extremely elaborate and exclusive. Thus the hall was a center for the most varied amusements and social activities, a real force in the development of the city as a community. Twenty years after it was put in service, its glory had begun to fade. It was somewhat renovated in 1911 but did not regain its place. It was last being used as a hostel for the unemployed, a long drop from the past.

In 1886 serious music was given a firm niche in the city by the formation of the Toronto Conservatory, by Dr. Edward Fisher. Eight years later, Dr. Vogt, Dr. Fisher's successor, also established the Mendelssohn Choir. In the same year a thoroughly adequate concert hall was opened—Massey Music Hall. Through the agency of the conservatory and the choir, Toronto came to know and appreciate fine music. The present Toronto Symphony is the concrete result—or one of the results. Developed by Dr. Ernest MacMillan, it is one of the fine symphonies that the continent has produced.

In sports Toronto is a curious blend of British and American. Its hockey team, the Maple Leafs, is one of the leaders of major-league hockey and attracts crowds of better than 13,000 at its home games. American football it has greeted coolly, not to say indifferently, preferring the British types, but baseball it has taken to its heart. It has hundreds of amateur teams and a professional team in the International League. Cricket, although much less popular with spectators, appeals to participants and holds its own.

Yachting, rowing and swimming are naturally at home in Toronto. For a time Toronto produced champion scullers known throughout the world. In swimming, Toronto was best known for its annual marathon swim. This race, because it forced each contestant to spend several hours in the paralyzingly cold waters of the lake, was perhaps the most sadistic sporting event of its kind, but because of a large cash prize it constantly attracted a big array of starters.

Unlike the seaboard cities, Toronto has no really old buildings. The greater part of its buildings were constructed within the period from 1850 to the present. A good many of the earlier buildings are classical in design, usually not a severe classical. Mixed with them are examples of many other styles. In the residential sections "Early Ontario," a simple brick style, is growing in popularity. Downtown there are some notable modern buildings. The skyscrapers are somewhat more similar to the big buildings of Chicago than to the thin spires of New York, being somewhat broader and with bolder set-back design.

No doubt it is partly because of the American business influence that Toronto's pace in trade and social life generally is swifter than in other Canadian cities. Toronto is particularly sensitive to the Americanizing trends which are feared by some and encouraged by others, trends which proceed steadily and without conscious forcing simply because they accord with the everyday needs of two great nations, their communities and citizens.

Religion usually walks hand in hand with respectability, and Toronto is a churchly city. In Victorian days "the Queen City" had one church for each thousand of its population, and Sunday was strictly observed in a conventional way. Toronto still takes orthodox religion with stern seriousness, and beneath its noble skyline of steel, brick and stone remains a church-going, God-fearing community.

Famous Yonge Street, the artery of business, runs northward from the lake's edge, dividing the city into east and west halves and continues under the same name to Lake Simcoe. The Provincial Parliament is housed in dignified buildings of the usual British types, as is the huge University of Toronto which has the largest student roll in the British empire—an annual enrollment, excluding students in affiliated colleges and in extension courses, of approximately 6,000. Central Technical School, with more than 5,000 students, is considered a model for the world. Where learning is encouraged, the press thrives; the city is the Dominion's publishing center. With a highly literate population, Toronto leads all Canada in sales of books, in publishing and in authorship.

With three commercial airports, four flying fields and an active flying club by 1930, Toronto was fully prepared to become the chief aviation center of a country whose wide domains seem likely to make its people the most air-minded on earth. The fields were most opportune for training young airmen for a stern purpose. Postwar plans encompass great commercial development of these facilities.

In normal times the city has another activity important in maintaining her prosperity, a lively tourist trade which pours sightseers and vacationers into Toronto by train, passenger steamer and automobile highway. Toronto woos tourists with easy travel, spacious hotels, notable stores which offer many bargains from Britain, horse races, International League baseball, big-time hockey, swimming marathons, beautiful beaches, an annual National Exposition on state-fair lines, kiltie bands and a delightful but not obtrusive hospitality.

Perhaps the most successful of Toronto's recreation travel enterprises are the Canada Steamship tours from Lake Ontario, the Thousand Islands, the St. Lawrence rapids to Montreal, Quebec, Murray Bay, Tadoussac and the Saguenay. The Canada Steamship Company, like the British and Canadian railroads, operates hotels where necessary and does it very well.

Toronto's shrewd travel planners anticipate an enormous air traffic with the North Country, a good part of which is expected to come from carrying fishermen to fine fishing waters. American businessmen who want to get their hip boots wet in a trout stream without delay will find Toronto's airports ready for them. Those in less of a hurry will find improved train schedules and an expanded system of motor conveyances penetrating lake and forest areas. Trains, airplanes and busses will connect with their American doubles; in fact American railroads and other travel services are counted on to assist in filling Toronto's depots, passenger docks and airports with paying guests from the States. And they, no less than Canadian residents, will feel quite at home in this most American of Canada's larger cities, Toronto.

# Chapter 22

## Of Ships and Ports

*Oh, those blessed times of old, with their chivalry and state!*
*I love to read their chronicles, which such brave deeds relate;*
*I love to sing their ancient rhymes, to hear their legends told,*
*But Heaven be thanked I live not in the blessed times of old.*

—FRANCES BROWN

No DOUBT the first sizable vessel to sail Ontario's waters was one of La Salle's construction at his seigneury near Kingston. Very likely it was the ten-ton shallop *Frontenac,* which with another smaller ship of his maintained for the French a rather sketchy control of the fur trade on the lake. The *Frontenac* carried supplies from Fort Frontenac to Niagara for the establishment of the post there and for the fitting out of the *Griffin.* There is a record that the *Frontenac* once ran into the mouth of the Humber River to evade a November storm, and stayed there ten days. Humber Bay has been definitely identified as the anchorage used by the French and the spot is marked by a green light buoy off the foot of Dufferin Street.

Governor Clarke of New York reported to London in 1743 that the French then had "on the Lake Cadaracquie" two sailing vessels. At least two schooners with square topsails were built by the French about 1755, *L'Huron* and *La Marquise de Vaudreuil. La Marquise,* after three busy years transporting men and supplies between Frontenac and Niagara, was captured in her home harbor by Bradstreet's raiders in 1758. Earlier in 1758, she is not specifically mentioned. Indeed, French chroniclers usually paid less attention to naval deeds than to their army's exploits. The sunken wrecks of two small ships in the harbor of Carleton Island, visible until quite recent times, were identified as those of the *Iroquois* and *Onatouise,* sunk by the French to prevent their capture in 1759.

Marine men think of these French ships as predecessors of slightly later schooners rigged with gaff topsails, which came to be regarded as the most effective type to combat Lake Ontario's high winds.

The last French vessel to take Ontario's waters was the brig *Ontario,* which was built near Pointe au Baril after the fall of Fort Frontenac. While under the command of Captain Labrocquerie, she was captured during Amherst's triumphant advance down the St. Lawrence from Oswego in 1760. In the following year she was wrecked near Oswego.

At the British port of Oswego, as at Frontenac, 1755 was a ship-building year, for Britain was preparing her initial challenge to the long-standing French control of the lake. On June 28 a little schooner of "40 foot keel with 14 sweeps of oars and 12 swivels" was launched, the first British ship. Keels were laid for two sloops-of-war, the *Oswego* and the *Ontario.* The French and Indians hindered their construction, but failed to stop the work even when they killed ten ship-wrights in a single raid on the yards. These sloops proved neat, swift-sailing vesels, with sufficiently light draft to make them handy in shallow waters. They were forty-three feet long, with a fifteen-foot beam, and carried ten light guns and swivels and crews of forty-two.*

Late in 1755—too late as it proved—construction of His Majesty's schooners *George* and *Lively* was begun at Oswego, and they were finished by the next spring. In the campaign against Oswego in 1756 the French fleet captured one of these new schooners at sea and the other was destroyed in Oswego Harbor by Montcalm.

Another product of the Oswego yards was H. M. S. *London,* the first British-built brig-rigged vessel on the lakes. Poor handling and delays in getting supplies and stores up from Schenectady so impaired the *London's* effectiveness that after a few uneventful cruises she too was caught and burned by Montcalm, despite her potential strength. All of the Oswego ships of 1755-1756 were built wholly of green timbers under extreme danger, yet they performed well.

The largest vessel laid down by the British at Oswego up to this

---

* In preparing this chapter the author has been greatly assisted by the water-color paintings of G. A. Cuthbertson, marine artist and author of *Freshwater,* many of whose paintings with those of other Canadian artists have been exhibited at many points under the sponsorship of Canada Steamship Lines. No comparable exhibition could be gathered relative to the American shore because shipbuilding is almost a lost industry there, though it remained vigorous in Ontario. Most helpful, too, were C. H. J. Snider's *In the Wake of the Eighteen-Twelvers* (New York: John Lane Company); Barlow Cumberland's *A Century of Sail and Steam on the Niagara River* (Toronto: Munson Book Company, Ltd., 1913); and Douglas S. Robertson's notes to Joseph Hadfield's *An Englishman in America* (Toronto: Hunter-Rose Company, Ltd., 1933).

time was the snow* *Halifax,* a craft of an unusual type somewhat resembling a brig. The *Halifax* sported three masts, was square-rigged on fore and main masts and had a lateen sail on the mizzen. Her over-all length was eighty-six feet six inches, and her displacement was 172 tons. Also destroyed in the Oswego debacle was the hull of the *Mohawk,* a schooner of the *Oswego-Ontario* type.

When the British struck back in Bradstreet's raid on Frontenac two years later, they sailed and portaged some 200 whaleboats from the Hudson through the interior waterway to Oswego. In their bows howitzers were installed, with shields to protect the gunners. These stout boats were thirty-five feet long and, fully loaded, they drew about a foot and a half of water. Each boat carried approximately thirty men, with six or eight of them at the oars and a big sail for favorable winds in open water.

While Kingston was still "Cadaracqui" the British selected Kingston as a base of the Provincial Marine on Lake Ontario and after 1788 it became their chief military and naval base. Its officers were usually naval men sent out from England, although the Marine was financially administered by the Army and its expenditures were controlled by the Quartermaster General. The yards at Kingston built the *Ontario,* which was lost in a storm on November 1, 1780, together with many officers and men of the Eighth Regiment, with a total loss of 350 persons, while proceeding from Niagara to Oswego.

Many ships built by the Provincial Marine continued in use as common carriers on Lake Ontario long after the Revolutionary War. They were relied upon for transporting general cargoes until the passage of Canada's Inland Navigation Act authorized the operation of mercantile vessels by private owners. At the close of the Revolutionary War General Haldimand forbade all trade with the United States. This decree could be enforced then because since 1777 only ships manned and armed by the Crown had been permitted to sail the lakes. Private traders could use the King's ships at fair rates, but in practice the Crown dominated trade. Many disturbing incidents occurred which aroused border friction. Schenectady traders were turned back at Oswego, and when American traders reached the Genesee in 1784, the long arm of Britain reached south of the lake

---

* This quaint nautical term derives from the Dutch *snaauw* and Low German *snau.* The word, as amended, entered English usage in 1676.

to bring Ebenezer ("Indian") Allen, formerly interpreter for the Canadians, to Quebec for trial. The effort was to shut Canada, particularly Canadian Indians, off from American contact.

An official return of 1787 lists only three war vessels as then in service on the lake: the *Limnade,* 220 tons, 10 guns; the *Seneca,* 130 tons, 18 guns; the *Caldwell,* 37 tons, 2 guns. Two schooners of 100 tons were building and there was one merchant vessel, the *Lady Dorchester,* of 80 tons.

In 1783, Ensign James Peachey painted a picture of a brig at Kingston which is now believed to be the *Limnade.* At that period, too, shipyards were turning out combined trading and fishing boats. Sailing pinnaces—small, light vessels usually two-master and schooner-rigged—also appeared in considerable number on Ontario's waters. Fortunately for history, Peachey painted all three types.

Western marine developments naturally lagged behind Kingston, because some of the western waters had not even been surveyed in the early days of the post-Revolutionary Provincial Marine. A tireless student of the marine history of Lake Ontario, C. H. J. Snider, reported in the Toronto *Evening Telegram* of May 20, 1944, an early survey of Toronto Harbor. Lieutenant Joseph Bouchette of the Provincial Marine made a signed survey of the bay (the present harbor) in November 1792, and drew a picture of his small survey schooner at anchorage there. At the time there were only some Indian wigwams or huts on the wilderness site of future Toronto, since the original trading post stood some miles away. Bouchette sketched his vessel for posterity as she rode in a scant two fathoms of water over a muddy bottom opposite the foot of what is now Parliament Street, but he neglected to name the schooner, which may have been the *Bear,* the *Buffalo* or the *Lively.* In the vicinity Bouchette spotted five anchorages and made ninety-two soundings, ranging from two feet at today's Hanlan's Point to thirty-three feet in a "deep" north of today's Eastern Gap. The harbor bottom he described as stony and rocky at the only entrance opposite the modern Queen's Wharf; elsewhere, muddy and sandy.

Bouchette's survey vessel sailed a huge commission pennant and ensign, both decked with crosses of the Union Jack, the better to symbolize the greatness of Britain to impressionable savages. Snider gives a precise description of this vessel's rig which we quote for

the benefit of those to whom such technical language is not unintel-
ligible. "The loose footed mainsail triced up from the boom; the fore-
sail brailed to the foremast, with the head hauled out on a standing
gaff; a squaresail for running (like a yacht's spinnaker), laced to a
yard which crosses the foremast and is lowered when not in use; a jib
which showed on the bowsprit. The mainsail hoisted with a 'tie'
or single peak halliard, with a bridle on the gaff, and the mainsheet
worked on another span or bridle on the boom. The rudder head
shows above the bulwarks and her trim appears to have been in three
colors, possibly yellow, black and white. Her boat is shown on its
painter astern and rowed three oars a side. Bouchette's detail is so
good that he shows the six tholepins of the rowlocks. The six-oared
boat would be 14 feet long, and with this yardstick we may assume
the parent schooner to have measured about 50 feet on deck. She
was probably 16 or 17 feet beam and not more than 5 feet deep in
the hold. That is why her stern is cocked up, to give head-room for
the officers in the cabin."

Naval uniforms were of blue and white cloth, coats fastened by
huge yellow buttons stamped with the image of a beaver under the
word "Canada." Discipline was rigid. Shore-leave privileges were
at the discretion of military commandants of the respective lake
ports—they decided whether naval officers and men might stretch
their legs on land when the King's ships touched port. Usually the
government vessels made straightaway runs from Kingston to Niagara, and vice versa, without stops at way ports.

Niagara shipbuilding, which grew to large proportions, began with
the schooner *York* in 1792. A few years later enterprise of all kinds
was vastly stimulated by visits of His Royal Highness the Duke of
Kent and the Duke de la Rochefoucauld Liancourt, who were well
entertained at Niagara. The French duke "told all" in his *Travels
through the United States of America,* published in Paris in 1799.
From 1786 to 1794 the senior naval officer on Lake Ontario had been
Captain David Betton, Acting Commodore. Under his successor,
waste and graft ruled among minor officers. The Lake Ontario fleet
consisted of half a dozen vessels of which only the twelve-gun schooners *Onondaga* and *Mohawk* could be considered formidable. Others
were an eighty-ton yacht (probably the *Mississaga*) and gunboats—
all of raw, unseasoned timber. Iron was expensive and sparingly

used; nevertheless the cost of the heavier vessels ran to 4,000 guineas each.

The *Mohawk* was selected to carry the Duke of Kent westward, and Commander Bouchette was in command. As the French duke noted, the commander of the fleet and most of his under-officers were French Canadians.

Among the good ships built on Lake Ontario before the War of 1812 began were:

1797—The *Governor Simcoe,* which brought to York in 1812 the captured American soldier, Winfield Scott, and also the news of General Brock's death.

The *Washington,* bought at Erie, portaged around the Falls and put into service as the *Lady Washington.*

1798—The *Prince Edward,* built of red cedar, and another vessel, unidentified, built of black walnut.

1799—The *Toronto,* very popular for speed and luxury, often called "the Toronto yacht." It was lost off Gibraltar Point, York, in 1811.

1809—The *Dove* and the *Reindeer,* which plied for some years between Kingston and Niagara.

Following declaration of the War of 1812, the Royal Naval Dockyard at Kingston, Upper Canada, hummed with feverish activity, as did its rival port across the lake at Oswego. Sailors' barracks occupied what is called "Old Stone Frigate," still used as company barracks for cadets of Royal Military College. At the dockyards were built the ships of Yeo's fleet.

The ships suffered more wounds than their crews. A common method of plugging shot holes was to tip or careen the hull and then fill the hole much as a dentist fills a tooth. Such an operation was performed on Commodore Chauncey's flagship, U.S.S. *Madison,* a frigate, during the brief occupation of York in 1813.

Armed schooners of United States Navy on Ontario during that war were often hurried along in calm weather by sweeps or extra-long oars. In this way they earned the amusing name of "Chauncey's Water Spiders" as they crawled along over the smooth surface.

In the fluctuating race for superiority in fleet tonnage between Chauncey and Yeo, the Englishman had the *Princess Charlotte* and the *Prince Regent* constructed at Kingston in 1814. The *Charlotte* was built originally as a brig, but later rebuilt, enlarged and rerigged. Her dimensions were almost double those of the largest warships built on the lake during the Revolution.

Shortly after the War of 1812 ended came the first challenge of steam on Lake Ontario. Sailing vessels put up a strenuous fight, which lasted for forty years before steam-powered ships definitely established their supremacy. Even yet a schooner or sloop arouses an affection that no steamer can match, but after Robert Fulton's *Clermont* had proved the practicability of his invention its broad adoption could not long be put off. Although neither admiral on Lake Ontario in the War of 1812 seems to have thought of building a steam-driven warship, two steamships were built in Lake Ontario shipyards, the *Frontenac* at Kingston and the *Ontario* at Sackets Harbor.

The Canadians started construction first. As soon as declaration of peace permitted, a syndicate of shareholders in Kingston, Niagara, York and Prescott contracted with two American assistants of Eckford's at Sackets Harbor to build a steamer at Finkle's Point, Ernestown, eighteen miles up the lake from Kingston. There the *Frontenac* was launched on September 7, 1816. No puny ship, she was 170 feet long, 32 feet beam and rated 700 tons displacement, nearly three times that of the rival *Ontario*. She proceeded from Ernestown to Kingston and laid up in that port for the winter.

On the American side Robert Fulton and his backer, Robert Livingston, possessed a monopoly on steamboat building in the state of New York. On January 2, 1816, Charles Smyth negotiated with those interests a contract permitting the construction of the *Ontario*. In December 1816 Smyth and his friends had applied to the New York legislature for incorporation of the Lake Ontario Steam Boat Company. While the language of their application is not clear, it indicates that the *Ontario* was then being built at Sackets with some assistance from the Navy, which was providing timber at a reasonable cost. The applicants apparently were stating their case as optimistically as possible, yet they do not mention a launching, which indicates that the honor of first launching a steamboat goes to Canada.

However, the same issue of the Kingston *Gazette* which describes the launching of the *Frontenac* also carried an item which read: "A steamboat was lately launched at Sackets Harbor." This item had been picked up from Niles' *Weekly Register* of Baltimore, which evidently erred in saying "launched" when it should have said "commenced." This can be deduced from several good witnesses. Records of the Collector at Sackets Harbor indicate that the *Ontario* made her first trip in the first part of April 1817. The *Register* later corrected itself by publishing in its issue of March 29, 1817, "The steamer *Ontario* is prepared for the lake." Finally Captain Van Cleve, sometime skipper of the *Mary Ogden,* the second American steamer built at Sackets, left behind a manuscript diary, now in the possession of the Buffalo Historical Society, which gives April 11, 1817, as the date of the *Ontario's* first enrollment in the customs office.

Apparently, therefore, the *Ontario* was launched late in March and moved on her own power for a maiden trip early in April. In this race for priority the Americans were favored by several factors. Ice clears out of Sackets earlier than out of Kingston. Their vessel was only 120 feet long, 24 feet beam and one-third the tonnage of the Canadian competitor, whose fitters were wrestling with suction pipes for their Boulton-Watt engines. The *Ontario* also had trouble, as the waves tore off her paddle wheels, but soon she was plying regularly between Ogdensburg and Lewiston at a speed of five miles an hour.

The first 1817 move of the *Frontenac*—"with majestic grandeur against a strong wind"—was from her winter anchorage to Government dock for repairs on May 23, and her second was to the Bay of Quinte for a cargo of wood. At first the steamer crew cut wood where they pleased; later a regular service was provided by wood-cutters and contractors at a dollar a cord. It was not until June 5 that the three-masted *Frontenac,* her hull painted black and with guards only at the paddle wheels, steamed forth on her first commercial journey to the head of the lake.

There is substantial backing for the conclusion reached by a Canadian vesselman, Barlow Cumberland, that while the *Frontenac* was the first steamship to be launched and to navigate the Great Lakes, the *Ontario* was the first to make a trip up the lake. Even that margin can be credited to a weather advantage as much as to American hustle. In planning, design and construction the Canadians led.

In passenger and freight service the *Frontenac* proved to be the more dependable pioneer. Right well did she live up to the promise of her Scots skipper, Captain James McKenzie, late of the Royal Navy, to make the scheduled ports "with as much punctuality as the nature of lake navigation will admit of." Rates were 3£ 15s from Kingston to Burlington, £1 from York to Niagara. Fifteen shillings would be charged for dogs. Deck passengers could bring their own victuals, but meals would be served by the steward.

The *Frontenac* proved to be a better ship than her rival, but neither of them had much luck. After running regularly from Prescott to Burlington for ten years, the *Frontenac,* then owned by the Hamiltons of Niagara, burned there, set on fire by incendiaries. Her hull was then broken up. The *Ontario,* less successful both commercially and mechanically, was broken up at Oswego in 1832. Thus steam navigation entered the Great Lakes with a construction race which finished with divided honors and dependable ships which recommended the new means of transport to a suspicious public.

The quick progress made by steam-powered vessels can be seen from lists of harbor entries about this time. For instance, Sackets Harbor was a busy place in 1819, with about a hundred vessels calling there during the season. George Camp's *Gazette and Advertiser* published the list of arrivals and departures each week. The list for the week of July 6, 1819, shows that even then steamers had drawn up almost even with sailing vessels:

| Schooners | Captain | From or to |
|---|---|---|
| Rambler | Wentworth | Ernestown, U. C. |
| Triumph | Cook | Kingston, U. C. |
| Farmer's Daughter | Sherwin | Pultneyville, Niagara |
| Monroe | Hubbard | Sodus, Oswego, Cape Vincent |
| Appelona | Knapp | Niagara, Sodus |
| Sachem | Rounds | Niagara |
| Blackbird | Silver | Sodus |
| Steamboats | | |
| Ontario | Lusher | Niagara, Genesee, Oswego, Ogdensburg |
| Sophia | Vaughan | Kingston |
| Jane | Dodd | Montreal, L. C. |
| Purser (Packet) | Schovill | Brownville |

VIEW OF TORONTO WATER FRONT FROM CENTRE ISLAND

## THE SCHOELLKOPF HYDROELECTRIC GENERATING STATION OF THE NIAGARA FALLS POWER COMPANY

This station is located on the gorge of the lower Niagara River, a short distance below the Falls. Its present capacity is 336,050 killowatts.

## GENERATORS IN THE SCHOELLKOPF STATION

In the stiff competition between the two types of ships, the steamers already showed an advantage in getting quickly in and out of port and in avoiding delays when the weather was contrary. The steamboat *Sophia,* for instance, arrived from Kingston on July 2, sailed the next day and was back in Sackets on July 6. The steamboat *Ontario* made the trip to Ogdensburg and back in one day. Of the schooners the *Farmer's Daughter* appears to have been the nimblest, making the round trip between Sackets and Niagara in three days.

After the *Ontario* six years elapsed before another steamship came off the ways at Sackets Harbor. Then came a beauty, the *Martha Ogden,* which held her own against the rising Canadian marine down to 1830, when she ran ashore off Stoney Point.

No doubt of it, the Canadians were gaining. They possessed certain advantages—better timber, less competition from other means of transport and a more deeply ingrained maritime training and tradition which gave even routine voyages authority and prestige. Superior men took command, and shipbuilding always had first call on capital provided by farsighted men who saw improved transport as a quick way to build up the country.

Such a man was Robert Hamilton of Queenston who, as a backer of good ships, shipbuilders and skippers, gave the lower Niagara River a marine leadership which endured until railroad coverage changed the traffic map. His example and wealth led the Niagara outlet to a position which lasted down to the time when steam competition became oppressive. His first ship was the *Queenston,* launched in 1825, his second the *Alciope,* vessels which had to compete with new vessels from other and better-established ports: the *Queen Charlotte* from Teobout & Chapman's yard near Kingston, which fixed a rate of £3 from Kingston to Niagara and the first *City of Toronto,* a 350-tonner, shortly broken up. Soon there were five steamers plying the trade-outlet ports of Lewiston, Queenston and Niagara.

There were special reasons for the Niagara River trade at the foot of the old carry around the Falls, considerations that brought both passengers and trade. Skilled men settled in the vicinity, both shippers and shipbuilders. The best known of these was Robert Gilkinson, Canadian-born but trained in Glasgow. Finding capital to match his experience, he opened at Niagara a yard where he designed and constructed one bonny ship after another; the *Commodore Barrie,* the *Transit,* the *Gore* and the *Queen Victoria.*

The *Queen Victoria,* 130 feet long and "fitted in elegant style," was launched by Gilkinson's Niagara Dock Company in April 1838. Under the command of Captain Thomas Dick she became a famous ship, amply fulfilling the promise of her maiden voyage—Niagara to Toronto, to Hamilton, to Niagara—121 miles in ten and a half hours, "a rate not exceeded by any boat on the lake." The *"Vic"* used both Lewiston and Queenston. She was the ship chosen to carry the wealth and beauty of the Dominion on high days and holidays, such as the commemoration of the Queen's coronation. During one season she served as a gunboat manned by the Royal Navy, received a rousing welcome at all the small ports visited to show the Flag during the later days of the Mackenzie troubles.

Through the 1830's and for many years thereafter fishing and trading luggers from twenty to forty feet in length and of four or five tons displacement were common on Lake Ontario. This type of craft proved popular with smugglers and those sly gentry who were helping along the rebel movements and Fenian raids on Canada.

A significant engineering development of 1838 was the building at Oswego of the *Vandalia,* second vessel to be activated by the screw propeller as perfected by John Ericsson. The first vessel of this revolutionary type was the launch *Francis B. Ogden,* built in England, but the *Vandalia* can be rated as the pioneer of lake cargo vessels in which the engines were located aft, thereby economizing space. This ship marks the peak of Oswego shipbuilding, which declined thereafter principally because near-by ship timber became scarce.

The first iron steamers on the lake were the *Passport* and the *Magnet.* The *Passport* was constructed of iron plates brought from the Scottish Clyde and put together at Niagara by James and Neil Currie for John Hamilton in 1847. The *Magnet,* too, was built of Scottish plates, but her principal owner was J. W. Gunn of Hamilton. Both vessels became part of the Royal Mail Line, which was later merged with the Richelieu & Ontario Navigation Company, predecessor to Canada Steamship Lines.

Signalizing the entrance of railroads into ship owning was the building of the *Zimmerman* at Niagara in 1853. Named for Samuel Zimmerman, promoter of the Erie and Ontario railway from Fort

Erie to Niagara, she was operated in connection with that railroad. Another famous ship finished at Niagara was the *Peerless,* built in Scotland, then taken apart and shipped to Lake Ontario. The *Zimmerman* and the *Peerless* led all others on the Toronto-Niagara run in the early 1850's, which proved to be the zenith for passenger trade. Against the stagecoach the steamers were a clear first choice; but against the railroads the steamships could no longer count on full passenger lists.

Great activity returned to Lewiston with the opening of the Niagara Falls-to-Lewiston Railway in 1854, and its excellent connections with the newly formed New York Central for transport to Albany by rail and then down the Hudson to tidewater. With the Crimean War on, British demand drew Canadian wheat and flour from Toronto to New York via Lewiston, at the boom price of 12½ cents per barrel for carriage from Queen's Wharf in Toronto to Lewiston, and another 6 cents for transshipment to the railroad at that point. Altogether it cost $1.19 to get flour from Toronto to New York. Mills in many Ontario communities such as Port Credit, Brampton, Oakville, Esquessing and Georgetown prospered during this sensational flurry. Return cargoes were mostly British teas, tobaccos and textiles "bonded through" from New York.

Decay set in soon afterward as railroad pressure increased. The Great Western Railway reached Hamilton from Niagara Falls in 1855, and Toronto in 1856. In the panic of 1858 all the American line steamers were tied up in bankruptcy and the *Zimmerman* abandoned the Niagara-to-Toronto trade to its rival, the *Peerless.* Vessel owners were somewhat relieved from this slump by the onset of the American Civil War early in 1861, when the United States soon needed ships to blockade the South and also to carry supplies to coastal garrisons. Uncle Sam bought not only the laid-up American vessels but also some Canadian ships, including the *Peerless.* The *Zimmerman* burned at dockside, so "a general clearance of distressed vessels had been effected." A third *City of Toronto* took over the Niagara-Toronto run after the war, while her predecessor, renamed the *Algoma,* went up the lakes to extraordinary adventures on the broader waters of Superior and Huron. The opening of the lumber, mining and fishing trades for Canada's part of the Upper Lakes drew away from Ontario not only her best ships, but her best skippers as well.

One early shipbuilding firm which has survived all vicissitudes and still carries on is that founded by Alexander Muir and his four brothers in 1850. Muir came to the Great Lakes in 1837 after four years on salt water, and Muir Brothers Drydock Company is a source of good ships and dependable marine history.

All through this period of steamer progress sail fought back and triumphed grandly but briefly on the Atlantic seaboard with clipper ships. Lake Ontario contributed two famous ships to this revival. One was the second *City of Toronto,* a full-rigged ship built in 1855, which sailed to Liverpool and back in her first season. Ten years later the *Sea Gull* of Toronto, a 105-foot brig, was launched. She started Canada-South Africa trade by carrying cargo from Toronto to Port Natal (Durban), but not being altogether suited to ocean travel, she returned from salt water to fresh, only to burn at Tawas, Michigan, in 1866 after a short but spectacular life of a single year.

In 1865, which marked the close of the Civil War and the subsequent rise of Fenian border troubles, a number of "imported" British warcraft traveled Ontario's waters. Among them were the *Heron,* the *Bramble* and the *Britomart,* the latter a wooden, screw-driven, three-masted gunboat built at Newcastle-on-Tyne in 1860 for the Royal Navy.

From 1870 to 1900 many single topsail schooners traversed the lake, but since the turn of the century these handy "coasters" have been replaced by package-freight steamers. These ships have in turn suffered from the competition of railroads and motor trucks, but there is now a trend toward increase in specialized ships designed and equipped to handle only a single type of cargo, often for the owners only.

The best-known passenger steamer on the lake and the St. Lawrence River is the old S.S. *Kingston* of the Canada Steamship Lines. This veteran still plies the Toronto-Kingston and Prescott line and proudly shows the colors of the Richelieu & Ontario Company under which she entered service.

Modern steam transportation on Lake Ontario reached a peak when Canada Steamship Lines brought to its home port of Toronto the S.S. *Lemoyne.* Although since outmatched by the new masters of the American steel trade, at the time of her launching the *Lemoyne* was the largest vessel on the Great Lakes and is still the largest to sail regularly out of a Lake Ontario port. During the 1928 season the

*Lemoyne* broke a world record as a grain carrier with 555,000 bushels.

As a result of World War scarcities of equipment for highly specialized steel ships, and also of the coal or oil necessary to fuel them, both salt and fresh water have seen a flash revival of the sailing ship. Lake Ontario's first entry in this interesting list is the *Swift,* built in 1942. Her Canadian architect, H. I. Chapelle, designed her from the lines of the British sloop *Swift* of 1783. This craft, seventy-nine feet long, has amply proved her cruising worth. The old *Swift* changed flags several times by capture in her sprightly career and sailed under French, American and British flags. Her beautiful design and speed under sail is thought to have influenced the construction of the *Sylph,* the queen of Yeo's fleet on Lake Ontario in 1813-1814. Thus marine construction on Lake Ontario has swung around a full circle from sail to steam and back to sail again in a little less than 150 years.

No better place could be found for testing and revival of sailing vessels than Lake Ontario, where the mariner finds plain sailing from Hamilton in the west to the St. Lawrence River in the east, with hardly a shoal between.

# Chapter 23

# Coal, Iron and Grain

*They that live in a trading street*
*Are not disturbed by the passing of carts.*
—Sir Richard Steele

LAKE ONTARIO, as must by now be apparent, is commercially the poor relation of the other Great Lakes. Not possessing the tremendous natural resources of the Lake Superior country or of the Erie coal fields or even the oil of the Michigan district, the Lake Ontario region has the choice of resigning itself to a comfortable mediocrity or of attracting to itself the natural wealth of other localities. But even that choice is not fully open. The main artery through which this wealth would have to flow runs east and west, and it is precisely this east and west route which is blocked and impeded. The Ontario region is screened off, if not shut off, by the St. Lawrence Rapids at the east end and separated from the other lakes at her left end by the formidable barrier of Niagara Falls.

Without the Welland Canal and the partial improvement of the St. Lawrence River, the east-west route would be for all practical purposes closed. As they stand, it is only partially open, for the St. Lawrence canals form a series of obstacles both as to depth and time of passage. Flanked by the Erie Canal, by water-level railroads on both sides of the lake, hampered by the international boundary, and off the direct route to New York, the water route east and west the length of Lake Ontario has not yet appeared either sufficiently profitable or sufficiently useful to justify further improvement.

The lake is not as isolated as it might be. It is easily accessible from either side, in a north and south direction. The rub here is that the available raw materials do not now justify any great increase in the north and south trade, all of which has to cross the international boundary. A good deal of coal comes up from the Pennsylvania fields

326

and is ferried across to keep fires in the furnaces of Canadian homes. So far Canada has not been able to provide a corresponding cargo for the coal boats to carry back on the trip south. The coal trade across the lake is substantial but it does not appear to have any tremendously enlarged future.

The three commodities which have made the fortunes of the other Great Lakes are grain, coal and iron. The oceans of wheat that grow on the western plains, both in the United States and in Canada, funnel down to Lake Superior ports and into freighters for cheap transportation to cities all the way from Chicago to New York and from there to foreign countries. Lake Superior iron and Pennsylvania coal, brought together by the bulk carriers of the Upper Lakes, have built a dozen great steel towns from Gary and Chicago to Detroit, Cleveland and Buffalo. Let us see what these three commodities, the wealth of the Northwest, mean to Lake Ontario.

Grain played a large part in the past of the Ontario region and may play a different and greater part in its future but at present the amount of grain handled is merely large, far from astonishing. It will be remembered that Rochester was for many years known as the Flour City. It is true that the grain, the bulk of it, reached the city through the Erie Canal, not via the lake. But from the earliest settlement down to the decline of the Rochester mills a good part of the grain and an even larger part of the flour accumulated in northern New York was shipped across the lake to Canadian ports. Thus for many years the grain business was vital not only to Rochester mills but to the carrying trade on the lake.

Now the centers where wheat is grown have shifted far to the west, to the plains of Minnesota and the Dakotas and the Canadian plains provinces. A flood of it comes pouring into Lake Superior ports. The elevators are usually overflowing when the spring break-up allows the grain ships to start east. Through the summer and early fall months the tide swells.

As the ships come down out of Superior with American wheat from Duluth they fan out to ports on Lake Michigan and Lake Erie, and on to the big population centers in a dozen parts of the East and Middle West and South. There is little reason to route it through the full length of Lake Ontario, since it is off the shortest route to New York and the Middle Atlantic, since it would have to be transshipped before going through the Welland Canal and since there are no large domestic markets on or close to the lake itself.

For Canadian wheat funneling down to Lake Superior at Port Arthur or near-by ports, the situation is different and somewhat more favorable. Tariffs put it at a disadvantage in United States markets, so only a part of it follows the route of much of the United States grain into ports on the south shore of Lake Erie. Much of it is shipped abroad, to England and the European continent. Some of it goes to the large domestic market of the Toronto region. Without the difficulty of transshipment, Lake Ontario would be the natural route for all this grain. Even as it is, a considerable amount does annually pass into Ontario.

Need to transship is created chiefly by the small bottleneck St. Lawrence Canals; but even the new, enlarged Welland cannot pass all the vessels bringing cargoes from the Northwest, as is evident from the following lock dimensions, in feet, of the three Great Lakes canal systems between Lake Superior and the Atlantic:

|  | Depth | Width | Extreme Length |
|---|---|---|---|
| Sault Ste. Marie | 30 | 80 | 1350 |
| Welland | 30 | 80 | 820 |
| St. Lawrence | 14 | 45 | 270 |

Of course, cargoes for the New York State Barge Canal must be transferred to barges at Oswego or before.

In 1928, a predepression year often used to indicate normal times, grain shipments from lower lake and St. Lawrence river ports totaled 163,000,000 bushels, chiefly from Buffalo and Port Colborne, the Lake Erie terminus of the Welland Canal. Shipments from each of these ports consisted chiefly of grain transshipped to the small-type vessels suitable for navigating both the Canal and the St. Lawrence. Volume at two key ports had declined more than thirty percent by 1935, which shows what a world depression can do to the most stable of foodstuffs. Translate into hunger pangs the wheat that never arrived at Colborne, Montreal, Liverpool and Bremen.

Port Colborne's harbor has a twenty-five-foot depth and 3,000,000 bushels of wheat capacity in its government grain elevator. Hard by the water front lie tracks of the Canadian National Railways with room for 200 freight cars, and rail connections with the Niagara, St. Catharines & Toronto Railroad, the Michigan Central and the Toronto, Hamilton & Buffalo Railway. There are privately owned elevators as well.

Toronto checks into the grain trade with a monster 4,000,000-bushel-capacity grain elevator located on the lake's northwest shore with berthing space of 600 feet and twenty-two feet of water alongside. Service is provided by the Canadian National and Canadian Pacific Railways.

Oswego's elevator of 1,038,000 bushels maximum capacity, state-owned and operated, is served by the Delaware, Lackawanna & Western Railroad. Vessels are loaded at a speed of 32,000 bushels, barges at 20,000 and freight cars at 20,000 bushels per hour. Definitely, New York State is equipping the Oswego end of its great canal system to relieve Buffalo's occasional congestion. As a result Oswego can now handle 15,000,000 incoming bushels of grain a year, a figure almost reached in 1939, which was nearly four times its 1932 grain trade.

On the Canadian shore at the eastern end of the lake, Kingston has local wooden-elevator storage of 250,000 bushels' capacity for distribution to local territory, served by both of Canada's great railroad systems. On near-by Cataraqui Bay is the Canada Steamship Lines' elevator of concrete construction, with Canadian National Service.

Prescott, Ontario, just above the Galops Canal, has a government-owned elevator on the St. Lawrence north bank with the impressive storage capacity of 5,500,000 bushels. Prescott can unload vessels at 65,000 bushels per hour or load 150,000 bushels per hour. The Canadians looked at the Oswego installation and then quadrupled it in loading capacity per hour.

At Ogdensburg, directly opposite Prescott and sixty-two miles by water from Lake Ontario, stands an elevator of 5,000,000 bushels' capacity owned and operated by the Rutland Railroad. Its principal function is to transfer grain from boat to car at 6,000 bushels per hour. Most of the grain thus rail-shipped goes to upper New York and New England points for immediate consumption.

From Montreal, Halifax, Portland, Boston and New York a considerable part of the golden grain which rides across Lake Ontario and through its elevators eventually crosses salt water to the mills and ovens of other and less fortunate lands. "To the tropics where wheat does not flourish, to the islands too narrow to till, to the mountains and deserts and marshes," but mostly, of course, to the overpopulated peninsula of Europe and the densely packed isles of Britain, weary but undaunted Mother of American Wheatlands.

If the Welland Canal is greatly enlarged and the St. Lawrence waterway is developed to accommodate the largest grain ships, then the bulk of Canadian wheat destined for export may quite possibly pass across Lake Ontario. The lake may take its place with the big Upper Lakes as a major link in the main export route. If . . . some-time—one of Lake Ontario's major industries is still a potential industry.

Like her grain trade, Lake Ontario's iron industry had a bright past and may have a brilliant future. This future, too, depends on a number of "if's" and "sometime's." Meanwhile, its present, except in the industrial district around Toronto, is good but not spectacular. It might be added here that even Toronto has to have both ore and coal imported, since it is a processing rather than a producing center. It is the best Canadian city available rather than the best natural location. If the route into Lake Ontario were improved, or if iron were available within the Lake Ontario region, this restriction would not be needed.

Northern New York is perhaps preparing to resume its place as one of the great iron-ore-producing regions of the nation, by virtue of its Adirondack mountain reserves. Long ago Lieutenant Governor Cadwallader Colden, a shrewd Scotsman, suspected that weighty riches lay hidden under these forest roots. In the course of an exhaustive report on trade and manufactures and resources of New York province, written in 1723, he relates, possibly because of reports from hunters with eyes open for more than game:

"The Northern parts of the Province bear large White Pines for Masts; and for iron we have great plenty of that Oar in many places close by the bank of the River, where ships of 3 or 400 Tuns may lay their sides the ground everywhere covered with wood for the Furnace and no want of Water Streams any where for the Forge."

Late in 1734, in a report to the reactionary Board of Trade in London, Governor Cosby related the presence of many other iron mines "both of the Bogg, and of Mountain Oar, but as yet no Iron Work is set up in this province if any encouragement was given upon the importing of it in Piggs and Bars, at least that it might be free of Dutys." Although development of mines of lead and iron ores was proposed in 1749, London discouraged the effort and the first systematic working of Adirondack ores followed colonial need for military supplies in the Revolutionary period.

Plentiful wood later helped to create a profitable but temporary charcoal iron industry, but in the process the forests were ravaged. During the 1870's Adirondack mines within easy distance of the St. Lawrence and the lake were producing nearly one-quarter of all iron ore mined in the United States. Then the iron-mining center shifted to the shores of Superior and operations in the Adirondacks died a lingering death. The last survival was the Port Henry smelter on Lake Champlain.

World War II revival of Adirondack mining has been tremendous, both in iron and titanium, and a steady postwar development is anticipated as the Michigan and Mesabi ores approach depletion. In quality Adirondack ores are frequently compared to those of Sweden, and they lie close to steel centers. While some of them require special treatment, technological process has overcome most of the difficulties due to magnetic properties. In 1943 engineers and mining investigators of the Division of Commerce co-operated with the New York State Geologist and the United States Bureau of Mines in investigating more than a hundred promising deposit-sites of iron, graphite and mica. During the war years $40,000,000 has been invested in milling plants, mining machinery and ore-processing equipment. Republic Steel, National Lead Company, Jones & Laughlin and the M. A. Hanna Company have all recently acquired mining properties in Northern New York, now recognized as one of the nation's chief ore reserves.

Coming down to localities near Lake Ontario, St. Lawrence County's varied mineral deposits were known more than a century ago but were then inaccessible. In the census year 1879-1880, however, 94,767 tons of hematite ore were produced within a limited area reaching from the village of Antwerp in Jefferson County thirty miles toward Gouverneur. In 1888 the output was 110,000 tons. Since 1910 there has been but little mining there, but with the renewed surge of activity the resources of this section are being reprospected.

The coal trade, unlike the grain business and the iron industry, seems to have more present than future. Since the coal comes up from the south it is not hampered by the obstacles at the ends of the lake. Railroad transportation to the lake shore is excellent. Handling facilities in ports on both sides of the lake permit quick and economical transshipment. As far as transportation itself is concerned, the coal-carrying trade is in good shape.

The limitation on the industry lies in the market problem. Without iron ore, one of the biggest uses of coal is not present in the Lake Ontario region. As Canadian water power is further developed, the use of coal for power in industrial plants cannot be expected to increase greatly. Indeed, the Canadian demand for coal may gradually narrow down to what is needed for heating.

All the coal has to cross the international border. At present the communities on the Canadian side have not been able to find a profitable commodity to exchange for American coal, at least in comparable quantities. A one-way traffic is naturally less satisfactory and less profitable than an exchange. The coal business is nevertheless one of the largest industries in the lake region.

The first cargoes of commercial coal brought across the lake were unloaded by laborers trundling wheelbarrows. At first, all coal received was reshipped direct by rail, there being no handling facilities or provisions for storage. By degrees came specialized docks and derricks, shovel buckets and finally the efficient clamshell bucket. With the turn of the century arrived the pioneer electric coal-handling plant. Today progressive types of electric-driven traveling coal bridges encompass the unloading, stocking, preparing, reclaiming and car-loading operations in a seeming miraculously meshed single unit.

Good, normal-demand years for the American-Canadian coal trade were 1923-1936. Bituminous, which constitutes ninety-eight percent of coal cargoes on the Great Lakes, reached a peak of nearly 38,000,-000 tons in 1929, then fell off and showed a prewar tendency to become stabilized at around 35,000,000 tons. The heaviest shipments, of course, cross Erie and Michigan because of their nearness to Pennsylvania, Ohio and Illinois bituminous coal fields.

Apparently the war has boosted coal shipments across Lake Ontario to new heights, particularly out of Oswego, but complete figures are not obtainable for the war years; and if obtained could not be considered typical. Three New York ports on Lake Ontario used to handle around 600,000 tons of bituminous a year—Sodus Point, 250,-000; Rochester-Charlotte, 225,000 tons; and Oswego, 135,000 tons. In addition 100,000 tons move into Lake Ontario from Lake Erie by the Welland.

However, the Lake Ontario coal ports make a better showing on anthracite, no doubt because the hard-coal mines lie directly south of the lake. When Canada buys around 700,000 tons of anthracite, the New York ports on Lake Ontario are likely to handle one-quarter of the total. The lion's share—twenty percent—goes to Rochester-Charlotte with its car ferry to Cobourg, while Oswego is second. Until recently Oswego would be called a poor second but that port is now growing rapidly on the basis of war demand and improved facilities for expeditious handling. But of course anthracite is even more of a luxury coal for Canadians than it is for Americans.

In general, coal statistics are often confusing because they do not always include coal ferried in cars across the international boundary, "vessel fuel," bunker or ballast coal. The net situation appears to be that while about ten tons of bituminous coal move across Lake Ontario for every ton of anthracite, Lake Ontario is a more important factor in the water-borne hard-coal trade than it is in soft coal.

Iron, coal and grain make a great part of the wealth of the Upper Lakes. On Ontario two of them are comparatively small businesses in the present, although offering a brilliant promise for the future of the region—sometime—perhaps. Both of these must come to the lake, at least for the present, from the west. The third, coal, is already at its peak or near it. Significantly, coal approaches the lake from the south and avoids the bottlenecks at each end of the lake.

Very clearly these industries feel the effect of the isolation of the lake both from the west and from the east. Comfortably prosperous, the Ontario country cannot expect to become fabulously wealthy while it is still cut off from the vital channels of the trade of a continent. The southern approach is a small channel, in keeping with the present commercial position of the region. The obstructed eastern and western gates open into great channels. Who can prophesy what Ontario might become if they were swung wide?

# Chapter 24

# Industrial Partners

FOR nations, cities and men a favorable economic position is often more a matter of luck and timing than of wise choice. A boom town may come to a bad end and even a Great Lake may find itself out of luck.

Early in this story I noted the backward state of commercial development on Ontario as compared with that of its sister lakes. For this the accident or design of prehistoric geological process is chiefly responsible. There were two portentous movements of earth and water. The Niagara River sliced its way through soft rock to tumble into the plain that lay at the foot of the Erie plateau, and a way opened for Great Lakes water to seek the sea through a rocky channel leading northeast to oceanic gulfs. West of the lake stood a lofty barrier of plunging water, east of it a series of stony rapids.

Both the exploration and the commercial development of Lake Ontario were thus retarded by its natural isolation, and commerce has only partially overcome the handicap by digging the Welland Canal. Buffalo, a huddle of settlers' cabins in the first decade of the 1800's, swiftly became a busy port for sound economic reasons. Eastbound cargoes perforce had to stop at Erie's foot for transfer to other carriers.

The Erie Canal provided a waterway from Buffalo to the Hudson and New York City. Cargoes of the same kind passing through the Welland Canal had to be transferred either to barges at Oswego or to shallow-draft vessels for the trip through the St. Lawrence to the sea and southward to Manhattan, a roundabout route four or five times longer than the Barge Canal.

So, with the Erie already available to through traffic, the Welland

Canal conferred chiefly local benefits. Conversely, the proposed St. Lawrence development, with its contribution of hydroelectric power and improved transport, would aid the Ontario border communities enormously. This gain would be at the expense of New York City and Albany, according to foes of the lakes-to-ocean waterway. Hence the long cat-and-dog fight over the proposal which entered a new phase with Governor Dewey's recommendation that New York should proceed with the improvement on its own if Congress proved unable or unwilling to act.

Rochester and Toronto, as they stand, are proof of human will to overcome economic odds set up by geography. It is partly because of the lake's isolation that the Lake Ontario cities are less developed than those of Lake Erie and Lake Michigan. But Ontario has in reserve two vibrant possibilities—access to the ocean and a new potential of 200,000 white horses harnessed for service.

Will the potential commerce of Ontario ever go freely to the sea? Since 1913 the farsighted have been predicting that a time will come when European-bound freight from the Upper Lakes will traverse Lake Ontario and the St. Lawrence and go straight on across the Atlantic without being unloaded until it reaches the docks of Europe.

Until electric power was harnessed for industrial use, this prospect remained dim. As long as coal was the dominant power for industrial production Lake Ontario was foredoomed to have few local goods for export. Considerable areas around the lake have always remained lightly populated and near it are two large undeveloped regions of wood and water, the Adirondacks and the Rideau Lake district. Nowhere in the immediate vicinity of Lake Ontario, either in the Empire State or in Canada, are mineral deposits developed so as to provide bulk cargoes, though Adirondack mining is again looking up after a long sleep. As the Mesabi range and Lake Superior lose tonnage, their successors may be the Adirondacks and Lake Ontario. But at present the thinly settled shore line of New York and the agricultural regions of Ontario do not create a heavy volume of goods suitable for water carriage. But what of cargoes from the West? That might well be quite another story. Large cities spring up where products can be most conveniently manufactured or distributed.

Here the postwar planners begin to advance their central theme of electric power as a substitute for coal. Electric power by itself is usually not sufficient to move population but electric power plus cheap, convenient transportation might move it. The planners foresee electrically operated hoists to lift or lower vessels from one lake to another, in which case cataracts could be mounted as easily as stairs. Even some hardheaded engineers among them really believe that bigger boats than any now on the lakes will steam from Chicago to the sea as easily as if Lake Erie and Lake Ontario were on the same level. What practical steps and working precedents nurture these vast hopes?

In her most industrialized provinces of Ontario and Quebec, both of which lack coal and natural gas in commercial quantities, Canada has 85 percent of her developed hydroelectric power—better than 10,000,000 horsepower. "Thus Canada has built her industries with water power . . . until now her central situations produce more than twice the power per capita (3,480 kwhr) that the United States generates (1,630 kwhr)." Even so, Canada has developed only one-quarter of its water-power potential of 40,000,000 horsepower described as ordinarily available through six months of the year.

For a survey of extraordinary hydroelectric developments in this region of abundant water, let us start west from Niagara, turn the corner and proceed along the north shore. The gap between the autocratic past of the Family Compact and the progressive twentieth century is nowhere better revealed than in this eloquent passage from the Hydro-Electric Power Commission's 1927 report: ". . . a successful public ownership enterprise whether it be of schools, of municipal works, of transportation systems, or of electrical utilities, cannot be successfully imposed upon an unwilling community; it must be broad-based upon the people's will. Unless there be a desire on the part of the citizens to proceed on a basis of public ownership; unless there be responsible and qualified public men ready to make sacrifices to achieve the results desired; unless competent technical assistance be employed under conditions which ensure continuity of administration, and unless the people themselves are ready to back the project with their financial resources, no program of public ownership can be expected to be satisfactorily initiated and carried forward on a basis of permanency."*

---

* *Hydro-Electric Power Commission of Ontario: Its Origin, Administration and Achievements* (Toronto, Ontario, 1928).

The Commission's declared intent is to supply electrical service to the citizens of Ontario Province "at the lowest possible cost consistent with sound economics." Service has been supplied on that basis since 1910 by the giant bond servant popularly known as "the Hydro." That term embraces both the official parent central body which sells power wholesale to the municipalities, and the municipalities or their commissions which distribute it to individual customers.

Development of this co-operative enterprise in basic energy is the greatest single factor in the recent progress of Toronto and the Canadian shore. Hydro's birth came in this way. By 1900 it was realized that manufacture was in an economic jack boot. Ontario's farm lands, forests and minerals could supply raw materials for industrial growth, but how about power? Dependence upon outside sources for a fuel supply constituted a heavy handicap. But "white coal" might serve as well as black, and of indestructible "white coal" well-watered Ontario possessed abundance.

In 1900 a special committee named by Toronto's Board of Trade reported favorably upon a plan to tap the Niagara River for hydro-electrical energy. Other Ontario towns and cities studied the situation from the consumer standpoint. The provincial government in 1903 empowered interested communities to proceed with investigation by local commissions. Manufacturing cities—notably Toronto, London, Brantford, Stratford, Woodstock, Ingersoll and Guelph—pushed through a special act creating the "Hydro" Commission in 1906. Its powers were legally extended the following year. In 1908 thirteen municipalities contracted with Hydro for transmission of energy from noisy Niagara, after Hydro had arranged to buy the current from the Ontario Power Company, purchasing electrical energy up to a maximum of 100,000 horsepower. At once the Commission began to build transformer stations and transmission lines, and by the close of 1910 power was being transmitted to several contracting municipalities. The initial capital cost to serve the first dozen municipalities was $3,600,000. Hydro, as a public agent, bought current in quantity for the benefit of municipalities and their citizens. The ultimate consumers kept calling for more and more.

By 1915, 130 communities were being served; in 1920, 263; in 1925, 436; and in 1928, 550 communities including 225 townships. This expansion went far beyond the contractual limit of the Ontario Power

Company. Additional power was bought from the Canadian Niagara Power Company and the Toronto Power Company. These various commitments led to government purchase of the Ontario Power Company in 1917 and the Toronto Power Company in 1920. Ontario Power's capacity was increased to 180,000 horsepower.

Further legislation provided the tremendous Queenston-Chippawa development, the first unit of which came into commercial use in 1922. Three years later, with installation of its ninth unit, horsepower rose to 550,000. By 1928 the Commission was distributing more than a million horsepower radiating from twenty-two harnessed waterfalls. Although under frequent attack, the Commission held to its expansion program, aiming at 1,400,000 horsepower.

The name of Sir Adam Beck, who pushed Hydro forward for nearly twenty years, is gratefully remembered in Ontario. A leading manufacturer of London, Ontario, Beck was named chairman of the Hydroelectric Commission when the body was created in 1906 and carried on stoutly until his death in 1925.

By the time Hydro was eighteen years old it had developed eight giant distributing systems which supplied the entire province. Four of the eight systems served districts on or near Lake Ontario. The others lay far to the west and north. The four grouped around the lake may be described as follows:

1. Niagara System, the largest, embraced all territory between Niagara Falls, Hamilton and Toronto in the east, and Windsor, Sarnia and Goderich in the west. Its source of energy was the Niagara plants, but arrangements had been completed to tap additional power potentials on the Gatineau River in the Ottawa River watershed. Thirty-five miles above Ottawa on the provincial boundary is the 224,000-horsepower Chat Falls plant jointly owned by Hydro and the Ottawa Valley Power Company. Hydro does the operating and buys the company's half of the output. Into the Niagara System has been merged the transmission networks formerly served by the Essex County and Thorold systems, the Ontario Transmission Company and the Toronto and Niagara Power Company. Of the 5,000,000 horsepower that could be developed on the St. Lawrence, Canada would have for disposal about four-fifths and the United States one-fifth on the basis of riverine geography and boundaries. But Amer-

ican companies could buy St. Lawrence current from Canada just as they buy Niagara current.

2. St. Lawrence System, serving the district immediately north of the great river between Brockville and Cornwall, distributed power bought from the Cedar Rapids Power Company on the St. Lawrence.

3. Rideau System, deriving its name from the chain of small lakes north of Kingston and its power from two stations on the Mississippi River of Ontario. This current served the vicinity of Smith Falls, Perth and Carleton Place. Other generating plants were being developed at Carleton Place and High Falls, and the Rideau Power Company at Merrickville was furnishing added power.

4. Central Ontario and Trent System had been formed to supply the district bordering the north shore of Lake Ontario, sandwiched between the territories supplied by Niagara and Georgian Bay on the West and by the St. Lawrence and Rideau Systems on the East. To create this system, the province bought private power companies and added new developments until it had nine installations on the Trent and Otonabee Rivers.

With the other four systems added in, it is obvious that Hydro's planners had a wealth of water at their disposal. Reserves were enormous and are still large in spite of steady expansion since the multiple distributing system was set up. Hydro's engineers by no means discount the advances of steam power in producing cheap electricity, but in a coal-less province they seek in flowing water the means of industrial growth up to full economic strength.

Rural electrification developed slowly but gradually gained headway. Thrifty Canadians well understood the handicaps in this field. Ontario's farms averaged in size from 100 to 200 acres apiece. In most districts no more than a half-dozen farms could be served by a mile of Hydro distribution line. The first Ontario rural power lines were built in 1912, and in 1920 amendments to the legal control gave some impetus to rural electrification. In 1924, as further encouragement, the province undertook to pay fifty percent of the capital cost of installing rural transmission lines and equipment from the distribution center to the boundary of the consumer's property.

An interesting commercial development was latent in rural electrification. In the 1920's a sharply increasing number of small plants in the hinterland turned to electric motive power. These included brick and tile yards, cheese and butter factories, gravel and stone plants, quarries, chopping mills and flour mills. Also some old-style portable sawmills are being converted from steam to electric power. Villagers and farmers began to back Hydro along with the towns-folk.

Ontario then became earnestly concerned with the prospect of developing St. Lawrence power to enhance and fortify southern Ontario's systems. One of Hydro's voluminous reports contains this:

"On the international portion of the St. Lawrence river, stretching from Lake Ontario to St. Regis below Cornwall, there is a fall of some ninety feet, and between eighty and eighty-five feet of this fall can be developed for power by building a series of dams and dykes, either concentrating the total fall near Cornwall . . . or making a two-stage development concentrating a portion of the head . . . near Chrysler Island or Morrisburg and the remainder at the foot of the Long Sault."

In other words, shrewd Ontario sought to get in early on the economic use of Great Lakes water as it flowed past her shores and those of neighboring Quebec.

The Commission perceived two other sources for additional hydraulic power. The Ottawa River, an interprovincial stream, held a potential of a million horsepower at several undeveloped sites, half of which would be Ontario's. Niagara's output, too, could be enlarged if authorization was secured to divert additional water beyond the amount made available by the Boundary Waters Treaty of 1909-1910. At the great cataract every cubic foot of water under the full head produces thirty horsepower. By virtue of getting the lion's share of Niagara water over its side of the Falls, Ontario now sells power in the United States.

Queenston generating station, a mile south of the village of Queenston, was for some years after completion the largest single hydro-electric-power development in the world. Its completion required several huge and original undertakings: providing an intake structure in the Niagara River at Chippawa; deepening and enlarging the Welland River with reversal of its flow for four miles; building a canal eight and three-quarters miles long from Montrose on the

Welland River to the forebay and screen house on the cliff above the powerhouse on the lower Niagara River, where the banks rise more than 300 feet above the water level.

The Queenston-Chippawa development required excavation of 17,000,000 cubic yards of rock and earth. Each of five electrically operated shovels loaded in a minute and a half a car of twenty cubic yards' capacity standing sixty feet above the shovel. What a contrast to the way the Erie Canal had been patiently dug by hand! Digging that power canal, concrete-lined and forty-eight feet wide, began in 1917. It carried a forty-foot depth of water which at one point was 140 feet underground. The opening ceremony took place at the Queenston powerhouse in December 1924. The development cost had been $76,000,000.

Hydro says that one of its nine great generating units at Queenston "will supply an industrial city of 200,000 people with electric energy to turn the wheels of its factories, to drive its street cars and elevators, to light its streets and business houses, to pump its water and to service its homes." Previous Niagara power developments used only the power of the river in the cataract's immediate vicinity. The Queenston-Chippawa layout sought to utilize all but twelve feet of the total fall of 326 feet of the Niagara River between Lakes Erie and Ontario. Of the remainder, the energy from twenty feet is required to convey the water through the canal, and of the rest power-hungry Ontario boasts its intention to utilize everything but the foam.

Throughout this development there were many doubters who stood ready to prove with pad and pencils that Sir Adam Beck was a waster, Hydro a farce and Ontario a ruined province because, as they were prepared to demonstrate, electric current could be generated more cheaply in steam plants. Perhaps so; such is often the statistical truth. But the social fact is that in a coal-less country not much enthusiasm can be worked up for building industries on power derived from coal imports which might one day be shut off, because of dwindling supplies or restrictions at the international boundary. As far as Ontario can read the future, its running waters seem likely to outlast all North American coal supplies.

As the most potent new factor in Lake Ontario's economy, therefore, the Province presents Hydro, a growing concern which has set a pattern for community and provincial co-operation.

Across Lake Ontario and the St. Lawrence the power picture is vastly different yet in its way equally fascinating. Only at Watertown does an American city in the Ontario region own and control its own water power. In her case power is generated from the Black River's fall of 112 feet within the city limits, and operation is in private hands—those of the capable and diligent Carlisle organization which has a contract with the city. Various Carlisle power and light branches own or control under long-term leases the installations for such communities as Malone and Oswego, using current derived from the Salmon and Oswego Rivers, and in the case of the Salmon, from storage reservoirs in the upper waters. Yet one of the great power producers of that region is the already described coal-burning central station on the Lake Ontario shore at Oswego.

An example of how water power can make over a community is furnished by the town of Massena. Once a sleepy health resort, Massena has been transformed swiftly into one of the chief American smelting centers for aluminum. The decisive factor in determining the choice of the old resort as the site of a great industrial plant was the potential power in the rivers converging there.

Massena is located where two sizable rivers, the Grass and the Raquette, each with a dependable flow of water, enter the St. Lawrence within close sight of one another. Both rise in the Adirondacks, drain large watersheds, approach each other, then turn and run parallel down to the St. Lawrence.

In 1792 Anable Fancher's mill attracted some workers and their families to the spot, where they built log cabins. After 1822 the village sprawling on the banks of the Raquette drew some attention because of its mineral springs, which the St. Regis Indians described as bad-smelling but healing for sick animals and sick Indians. But in 1900 Massena contained less than a thousand residents, half of whom were engaged in the dairy business while the other half supported themselves by taking care of the ailing who came to take the waters.

Then came Henry H. Warren, who recognized a power site when he saw one. Warren organized a company which dug a canal connecting the Grass River with the St. Lawrence. The water sluiced through the canal on a shelving grade, with a fall of forty-five feet in three miles, to generate 200,000 horsepower. The rivers are now interconnected and their efficiency further developed.

This power now operates the Massena Works of the Aluminum Company of America. This great plant, occupying fifty acres of mills, shops and warehouses, is the only one in the country that produces aluminum cable for electrical transmission, along with the more usual goods and the standard aluminum biscuits shipped out to machine shops and forges. The giant Massena Works include the world's largest mill for the production of aluminum structural shapes. On seeing Massena, which now has 12,000 residents drawn from thirty nations, the visitor must admit that power alone can sometimes draw heavy industry to a new location, and that something comparable might happen at many sparsely settled points in the region. Projected Seaway plans call for another huge power installation at Massena.

The village of Waddington, eighteen miles up the St. Lawrence from Massena, is a historic community now apparently content to bask in the summer sun and hug the stove in winter. Here part of the river water flows through a ruined eighteenth-century lock, one of the first built to help river traffic pass the Plat Rapide.

At Ogdensburg, where the St. Lawrence is about a mile wide is a wharf-lined Federal-built channel twenty-one feet deep, extending up the Oswegatchie River which enters the St. Lawrence there. A twelve-foot dam furnishes water power for mills, factories and hydroelectric plants.

Another pioneer in North Country electricity was the late John Byron Taylor of Watertown, head of a local light and power concern which later took the name of Northern New York Utilities. He harnessed river power and agitated successfully for the impounding of waters in state storage reservoirs. The Taylor interests were purchased by the Carlisle brothers, Floyd and John N., and their associates in the so-called "Carlisle powers" already mentioned in connection with Oswego and Watertown. Communities and industries have profited much from the development of several rivers in the Lake Ontario watershed during the past twenty-five years.

Among the Carlisle projects was the creation of a storage reservoir on the upper Beaver River in Lewis County, some twenty years ago. This Adirondack foothills construction involved sealing a dam with sand, an experiment which went off successfully.

At the turn of the century the power streams of northern New

York were losing their mills, which were largely devoted to turning out paper and pulp. Deforestation had decreased their raw materials and so denuded the watersheds that the flow was uneven, with alternating freshets and drouths. Reservoirs relieved the situation somewhat but not sufficiently. The state of New York came to the rescue with enlightened control of forest-reserve areas, and hydroelectric companies and some paper manufacturers have followed the state's example. The flow of water for power has been saved, but pulp manufacturers are now mainly dependent for their spruce supply on the forests of Quebec and Ontario Provinces. Many bargeloads of Canadian spruce are delivered at Oswego and St. Lawrence River ports, and New York's past wastefulness is Canada's present gain.

At Oswego the power situation is most encouraging. Two hydroelectric plants plus a giant steam plant, erected in recent years by the Niagara-Hudson Power Company, are of sufficient capacity to serve many new industries. Engineers made the most of the fall of the Oswego River in its last half-dozen miles. A concentration of power also was developed in the eastern end of Oswego County. The surrounding rural territory is being generously served from this central source.

At Rochester the turbulent Genesee, whose power gave the city its industrial start, has been harnessed pretty thoroughly but not enough to destroy all its scenic possibilities. Rochester's industries now draw on Niagara power, which is supplemented in its turn by power purchases from Canada.

From this discussion of power developments on both sides of Lake Ontario, two broad conclusions emerge. The American side has almost reached the end of its water-power possibilities for electrical development and needs still more power, while the Canadian side still has undeveloped hydroelectric resources and, in a sense, needs more industries. Both shores, however, feel that they can profitably use part of the potential power now being wasted in the St. Lawrence rapids. They believe, too, that the lakes-to-gulf waterway for ocean commerce, built in conjunction with proposed power development on the great river, would stir this country to new heights of prosperity, by bringing in raw materials for manufacture and carrying away surplus products to the markets of the world.

# Chapter 25

## Hands Across the Lake

---

*When I was walking near the Capitol in Washington with James (afterwards Lord) Bryce, author of* The American Commonwealth *and, at the time, British Ambassador to the United States, suddenly he stopped, waved his hand towards the great dome, and said: "If Canada did not exist, it would be in the interests of the United States to create it." He meant that North America is too vast a territory to be governed from one centre.*
—George M. Wrong

---

MYRIADS of words have been printed of the vision of those who found nations and communities, yet upon close examination it usually appears that founders wander through the same wilderness of trial and error as do their grandsons. Each generation is given its chance to muddle through. One of the paramount blunders of our early statesmen was the War of 1812, which poisoned American-Canadian feeling for a century, but to the credit of the border be it said that Lake Ontario folk on both sides were never eager for that conflict. Since then, in spite of all misunderstandings, the two peoples have rubbed along together with growing confidence in the purposes of each other.

The Lake Ontario region, too, has seen its share of missteps in the general advance. Many a deserted village on Ontario's shore testifies to failure, and even the cities which have succeeded pulled through despite errors in judgment by their leaders.

Take Rochester, for instance. Completion of the Erie Canal created the impetus to growth that every progressive modern community craves. Freight shipments eastward over the canal began in 1823, though the Big Ditch was not finished westward to Buffalo until late in 1825. Transportation rates from Rochester to Albany were hacked from $60 per ton by wagon to a maximum of $10 per ton by boat. Meantime the little village by the Falls of the Genesee had been recommended by state surveyors as the point for the Genesee crossing which would automatically make Rochester the prime gateway on the canal route. By 1826 flour shipments reached 202,000 barrels annually, and 1827 saw total canal exports of $1,200,000 while the boats brought back $1,020,000 in goods for the merchants' shelves. Nevertheless many leading citizens opposed the canal's coming and thought it spelled doom.

". . . those early Rochesterians while individually energetic perhaps in their businesses, were reactionary in the mass. An economy drive launched by the frugal-minded in the early 1840's stopped an ambitious program of street paving and other civic improvements. The State legislature's slow and timid grant of banking powers and the resulting invalidism of Rochester's five weak banks which commanded a total over-all capitalization of $1,500,000, placed Rochester twenty-sixth in rank as a banking center, when by 1849 population she should have rated as seventeenth."*

It appears that Rochester could hardly have avoided prominence arising from its almost ideal location, a primary advantage also enjoyed by Buffalo and Toronto. Such well-placed communities forge onward in spite of early blunders. Rochester on the south shore, Toronto on the north shore, were both hampered by initial mistakes, but the physical location of each triumphed over all errors of judgment and reactionary setbacks. Such blunders are not likely to happen again. Enlightened civic spirit mobilized for action in communities is a relatively new expression of human initiative. In the old days there were no Chambers of Commerce to oppose the village cynics. Both of the great cities on Lake Ontario now have institutions which are remarkable of their kind, alike for business vision and solicitude for social and cultural development.

As with border towns all the way to the Pacific, Rochester and Toronto profit reciprocally from international commerce. This traffic dates from potash-smuggling days when new settlements were rising in the thick forests. Free trade, even on a smuggling basis, is a practical reciprocity that encourages peace. There was the ancient profit motive, to be sure; but from the time of those early traders there has also been mutuality of interest based upon fair exchanges.

---

* *Rochester History,* edited by Dexter Perkins, City Historian, and Blake McKelvey, Assistant City Historian, Vol. iii, No. 4 (October, 1941).

The bulk of international trade has helped enormously in the up-building of both shores along the great river and the lakes.

The sweep of scientific industrialism—or big business, if you like—has profoundly influenced the relations of Canada and the United States, of Ontario and western New York. When Toronto can telephone Rochester, there is no insuperable obstacle against a man of Toronto launching a branch of his business in Rochester, or vice versa, merely by using the appropriate corporate form. And the corporation itself, remember, is at once a most substantial and adaptable modern invention. Hence we have the phenomena of the Canadian branch industry and its counterpart, the American branch.

Some of the Canadian branches of American manufactures have already been mentioned in connection with the Rochester, Hamilton and Toronto narratives. Toronto is also headquarters for five great American steel companies and four of the five largest tire companies. In exchange a British and Canadian tire company operates out of Toronto a large rubber factory near Niagara Falls. All of Rochester's leading nursery and seed farms are well established across the lake, where soils and agricultural problems are almost identical.

Bell Telephone, Stromberg-Carlson, the Radio Corporation of America and its giant subsidiaries in communications and broadcasting, represent the continuous forging of a community of thought and idea between the two nations. There are no customs houses or immigration inspectors on the air waves.

Firms in Toronto and other parts of Canada maintain connections, and sometimes even commercial subsidiaries, in Rochester, Niagara Falls, New York and Oswego as well as in communities to the southward in the Finger Lakes region of the Empire State. This is particularly true of lumber, wood-pulp and paper-products concerns.

The American Salesbook Company, originating in Canada and managed from Toronto, has several plants in the United States, one of them at Niagara Falls.

To a truly amazing degree business and industrial interests on both sides of Lake Ontario interlock. Consider, for instance, the border activities of a non-profit organization—Better Business Bureaus, Inc. Amid the increasing business relationships between Canadians and Americans a whole new field of fraud and near-fraud has been opened to shady operators. Such crooked transactions may be as simple as selling Americans stock in a nonexistent Canadian company, or promoting in the United States an Ontario gold mine which those on the ground know to be worthless. Another favorite scheme is built upon swindling small Canadian communities that dearly want American branch factories, and will hopefully put up money for expenses, fees and bonuses for agents who cannot perform.

Far wider than the field of fraud is the domain of legitimate trading and contractual risks entered into by citizens and corporations dealing across a border at which laws, customs and even business ethics in some degree change. In these transactions, losses through ignorance or error are far more likely to occur than in domestic trade, and as these dangers exist in a realm of action not easily reached by law, business itself has devised ways and means of coping with these entanglements that arise in United States-Canadian business.

The most outspoken of these regulators of private enterprise are the Better Business Bureaus. These organizations frankly state that they are descended from the old Vigilance Committees of pioneer days. Below the border there are some eighty affiliated agencies, and in Canada there are five. Their information service not only provides usual trade information but also discovers and unmasks rackets of all descriptions, those undercover activities which so often escape the attention of police and public prosecutors. During the 1930's the United States Bureaus made themselves solid in Ontario by trailing fraudulent stock promoters who fled into Canada when the depression blighted their trade in New York.

As a way of blocking spurious transactions, Canadian bureaus—the one at Toronto is extremely wide awake—warn their United States associates of peddlers of stolen or imitation furs, solicitors for racketeer war funds, promoters of salted gold mines, leaders of illegal immigration schemes and impecunious gentry who know how to make their fortunes by beating the regulations on currency transfers. A sleepless defense is maintained on both sides of the border.

Aside from detection, the effort is to maintain standards of fair business practice in both countries, with bilingual attention to Canada. This entire movement is financed by business on a co-operative basis, and the boards of directors of all the separate Bureaus serve without pay. Originally created to promote and defend truth in advertising, B.B.B. still carry on that function but have added many others, and present policy-makers consider that one of their most important fields of action is that of United States-Canadian business relationships.

As W. D. Bell, executive director of the National Association of Better Business Bureaus, Inc., says: "We feel that these services will be especially valuable along the borders of Ontario and its sister lakes in the approaching mass of postwar business. There is no boundary line between fraud, deception and unethical practices, and fortunately there are no international barriers to impede cooperation and friendship in border trade."

To this extent the impediments created by the international border through Lake Ontario have been overcome. Business has a way of overlaying with system and order those difficulties which it is powerless to uproot. But the lone traveler and people overawed by officials in uniform, occasionally find themselves wishing that the international border would vanish from the maps and never be heard of again. A relaxation of many bothersome regulations may be reasonably expected to follow hard on the heels of the partnership in arms brought about by World War II, to the end that these two peoples can trade together, work together and play together for their own good and comfort as distinct from the revenues and glories of their respective commonwealths.

As in things material, so also in things cultural. In motion pictures with their accompanying miscellany, Hollywood is as dominant in Ontario as in New York. Behold here the continuing invasion power of two great Americans—Thomas A. Edison and George Eastman, whose work combined to provide the motion-picture industry with its basic needs.

At Toronto's "474 Wellington W" is domiciled the familiar American News Company (Limited). The name will recall to many a graybeard old days when he entrained with his parents from somewhere to elsewhere, and the American News man or "butcher" boy came through the cars with everything from newspapers to popcorn, candy and pop in his bag or basket. Of course the American News Company has long since become a tremendous distributor of books and magazines with branches everywhere.

Most book publishers and practically all periodicals of New York City maintain offices of their own or close affiliations with Canadian publishers in Toronto and Montreal. Some of the larger ones have their own complete organizations, replicas of those in New York or Philadelphia, with the printing done by Canadian concerns. The so-called pulp magazines from the United States are stocked across the border in tiers and masses, competing with Canadian publications, many of which issue from Toronto. Everything in "thrillers," including fictional adventures of the "Mounties" too frequently written by authors who never set foot in Canada and know its forests only by what others' pens have written, load the stands in Toronto and in all the Dominion's other communities.

As for railroads, a web of steel of connecting American lines has spread over the Ontario border, competing and co-operating with the Canadian systems. In Toronto you can do business directly with the Baltimore & Ohio; Chesapeake & Ohio; Chicago, Milwaukee, St. Paul & Pacific; Chicago, Rock Island & Pacific; Delaware, Lackawanna & Western; Erie; Great Northern; Illinois Central; Lackawanna; Lehigh Valley; New York Central; Pennsylvania; Pere Marquette; Rock Island; St. Louis Southwestern; Union Pacific; and Wabash. Their offices and various facilities in Toronto consolidate freight and passenger transportation for the convenience and prosperity of the two good-neighbor countries which form this continent.

Thirty-one steamship lines, ranging in size from carriers on the lakes and the St. Lawrence to ocean-girdlers, occupy quay-space along Toronto's harbor and elsewhere. Directly connected with the Lake Ontario trade are: Canada Steamship Lines, Limited; Canadian National Steamers; Niagara, St. Catharines & Toronto Line; Northern Navigation Company, Limited; Free Line Navigation Company, Limited; and Upper Lakes & St. Lawrence Transportation Company, Limited.

Tied into this financial, industrial and cultural net which criss-crosses the border are two considerations portentous for the future. Under Imperial preference, which by tariff advantage provides members of the British Commonwealth of Nations with favorable access to one another's markets as against outsiders, the Ontario branch of an American corporation may do business more cheaply than its parent company on shipments to that considerable part of the planet on which "the sun never sets." There are cases where the foreign trade of a Canadian subsidiary exceeds that of the American principal—partly because of Imperial preference, partly because Canadians have learned from long British association how to foster and develop overseas commerce. These aspects have not been lost on American enterprise, and will influence continued northward expansion of American business unless Uncle Sam considerably modifies his own tariff policy.

The second consideration of utmost significance is Ontario's wealth of natural resources, both in production and in reserve. When Ontario's lumberjacks go to war, American housewives are asked to carry their packages home unwrapped. I have stood in a magnificent American-owned paper mill—the Kimberly & Clark—on Kapuskasing River, not so far from James Bay, and there have seen paper on which the New York *Times* is printed being pulped from trees grown in forests as yet mapped in only the sketchiest manner. Add to lumber all the other gifts of nature—metals and minerals, water power, furs, arable land waiting for the plow. So vast a country must have capital for development, and pay for its use with exports to lands which in an earlier period have consumed enough of their natural assets to create import markets. The United States is already in such a position as to lumber, and is rapidly approaching that position in other respects. The development of Canadian natural resources by American capital is as inevitable as the march of the seasons.

"Ah, yes," say the bankers and manufacturers of Ontario, "of course, of course. But really, we want to do the business ourselves, you know, and get a bit out of it for ourselves. Not as hired men, you understand, but as employers and enterprisers in our own right."

Quite so, a natural and laudable ambition which Americans will do well to note before they take their checkbooks northward! The best arrangement they can possibly make is to join with Ontario firms, find Ontario managers for their Ontario properties and see to it that the managers become part owners. There is an old saying that a rich man for his own protection should devote some time to creating other men of property; the more proprietors the better for himself. Such is surely the case between nations. The United States stands to benefit greatly from the prosperity of Canada's richest and most populous province, not merely in the profits which accrue from trading with a solvent neighbor, but also in the delights of associating in trade and travel with an able people full of confidence in itself. Out of Armageddon should flow a sense of partnership deeper than economic, a kinship mellowed by comradeship in the supreme test.

Canada is more than Canada—an independent, self-reliant nation. She is also a link between America and Britain. The relations of these three nations are fascinating both historically and prophetically; inside the triangle of that future may be read the fate of the fairest dreams of mankind. As these dreams unfold in the future out of the past and present, the Lake Ontario region is likely again to be the scene of historical events and the epochal adaptations of great peoples who have foresworn war except in mutual defense of their home-lands. For it is across Lake Ontario that the strongest Canadian province and the richest and most populous of these United States face each other. May they read in the clear waters of that lake true portent of a fair and smiling destiny!

**THE END**

GENERAL ZEBULON PIKE MEMORIAL

The memorial is built on the spot where General Pike, discoverer of Pike's Peak, fell at Fort York, Toronto, in 1813.

*Courtesy of William C. Muir*

MUIR BROTHERS DRYDOCK AT PORT DALHOUSIE

# ACKNOWLEDGMENTS

# AND

# BIBLIOGRAPHICAL NOTE

# ACKNOWLEDGMENTS

THE author is grateful for assistance from many persons and institutions, among them the following:

Ottawa. The Public Archives of Canada.

Toronto. The Corporation of the City of Toronto.

A. A. McIntosh, Editor-in-chief of *The Globe and Mail*.

The Board of Trade of the City of Toronto.

The Toronto Convention and Tourist Association, Inc.

Toronto Industrial Commission.

Ontario Travel and Publicity Bureau.

Board of Harbour Commissioners.

Kingston. *The Whig-Standard,* W. Rupert Davies, President, and Robert D. Owen, Managing Editor.

Niagara Falls, Ont. A. S. Robertson, The Hydro-Electric Power Commission of Ontario.

Hamilton. The Chamber of Commerce.

London, Ontario. Fred Landon, historian, University of Western Ontario; author of *Lake Huron* in this series.

Port Dalhousie, Ont. Muir Bros. Dry Dock Co.

New York City. New York Historical Society.

The Macmillan Company, for permission to quote.

Rochester. City Historian's Office and Blake McKelvey, Assistant City Historian.

The University of Rochester.

Public Library.

Rev. A. M. Stewart, antiquarian.

Rochester Museum of Arts and Sciences, Dr. Arthur C. Parker, Director.

The Chamber of Commerce and Dr. Milton E. Loomis, Director.

Eastman Kodak Company.

The Better Business Bureau of Rochester, Inc.

Albany. The State Library and State Historian's office; Dr. A. B. Corey.

Oswego. *The Palladium-Times.*

County Historian, R. M. Faust.

Watertown. Harry F. Landon, Managing Editor of the Watertown *Times;* author of *The North Country*.

Jefferson County Historical Society. Also Miss Faith Common, secretary and curator, Jefferson County Historical Society.

Fonda. Department of History and Archives of Montgomery County, Edward F. Sheehan, Director.

Cooperstown. New York Historical Association, Dr. Dixon Ryan Fox, President; Miss Janet McFarland, Acting Director.

Niagara Falls, N. Y. Niagara-Hudson Power Corporation.
E. T. Williams, City Historian.

Cleveland. National Association of Better Business Bureaus, Inc.

Detroit. Dr. M. M. Quaife, editor of this series, for permission to use valuable unpublished material from his monograph on the burning of Parliament buildings at York, and other expert assistance.

Also to these persons who helped in research, editing or correspondence—O. L. Lyman, E. B. Davis, Irving Adler and Mrs. Henrietta Sann.

—ARTHUR POUND

# BIBLIOGRAPHICAL NOTE

For the geology and geography of the Lake Ontario region, official bulletins of New York State and the Province of Ontario are available, but most of them are heavy going. A competent résumé of the material appears in the *History of the State of New York* (New York, 1933) edited by the late State Historian, Dr. Alexander C. Flick. The first chapter of Volume I, written by Dr. Chris A. Hartnagel, State Geologist, gives a good description of early geologic changes. Two lively books on the same subject are Arthur P. Coleman's *The Last Million Years* (Toronto, 1941) and Herman L. Fairchild's *Geologic Story of the Genesee Valley and Western New York* (Rochester, 1928). On physical geography, climate, rainfall, agriculture and horticulture the best references are J. Russell Smith's *North America* (New York, 1925) and Dr. U. P. Hedrick's *History of Agriculture in the State of New York* (Albany, 1933).

The outstanding American authority on the archaeology and anthropology of this region is Arthur C. Parker, former State Archaeologist of New York and now director of the Rochester Museum of Arts and Sciences. His *Archaeological History of New York* (1920) and his stimulating article, "The Origin of the Iroquois as Suggested by Their Archaeology" in the *American Anthropologist* of December 1916 (Vol. XVIII, No. 4) are especially useful. More information can be found in the *Researches and Transactions* of the Lewis H. Morgan chapter of the New York State Archaeological Association (Rochester, 1925-1927). A more general treatment of archaeological discoveries about the North American Indian is seen in the beautifully illustrated *Romance of Archaeology* (New York), by R. W. Magoffin and Emily C. Davies, originally issued in 1929 as *Magic Spades*.

Some of the first studies of Iroquois history were Henry R. Schoolcraft's *Notes on the Iroquois* (Albany, 1847) and J. H. V. Clark's *Onondaga, or Reminiscences of Earlier and Later Times* (Syracuse, 1849); but Lewis H. Morgan was the first to treat the Confederacy as a subject of high politics in his *League of Hodenosaunee, or Iroquois* (Rochester, 1851). Several Indian treatises have been published by the New York State Museum; among them W. M. Beauchamp's *Aboriginal Occupation of New York* (1900) and *History of the New York Iroquois* (1905), Arthur C. Parker's *Code of Handsome Lake* (1913) and the precious *Constitution of the Five Nations* (1915). A brief account of Iroquois organization by clans, nations

357

and federation appears in *Johnson of the Mohawks* (New York, 1930) by
Arthur Pound and Richard E. Day. Two articles by the late Robert M.
Lansing in *The Independent* (Oct. 4-Oct. 11, 1924) give a modern statesman's appraisal of the League. The extent of Iroquois control over waterways, trade routes and trails is best indicated in Seymour Dunbar's
monumental *History of Travel in America* (New York, 1937).

Abundant material on French discovery, exploration, colonization and
trade is available in several great compilations: *The Jesuit Relations and
Allied Documents* (Cleveland, 1896-1901), edited by R. G. Thwaites; *The
Documentary History of New York* (Albany, 1850) and *Documents Relating to the Colonial History of the State of New York* (1855), both edited
by E. B. O'Callaghan, M.D.; and *The Works of Samuel de Champlain*,
edited by H. D. Biggar, and published by the Champlain Society of
Toronto (1922-1936). Much of this documentary material is condensed and
interpreted in J. G. Shea's section on the Jesuits, Récollets and Indians in
the *Narrative and Critical History of America* (Boston, 1884-1885), edited
by Justin Winsor. Other narrative histories are the vivid works of Francis
Parkman: *Jesuits in New France, Pioneers of France in the New World*,
and *Count Frontenac and New France under Louis XIV*. More popular in
tone is William B. Munro's *Crusaders of New France* (New Haven, 1918)
in the Chronicles of America Series.

The Lake Ontario fur trade is mentioned in many books, but dominates
no important publication. A. Everett Peterson touches on the subject in the
last chapter of Volume I of the *History of the State of New York* mentioned earlier, but the really choice bits are scattered through the first two
volumes. E. A. Jennings' *History of Economic Progress in the United
States* (New York, 1926) gives some facts and figures on the role of furs
in both the foreign and domestic commerce of colonial America. Brief but
convincing accounts of the Canadian fur trade are contained in introduc-
tions to the Journals of Sir George Simpson. The first is that by Frederick
Merk in his *Fur Trade and Empire; Sir George Simpson's Journal* (Cambridge, Mass., 1931); the second is by George Martin in Simpson's *Atha-
basca Journal* (London, 1838), edited by E. E. Rich. *The Life and Times
of Sir William Johnson* by William L. Stone (Albany, 1865) was the first
and is still one of the best of many biographies of the family. *Johnson of
the Mohawks,* by Pound and Richard E. Day, who edited the *Sir William
Johnson Papers* (Albany, 1921-1938), is now more readily available than
Stone's book, and its authors had access to material unknown to Stone.

The course of the Seven Years' War in the Lake Ontario region can be
followed in several notable books. Professor George M. Wrong's *Fall of
Canada: A Chapter in the History of the Seven Years War* (Oxford,

1914), *Conquest of New France* (New Haven, 1918), and his two-volume *Rise and Fall of New France* (New York, 1938) make a noble trilogy by a great interpretative historian. The New York point of view on these epochal events is well set forth in state publications mentioned earlier. The best source material for Colonel John Bradstreet's campaign is an unpublished journal, now in the New York State Library, by Colonel Charles Clinton. Oswego's part in the war is sketched in *The Story of Oswego* (Oswego, 1934), an excellent local history.

The history of Lake Ontario in the American Revolution is available in many publications. Professor John C. Miller's *Origins of the American Revolution* (Boston, 1943) takes proper note of Western causations and George M. Wrong's *Canada and the American Revolution* (New York, 1935) provides urbane and balanced interpretation from the Canadian point of view. The University of the State of New York issued two sesquicentennial publications of great merit by Dr. Alexander C. Flick: *The American Revolution in New York* (1926) and *The Sullivan-Clinton Expedition in 1779* (1929). *War Out of Niagara* (New York, 1933) by Harold Swiggett makes spirited use of scant material. A short biography of the Revolutionary leader, Brigadier General James Clinton, appears in *My Native Stock* (New York, 1932). The Iroquois leader, Joseph Brant, was done full-length long ago by W. L. Stone in his *Life of Joseph Brant* (Albany, 1838), and more informally of late by Harvey Chalmers II, in *West to the Setting Sun* (Toronto, 1943). The Public Archives of Canada have disclosed valuable material on Walter N. Butler, on the construction of the Carleton Island fortress and raids into the Mohawk country. In addition, I have drawn upon two large Canadian compilations for information and likenesses of various British and Canadian leaders of this period and the War of 1812—*Chronicles of Canada* (Oxford, 1911-1928), edited by George M. Wrong and H. H. Langton; and *Canada and Its Provinces,* edited by Adam Shortt and A. G. Doughty of which two volumes dealing with the province of Ontario were issued in 1914.

Of the massive literature on the Mohawk Valley I can mention only a few books. F. W. Halsey's *Old Frontier of New York* (New York, 1901) expounds well the historical and imperial significance of the water-level route. John J. Vrooman's exceptionally well-illustrated *Forts and Firesides of the Mohawk Country* (Philadelphia, 1943) reveals how the people of the valley suffered under the British raids of the Revolution. The savage nature of this warfare is also attested in Dr. T. Wood Clarke's *The Bloody Mohawk* (New York, 1940), and close knowledge of a complex and confused military movement distinguishes *Fort Stanwix and Oriskany* (Rome, N. Y., 1927) by John A. Scott. Mohawk Valley has also been a favorite subject for historical novels, the most popular one of recent years being *Drums Along the Mohawk* (Boston, 1936) by Walter D. Edmonds. The publications and collections of numerous county and local historical societies teem with material bearing upon the importance of the Mohawk gateway to Lake Ontario in three wars.

The history of Niagara and Upper Canada is best covered in several excellent Canadian books, though Frank W. Severance's graceful *Old Frontier of France* (New York, 1917) is one of the masterpieces of New York historical writing. For the Canadian side of the river the best books are Brigadier General E. A. Cruikshank's *Butler's Rangers and the Settlement of Niagara* (Toronto, 1904) and *Ten Years of the Colony of Niagara, 1780-1790* (Welland, Ont., 1893). Upper Canada history has likewise been enriched by his editing of the *Correspondence of John Graves Simcoe, Lieutenant Governor* (Toronto, 1922-1931), which was published by the Ontario Historical Society. Mrs. Simcoe, however, still outshines her husband by reason of her justly famous diary which was published by W. Briggs, Toronto, in 1911. *Early Life in Upper Canada* (Toronto, 1933), by E. C. Guillet, is a semipopular work, with good maps and portraits, dealing with social life down to about 1850.

No work on Loyalism has superseded Dr. C. H. VanTyne's *The Loyalists in America* (New York and London, 1902, 1929), though Dr. Alexander C. Flick's *Loyalism in New York in the American Revolution* (New York, 1901) has a real flavor of the local scene. Canadians have Egerton Ryerson's excellent *The Loyalists of America and Their Times* (Toronto, 1880), and two books by A. G. Bradley: *The United Empire Loyalists* (London, 1932) and *Colonial Americans in Exile* (New York, 1932), vigorously written though they contain some errors on the New York side. An excellent source study is General Cruikshank's *Settlement of United Empire Loyalists on the Upper St. Lawrence and the Bay of Quinte, 1784* (Welland, Ont., 1898). *The Family Compact,* by William S. Wallace (Toronto, 1915), shows how oligarchic rule grew from Loyalist roots. I should mention, too, Bruce Lancaster's novel, *Bright to the Wanderer* (Boston, 1942), which pictures the Loyalist migration, the Reform movement and the Rebellion.

Material on the Holland Purchase can be found mainly in publications issued by the Buffalo Historical Society: *The Holland Land Company* (1924) by Paul Demuth Evans, and *The Reports of Joseph Ellicott as Chief of Survey (1797-1800) and as Agent (1800-1821) of the Holland Land Company's Purchase in Western New York,* edited by Robert W. Bingham in 1927. The New York State Library contains several rare pamphlets on agrarian conventions from 1827 to 1834.

For vessels, armaments and tactics I have followed Theodore Roosevelt's *Naval History of the War of 1812* (New York, 1883). Gerald S. Graham's *Sea Power and British North America* (Cambridge, Mass., 1941) is helpful on strategy, and a good contemporary account can be found in Robert Christie's *Military and Naval Operations in the Canadas* (Quebec, 1818). Canadian scholars have given the war thorough attention in the *Select British Documents of the Canadian War of 1812* (Toronto, 1920-1928), edited by William Wood and published by the Champlain Society, and in the *Campaigns of 1812-14* (Toronto, 1902) published by the Ontario Historical Society. General Cruikshank was first known as a precise chronicler of the military history of this war. His *Battle of Lundy's Lane* (Welland, Ont., 1893), *Battle of Fort George* (Welland, Ont., 1912) and similar works led to his appointment as editor of the excellent *Documentary History of the Campaign upon the Niagara Frontier* (Toronto, 1923).

Walter D. Edmonds' tales of the Erie Canal do much to catch the color and spirit of the enterprise. *Rome Haul* (1929), *Erie Water* (1933) and *Mostly Canallers* (1934) are all published by Little, Brown and Company, Boston. The effect of Clinton's Big Ditch on the economy of the Lake Ontario region is also well revealed in local histories. Dr. Alexander Coventry's unpublished diary, now in the New York State Archives, is rich material which has been available to this author.

Dunbar's *History of Travel* does full justice to Elkanah Watson and his writings on canals here and abroad, of which the most inclusive was *The History of the Rise, Progress and Existing Condition of the Western Canals in the State of New York, etc.* (Albany, 1920). Watson's canal leadership is also covered in his semi-autobiographic *Men and Times of the Revolution* (New York, 1856), prepared jointly with his son, W. C. Watson, but published after the father's death. A modern account of the Erie and of its successor, the New York Barge Canal, is *New York—The Canal State* by Francis P. Kimball (Albany, 1937).

The whole parade of events on the Canadian Reform Movement and the Rebellion of 1837 can be followed in Charles Lindsey's *Life and Times of William Lyon Mackenzie* (Toronto, 1909), and in *The Crisis of 1830-42 in Canadian-American Relations* (Toronto, New Haven and Oxford, 1941) by Dr. A. B. Corey. The disorders and confusion of the times are described in E. C. Guillet's well-documented tale, "The Cobourg Conspiracy," in the *Canadian Historical Review* for March 1937, later reprinted in pamphlet form. Numerous accounts were written by captives and refugees from the Rebellion, one of the most revealing of these being Donald McLeod's *Brief Review of the Settlement of Upper Canada* (Cleveland, 1841). One refugee re-established in the States, Dr. E. B. O'Callaghan, edited the important collections of early documents for the state of New York. Francis White's *1837—The Birth of Canadian Democracy* (Toronto, 1941) is also of interest in this connection.

The fascinating subject of Canada's political evolution toward federation has often been treated. It is well though briefly covered in *The Federation of Canada* (Toronto, 1917), a symposium of University of Toronto lectures by four Canadian scholars. Sir John G. Bourinot's *Canada under British Rule, 1760-1905* (New York, 1900) is another study of great worth. The great Macdonald's influence on the development of Ontario and the Dominion after federation is handled well in two meritorious biographies of this statesman: George R. Parkin's *Sir John A. Macdonald* (Toronto, 1906) and *The Day of Sir John A. Macdonald,* in the Chronicles of Canada Series, by Sir Joseph Pope, Macdonald's former secretary.

For the journey around Lake Ontario on the American side one of the best books is the WPA opus, *New York: A Guide to the Empire State* (New York, 1940), and local histories are also invaluable aids. A masterly work of this character is the *History of Jefferson County in the State of New York* (Watertown, 1854) by Franklin B. Hough. Harry M. Landon in his three-volume history, *The North Country* (Indianapolis, 1932), does well by the southeast corner of the lake, and *Émigrés in the Wilderness* by Dr. T. Wood Clarke (New York, 1941) describes vividly the picturesque French migrants to the North Country. An excellent book of reminiscential travel is Edward Hungerford's *Pathway of Empire* (New York, 1941).

The port of Toronto and the city itself are intelligently represented in centennial booklets—particularly *Toronto's 100 Years,* the official centennial book by Jesse Edgar Middleton, published in Toronto in 1934. E. C. Guillet's *Toronto from Trading Post to Great City* (Toronto, 1934) is another valuable history. In all the prominent Lake Ontario ports— Oswego, Rochester, Niagara Falls, Hamilton, Toronto and Kingston— information and illustrative material, with a decided accent on the history and culture of the localities, can be obtained from the respective Chambers of Commerce. For the state of New York the new Department of Commerce performs a similar function on a larger scale.

For merchant shipping of the past on Lake Ontario the best material is to be found in old newspapers, in the columns of marine reporters, in the collections of historical and art societies and in collections of old prints. The book, magazine and newspaper writings of C. H. J. Snider of Toronto and the publications of the Harbour Commissioners of Toronto also prove helpful. Commerce and industrial development on both sides of the international border naturally have a flourishing press, and Canadian business enterprise is also discussed in James A. Aiken's *Economic Power for Can-*

*ada* (Toronto, 1931) and D. G. Creighton's *Commercial Empire of the Saint Lawrence* (Toronto, 1937). Hydroelectric developments are publicized by both the companies and the localities involved. Hydro's comprehensive report of 1928 can be checked against reports for succeeding years and statistics of the *Canada Year Book*. Professor James Mavor of the University of Toronto took a decidedly adverse view of Hydro in *Niagara in Politics* (New York, 1925) and in various pamphlets and articles, but Hydro seems to have lived down the serious criticism of laissez-faire economists. The *Canada Year Book* and the publications of the Province of Ontario are excellent on population, trade and maritime statistics.

A keen, stimulating book on Canadian-American affairs and prospects is André Siegfried's *Canada* (New York, 1937), which brings up to date the conclusions stated in his *Race Question in Canada* (New York, 1907). *Canada* dwells on the problems between the French-speaking and the English-Scottish-Irish peoples of the Dominion, but for Americans the book's high point is probably its penetrating discussion of American influence, the unpromoted Americanization of the Dominion. Other books bearing on the relations between the two countries include Hugh L. Keenleyside's *Canada and the United States* (New York, 1929), and two other volumes by Professor George M. Wrong: *The United States and Canada* (New York, 1921) and *The Canadians: The Story of a People* (New York, 1938). Three publications edited by Professor James A. Shotwell for the Carnegie Endowment for International Peace also deal with this subject. All issued by the Ryerson Press, Toronto, the Yale University Press, New York, and the Oxford University Press, Oxford, they are: *Canada and her Great Neighbor,* edited by Henry Forbes Angus (1938); *Great Britain, the United States and British North America, from the Revolution to the Establishment of Peace after the War of 1812,* by A. L. Burt (1940); and Fred Landon's *Western Ontario and the American Frontier* (1941). The most recent discussion of Canadian-American relations is to be found in *The Dominion of the North,* by D. G. Creighton (New York, 1944).

# INDEX

# INDEX

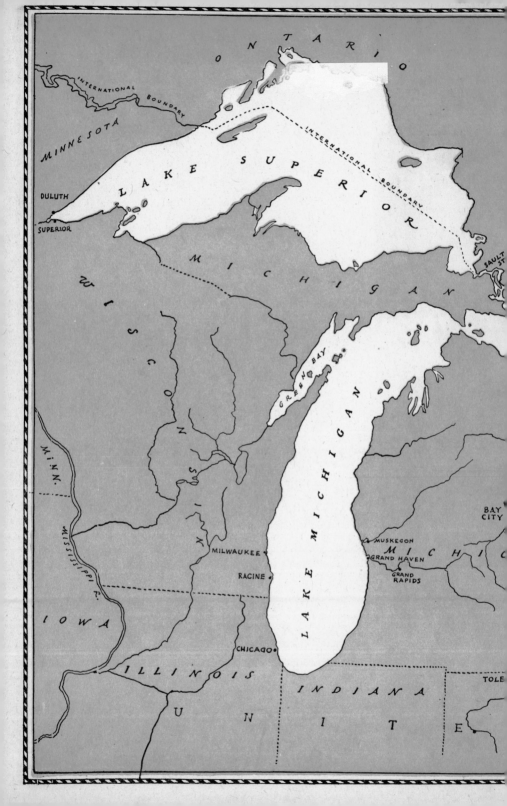